FOSSIL LEGENDS OF THE FIRST AMERICANS

FOSSIL LEGENDS
——— OF THE ———
FIRST AMERICANS

Adrienne Mayor

PRINCETON UNIVERSITY PRESS

PRINCETON AND OXFORD

First edition, 2005
New paperback printing, 2023
Paperback ISBN 9780691245614
ISBN (E-book) 9781400849314

The Library of Congress has cataloged the cloth edition of this book as follows:

Mayor, Adrienne, 1946–
Fossil legends of the first Americans / Adrienne Mayor.
p.   cm.
Includes bibliographical references and index.
ISBN 0-691-11345-9 (cl : alk. paper)
1. Indians—Antiquities. 2. Indians—Folklore. 3. Fossils—America—
History. 4. Fossils—America—Folklore. 5. Tales—America.
6. Paleontology—America. 7. Paleoanthropology—America.
8. America—Antiquities. I. Title.
E58.M36   2005
398'.36—dc22   2004053234

British Library Cataloging-in-Publication Data is available

This book has been composed in Galliard
and Copperplate Gothic

Cover image by Anne Mathiasz / Shutterstock
Cover design by Chris Ferrante

press.princeton.edu

Printed in the United States of America

For Josiah

CONTENTS

ILLUSTRATIONS

MAPS

FIGURES

GEOLOGICAL TIME SCALE

Era	Period	Epoch	Years Ago
Cenozoic	Quaternary	Holocene	Recent
		Pleistocene	1.7 million to 10,000
	Tertiary	Pliocene	5–1.7 million
		Miocene	23–5 million
		Oligocene	34–23 million
		Eocene	55–34 million
		Paleocene	65–55 million
Mesozoic	Cretaceous		145–65 million
	Jurassic		215–145 million
	Triassic		248–215 million
Paleozoic	Permian		286–248 million
	Carboniferous		360–286 million
	Devonian		408–360 million
	Silurian		438–408 million
	Ordovician		505–438 million
	Cambrian		570–505 million
Precambrian			4.6 billion to 570 million

ACKNOWLEDGMENTS

As I NOTED in *The First Fossil Hunters* (2000), the original pathbreaker in combining folklore and paleontology was the French naturalist Georges Cuvier (1769–1832). If any historical scholar could have conceived of a book like this one, it would have been Cuvier. As he was forging the new discipline of paleontology, Cuvier was also gathering the world's fossil legends from classical antiquity and the New World. This evidence helped him devise the theory of global extinctions. Yet Cuvier's comprehensive knowledge of Native American fossil discoveries and interpretations is little known today.

After Cuvier, Thomas Jefferson, Othniel Marsh, William Berryman Scott, and Edward Kindle were paleontologists who paid serious attention to Native American traditions about fossils. But the strangely ambivalent skepticism about the value of Indian discoveries expressed by the eminent modern American paleontologist George Gaylord Simpson in the 1940s also fueled my project. I really wanted to find enough evidence to impress Simpson were he still alive. My friend the paleontologist Peter Dodson helped me to understand what sorts of Native knowledge might have stirred Simpson's interest.

In the summer of 2000, I was fortunate to participate in excavations of fossil marine reptiles from the era of dinosaurs on Crow Creek Sioux Reservation, sponsored by the South Dakota School of Mines and Technology. Conversations with the leaders, Jim Martin and David Parris, and the other team members were very helpful. I began interviewing Native Americans and paleontologists that same summer (see the bibliography for a list of interviewees). A writer's residency at the Ucross Foundation, Wyoming, in fall 2000 enabled me to organize my research and begin writing. In

2001, I benefited from discussing my methods and preliminary findings at the University of Oklahoma (thanks to Laura Gibbs) and the University of Puget Sound (thanks to Mott Greene). Conversations with the rock art specialist Peter Faris in Colorado were also enlightening.

This book was enriched by Sam Elworthy's editorial guidance; the substantive comments on early drafts from Peter Dodson, Roger Echo-Hawk, Josiah Ober, and Pat Shipman; the critiques of the LPG members of Princeton; Michele Mayor Angel's mapmaking; Lauren Lepow's copyediting; Frank Mahood's book design, and Barbara Mayor's proofreading. For extra assistance with illustrations I am indebted to Michele Angel, John Blazejewski, Linda Coldwell, Joyce Gherlone, Dimitri Karetnikov, Barbara Mathé, Russell Maylone, Barbara Narendra, and Annalee Pauls. Heartfelt appreciation goes to Michele Angel, Peter Faris, Ed Heck, Patti Kane-Vanni, Linda R. Martin, Rick Spears, and Pete Von Sholly for contributing wonderful original artwork.

I received early encouragement from Richard Greenwell; Elsie Herten; Jack Horner; Jenny Herdman Lando; Matt Smith; my two-fisted agent, the late Clyde Taylor; and John Noble Wilford. I'm grateful for the enthusiastic advice and expertise of countless paleontologists who helped me understand the fossil evidence behind the early historical accounts and traditional stories. Finally, this project would have been not only impossible but unthinkable without the help of so many generous Native Americans who believed in sharing what they know about their cultures' encounters with fossil remains.

Sincere thanks to a circle of helpers: John Allen, Jr.; Warren Allmon; Paul Apodaca; Wayne Archambault; Steve Brusatte; Kyril Calsoyas; Ken Carpenter; Dan Chure; Robert Cox; Vine Deloria, Jr.; Mike Everhart; Michael Flynn; Tracy Ford; Mark Goodwin; C. Richard Harington; Johnson Holy Rock; Mark Isaak; Jason Jackson; Robert Ketelsen; Ruthann Knudson; Léo Laporte; Tim McCleary; Greg McDonald; Barbara Mann; Nita Manning; Harry Manygoats; Michelle Maskiell; Patricia Mason; Bill Matteson; Marcia Mogelonsky; Fred Shaw (Neeake); Mike O'Neill; Juanita Pahdopony; Zeese Papanikolas; Dee Pinkney; David Reese; Timothy Rowe; Max Salas; the late William A. S. Sarjeant; Billy G. Smith; David Spalding; Alison Stenger; Barry Strauss; Darren Tanke; Pascal Tassy; Tim Tokaryk; Gerard Tsonakwa; Dan Varner; Isabelle Walker; Glenn Welker; Richard White; and Douglas Wolfe. Many other individuals are thanked in the notes for their specific contributions.

Sitting Lizard and Hummingbird were there when I needed them; and Josh has always been my safe harbor. My lifelong curiosity about natural history lore is a legacy from my great-grandfather, George Halleck Center, a self-taught naturalist and medicine man who first collected fossils as a boy of nine laboring in the coal mines of Illinois.

PREFACE

THE ONLY other vehicle on the long dirt road to the Hell Creek field camp was a dusty pickup truck carrying a *Triceratops* skull encased in plaster. I was on my way to visit the new excavation site in the badlands of eastern Montana, directed by Jack Horner (curator of the Museum of the Rockies, in Bozeman, Montana). Horner's team was searching for dinosaur bones in the same landscape where the fossil hunter Barnum Brown had discovered *Tyrannosaurus rex* almost a century earlier, in 1902. The chalk-white, burnt red, and charcoal layered hills and ravines, dotted with sagebrush and home to rattlesnakes, are a vast burial ground of Cretaceous dinosaur species that lived here 68–65 million years ago.

A hot wind was gathering force. At the campsite, the field crew handed us railroad spikes to use as tent stakes. We zipped up our tents against rattlers, filled our canteens, and set out to look for fossils.

By the end of a scorching day of climbing hills, scrabbling down clay cliffs, and walking along dry alkali washes, scanning constantly for bits of bone and tooth, everyone's canteen was empty. But each person in the group had found at least one piece of dinosaur bone or tooth. Horner pointed out the tip of the horn of a *Triceratops* skull he'd found the day before, poking out of a rocky ledge. He didn't plan to take the skull back to the museum in Bozeman. After measuring it, he would rebury the fossil. "It's been here for 65 million years. This is a pretty good place to keep it."

Among the workers in Hell Creek that season was Joe Johnston, the director of *Jurassic Park III* (Horner is the paleontological con-

sultant for the movie series). When our group met up with Johnston in the late afternoon, his face could not conceal his excitement—and Horner immediately asked what he had found.
Grinning, Johnston pulled from his pocket a black fang, about five
inches long, the point and serrated edges still razor sharp. It was so
obviously the tooth of a terrible predator that we were all struck
silent by the *reality* of dinosaurs. Horner pulled out a plastic bag.
"Yup, that's a fine *T. rex* tooth. Thank you for your contribution to
the Museum of the Rockies dinosaur dig!" Tomorrow the director
would spend the day scouring the ridges above his find, hoping to
locate the rest of the monster's skeleton.

Around the campfire that night, we watched the black skies for
falling stars and satellites. Besides the museum field crew and Joe
Johnston, the visiting paleophiles included a special effects expert
for *Jurassic Park*; Homer Hicks, the science teacher who had inspired Johnston's 1999 film *October Sky*; the director of the Museum of the Rockies; a handful of National Science Foundation
representatives from Washington, DC; and a trio of teenagers from
Portugal studying paleontology. The talk drifted to the people who
had known these fossil-rich badlands better than anyone else ever
would: the Crow, Blackfeet, and Sioux. Long before the arrival of
Europeans, Native people had been the first to experience the thrill
of discovery that we had felt today. They were the first to encounter
dinosaur bones and other fossils buried in the earth for eons and
then exposed, like our finds, by wind and rain.

Suddenly we all were wondering out loud: What did Native
Americans think of these bizarre skeletons mysteriously turned to
stone? How did they explain the bones and teeth and claws of gigantic creatures that no one had ever seen alive? Did they speculate
about what could have destroyed such monsters? Did they collect
fossils?

As a scholar of natural history legends, I had written a book about
how the ancient Greeks and Romans interpreted the remains of
enormous, extinct creatures buried around the Mediterranean.
And I'd read about the pioneer paleontologists Edward Drinker
Cope and Othniel Marsh battling over fossil bones in the American
West. But Native American discoveries and conceptions of fossils—

this was unexplored territory, full of exciting possibilities for understanding pre-Darwinian ideas about paleontology.

What did fossils mean to Native Americans? It was something I'd
wondered about every time I had gazed at arrowheads and fossils
exhibited side by side in museums. I knew that Plains Indians had
gathered certain iridescent marine fossils for their magical power
to summon buffalo herds. Growing up in South Dakota, I had read
Sioux myths about Thunder Birds fighting Water Monsters. Now I
was curious to know whether those stories had been woven around
dinosaur and other giant reptile skeletons that people had observed
weathering out of the Badlands.[1]

I recalled an object I'd seen earlier that summer in the Phillips
County Museum in Malta, Montana, a small town northwest of
Hell Creek. Indian artifacts were displayed along with impressive
dinosaur remains, just as they are in countless other American museums. This juxtaposition, which seems to equate the human artifacts with the animal fossils as relics of extinction, would become a
common sight as I visited natural history collections across the
country. I had always wondered why museum curators never made
what seemed to me the obvious connection between the local Native cultures and the conspicuous evidence of remarkable creatures
from another age that they had encountered in their lands.[2]

The arrowheads and the dinosaur fossils in the Malta museum
had been discovered by amateur collectors and professional paleontologists on ranch land around Phillips County. In a glass case just
a few feet away from a menacing *T. rex* skull full of denticulated
teeth like serrated steak knives, one large, black obsidian blade
stood out. Long and slightly curved, the obsidian knife also had
serrations on both cutting edges.[3] Now it struck me how much that
artifact resembled the long black *T. rex* tooth discovered by the
Hollywood director at Hell Creek. Had the Native American stone-
knapper created a replica of his own similar find?

Pondering these questions kept me awake in my tent late into
the night. By morning I had decided to learn as much as I could
about the paleontological knowledge of the First Americans. I realized that much of this untold story had been lost and that extensive
detective work would be required to recover it. The sleuthing

would send me to American and European libraries and archives, to world-class museums and small, out-of-the-way fossil collections, and to dinosaur and mastodon excavations across the country. I drove more than eight thousand miles, talking with Native American people who live on reservations near renowned bone beds in the western United States, visiting historical paleontological sites, viewing fossil remains, and consulting with paleontologists about fossil exposures across the country. I excavated giant water monsters buried on the South Dakota prairie and helped uncover a dinosaur backbone on the Wyoming-Montana border. I listened, rapt, to old stories about Thunder Birds told by Johnson Holy Rock, an Oglala elder on Pine Ridge Reservation in South Dakota; I sought out the Navajo cultural leader Harry Manygoats in Tuba City, Arizona; and I found myself scrambling over Montana badlands with an Assini- boine fossil hunter, searching for buffalo-calling stones.

Most historians of science assume that traditional Indian knowl- edge of fossils is irretrievably lost. As the paleontologists David Weishampel and Luther Young recently put it: "Native Americans, so in tune with Earth and sky and water, surely noticed the giant bones weathering from the ground and the birdlike footprints pre- served on slabs of stone. But their discoveries are lost to modern science; only their legends survive."[4] Recovering the details of early fossil discoveries and insights preserved in those oral legends is the primary goal of this book. The research was arduous but rewarding. What may have seemed a hopeless task turned up results far richer and more exciting than anyone could have imagined.

•   •   •

The folklore of paleontology is a new field of study. Combining oral traditions and paleontology, and drawing on history, archaeology, anthropology, and mythology, the investigation of fossil legends offers a new way of thinking about pre-Darwinian encounters with prehistoric remains. This book on Native American fossil folklore is a contribution to an emerging discipline. But, in fact, the collec- tion of New World oral paleontological traditions began nearly five hundred years ago, in 1519, when Hernando Cortés brought Aztec fossil legends and a huge mastodon bone from Mexico back to the king of Spain. And it turns out that many of the great figures in early modern scientific history—from Georges Cuvier and Alexander von Humboldt in Europe to Benjamin Franklin and Thomas Jefferson in America—were avid investigators of indigenous American fossil lore.

The deep involvement in Native folklore of these scientifically oriented individuals—especially Cuvier, the father of paleontology—was one of the most surprising discoveries of my research. Their interest points to an important theme of this book: even though Native American understandings of the fossil record were not scientifically methodical in the modern sense, they offered an alternative, coherent way of interpreting Earth's history at a time when Europeans were questioning their own mythic explanations for fossils and just beginning to develop the formal disciplines of geology and paleontology. Many of the Native approaches to the fossil record—based on their careful and repeated observation of evidence and on rational speculation—are compatible with scientific inquiry. Observations of remarkable natural evidence stimulated explanations that became part of traditional Native knowledge, and those traditions were often verified and revised over time—activities that spring from the same impulses to "get it right" that led to the creation of scientific methods.

The interest in Native American fossil knowledge continued among scientific thinkers for four hundred years after Columbus, but it had already begun to wane by the time Marsh, Cope, and the other pioneer paleontologists hunted fossils in the American West in the late nineteenth and twentieth centuries. These men depended on the help of Indian scouts to locate the bone beds, but they rarely preserved any traditional notions about the extinct remains offered by the guides—or even their names. I have made a special effort to recover the names of Indians who helped the early paleontologists find and collect fossils. They deserve no less than what the famous bone hunter Charles H. Sternberg claimed as his "inalienable right." "I demand that my name appear as collector on all the material which I have gathered from the rocks of the earth," he wrote in 1909.[5]

Othniel Marsh of Yale became personally involved with Native Americans through his friendship with the Sioux chief Red Cloud.

The names of three of Marsh's Indian scouts were recorded, and there is evidence that he discussed fossils with Pawnee and Sioux leaders. Inspired by Marsh's discoveries, the Princeton paleontologist William Berryman Scott led expeditions in the Dakota Badlands, Wyoming, and Montana. I was able to find the names of one Crow and two Sioux scouts hired by Scott—and even recovered rare photographs of two of the men. Scott became quite interested in Native legends relating to extinct creatures and published a now forgotten survey of traditions about prehistoric elephants in a popular magazine of 1887.[6]

In 1935, the Canadian paleontologist Edward M. Kindle (1869–1940), in a brief paper in the *Journal of Paleontology*, was the first scientist to suggest that Native Americans should be credited with several significant fossil discoveries. But in 1942–43, the eminent U.S. paleontologist George Gaylord Simpson (1902–84) strenuously rejected Kindle's suggestion, classifying all Indian fossil discoveries as "casual finds without scientific sequel." Simpson, curator and chair of the newly formed Department of Vertebrate Paleontology at the American Museum of Natural History (AMNH), effectively ended the earlier conversations between Native Americans and Euro-American scientists about the fossil record. And his pronouncements are one reason why the history of Native encounters with fossils is so little known today.[7]

In his definitive history of vertebrate paleontology in the Western Hemisphere from the Spanish Conquest to 1842, Simpson declared that Native Americans had made no real contributions to paleontological history. Why? Because, he maintained, Indians only picked up fossils out of "idle curiosity," without ever recognizing their organic nature, and all their ideas about fossils were based on superstition. Since there was no record of "continuous consciousness" of fossil knowledge in Indian culture, argued Simpson, their discoveries did not result in scientific advancement and had "no real bearing on paleontological discovery." Why would Simpson go to such lengths to deny Native Americans a role in the early history of paleontology?

Some who knew Simpson regarded him as a racist. I asked Léo Laporte, Simpson's biographer, about Simpson's attitude. Laporte pointed out that Simpson was above all concerned with defining "science as science," and he doubted that Simpson "bore any animus toward Native Americans. If he did not give them sufficient credit, it was probably because he was not aware of their traditions accounting for fossil remains."[8]

Paleontology was just coming into its own as a scientific field of study in the 1940s, and Simpson's rigid standards were intended to define its disciplinary borders. In the drive to modernize and demythologize the new, formal science, Simpson even asserted that "various reported Indian legends of fabulous beasts represented by fossil bones have little ethnological and no paleontological value." Such legends, he said, are "untrustworthy, and carry little conviction of genuine and spontaneous (truly aboriginal) reference to real finds of fossils." In other writings, Simpson went out of his way to denigrate the intellectual capacity of "men who live close to nature." They may be meticulous observers, he wrote, but their "acuteness of physical observation is . . . generally linked with peculiarly dull" understanding. "Men who pass their lives out of doors commonly have a vast store of objective knowledge, but their comprehension of any real interpretations of those facts . . . is usually ludicrously scanty."

Yet there are hints of ambivalence in Simpson's attitudes. In a revealing moment, he noted that early finds by Indians and their knowledge of fossils offered "sentimental and literary" interest, but "the temptation to consider them in more detail must be resisted" in favor of "true scientific discoveries." At another point, Simpson credited his uneducated Patagonian guide Justino with the discovery of many important fossils now in the American Museum of Natural History, remarking that Justino possessed that "consuming curiosity which is the real reason for any scientific research."[9]

Had Simpson known more about genuine Indian fossil knowledge and the perceptive creation stories collected for the first time in this book, I like to think that he would have been impressed by the levels of understanding of Earth's past that could be expressed in mythic terms. But, because he was unaware of the early French and English, and later American, records of Native fossil observations and interpretations, Simpson was led to make a patently false claim: "The abundant occurrence of fossil bones in North America was not widely known among Indians and not a common subject of remark by them."[10]

Numerous examples in this book prove Simpson wrong on all counts, but until now his assertions have been accepted uncritically by most historians and scientists. In 1943, Simpson concluded his grand history of American paleontology—which he considered "definitive"—with these words: "Now [that] the thin trickle of fossils collected in America" has become "a flood, . . . the study of the beginnings of this phenomenon need go no further." But to-day, now that the field of paleontology is mature and secure, I think paleontologists have much to gain by considering wider horizons of paleontological inquiry, and perhaps even being more open to Native insights about fossil remains expressed in mythological terms.[11]

If the ghost of George Gaylord Simpson seems to hover over these pages, it is because he was the imaginary scientific reader I would most hope to convince of the worth of this project. Paleontologist Peter Dodson helped me in formulating this goal by musing: "If I were Simpson, I would distinguish three levels of pre-Darwinian thought or interpretation: first, a legend based on interpretation of a single fossil or a single kind of fossil [such as belemnites or giant bison bones]; second, a reconstruction of an entire fauna of diverse extinct creatures [such as Pleistocene megafauna fossils interpreted as giants and various monsters]; and finally, the concept of successive faunas over deep time [such as water and sky monsters succeeded by land monsters]. If I were a real scientific snob, I would dignify only the third level as worthy of serious consideration by the scientific community." In analyzing the fossil legends presented here, I apply Dodson's useful tripartite "Simpsonian" criteria to Native American insights about the fossil record, along with other concepts such as deep time and extinction.[12]

• • •

Following the definition and methods I introduced in *The First Fossil Hunters: Paleontology in Greek and Roman Times* (2000), I consider traditional tales about giant creatures and monsters to be "fossil legends" only when they refer to physical evidence, to the bones or other traces of strange life-forms. Myriad myths around the world describe giant or monstrous creatures or explain the history of the earth and origins of life *without* ever referring to unusual fossil remains, of course. Many fantastic creatures of myth are imaginary or symbolic, and their origins and meaning may have nothing to do with paleontology. But a culture's mythic panorama of the history of the earth and fantastic life-forms of the past provides the context—the matrix, to put it in paleontological terms—for legends that *do* explicitly refer to unusual bones and other remains, and for traditional accounts that describe discoveries of fossils. That mythic context is important to an understanding of enigmatic or fragmentary oral narratives about the traces of extinct creatures.

For example, tales about horned water monsters or giants destroyed by landslides or sacred bison hidden underground form the mythic matrix that can help illuminate incomplete narratives or myths of observation that describe actual discoveries of "magic tusks" in riverbanks or enormous petrified bones in the earth. Moreover, the stratigraphy of traditional folklore is seldom simple. Because a living culture's folklore is a cumulative process, some very old Native traditions about giants and monsters, as they were retold over time, have integrated or accrued new layers of modern knowledge about dinosaurs or extinct mammals.[13]

I define a *fossil legend* as a story or belief that relates extraordinary creatures of myth and legend to observations of the mineralized remains of extinct animals, or otherwise attempts to explain fossil traces of prehistoric species, including marine and plant fossils, and the bones, teeth, claws, burrows, nests, eggs, and footprints of extinct animals. In the nineteenth century, traditional tales based on empirical evidence of fossilized remains were classified as "myths of observation" by Edward Burnet Tylor (1865). A century later, in 1968, the geologist Dorothy Vitaliano established "geomythology" as a new discipline that attempts to match traditional, prescientific accounts of Earth's history with modern geological knowledge. Although Vitaliano did not analyze fossil legends as such, they are a type of geomyth.[14]

Fossil legends in the Americas come from a wide range of sources, and many oral narratives about discoveries of remarkable remains can be traced back to the time before European Contact. The earliest documented oral fossil lore in America was preserved in writing by the Spanish in the sixteenth century, and the most recent were recounted yesterday by some Native American storyteller. For this book, I pored over the writings of Euro-American explorers, colonists, travelers, missionaries, ethnologists, naturalists, geologists, paleontologists, and Native American writers. I also interviewed numerous Native Americans about fossil traditions.

The paleontological lore gathered here is not meant to be all-inclusive, of course. A great many more fossil legends and insights from other groups in North and South America could be identified and studied.[15] But this survey displays for the first time the great wealth of Native American ideas about the fossil record expressed in traditional ways, and I hope this initial step will encourage other scholars of mythology and historians of science to delve deeper into pre-Darwinian fossil traditions.

The early discoveries by the First Americans and their attempts to understand fossils represent a crucial chapter in the history of paleontological inquiry. But much of that story has been obscured or lost. One reason, discussed above, has to do with the way the history of paleontological discovery has been defined by Simpson and others. The other reason is the fact that Native American culture is mainly oral.

In 1812, a famous memory contest pitted the Seneca chief Red Jacket (Sagoyawetha) against Governor Daniel Tompkins of New York. Regarding a disputed detail of a treaty signed in the previous century, the governor claimed that his own memory must be accurate because "we have it written down on paper." But Red Jacket's memory turned out to be correct—as was confirmed by the actual treaty. Red Jacket blamed the governor's forgetfulness on his psychological reliance on written records: "You Yankees are born with a feather [quill] between your fingers, [but] I have it written here," he said, pointing to his head. "The Indian keeps his knowledge here! This is the book the Great Spirit gave him."[16]

When a culture's history and wisdom are not written but transmitted by word of mouth, attention to consistent details is an essential skill, and an accurate memory is a matter of necessity and pride.

As Wayne Archambault, an Assiniboine fossil hunter in Montana, remarked to me, "Our tales are very consistent through time because we strive to remember the details." Traditional knowledge based on accumulated experiences and memories of historical or geological events is often marked by accurate details, even though they may be couched in mythic language. European colonists were impressed by the depth and sharpness of Native people's oral memories, honed by the custom of learning traditions by heart at an early age and the courtesy of repeating an orator's speech before replying. Even the skeptical George Gaylord Simpson expressed admiration for the way feats of memory often took the place of written records in the oral cultures that he encountered in South America.[17]

But it's also important to consider what may have been left out, misinterpreted, or garbled when information was passed down over generations and across cultures. Like fossil evidence itself, traditional oral knowledge about remarkable remains was often scattered and long buried; important details and connections may have dropped away. Tribes traveled very long distances and many groups migrated far from their homelands; ancient creation myths may no longer coincide with the landscapes of a people's new locations. Names of storytellers, elders, and fossil guides may have been forgotten. And much was lost during the violence of colonization, epidemics, the Indian Wars, and the forced removals to reservations.

Yet much more historical and natural knowledge has been retained and for a longer time span than is generally appreciated. To find these nuggets of genuine knowledge, the Iroquois scholar Barbara Mann suggests that one should look for the "consistent elements" in the layered matrix of storytelling over the ages. Many scholars have questioned whether oral traditions are "real history." Anthropologist Robert Lowie, for example, who studied several Native American cultures in the 1930s, famously declared in 1915 that "oral traditions [have no] historical value whatsoever under any conditions whatsoever." But Lowie's grip is loosening: today many mythologists and historians would agree with Roger Echo-Hawk, a Pawnee historian, that oral histories should be treated as "respectable siblings of written documents," as valuable sources for reconstructing "ancient American history." The most recent analyses of the mythmaking process, drawing on modern linguistics and cognition studies and matching details in traditions with datable historical, astronomical, or geological events, are revealing that accurate geomythology can extend back over millennia.[18]

•   •   •

Gathering surviving accounts about extraordinary skeletons, figuring out which fossil species could have been observed in specific landscapes, filling in gaps in incomplete or cryptic narratives while hewing to historical, cultural, and geological realities—this endeavor entails a new and experimental kind of scholarship. To uncover the paleontological folklore of the past, one must become a kind of paleontologist of folklore, sifting through sediments of historical writings and living oral lore for meaningful bits of fossil knowledge.

And indeed, my method resembles some techniques of modern paleontology. Like a fossil hunter scanning for fragments of bone and carefully noting their context, I searched the literature for Indian accounts about finding bones of unusual size and shape, or stories describing the physical remains of mythical giants, monsters, and other special creatures. Other, mute, evidence for ancient curiosity about fossils is literally buried in the ground, since modern archaeological excavations have shown that many kinds of fossils were collected and used in various ways by paleo-Indians. Further evidence for interest in fossils is also stored in museum collections, in the form of medicine bundles and amulets containing petrified wood and fossil shells and bones.

Trying to reconstruct the outlines of an incomplete and ancient body of oral fossil knowledge is like trying to reconstruct a skeleton from disarticulated and incomplete remains. As in paleontology, luck plays a role and so does conjecture. The paleontologist assembles a framework from the fragmentary traces of a creature that were accidentally preserved in stone by a capricious geological process—a process as unpredictable as the preservation of spoken folklore over countless generations and upheavals. Gaps are filled in with hypothetical bones. The reconstructed dinosaur skeleton is truly impressive, but it is still only a lifeless armature; one longs for so much more than dry bones. I remember Jack Horner exclaiming, as he pointed out the remains of *T. rex* and *Triceratops* at Hell Creek: "But these are just skeletons! I wish I could see the. *real* dinosaur, the living, breathing creature!"

Thomas Jefferson felt that same desire in 1775, as he eagerly questioned Delaware elders about the great heaps of mastodon fossils along the Ohio River. Jefferson yearned to see those behemoths alive, and he hoped that Lewis and Clark would discover living mastodon herds in the Far West. A century later, after digging all day in the dinosaur bone beds of Montana in 1876, the pioneer paleontologist Edward Drinker Cope wrestled every night with the fearsome monsters resurrected in his dreams. In the 1950s and 1960s, for a wide audience that included Indian kids on reservations as well as many future paleontologists working today, the popular comic book series *Turok, Son of Stone* brought dinosaurs and Native Americans of the past alive, in the adventures of a pair of Plains Indians who discover dinosaurs populating a lost valley of time. Today, Hollywood movies and animated documentaries feed our dreams of visualizing the never-to-be-encountered but very real creatures of deep time.[19]

To help reanimate long-forgotten tales in their cultural landscape and fill in the gaps, many Native American elders, historians, teachers, storytellers, healers, and others provided details about traditional ways and told me some old fossil tales that they had heard as youngsters. In interviews and personal correspondence, they also pointed out nontraditional elements embedded in early fossil narratives that were recorded by Euro-Americans and Christianized Natives. Like the models of dinosaurs created by scientists and artists working with incomplete evidence and educated guesses, the resulting picture of Indian fossil knowledge is never final, of course— it will always be subject to revision in light of new information.[20]

The Native American historian Vine Deloria, Jr. (Standing Rock Sioux), believes that through the publicizing of Indian contributions to science and insights into nature's history, more hidden "data will come to light or be made available by our elders" before they pass on. Estimating that perhaps only 10 percent of the natural knowledge, the "distilled memories of thousands of years of living in North America . . . is presently in print and available for discussion," Deloria hopes that new generations of Indians will "rescue the remaining bits of information our people possess." It is my hope that this book will encourage that process.

Like paleontological resources on Indian lands, however, traditional fossil knowledge can be fraught with issues of ownership. Some oral knowledge is considered sacred or kept secret from outsiders. Deloria approaches the problem of sacred knowledge by trying to avoid being the first to publish oral material unless a comparable version has already appeared in print. This approach is generally accepted among Native Americans as they balance the tensions between conserving and sharing cultural wisdom. Juanita Pahdopony, a Comanche storyteller who related some personal memories about fossil-bone medicine in Oklahoma, remarked: "I would not like to be the first to reveal a tribal knowledge that is kept by our people. After all, what is left that hasn't already been taken from us?"

Some traditional stories are the private possessions of individuals. The early ethnologists learned that offering something of value was often the price of a hearing a story. A rare few today feel that their stories remain personal possessions even after publication. For example, Virginia Driving Hawk Sneve, a Lakota writer in South Dakota, told me that I needed her permission to quote from books she has published with a university press. John Allen, Jr., an Assiniboine spiritual leader in Montana, on the other hand, says that it honors his culture whenever oral traditions are retold in writing.

Some elders believe that oral stories should never be put in print, for they "must have human breath or they will die," in the words of the Shawnee storyteller Neeake. And sometimes stories are not recalled until the right question is asked, continued Neeake. "People may suddenly give a story if they have found someone who knows how to listen with the heart, but at other times they decide not to share. A cardinal rule of Indian teaching must be followed: If you don't know the proper question, or how to pose it properly, then you don't need to know the answer."[21]

I tried to keep this rule in mind during my interviews. And it occurred to me that the concern with seeking truth by framing the right questions happens to be a basic value of modern science. To elicit answers from the natural world, the scientist's first task is to formulate elegant questions. As one reads the lively dialogues of the sixteenth to the eighteenth century among Euro-Americans and Native Americans, one has the sense that many early colonists, like Charlevoix, Morgan, Croghan, Jefferson, and the Spanish Jesuits in New Spain before them, understood how to ask the right questions in the right spirit. Such an understanding seems to have been lost to more recent fossil collectors in the American West in the nineteenth and twentieth centuries.

● ● ●

Unlike the paleontological interpretations of the classical Greeks and Romans, the pre-Darwinian ideas about fossils collected here do not fall neatly into one overarching mythological explanation. The sheer range of geological ages represented by fossils in different regions and the diversity of cultures in the New World preclude a single conceptual picture. This book reveals the many unique ways that the First Americans have interpreted the observed evidence of the fossil record in various landscapes. One recurring theme, however, is the eternal struggle for natural balance among earth, water, and sky forces in mythologically based explanations of fossils. Fascinating resonances exist not only among various tribes' creation and extinction scenarios, but also with the emerging European ideas about the disappearance of giant creatures in geological eras long past. Most pre-Darwinian fossil legends are expressed in symbolic or mystical language, and many of the interpretations and uses of fossils seem far removed from modern science. But many other examples in this book show how traditional concepts sometimes anticipated the development of modern theories of geological ages and life-forms in the deep past, the relationships among species, changes over time, and extinctions.

The term *fossil* usually refers to the preserved remains or traces of organisms that died about ten thousand years ago or earlier in the geologic past. Fossils take many forms: plants, wood, shells, insects, bones, teeth, claws, footprints, impressions or casts, eggs, nests, burrows, and even excrement. To become fossils, dead plants or creatures were buried rapidly, usually near water, and the remains were infiltrated by minerals that turned them to stone (although teeth can survive unchanged for eons). Sometimes fossils are preserved in anoxic conditions such as burial in sand, volcanic ash, ice, or tar. The most plentiful fossil remains are marine organisms, followed by animals or plants that dwelled in or near lakes or rivers. The rarest fossils are of land animals, such as dinosaurs, that died and were mineralized near bodies of water.

The large fossils of Pleistocene megafaunas, such as mastodons, mammoths, huge bears and sloths, giant bison, and very large raptor birds occur across the North American continent and in Central and South America. Indians, and later the Europeans and American colonists, were aware of numerous sites in eastern North America where Ice Age remains often come to light, especially in watery locales. West of the Mississippi, similar Pleistocene remains occur in dry caves or in alluvial deposits that overlie much older fossil material. In the western Great Plains, for example, the bones of Tertiary mammals of strange and immense proportions—colossal rhinoceroses and mastodons, bizarre chalicotheres, and giant pig-like carnivores—emerge in badlands terrain. On the prairies, one also finds copious marine fossil deposits and the impressive skeletons of flying reptiles (pterosaurs) and enormous marine reptiles (mosasaurs and plesiosaurs), former denizens of the vast inland sea that bisected the continent during the Cretaceous epoch. The most prolific locales for dinosaur fossils are in the arid Southwest, the Great Basin, and the badlands of the High Plains, where the ancient sediments of the Mesozoic era were uplifted and then dramatically carved and eroded away by water and wind. In the regions that were under water during the Cretaceous era, dinosaur skeletons are rarely preserved: very few have been found on the West Coast or in the eastern half of the United States, although dinosaur footprints are plentiful in the Connecticut Valley.[22]

The chapters are organized geographically, more or less by Native American culture areas, moving clockwise from the Northeast

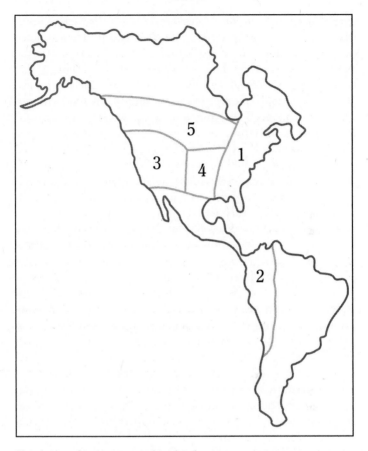

Sketchmap of regions covered in the chapters

down the Atlantic coast to Mexico and South America, and then
north to the southwestern United States and the Great Basin, up
through the midwestern prairies, and then to the High Plains (see
sketchmap).

The sequence of the chapters also roughly follows the chronological advance of European Contact—and that history revealed an un-
anticipated aspect of paleontological folklore in the New World.
Expecting to find more records of oral fossil legends preserved with

the passage of time, as Euro-Americans explored the western geographies with the most spectacular dinosaur remains, I had assumed that the period of earliest contact with Native Americans on the Atlantic coast would produce only sketchy material. I thought that the greater body of fossil traditions would emerge along with westward movement and modern record keeping. To my surprise, however, very rich lodes of oral fossil lore were preserved from the earliest colonial period, from the sixteenth to the eighteenth century, and the recorded material began to taper off in the nineteenth and twentieth centuries.

There is a logic behind this inverse relationship. It's not that Native Americans of the West encountered fewer conspicuous fossils or thought less about their meaning. And the nineteenth and twentieth centuries saw the development of the new fields of ethnology and anthropology, which focused on preserving Native cultural knowledge. Nevertheless, with the rise of the formal science of paleontology, scientists' interest in recording traditional interpretations of fossils diminished. As historian Richard White showed in *The Middle Ground*, the early colonial era was often marked by friendly and accommodating exchanges among Europeans and Native peoples. But that positive mutual respect disappeared in the nineteenth century as whites pushed west and Indians were recast as uncivilized aliens to be subjugated.[23] One result of the new attitude was that the fossil traditions of Native cultures that came into European contact most recently are the least preserved in writing. To help compensate for that fact, I focused special attention on interviewing Native Americans in the West.

Fossils of all sorts were collected in the Americas for a wide range of uses: as "deeds" to land, as historical evidence, as weapons, as healing medicine, and as personal amulets for protection or other special powers. Their mysterious presence in the earth inspired explanatory narratives both simple and surprisingly sophisticated. In the introduction, we accompany a party of French and Indian warriors down the Ohio River in 1739 to find out who really deserves credit for the historic discovery of the first vertebrate fossils from the New World ever to be studied by scientists. The introduction also shows how much fossil-oriented knowledge—often of unex-

pected antiquity—can be recovered by careful analysis of long forgotten or misunderstood Abenaki, Iroquois, and Wyandot oral narratives, first recorded by Euro-Americans who may not have
realized what valuable material they were preserving.

Chapter 1 reveals the depth of Iroquois, Shawnee, and Delaware
(Lenape) familiarity with the fossils of mastodons and giant bears
and bison—and even some Cretaceous creatures—in New England,
the Mid-Atlantic, and the Ohio Valley. Their traditional knowledge
of these fossils was eagerly sought in the eighteenth century by early
scientific investigators such as Cotton Mather, Thomas Jefferson,
and Georges Cuvier.

Even earlier, however, the Spanish conquistadors and missionaries of the sixteenth to eighteenth centuries recorded chronicles of
the Aztecs and Incas to explain the presence of immense Pleistocene
skeletons in Central and South America. Chapter 2 presents the
evidence for indigenous fossil knowledge in Mexico and Peru before the arrival of Columbus.

Next, chapter 3 looks at how the dinosaur remains of the Southwest and Great Basin figured in Zuni, Navajo, Apache, Hopi, Ute,
and Pit River creation stories. Chapter 4 presents fossil lore from
the prairies, where Pawnee, Cheyenne, Comanche, Yuchi, and
Osage fossil hunters observed the enormous bones of Cretaceous,
Tertiary, and Quaternary creatures.

In chapter 5, about the High Plains and Badlands of the Dakotas,
Montana, Wyoming, and western Canada, we'll see how the impressive bones of extinct land mammals, huge marine reptiles,
winged pterosaurs, and dinosaurs were explained in Sioux, Crow,
Kiowa, Ojibwe, and Blackfeet stories long before the pioneer bone
hunters came West to claim trophy fossils for famous museums.

In the spirit of reviving the rapport that once prevailed between
early paleontologists and Native Americans, the conclusion points
toward synthesis: a reconciliation of differences over the possession
and meaning of fossils.

INTRODUCTION

Marsh Monsters of Big Bone Lick

> We are indebted to the Indian for finding and collecting the
> first fossil bones that received scientific study.
> —*Edward M. Kindle, 1935*

> Indians certainly found and occasionally collected fossil
> bones . . . but these discoveries are no real part of
> paleontological history.
> —*George Gaylord Simpson, 1943*

OHIO RIVER, SUMMER 1739

TOWARD dusk, the Indian hunting party returned with game to feed the army of French Canadians and Indians camped along the Ohio River in what is now Kentucky. But tonight the hunters' canoes are laden with more than fresh venison. Curious soldiers gather to watch the Indians unload a strange cargo—an enormous, fossilized femur nearly as tall as a man, several huge teeth, and great ivory tusks darkened by time.

The expedition of 442 men (123 French soldiers and 319 Native American warriors) from Quebec was commanded by Charles Le Moyne, Baron de Longueuil. Traveling by waterway, the fleet of war canoes left Montreal in July 1739, paddling down the St. Lawrence River, Lakes Ontario and Erie, and the Allegheny and Ohio rivers, heading for the Mississippi River (see map 1 on page 35). Their destination was the French port of New Orleans. It was the height of the great colonial wars for empire, as the English and

French and their Indian allies battled for control of North America (the French and Indian Wars, 1689–1763). In 1739, Longueuil's mission was to help repel the pro-English Chickasaw Indians who were besieging New Orleans and blockading the Mississippi.

Longueuil's expedition was a military failure. The Chickasaws defeated the French and Indian armies, and the French ultimately surrendered to the English in 1763. But the big bones collected by the unnamed Indian hunters in Longueuil's army made scientific history.

After the perilous river journey down the Mississippi, the fossils arrived unscathed in New Orleans. From there, they sailed with Longueuil to France. Reaching Paris in late 1740, the fossils were placed in Louis XV's cabinet of curiosities, under the direction of the famous naturalist Count Buffon. A few years later, those bones and teeth from the Ohio River became the first American fossils ever studied by scientists.

In 1762, Louis Daubenton read his scientific paper on the Ohio fossils to the French Royal Academy (scientific drawings of the fossils had been made six years earlier). Crediting the anonymous Indians ("les Sauvages") with the finds, Daubenton sketched the circumstances of their discovery and established for the first time a comparative procedure for identifying vertebrate fossils. The method was far from perfect. Daubenton concluded that the remains belonged to two separate living species. The femur and tusks he recognized as elephantine, but he thought the molars must belong to a species of carnivorous hippopotamus (the reasons for this mistake are discussed below). He imagined that both animals were to be found alive in the swamps of America. As more fossils from the New World were studied and compared over the next century, however, it eventually became clear to scientists that the Indian hunters had actually found the remains of a single species: the extinct American mastodon, *Mammut americanum* (fig. 1).[1]

The discovery in 1739 that led to Daubenton's paper is hailed in the annals of scientific history as the birth of American paleontology. In 1821, the great French naturalist Georges Cuvier credited the Indian hunters in Longueuil's army with discovering the first specimens of the "mammouth d'Amérique" to be studied in Eu-

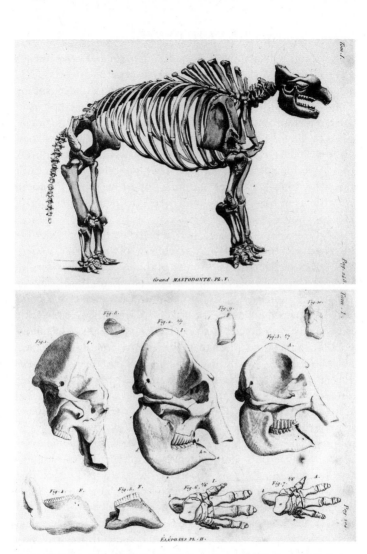

1. Cuvier's *mastodonte* skeleton, above; mammoth/elephant skulls below. Mastodons and mammoths are often confused, especially since Cuvier named the American mastodon *Mammut americanum*, while *Mammuthus* refers to the mammoth genus. Both are ancestors of elephants and survived till the end of the Pleistocene, but mastodons have pointed molars, while mammoths and living elephants have flat "grinders." Engravings from Cuvier, *Recherches sur les ossemens fossiles* (Paris, 1821–24).

rope. From the beginning, Daubenton, Cuvier, and other French scientists included "les Sauvages" as partners in the discovery. And partners they were. Even though their approach to understanding giant bones was quite different from the comparative method inaugurated by Daubenton and the paleontological theories later established by Cuvier and other scientists, the Native Americans knew where to find large vertebrate fossils of animals that no longer lived. They collected specimens for their own uses, and they had their own ideas about the bones' meaning—at a time when European scientists were struggling to understand the petrified remains of large, unknown creatures.

The 1739 episode at what came to be called Big Bone Lick has often been recounted from the point of view of the European scientists, but never from the perspective of the Indian fossil finders. In his authoritative history of American paleontology (1942), George Gaylord Simpson wrote that "although Indians were probably involved in the real discovery" of Big Bone Lick, "they cannot fairly be called the discoverers." Just as "Columbus discovered America in 1492," he asserted, "Longueuil discovered American fossil vertebrates in 1739." According to Simpson, "Longueuil's claim as the true discoverer of North American fossil vertebrates depends more on the results than its absolute priority."

To sidestep what he acknowledged was the Indians' absolute priority, Simpson argued at length that full credit should go to Longueuil alone, "the star . . . of the paleontological drama." Rejecting Daubenton's clear statement that the Indian hunters were the only ones actually to observe the fossils in situ, and that they were solely responsible for their collection, Simpson insisted—on no evidence—that Longueuil himself surely observed the fossil site, too. Simpson claimed that the marsh must have been less than an hour's "walk" from camp, and that Longueuil personally ordered that the remains be gathered up. Simpson was a fine paleontologist, but his eagerness to put the European "star" at center stage led him to construct a historical fantasy. He even stated that the French defeated the Chickasaws, when in fact the Chickasaws were victorious.[2]

Simpson's scenario has become entrenched in paleontological and popular history. A recent example appears in the chapter on the discovery of Big Bone Lick in Paul Semonin's comprehensive study of mastodon fossils in colonial America, *American Monster* (2000). Semonin elaborates on Simpson's imaginary version, writing that "Longueuil's Indian guides led the French soldiers several miles up a buffalo path from the Ohio River to the large muddy pond" where they saw "a multitude of enormous bones."[3]

In April 2001, I visited Big Bone Lick State Park in Kentucky. The heaps of mastodon and other large skeletons that used to loom out of the brackish backwaters along the Ohio River here are long gone, though the occasional big bone sometimes comes to light. The official museum texts state that the original discovery of the fossils was made "by a French soldier . . . Longueil [*sic*] . . . and his troops. They discovered a marshy area scattered with large bones and teeth they believed came from an elephant. They gathered . . . a tusk, a femur, and molars" that were later sent to France. There is no hint that Indian hunters actually discovered the fossils and brought them back to Longueuil in camp. Indeed, the illustrated markers at the site depict a group of French soldiers in tricornered hats standing next to the big bones. Here, too, at the "Birthplace of Vertebrate Paleontology," Simpson's ahistorical vision—Baron de Longueuil strolling along a path to view the site of the Native fossil find—holds sway.[4]

Clearly it was the Indians' decision to collect extraordinary bones that day in 1739 that initiated paleontological inquiries by Europeans in the New World. For me, learning of the hunters' action opened up an unexplored world of early Native American encounters with fossils. How much of their story could I recover? Could I identify the unknown Indians who made the discovery? Why would hunters looking for game go to the trouble of collecting the heavy bones of bizarre creatures? All I had to go on were two facts: the physical evidence of the fossils themselves and the French historical record that it was "les Sauvages" supplying meat for Longueuil's army who discovered the fossils in 1739. By working with these facts and filling in their context, I think we can reconstruct a plausible story to counter Simpson's fabricated version of this historic milestone.[5]

My first step was to try to determine the tribal affiliation of the fossil hunters. Although the French sources credited the Indians with the discovery of the fossils in 1739, they did not name the tribe, and no modern historian has ever attempted to identify the Indians. Historical and cultural detective work allows us to figure out who they were. The Natives in Longueuil's army came from New France, eastern Canada, home of Algonquian and Iroquoian cultures. In the seventeenth century, French Jesuits had established missions among the Algonquian-speaking Abenakis and the Iroquoian-speaking Iroquois and Hurons (Wyandots) of New France. Longueuil's father, a founder of Montreal, had come to New France in 1641 as an interpreter for the Hurons and Iroquois. As early as 1681–82, a group of Abenakis had accompanied the French explorer La Salle on his historic voyage down the Mississippi to the Gulf of Mexico. By 1700, many Abenaki and Iroquois Indians spoke French and had some European education, and some were literate in French and Latin. But by that time, the Iroquois had become very hostile toward the French missionaries and their converts, the "praying Indians." Meanwhile, Abenaki men regularly joined the French military campaigns, and, as historian Richard White points out, the Chickasaw Wars increased the French need for Algonquian warriors.[6]

In 1739, Longueuil recruited Indian men for his army in southern Quebec, with the help of the Jesuit missionaries. At that time and place, the Christianized Abenakis were the most powerful and loyal allies of the French, while the pagan Iroquois and Hurons were their enemies (and in the Ohio Valley, the Shawnees and Delawares leaned toward the English and opposed the French). Since the 319 Indians in Longueuil's army were persuaded to enlist by the Jesuit priests, we can safely assume that they were almost all Abenakis, with perhaps a few "praying" Iroquois living at the missions. In all likelihood, then, the hunters who found the fossils on the Ohio River were Abenaki.[7]

To fill in cultural details about these men, I talked with Gerard Tsonakwa, an Abenaki historian-storyteller. Tsonakwa also happens to be an amateur paleontologist, so he was intrigued by the idea that his ancestors may have been involved in the famous discovery. He confirmed that a great many Abenaki warriors in Quebec joined French military expeditions at that time. By consulting historical records, and drawing on Tsonakwa's knowledge, I set about reconstructing the circumstances of the discovery along the Ohio.[8]

A large war canoe of that era carried ten men. With supplies and the traveling armory, Tsonakwa estimated that Longueuil's fleet probably consisted of more than a hundred large birch-bark canoes. "To avoid scaring away game and attracting the attention of hostile enemies—or water monsters," said Tsonakwa, "Abenaki war parties followed a strict protocol on the water. Silence was the rule—no splashing, no shouting or cursing, and nothing was thrown overboard."

How many Indians would have been in the deer-hunting party that found the skeletons? Tsonakwa estimated that meat for the army of nearly 450 men could have been provided by a small hunting group of about six Indians. But contrary to Simpson's notion, it seems unlikely that the hunters simply walked "less than an hour away" from the camp. To carry back enough dressed venison, the men probably set off in three canoes, going a good distance away from the noisy encampment. Armed with flintlock muskets and bows and arrows, they would then beach their canoes and stalk deer on foot, paying special attention to salt licks, which attracted game. After gutting the carcasses, they would drag the venison back to the canoes.

According to early French maps indicating the "place where elephant bones were found" in 1739, the Indians went hunting on the southern side of the lower Ohio River. They were in the vicinity of the rapids some miles east of modern-day Louisville, Kentucky, and not far from Big Bone Lick, which would later become the most famous fossil site on the Ohio River. The impressive bones of Pleistocene mastodons and other very large mammals, extinct for about ten thousand years, were abundant in the salty, sulfurous back-channel bogs. The deer hunters from Quebec came upon the skeletons of three immense creatures at the edge of a swamp reeking of sulfur (fig. 2).[9]

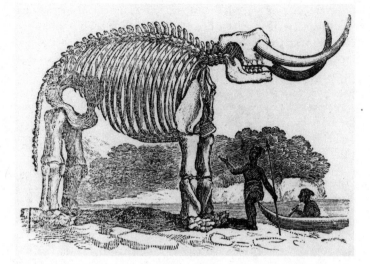

2. This wood engraving of 1804 shows two Indians in a canoe, discovering a fossil mastodon skeleton along a river. Engraving by Alexander Anderson, for Thomas Bewick's *A General History of Quadrupeds* (1804). Photo: Graphic Arts Collection, Department of Rare Books and Special Collections, Princeton University Library.

Ivory and Monsters

Seeking to understand why the hunters decided to carry away heavy tusks, teeth, and bones, I asked Tsonakwa to imagine his ancestors' reactions. First, he pointed out, even though they were unfamiliar with elephants, Abenakis would have immediately recognized ivory tusks as a precious commodity. The Abenakis prized the ivory teeth of whales that they hunted in the Atlantic, and they also acquired pieces of fossil mammoth ivory through trade with Arctic people. Historical records show that Abenakis and other Natives encountered European explorers and traders in Canada looking for sources of ivory to compete with the Russian trade in Siberian fossil mammoth ivory—these traders routinely asked about ivory "horns" and teeth. Since isolated mastodon fossils and tusks are found in eastern

Canada, New England, and around the Great Lakes, the Indians in Longueuil's army might also have observed or heard about similar remains closer to home.[10]

Historical evidence indicates that Algonquians, including the Abenakis, were actively collecting and trading fossil ivory at a very early date, and there were stories to explain the remains of huge animals in the Northeast. The Algonquians, for example, referred to the "bones found under the earth" as ancient monsters killed by their culture hero Manabozho. In the seventeenth century, a French missionary in Canada reported a "strange legend" circulating among the Hurons. They told of a monster with a "horn" that could pierce anything, even rock. "Anyone possessing a piece of it was supposed to have very good fortune. The Hurons did not know where the creature was to be found, but [they] said that the Algonquins were in the habit of selling them small pieces of the magic horn." These talismans were probably chunks of fossil ivory, gathered by Abenakis and other Algonquians.

In a similar practice, the Creek Indians of the Southeast fashioned amulets of pieces of "horn" that they sawed off from monsters found lurking in water holes—most likely the tusks of fossilized Columbian mammoths preserved in bogs, like the mastodons of the Northeast. Archaeologists at the paleo-Indian Hiscock Site in western New York (occupied in the Ice Age) have found numerous mastodon fossils and tusks along with tools made from mastodon bone. The mounds built by paleo-Indians in Ohio also contain pieces of fossilized ivory tusks collected more than two thousand years ago.[11]

So Abenaki huntsmen would have taken tusks and teeth back to show Longueuil because they themselves valued ivory and because they knew that the Europeans were eager to obtain such things. Indeed, within a few years of Longueuil's expedition, the competition had became fierce among French and English tusk collectors in the Ohio Valley (dominated at that time by the French and their Indian allies). The dangerous rivalry was vividly described in explorers' journals. For example, Colonel Christopher Gist, of the British Ohio Company, purchased several great molars and tusks from another English trader. The trader told Gist that earlier, in

1744, he had buried a prize five-foot-long "horn" in a secret cache "lest the French Indians should carry it away." The French-allied Indians were known to acquire ivory for French traders. Gist also met four friendly Shawnee men canoeing upriver who warned him that sixty French Indians were encamped nearby. Gist abandoned his fossil-hunting expedition after he heard the French Indians firing their muskets.[12]

By 1766, only four years after Daubenton's landmark paper made the Ohio fossils so famous in Europe, a "considerable quantity of elephants' teeth from the banks of the Ohio" was already stored in the Tower of London, in the royal cabinet of curiosities. Some of these may have been shipped to England by the Indian trader George Croghan (1720–82), an adventurous Irishman who collected mastodon tusks despite the perils. Croghan, who had arrived in America in 1741, learned Shawnee and Iroquois languages and became an important diplomat and Indian agent for the British. He knew of the bone beds in the 1740s, years before he began deliberately collecting specimens in the 1760s. In his letters, Croghan stated that local Indians guided him to the "extraordinary Bones of Elephants" at the place they called the Great Buffaloes' Lick. And he made the important point that even the "oldest Indians had no traditional Trace" of seeing these beasts alive (the local knowledge of the Shawnees and other tribes in the Ohio Valley and eastern United States is discussed in chapter 1).

In 1765, Croghan, with an escort of Shawnee men, began gathering Ohio fossils intended for the English king's collection and for others, such as Benjamin Franklin in Philadelphia. The Shawnee guides were never named; however, searching old records for possible candidates, I found that a few years earlier, in 1759, Croghan had negotiated with five Shawnee chiefs and sixty-four warriors at Fort Pitt (now Pittsburgh) on the Ohio River some miles above the big bone deposits. He listed the chiefs' names in his notes: they were Misquepalothe, Waconathechea, Othoaway, Weseloutha, and Woppepalathe. There is no way of knowing for sure, but it is quite possible that some of these chiefs or their men joined Croghan's fossil-collecting expeditions.

At Big Bone Lick, Croghan and the Shawnees loaded a flatboat with fossils, including a magnificent tusk seven feet long. But the precious cargo was lost when eighty French Indians (in this case, Mascoutins and Kickapoos from the Great Lakes) attacked the party. Several of the Shawnees were killed, and Croghan survived a bloody hatchet blow to the skull and was captured. But by summer of 1766, Croghan had escaped and set out to gather more fossil ivory tusks on the Ohio, as will be described later.[13]

Besides ivory, however, there was another compelling reason for Abenaki hunters' interest in the strange remains in the marsh, hinted at in the early Huron legend of collecting "magic horns" from monsters. Stories about dreadful monsters would have influenced the men's reaction to the eerie sight of many gigantic skeletons emerging from the foul-smelling mire. Around the time of Longueuil's expedition, Father de Charlevoix, a French missionary in eastern Canada, recorded a fascinating Abenaki legend about the Great Elk, a beast that despite its name sounds decidedly elephantine. (Notably, the Iroquois knew this creature as Big Elk; see chapter 1.) This animal's bulk made other animals seem like ants; it had an extremely tough hide and could stride through eight-foot snowdrifts. And the Great Elk had a peculiar, prehensile "extra arm" extending from its upper body. Did some of Longueuil's marksmen associate the mastodon skeletons they discovered in the Ohio marsh with the legendary Great Elk?

Some scholars have suggested that the mythology of the Abenakis and other tribes may actually preserve ancient memories of living mastodons and mammoths hunted by distant ancestors in the Ice Age. Humans and Pleistocene megafaunas did coexist for many centuries, until the large mammals died out between eight and ten thousand years ago. It has been demonstrated that oral narratives about datable geological events can extend back at least seven thousand years, and perhaps further. The notion that ancestral memories of Pleistocene-Holocene creatures persisted in folklore is a possibility, but it is difficult to prove. On the other hand, stories of such creatures could also have arisen from observations or reports of well-preserved woolly mammoth remains in Arctic ice or in New England bogs. Water monsters with horns constitute a

3. Horned Water Monster and a war canoe; note two large serpents below. Algonquian rock art, Great Lakes. After Conway 1993. Drawing by Peter Faris 2004.

pervasive motif across North American Indian cultures where prehistoric elephant remains occur. The image of a horned water monster may have been a way of explaining mysterious tusked skeletons eroding out of marshes and riverbanks.[14]

Abenaki tradition also featured a terrible water monster known as *Meskag-kwedemos* ("swamp creature"). These monsters were said to lie in lakes, rivers, and marshes, posing great danger to canoes (fig. 3). According to Abenaki historical records (beaded mnemonic devices known as *wapapi*), in the early seventeenth century Abenaki guides warned French captains in Quebec to be "respectful" of Meskag-kwedemos. Men in canoes "should not make loud noises or fire their muskets without good reason." War canoes were especially at risk, because "in the bloody days of the wars, the monsters are numerous; there is much to eat." When fighting the Mohawks, for example, the Abenakis would "take hold of the enemy's canoes to capsize them . . . so the Meskag-kwedemos will rise from the depths to eat them."[15]

When hunters from Quebec encountered the unusual, oversize animal bones and tusks in the Ohio marsh, they may have associated them with water monsters. That would parallel the reports of early French explorers in the Great Lakes region who learned that when Natives discovered massive mastodon bones and tusks in swamps and streambeds, they also identified them as underwater horned monsters. Perhaps the Abenaki hunters believed that the bones and teeth from the swamp carcasses would convince the French that the fearsome Meskag-kwedemos really existed.

Is it possible that an Abenaki narrative about water monsters actually accompanied the fossils to Paris? It's an intriguing thought. Consider how Daubenton came to know the facts of the 1739 discovery. As we have seen, Daubenton stated that the discovery was made by "les Sauvages," and that they were the only ones to see the fossils in situ. The description of their discovery came either from Longueuil himself before his death in 1755 or from other Frenchmen on the Chickasaw campaign of 1739—or perhaps (as George Gaylord Simpson suggested) from written notations about the Indian discovery that accompanied the specimens when they were placed in the Cabinet du Roi in 1740. In any of these cases, an oral or written account may well have mentioned an interpretation of the remains offered by original finders. Keep in mind that the Indians spoke some French and Longueuil and his men knew some Algonquian, so they could have conversed about the hunters' remarkable discovery in the salt marsh.

French explorers and scientific thinkers of Daubenton's era (and earlier) were very interested in recording what Native Americans thought about large vertebrate fossils. In 1748, for example, Count Buffon, Daubenton's colleague in Paris, received a letter from a French officer named Fabri who had accompanied Longueuil to New Orleans. Fabri recounted a Louisiana tribe's tradition about monsters based on mastodon fossils. He also told Buffon that similar fossils were known to Natives in Canada, and Fabri remarked that some Indians referred to mastodons as "the grandfather of the buffalo." We know that Fabri (and another Frenchman named du Hamel) also detailed for Daubenton the circumstances of the 1739 discovery on the Ohio. Little is known about Fabri except that he participated in the campaign from Montreal down the Ohio and on to New Orleans, and he obviously maintained an active interest in Indian fossil lore.[16]

If Daubenton knew of Canadian Indian traditions about carnivorous water monsters that suddenly emerged to attack canoes, it would help explain his erroneous conclusion that the giant molars belonged to a *living* species of gigantic carnivorous hippopotamus. He was unfamiliar with mastodon molars, which—unlike flat elephant molars—have sharp points, and in his day, pointed teeth were taken to indicate a carnivore. Mastodon teeth do resemble hippopotamus teeth, so it was logical for the French naturalist to visualize a New World version of the terrible African water monster feared for its attacks on boats.[17]

Indeed, in Europe, knowledge of the hippopotamus was "wondrously vague" until the end of the eighteenth century (the first live hippo was not displayed in Europe until 1850). In Daubenton's day, the mid-1700s, information about the hippopotamus came primarily from the Bible and from classical Greek sources, which described the animal as a monstrous water beast that overturned boats and killed men, something like the Meskag-kwedemos. In about 1760, a French explorer in the Congo sent a letter to Paris describing an enormous water beast, apparently a hippopotamus, that suddenly surged up to smash boats, and Daubenton would have known Konrad Gesner's illustration (1563) of a hippo as an aquatic, carnivorous monster attacking a crocodile, and other seventeenth-century engravings of savage Hippo-Behemoths (fig. 4). As late as 1711, Siberian mammoths were confused with the biblical Behemoth, identified by theologians as the hippopotamus.[18]

And, since the early 1600s, we know that the Abenakis had warned French captains about very similar water monsters. Such tales filtered back to France, through traders, explorers, and soldiers like Fabri. All these facts suggest that Daubenton may well have been influenced by American Indian lore about dangerous water monsters when he postulated that the great molars belonged to a giant hippopotamus living in the Ohio River. Unfortunately, any written notes once attached to the fossils about the hunters' discovery have been lost. All we can say for sure is that the hunters decided

4. Hippopotamus attacking a crocodile, woodcut by Konrad Gesner, 1563. Until the mid–nineteenth century, Europeans imagined the hippopotamus as a carnivorous "water monster." Dover Pictorial Archives.

it was worth the extra work and weight to collect specimens from the three monstrous creatures. They took a tooth from each jawbone and dragged some tusks and one immense thighbone from the bog and loaded them into their canoes.

The Ohio Fossils in Paris

As I delved deeper into this story, I became ever more curious to know what finally happened to those historic fossils. In 1943, George Gaylord Simpson had also wondered whether Longueuil's specimens might still be in the museum in Paris, but the German occupation of France during World War II made it impossible for him to confirm their whereabouts. In December 2000, more than 250 years after the Ohio fossils were found by Native American hunters, I arrived in Paris hoping to learn the fate of the relics. Would they still be in the old Museum of Natural History?

Walking in the cold rain along the Seine, I turn onto the rue Cuvier and enter the gate of the Jardin des Plantes, the royal botanical gardens founded in 1635. Passing by Cuvier's house, the site of his study and anatomy laboratory, I remind myself of the arduous odyssey of the specimens. After traveling down the Ohio and Mississippi rivers in 1739, and withstanding attacks by the Chickasaws, the fossils arrived in New Orleans, were loaded on a French ship, crossed the Atlantic, and were finally placed in the Cabinet du Roi, in the Jardin des Plantes. Between 1740 and 1861, the fossils had been stored in at least three different buildings. I knew that the femur and two of the three teeth (but not the ivory tusks) had somehow survived the upheavals of the French Revolution (1789), because Cuvier had mentioned their existence in 1834. But after that the fossils seem to have dropped out of sight.

Paleontologists had advised me that the Paris museum's dust-laden collections were disorganized, last cataloged in 1861. To find a particular specimen would require luck; it would also require the help of some individual in the laboratory who happened to have studied that particular fossil and might remember its location in the museum's vast holdings. I had arranged to meet Pascal Tassy, curator of vertebrate fossils in the Museum of Natural History, at his office on the rue Buffon. The lanky paleontologist hears my request with delighted surprise. By an amazing coincidence, he says that he himself unearthed the two Longueuil specimens from deep in the museum that very week. Tassy was comparing the teeth with other mastodon teeth from America, in an attempt to find the lost third tooth from Longueuil's expedition. *Voilà!*—there are the two big molars on his old oaken desk, amid a jumble of other American mastodon teeth, including one sent to Cuvier by Benjamin Franklin (fig. 5).

Tassy places one of the molars in my hands. I turn the heavy, burnished tooth over in my palms and read Daubenton's inscription in faded black ink: *b. de Longueuil 1739*. We marvel over the fact that we are holding the very same molars wrested from the stony jaws of marsh monsters so long ago in America. "What a story these relics must hold," Tassy reflects. He confides that he hopes someday to visit Big Bone Lick in Kentucky, "the place where American paleontology *and* bourbon were invented." Then he confides another secret. The huge femur that was discovered by the Indians is prominently displayed here in the museum. But few people know it, says Tassy, because the label is wrong.

5. Pascal Tassy, curator of vertebrate paleontology, National Museum of Natural History, Paris, holding one of the mastodon molars discovered by the Indian hunters in Longueuil's army near Big Bone Lick on the Ohio River, 1739. Photo: Adrienne Mayor.

Sure enough, at the top of the curving wrought-iron staircase, two great mastodon femurs from the New World have guarded the entrance to the Paleontological Gallery since about 1865. Held upright by iron bands, the South American bone on the left is labeled as a gift to Cuvier from the great naturalist Baron Alexander von Humboldt. The North American mastodon femur on the right is labeled "Gift of Thomas Jefferson" (fig. 6).

Going through the museum archives, however, Tassy was surprised to find that Thomas Jefferson had never shipped a mastodon

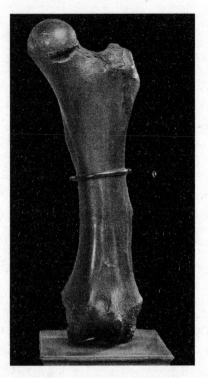

6. The fossil mastodon femur discovered in 1739 by Indian hunters on the Ohio River, now at the entrance to the National Museum of Natural History, Paris. Courtesy of Pascal Tassy, *Geodiversitas* 24 (2002).

femur to Paris. Jefferson, America's third president and a paleontological scholar, did collect many fossils from Ohio, Kentucky, and Virginia, and he sent several important specimens to Cuvier in Paris. But that was half a century *after* Longueuil's expedition, after Big Bone Lick had become famous.

Mystified, Tassy dug further and learned that an American scholar studying Jefferson's papers in Paris, Howard Rice, had uncovered the mistake in 1951. By comparing the meticulous records kept by Jefferson of the specimens he sent and Cuvier's record of fossils received, he established that the great thighbone long thought to have been donated by Jefferson exactly matches

Daubenton's detailed drawing of the femur brought to Paris by Longueuil in 1740. It was a natural mistake for later curators to assume that the venerable pair of American fossils must have been donated by the two most celebrated scientific friends of Cuvier, Baron von Humboldt and President Jefferson. There is no doubt, however, that this femur is the very same one found by Abenaki hunters in the marsh in 1739. In 2001, the labels were corrected.[19]

In summer of 2002, a bulky package from Paris was delivered to me in Bozeman, Montana. Inside were realistically painted casts of the two great molars discovered by the hunters, the specimens that Tassy had shown me. But there was a third colossal molar, twice the size of the others (fig. 7). It turned out that Tassy had solved the case of the missing third tooth, lost for two centuries in the bowels of the Paris museum. By comparing the original 1756 drawing of the three molars with all the other mastodon teeth from America that I had seen spread out across his desk that day in 2000, Tassy was able to identify the lost molar. The third molar had been mislabeled sometime after Cuvier's statement of 1834, identified as a gift to Buffon from the British naturalist Peter Collinson, an avid collector of American mastodon fossils. At last, all of the relics collected by the Abenaki huntsmen have been accounted for, except for the ivory tusks, which were probably looted during the French Revolution.[20]

"The Indian hunters knew that these bones and teeth were strange and important," remarked Tassy that day in Paris. "Accordingly, all the early French scientists who studied these fossils credited the American Indians with the discovery." How many other Indians had observed mastodon or dinosaur fossils in America, mused Tassy, and what stories did they tell? It was a paleontologist's question that only a folklorist could answer. Tassy's curiosity spurred me to search for evidence that the remarkable mastodon remains of the Ohio Valley had captured the attention of other Native American groups who traveled in the area. The earliest oral legend told by northern tribes about the Ohio fossils was written down twenty-seven years after the Abenaki discovery of 1739, by a trader named George Morgan.

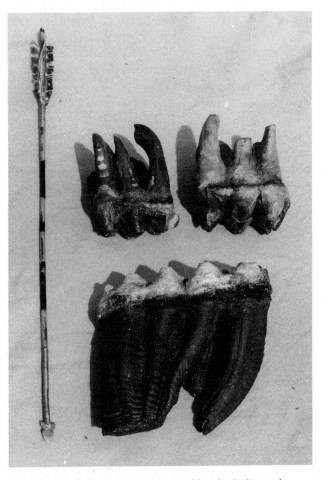

7. The three mastodon molars discovered by the Indians who accompanied Longueuil down the Ohio River in 1739, now in Paris. Arrow = twenty-four inches long. Casts created by the Laborotoire de Paleontologie, Muséum National d'Histoire Naturelle, Paris. Photo: Adrienne Mayor.

IROQUOIS AND WYANDOT KNOWLEDGE OF BIG BONE LICK

In 1766, George Morgan accompanied the indomitable Irish trader George Croghan on his return to the salt licks on the Ohio, a year after the boatload of fossils and ivory had been sunk during the Indian attack described above. Morgan, age twenty-three, was the junior partner of a trading company in Philadelphia. (Later, during the Revolutionary War era, Morgan won the trust of the Indians by his passionate defense of their territorial claims, as George Washington's Indian agent for the Continental Congress, and helped to instill the Founding Fathers' admiration of Indian democracies.)

In 1766, Croghan's party discovered the remains of at least thirty mastodon skeletons at the edge of a swamp. Morgan personally packed a large box full of mud-encrusted bones, including a femur, a very large tusk, and huge jawbones with molars (fig. 8). But Morgan also collected one of the oldest recorded Indian traditions about the Ohio fossils. By this time, George Croghan had become a celebrity whose exploits were narrated in the newspapers along with reports about Big Bone Lick, and Morgan was equally famous. Remarkably, however, modern historians of Big Bone Lick are unaware of Morgan's account—which was published in London and New York in 1795–96 by William Winterbotham, cited in 1803 by Rembrandt Peale, and reprinted in America by Henry Mercer in 1885.[21]

Morgan recalled his trip to Big Bone Lick in correspondence to a Mr. Morse (probably Jedidiah Morse, the "father of American geography," a scholar sympathetic to Indian causes). Morgan remarked that he and other traders in the Colonies had already seen many large molars from the Ohio Valley, which had been collected by various Indian war parties. When Croghan and Morgan arrived at the salt licks in 1766, they traded with several Iroquois war parties who were on their way "to fight the southern Indians."

From earliest times, the Iroquois of the area around Lake Ontario and New York State routinely traveled down the Ohio River on their way to make war in the deep South. The powerful Six Nations of the Iroquois Confederacy (Seneca, Cayuga, Mohawk,

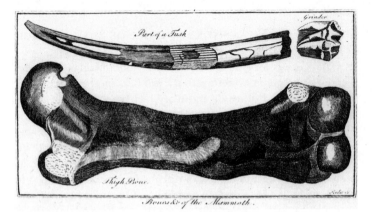

8. Mastodon tusk, tooth, and femur, collected by George Morgan in 1766, at the time of his conversation with the Iroquois-Wyandot chief at Big Bone Lick. Engraving published in Winterbotham 1795.

Oneida, Onondaga, and, after the early 1700s, Tuscarora) had controlled the Ohio Valley for centuries—even before Columbus, according to Iroquois historians. The Iroquois had turned against their Huron neighbors in Canada in the early 1500s, and in the 1600s they had nearly wiped them out. By about 1700, the Huron survivors left Canada for Ohio, where they became known as Wyandots. Subsequently, the Iroquois made peace with the Wyandots and included their "little brothers" in raids against southern enemies, such as the Cherokees and Chickasaws.[22]

At Big Bone Lick, Morgan and Croghan met a large party of Iroquois and Wyandot warriors traveling south to fight the Chickasaws. The head chief was a very old man of about eighty-four, wrote Morgan. "I fixed on this venerable chief as a person from whom some knowledge might be obtained." After presenting him with tobacco, paint, and ammunition, Morgan, with careful courtesy, asked the old man what his people knew of the immense skeletons in the marsh. Croghan, who spoke Iroquois, may have translated, as Morgan wrote down the story. "Whilst I was yet a boy," began the old chief, "I passed this road several times, to war against the Catawbas."

Morgan failed to record the old chief's name or tribe. The Iroquois and Catawbas of South Carolina had engaged in fierce warfare between 1650 and 1760, and the Huron-Wyandots fought Catawbas until a treaty was made in 1729. So the chief may have been a Wyandot who had fought Catawbas as a boy, or he may have been an Iroquois. In treaty archives and the diaries of Croghan, Gist, and George Washington, I found the names of several Iroquois chiefs who conversed with British colonists in the period 1740–60. For example, the Onondaga orator Canassatego attended a council in Philadelphia in 1742, and the Seneca chief Canagaat came from his "castle" on the Allegheny to deliver speeches at Fort Pitt in 1759 and 1761. The Iroquois chiefs Iononerissa and Cosswertenicea had dealt with Croghan in the Ohio Valley in 1749, as did Tanacharisson and Monacatoocha, who also met with George Washington on the Ohio River in 1754 (Washington himself collected fossils at Big Bone Lick). One of these men may have been the old chief who spoke with Morgan in 1766. Monacatoocha would be a good candidate: in 1754 Washington had recorded his speech castigating white intruders and "Disturbers in this Land [which] is our Land, and not yours, [given to us] by the Great Being Above."[23] Similar sentiments are prominent in the old chief's fossil story of 1766, which continued as follows:

> The wise old chiefs, among whom was my grandfather, then gave me the tradition, handed down to us, respecting these bones. After the Great Spirit first formed the world, he made the birds and beasts which now inhabit it. He also made man, but having formed him very white, and imperfect, and ill-tempered, he placed him on one side of it [the world], where he now inhabits, and from whence he has lately found a passage across the great water, to be a plague to us.
>
> As the Great Spirit was not pleased with his work, he took of black clay and made what *you* call a negro, with a woolly head. This black man was much better than the white man, but still he did not answer the wish of the Great Spirit. . . . At last, the Great Spirit having procured a piece of pure, fine red clay, formed from it the Red Man, perfectly to his mind, and he was well pleased with him, that he

placed him on this great island, separate from the white and black
man, and gave his rules for conduct, promising happiness in proportion as they should be observed.

At last the old man turned to the fossils. The red man "was perfectly
happy for ages, but foolish young people, at length forgetting his
rules, became exceedingly ill-tempered and wicked." Therefore,
"the Great Spirit created the Great Buffalo, the bones of which you
now see before us. These made war upon the human species alone,
and destroyed all but a few, who repented and promised the Great
Spirit to live according to his laws if he would restrain the devouring enemy. Whereupon he sent lightning and thunder, and destroyed the whole race [of giant bison] in this spot." But a pair of
these great bison, male and female, "he shut up in yonder mountain, ready to let loose again should the occasion require."

The Creator relented and destroyed the giant bison before they
completely wiped out the Indians. With the aid of scholar Barbara
Mann's insights about Iroquois beliefs, we can imagine that the
original Iroquois and Wyandot tale was a story of restoring harmony and balance in nature. Instead of totally destroying dangerous earth-water monsters, sky spirits "neutralized" them with lightning and buried them in the earth, where they remain "dormant."[24]

The introductory part of the chief's story about the geographic
distribution of three human races was obviously recent oratory, intended for European ears. The chronology of creation progressing
from imperfect white men to black men and culminating in morally
advanced red men veers from older, traditional Iroquois belief that
Natives were created before Europeans. References to race were
common in Indians' speeches to whites at this time, and the chief's
criticism of Europeans was meant to support Native claims to the
god-given lands being stolen by the encroaching settlers. The chief
viewed the ancient bones as markers of territorial rights, as physical
memorials of the sky spirit's intention to make the land safe for
Indian ancestors. The concept that fossil legends could serve as historical "deeds" to land to contest Euro-American appropriations
was suggested to me by Paul Apodaca, a Navajo-Mixtec scholar of
Native American mythology. It is a theme that recurs as we travel

across the New World, and it also figures in modern disputes over fossil ownership.[25]

The rest of the chief's tale, about the giant buffalo, had probably circulated for at least three generations. If the chief in his eighties had heard the story as a boy from his grandfather, that means the story explaining the great bones was already being told by about 1690—a generation before Longueuil's expedition. The Iroquois, and later the Wyandots, on the warpath against the Cherokees and Catawbas followed the old Iroquois Trail south (the same route taken by the Canadian Indians who canoed with Longueuil down the Allegheny and Ohio rivers in 1739). As Iroquois and Wyandot warriors of the Northeast traveled back and forth to raid in the South, they became aware of the masses of oversize animal skeletons submerged along the Ohio.

The obvious antiquity of the tradition recorded by Morgan led me to search for further evidence to indicate just how long ago the Iroquois and Wyandots from the North had first discovered the big bones in the Ohio marshes.

Giant Bison and Witch Buffalo

It was thanks to the long-standing French fascination with Native American fossil lore that I began to recover the evidence I was seeking. During my visit with Pascal Tassy and other paleontologists in the Paris Museum of Natural History, Madame Françoise Ozanne, the elderly librarian of the French Geological Society, took an interest in my project. She showed me "Les Légendes des Iroquois," an article penned in an ornate style in 1885 by the Marquis de Nadaillac. He included a French translation of a curious tale about pygmies killing gigantic buffalo at a salt lick, a tale that had been translated from Iroquois into English only a few years earlier. I would eventually discover that this story was a real fossil legend, probably dating to the 1500s.

Back in the United States, I consulted the original report to the U.S. Bureau of Ethnography cited by Nadaillac. There I read the story, "The Warrior Saved by Pigmies," told by an unnamed Iroquois storyteller in his or her native tongue to Mrs. Erminnie Smith, an ethnologist-linguist born in 1836. Smith lived many years with the Iroquois, spoke their language, and was adopted into the Tuscarora nation. But neither Erminnie Smith nor the Marquis de Nadaillac had any idea that they were translating an account of an early Iroquois encounter with the Ohio fossils. Nadaillac noted elsewhere that the Iroquois credited thunder spirits with the destruction of giants, and suggested that chance discoveries of huge bones and teeth of pachyderms of Tertiary and Quaternary times must have confirmed such legends for the Iroquois, but in this case somehow he failed to connect the striking story about enormous bison remains to fossils. In 1914, the British mythologist Lewis Spence retold the same tale—his version was illustrated with a romantic painting of the pygmies—but he too missed the story's paleontological meaning. Like Nadaillac and Smith before him, Spence focused on the supernatural pygmies in the story. But for a folklorist searching for fossil legends, the story's geographic and historical significance stands out. It remained to discern how old the tale really was.[26]

The tale begins, "It was customary for the Iroquois tribes to make raids upon the Cherokees while the latter inhabited the swamps of Florida." That was an important clue—I asked Barbara Mann what time period was signified by this phrase. The storyteller had used the old Spanish designation "La Florida," which meant the entire Southeast, from Carolina to Florida to the Mississippi River. This indicated that the story had been told during the Spanish colonial era. Other clues to the tale's age lay in the enmity between Cherokees and Iroquois. According to Mann, the Iroquois had driven the Cherokees south from the Ohio Valley in about A.D. 500, and according to the Iroquois historian David Cusick (writing in 1825), the Iroquois were already battling the Cherokees in the Southeast by the time of Columbus, although many modern historians conservatively date the hostilities to the late 1500s. Notably, the English colonist John Smith met an Iroquois war party in Virginia in 1608.[27]

The Iroquois were adventurous long-distance explorers, bringing back reports of strange sights and exotic folklore, including fossil lore. For the Iroquois, a journey from upstate New York to the southern Alleghenies "was regarded as a mere excursion or scouting trip," and journeys of thousands of miles were ordinary for them. They routinely brought back captives from distant locales, Shawnees and Cherokees, who were adopted into the Iroquois nations. Some captives became storytellers, integrating their own traditions with those of their new tribe. In this way, the Iroquois probably heard Shawnee ideas about Big Bone Lick and perhaps learned that the Cherokees called the Ohio Valley "the Land of Horned Water Monsters," or *Ukténa*, who were the enemies of the Thunder Birds (*Tlanuhwa*) of the Tennessee River.[28]

Still tracking the date of the tale of the pygmies and giant bison, I searched out other tales of early Iroquois explorers. In Native cultures, scouts and explorers were trusted reporters and often became storytellers, or repositories of oral traditions. According to David Cusick, his tribe's oral histories stated that some centuries before Columbus the Iroquois had sent an expedition party of fifteen men and two chiefs to explore west of the Mississippi River. Just before reaching the Rocky Mountains, however, they encountered "a giant" and turned back. After many years, the explorers returned home with amazing tales of the strange people and animals of the West. Around the same time, wrote Cusick, the first Iroquois war party crossed the Ohio River and camped on the bank on the Kentucky side, where a monstrous "furious Lizard" killed all the warriors except for one, who killed the monster and survived to tell the tale. Although there is no mention of unusual skeletal remains in these two ancient accounts in Iroquois oral history, it's tempting to speculate that the giant and the monster lizard might have reflected attempts to describe some extraordinary fossils in the Badlands and the Ohio Valley, respectively. At least, I was beginning to fill in the cultural and chronological background of Erminnie Smith's story of pygmies and giant bison.[29]

According to that tale, after more than two years of fighting Cherokees in the "Southern country," a party of Iroquois warriors was returning home. When one of the men fell deathly ill, the group abandoned him on a river south of the Allegheny Mountains, the Ohio. On their arrival back in their village, the men claimed that their companion had died in battle. But the warrior eventually recovered and made his way home, where he told this story: One night, near death and lying by the river, the warrior had a vision in which three pygmies or Little People arrived by canoe. The Little People told him that they were on their way to a nearby salt lick where there were "many strange animals." They planned to ambush these giant beasts as they emerged from the earth. The sick warrior watched as a huge male and two female animals "arose out of the lick" and the Little People killed them with arrows.

The Little People cared for the warrior until he was well, and escorted him back to his village. After he told his tale, the men who had abandoned him were punished. But the warrior's compelling description of gigantic "buffalo" rising from the murky salt marsh caused the Iroquois to develop a "strong desire to see the lick." Accordingly, a large party of Iroquois was organized—not for war, but to rediscover the bone bed. The Iroquois "searched for it and found it surrounded with the bones of various large animals killed by the pigmies."

The hallucinatory vision of giant buffalo emerging from the swamp could be interpreted as the delirious warrior's efforts to make sense of the sight of large, ghostly animal skeletons partly submerged in a swamp of the Ohio River. His feverish condition, brought on by illness, was like a vision quest, in which dreams of the past or future are sought through fasting. The idea of special, sacred animals hidden in the ground is a widespread Amerindian motif, and the theme of a warrior abandoned by companions frames many other vision-quest stories; for example, a Wyandot story about a warrior's discovery of the Thunder Beings begins with a similar abandonment. To his observation of the real but mystifying natural phenomenon of remarkable bones, the warrior added some familiar elements from Iroquoian mythology. The Little People (translated by Smith as "pigmies") were small folk of supernatural strength, legendary protectors of isolated people and hunters, and they had helped the early Iroquois by slaying monsters, serpents, and other dangerous, primeval creatures.

The Wyandots also had a legend about Big Bone Lick, collected by an ethnologist in 1850–90. In the Wyandot story, the bones were identified as those of Witch Buffaloes, immense female bison as high as trees with horns extending straight out from their foreheads as long as a man is tall. Long ago, these Witch Buffaloes ruled the "great and ancient spring" of pure water at Big Bone Lick, and so dominated the spring that other, smaller game animals were forced out. The Wyandots could no longer hunt or gather salt there, until the Little People wiped out the Witch Buffaloes, leaving the vast heaps of big bones at the spring. Then, as the pure spring shrank in size over the ages, it came to be called *Oh-tseh-yooh-mah*, "Spring of Bitter Water."

The Wyandot tale accounts for both the salty water and the masses of bones at Big Bone Lick. Notably, among the Pleistocene fossil remains of the Ohio River are the skulls of extinct, giant bison with straight horns that span six feet, and these were apparently recognized by Wyandots, Iroquois, and other early Indian observers as much larger relatives of living buffalo.

A crucial aspect of the Iroquois fossil legend preserved by Erminnie Smith is that the warrior's discovery of strange remains in a faraway land inspired his tribe to organize an expedition to investigate the big bone site. According to Barbara Mann, bones and parts of animals, including fossils, were considered powerful "earth medicine." Noting that the Iroquois often went on "pilgrimages to such spiritual spots and bone heaps," Mann suggests that the Iroquois in the tale intended to gather some of the bones of the giant game from the deep past to use as hunting medicine. And, indeed, among the Wyandots, too, there are old traditions about going out to collect the "calcified bones of destroyed monsters" to make hunting amulets, described by a Wyandot elder in 1912.[30]

The story of the Iroquois warrior at Big Bone Lick is the first of many examples described in this book of active verification of paleontological finds undertaken by various Native nations. These widespread examples counter George Gaylord Simpson's assertion that Indian discoveries were always accidental, never purposeful, that they were casual finds without sequel, and that they never resulted in "permanent record or continuous development."[31] The reports and investigations by the Iroquois and others were not scientific in the modern sense, of course, but there is something akin to scientific inquiry in these activities. Scouts and explorers were expected to bring back accurate, verifiable reports of their observations. Deliberate efforts were made to authenticate empirical evidence: witnesses seeking reproducible results traveled to view the firsthand reports of big bone sites. The authentication led to narrative theories explaining the giant bones, which were recognized not only as organic remains but also as related to smaller, living species. These explanations were then integrated into oral histories and maintained over centuries in an oral culture, satisfying Simpson's requirement of "permanent record and continuous development."

Some significant details of the original Iroquois and Wyandot stories were almost certainly lost or mangled in translations, and Morgan's translated tale of 1766 has strong biblical overtones. One longs to know the chief's exact words without the eighteenth-century European filter. As many Native American scholars have pointed out in conversations with me about the fossil legends gathered here, European concepts such as "Great Spirit" or "Creator" ring false in original Indian cosmology. The traditional view of the cosmos was based on the maintenance of a precarious balance among earth, water, and sky powers, so that no one force "runs amok," explains Barbara Mann. Sky, earth, and water powers (often represented by large birds, giant buffalo, and various land and water monsters) were in eternal and sometimes violent tension but could never totally destroy each other.

Applying Mann's insights, one realizes that many fossil tales concerned restoring natural harmony and balance. Rather than eliminating all of the earth-water monsters, sky spirits struck them with lightning and buried them in the earth, where they continue to exist in a kind of mystical suspended animation.[32]

In many oral fossil legends recorded by Europeans, distortions and misinterpretations can make it difficult to untangle what the Native speakers really intended to say. Yet it seems well worth the effort to try to understand these extremely rare written records of ancient oral traditions. The Iroquois account of the giant bison bones in the Ohio Valley probably dates back to the 1500s, the era when most historians believe that the Iroquois-Cherokee conflicts began, calling into question Simpson's argument that most Indian fossil finds were "relatively late, long after white men were thoroughly familiar with similar fossils."[33] The Iroquois had observed the Ohio fossils at least two centuries before Longueuil's expedition, and as Mann points out, the story of the warrior's experience at Big Bone Lick has none of the European influences so obvious in Morgan's story of 1766. But Morgan's story is significant because it confirms that by the late 1600s the Iroquois (and Wyandots) had devised a coherent theory to explain the oft-observed evidence of extraordinary animal bones in the Ohio Valley.

The Abenaki discovery of mastodon fossils at Big Bone Lick in 1739 and the even older Iroquois and Wyandot interpretations of Pleistocene fossils on the Ohio River as the remains of giant bison show that, before the arrival of Europeans, Native Americans had already observed large vertebrate fossils as organic evidence of animals of the distant past and had tried to understand their disappearance. Unlike the explanatory narratives of the ancient Greeks and Romans and medieval Europeans, who commonly identified Pleistocene mammal bones as those of human giants, the legends collected by Smith, Morgan, and others indicate that many North American Indian groups understood that some of the extinct mammal skeletons belonged to larger ancestors of modern bison.

This introduction has opened a window onto the earliest interpretations of remarkable fossil bones encountered by Abenakis, Iroquois, and Wyandots of the Northeast on their adventures in the South. The following chapter shows that these groups and others were also aware of large vertebrate fossils in their own lands, and their local knowledge was of considerable interest to such investigators as Cotton Mather, Thomas Jefferson, and Georges Cuvier.

1

The Northeast: Giants, Great Bears, and Grandfather of the Buffalo

There is very Little in any Tradition of the
Salvages [*sic*] to be relied upon.
—*Cotton Mather, 1712*

This is their Tradition and I see no reason why it should
not be received as good History, at least as good as a
great part of ours.
—*George Rogers Clark, 1789*

AFTER the Abenaki discovery
of 1739 and the American fossils' scientific debut in Paris in 1762,
the mastodon, Columbian mammoth, and giant bison deposits at
Big Bone Lick began to attract the interest of European and American scientists. The early investigators sought out the traditions of
the Shawnees and Delawares in their efforts to understand the extensive bone beds in the Ohio Valley. But Pleistocene mastodons
and oversize buffalo and bears—as well as dinosaur tracks and even
rare dinosaur bones—also existed in the Northeast, and these

conspicuous remains had influenced exciting tales of giant creatures among the Iroquois, Delaware, and other nations. European colonists first learned some of these stories as early as 1705, when some stupendous "bones of giants" suddenly appeared along the Hudson River.

At the turn of the eighteenth century, there was no European science to contrast with Native American interpretations of big bones. Until 1793–1806, when Georges Cuvier published his scientific discovery that mastodon and mammoth fossils were the remains of long-extinct elephant species, Europeans and colonists in America were struggling to understand the reports of skeletons of startling magnitude from around the world. According to traditional biblical interpretation, the petrified bones belonged to giants drowned in Noah's Flood, and their presence in far-flung lands was believed to demonstrate the Flood's global effects. Many Europeans believed that the mammoth remains in Siberia, for example, had been carried there by the vast waves of the Deluge. In 1804, Cuvier formally described and named the American mastodon, and he devised a scientific theory of catastrophism to replace the Flood myth. But references to the biblical Deluge to explain the huge skeletons recurred through the mid–nineteenth century. Meanwhile, some early naturalists speculated that the great bones of the "American *incognitum*" or "Ohio animal" belonged to whales, or to carnivorous beasts that would be found alive in the unexplored wilderness further west.[1]

Pre-Darwinian European and American theories about the meaning of the fossil record have received considerable attention in paleontological literature, but the fact that Indians of North America had observed large vertebrate fossils and created their own explanations is little known. Those traditions, like those of the Iroquois and Wyandots retold in the introduction, were part of a rich body of lore handed down orally over generations, now mostly lost to us. Tantalizing fragments of those ideas are preserved in colonial accounts of fossil exposures in the Ohio Valley, New England, and the mid-Atlantic, and in recorded conversations with Native people. And by the early nineteenth century, some literate Native historians began to publish (and update) their people's oral traditions. Drawing on all these sources, this chapter explores how the cultures of the Northeast viewed the physical evidence of strange creatures that had disappeared in the deep past.

GIANTS AT CLAVERACK, NEW YORK, 1705

The spectacle of enormous bones and teeth eroding out of the banks of the Hudson at Claverack (south of Albany, New York) in 1705–6 drew curious crowds from miles around (see map 1). Two groups in particular—the Indians of the Hudson Valley and Dutch and English farmers—debated the identity of the remarkable remains, and word of the New World "giants" electrified intellectual circles in the Colonies and Europe.

Indian tales about giants fascinated the Puritan poet Edward Taylor, who examined some of the Claverack creature's great "fangs" (one was said to hold a pint of liquor) and bones (one thighbone was claimed to be seventeen feet long—three times the actual length of a mastodon femur). In his letters, his diary, and a long, romantic poem about the giant based on local Indian lore (1705–8), Taylor gives us a sense of the conversations between colonists and Native Americans about the fossils. Some colonists thought the remains were whale or elephant bones, but those who believed literally in Noah's Flood agreed with the Indians who thought the remains had belonged to extinct giants.

The Indians "flocking to see the monstrous Bones upbraided the Dutch farmers" for not believing what the Indians had already told them, that giants once inhabited the Hudson Valley. In about 1668, as a young man, Taylor himself had heard local Indians describe a "Gyant of incredible Magnitude," but he had "disbelieved it till he saw the Teeth" of the Claverack skeleton in 1705. According to the Indians (probably Iroquoian-speaking Mohawks, Algonquian Mohicans, Abenakis, and Pequots, among others), the Claverack remains belonged to a giant called *Weetucks* or *Maushops*, who lived about eight or ten generations ago (some said it had died out "centuries ago").

Map 1. Eastern North America (map by Michele Mayor Angel)

The description of the giant, as "high as the Tops of the Pine Trees," seems to conflate the behavior of a marauding elephant with that of a huge bear. Weetucks hunted bears by knocking them out of tree branches, and it could wade into "the River 12 or 14 feet deep and catch many Sturgeons at a time." (Keep in mind that in many Native traditions, "giants" of ancient eras were often understood to be primeval beings that were neither animal nor human. The traditional Abenaki saying is typical: "In the beginning when everything started, men were like animals and animals were men.")

There was controversy among the Indians over whether these giant beings were humanlike or dangerous to humans. According to Taylor, "the Tradition among the Indians" was that although the giants were carnivorous, they were "peaceable and would not hurt the little Indians." Nevertheless, people of the old days were always afraid of them, even though it was possible to approach them cautiously with offers of meat. A contrasting version of the fossil legend was told by the Mohican and Delaware people. In their traditions, a small population of gigantic "naked bears" had once preyed on humans in the East, but the last of the species had been slaughtered long ago on a precipice of the Mahicanni Siper (Hudson River).[2]

In 1712, the erudite Puritan minister Cotton Mather wrote to the Royal Society of London to describe the colossal Claverack skeleton (probably a mastodon's), which he identified as a giant human victim of the Deluge. In his letter, he strove to show that such remains were "scientific proof" that the biblical Flood had inundated the Americas. A complex individual, Mather had a strong interest in Native knowledge of natural history, and he had learned Native languages in order to publish biblical tracts in Algonquian. To support his argument that antediluvian giants had once existed in America, he began to recount Hudson Valley Indian lore. "Upon the Discovery of this horrible *Giant*," Mather wrote, "the *Indians* within an Hundred Miles of the place" all agreed that they had an old tradition, passed down over "some hundreds of years," concerning giants. According to the "Albany Indians [the giant's] Name was *Maughkompos.*"

But here Mather suddenly breaks off to mock the Native language, with its "disagreeable" sounds and ridiculously long names. His narrative ends abruptly: "There is very Little in any Tradition of the Salvages to be relied upon." Ironically, Mather was well versed in many paleontological legends of North American Indians, and he even knew about the Inca and Aztec giant-bone legends reported by the Spanish in Mexico and Peru (presented in the next chapter). Yet, anticipating George Gaylord Simpson's attitude by more than two hundred years, Mather was the first authority in America to deny Indians a role in interpreting important fossil evidence. Mather seems to have made this decision in midsentence. I think he sensed that opening the door to alternative, diverse ideas about giant bones threatened his dogmatic "science" based on a literal reading of the Bible. Unlike his fellow Puritan Taylor, who maintained that the evidence of the bones at Claverack *legitimized* the Native traditions, Mather believed that pagan mythology was inspired by the devil. That belief clashed with his initial impulse to cite the Indian giant legends as proof of Christian doctrine.[3]

Given our fragmentary knowledge of oral traditions, there is no way to know whether ancient legends about Weetucks and Maughkompos and other giant beings of Indian mythology actually originated as attempts to understand large, puzzling skeletons of Pleistocene mammals that no longer lived. But the incomplete accounts preserved by the Puritans are real fossil legends because they show that when extraordinary bones *were* found, like those at Claverack, Native Americans turned to mythic traditions about giants and monsters to account for them (just as many Europeans of the era relied on biblical traditions to explain fossils). Yet, as we will see, the Indians' approach could be more open to integrating new evidence and modern knowledge than was Mather's.

GIANTS AND MONSTERS IN IROQUOIS MYTHOLOGY

The Mohawks who argued with the Dutch farmers over the identity of the Claverack giant belonged to the Iroquois Confederacy, which also included the Cayuga, Oneida, Onondaga, Seneca, and Tuscarora nations. Iroquois folklore features many mysterious creatures that may have been purely imaginary but *might* have been related to observations of large fossils. These tales form a vivid backdrop, a context for Iroquois fossil-finding tales that do relate remarkable remains to mythic creatures.

The oldest oral chronicles spoke of primal times characterized by monsters and giants, such as *Ro-qua-ho*, a gigantic lizardlike beast that killed with violent blows of its tail, and the fierce Stone Giants. This idea of past ages distinguished by different kinds of creatures was a long-standing concept in many Native American traditions, and discoveries of unusual vertebrate fossils would certainly reinforce the idea. The notion of extinction was more easily applied to *land* creatures, because one could see and touch the fossilized remains of extraordinary animals found in the ground and verify that no one had ever seen them alive. But the unknown, unfathomable realm of water was a different matter. I discussed this with Clara Sue Kidwell, a myth scholar of Ojibwe (Chippewa) heritage, who explained that bodies of water evoked awe in Native American mythology. Water's frightening power to swallow and conceal drowned people and animals, and the impossibility of knowing what sorts of primeval monsters might lurk undetected for eons in the dark depths, made lakes, rivers, and swamps places of mystery and danger. Rarely seen denizens of the deep could include primitive "living fossils" that grow many feet long and weigh hundreds of pounds, such as alligator gars, sturgeon, and paddlefish, or alligator snapping turtles, which can reach two hundred pounds.

The Abenakis and other groups feared that monsters could surge up from watery places, as we saw in the introduction, and they often identified the large vertebrate fossils and tusks that emerged along riverbanks, lakes, and marshes as the remains of horned water monsters. An Iroquois tradition recorded in 1825 by the Tuscarora historian David Cusick is especially striking. Some two thousand years before Columbus, a great horned monster killed by thunderbolts appeared on the shore of Lake Ontario, and its stench brought disease. The overpowering stink of rotting frozen mammoths emerging from Arctic ice is a well-known phenomenon. Perhaps a similar event attracted notice in very early times as ice receded from Lake Ontario.[4]

The well-educated David Cusick was the first Iroquois to write a history of his nation, based on oral chronicles extending back many centuries (fig. 9). The Iroquois creation myth, published in 1825 by Cusick, contains an anticipation of evolution theory that

9. David Cusick, Tuscarora (Iroquois) historian, portrait painted by George Catlin, 1837–39. "Cú-sick, Son of the Chief." Smithsonian American Art Museum, Gift of Mrs. Joseph Harrison, Jr.

would have interested George Gaylord Simpson. Cusick interpreted the origin of human "prototypes" in Iroquois oral history to include primates, suggesting that humans and apes were related in primeval times. Apes would have been unknown to the ancient Iroquois (the closest living primates are in Mexico), but Cusick had read about apes and perhaps observed monkeys in zoos in New York in the early 1800s. Cusick's insight foreshadowed by three decades the link that Charles Darwin would propose in *Origin of Species* (1859).[5]

According to Cusick's sources, northern giants, called *Ronnong-wetowanea*, had harassed the early Iroquois in the past, but the giants all died out about twenty-five hundred winters before Columbus discovered America. In 1881, after Darwin's theories had been well publicized, another educated Tuscarora historian, Chief Elias Johnson, wrote that these giants, which he called *Ronong-waca*, had "gone extinct" along with the great mammoths in the "age of monsters." Cusick and Johnson agreed that in ancient times the Iroquois had been obliged to build strong forts to protect themselves from giants and monsters. Interestingly, in the late nineteenth century, mastodon fossils were found at the site of a fortified Iroquois village known as Seneca Castle.[6]

Ko-nea-rau-neh-neh ("Flying Heads") were another type of monster. These terrible heads "disappeared and were . . . concealed in the earth," a detail that seems to hint at fossil skulls in the ground. Other Iroquois tales describe dragons or serpents and water monsters with horns like a giant buffalo's, destroyed by Thunder Beings and by the Little People (small folk with superhuman strength; see introduction). As noted earlier, water monsters may have been visualized with horns because all large, familiar land animals (buffalo, moose, elk, deer) have horns or antlers, and the appearance of tusked mammoth or mastodon remains, eroding out of riverbanks or lakeshores and swamps, would encourage the idea of mysterious water creatures with horns. What about the water monsters' black "scales," which were worn as protective amulets and placed in medicine bundles? The Navajo sometimes identified scutes (horny plates) of dinosaurs in the desert as the scales of a legendary monster. Were the scales collected by the Iroquois large fossil fish scales, I wondered, or scutes from prehistoric crocodiles or giant extinct turtles? But when I asked Iroquois scholar Barbara Mann about this possibility, she informed me that in the case of the Iroquois amulets, the black scales were not fossils but sheets of black mica.[7]

10. Stone Giant of Iroquois legend. Woodcut by David Cusick, *Ancient History of the Six Nations* (1828).

Many Iroquois stories tell of Stone Giants, ferocious men and women called *Ot-ne-yar-heh* who lived about 1,250 years before Columbus, according to Cusick (figs. 10 and 11). They were destroyed by rock slides or trapped in marshy pits, and finally disappeared, although perhaps a few migrated to northern or western lands. In Seneca lore, the Stone Giants were destroyed en masse by fire and earthquake, and the last survivor was killed in a cave. According to Onondaga legend, a Stone Giant had died in a marsh near Cardiff, south of Syracuse, New York. When the Cardiff Giant, the figure of an enormous petrified man, was exhumed with great fanfare in 1869, some Onondagas were excited by the possibility that it was the ancient Stone Giant. But the figure proved to be a white man's hoax, exposed by America's first professor of paleontology, Othniel C. Marsh of Yale.[8]

Other Iroquois legends tell of frightening beasts such as Big Elk (recalling the Abenaki Great Elk; see introduction); enormous serpents, a Monster Bear called *Nya-Gwahe*; a giant animal of the "cat kind" (perhaps the Pleistocene saber-tooth cat); the horrible *Quis-quiss* (which furiously toppled houses), and a huge monster called *Bosh-kwa-dosh*. Speculating in 1825 that *Quisquiss* may have referred to "the Mammoth," David Cusick was the first Indian writer to make an explicit connection between the real, extinct mastodon fossils being discussed by scientists of his day and traditional Indian

11. "The Stone Giants." Painting by Gaon Yah (Ernest Smith), Seneca artist, Tonawanda Reservation, New York, 1936. From the Collections of the Rochester Museum & Science Center, Rochester, New York.

myths about giants and monsters. A half-century later, in 1881, the Tuscarora historian Elias Johnson identified beasts from the "age of monsters," the *Oyahguaharh*, as "some great mammoth." Non-Indians were also beginning to make the connection between the monsters of Native myth and mastodons. In 1856, for example, the ethnologist Henry Rowe Schoolcraft had identified Bosh-kwa-dosh as the mastodon. When the Seneca artist Gaon Yah (Ernest Smith, b. 1907), of Tonawanda Reservation, New York, illustrated the old Iroquois monster legends in 1936, he depicted one of the monsters as a rampaging mammoth (fig. 12).[9]

Iroquois myths of giants going extinct by fire and earthquake, trapped in marshy pits and under landslides, and huge bears, horned monsters, and monstrous heads buried in the ground raise the pos-

12. In this painting of 1936 by Seneca artist Gaon Yah (Ernest Smith) of the Tonawanda Reservation, one of the monsters of Iroquois legend is portrayed as a mammoth. "The Mammoth," from the Collections of the Rochester Museum & Science Center, Rochester, New York.

sibility that fossils may have contributed to the images. But these are not really fossil legends unless some version of the story directly connects the monstrous creatures with unusual remains, such as skeletons, skulls, bones, teeth, tusks, or footprints in stone—as in the following narratives.

The Tooth of the Monster Bear

Many versions of the well-known Iroquois tradition of the Monster Bear, Nya-Gwahe, are authentic fossil legends. As narrated by Taha-dondeh, a Seneca elder in Cattaraugus County (western New York) in 1903, the original event took place "in olden times" and was

13. Iroquois boy racing the Monster Bear. Drawing © Ed Heck 2004.

first described by Hahyennoweh, an old warrior who had been a champion runner. As a boy, Hahyennoweh ran a race with the Monster Bear around a swamp. The swift-running youth managed to kill the great bear and took one of its big tusks to his father. Ever after, the Senecas considered the Monster Bear's fangs to be "magic medicine," and if one ingested the dust or powder from one of the Bear's leg bones as a medicine, one could become an invincible runner (fig. 13).

When the old warrior-runner first told his tale, however, the Seneca youth scoffed until the old man took them on "the journey and showed them the place where the beast had fallen. They dug into the soft soil and found the huge bones and the jaw where he had broken out the tusk." The storyteller Tahadondeh concluded this traditional fossil legend in 1903 by citing modern scientific discoveries: "White man find bones right where the [giant bear] fell long after, to this day. Put them in big musees, so story real true I guess!"[10]

Another fossil-related version of the Monster Bear tale comes from the Seneca storyteller and artist Jesse Cornplanter in 1937 on the Tonawanda Reservation (western New York). Cornplanter's story also describes the discovery of the tooth of a gigantic bear in a vision quest. Set in the earliest days of his nation, Cornplanter's narrative described a swift runner who hunted down the Monster Bear in an eerie landscape littered with the bones of its human victims. The Bear appeared to the runner in a dream and broke off his own tooth as a promise that he would disappear forever and no longer prey on people. When the runner awoke, he found an enormous fang nearby, left by the Monster Bear as a token of its voluntary extinction to restore balance to nature. The great tooth was kept by the Senecas as a lucky charm, and in return they promised to remember the bear's name in their stories.

The Monster Bear tale, one of the earliest of many North American accounts of fossils collected for medicine and special powers, especially running speed, was apparently woven around an Iroquois warrior's chance discovery of the fossils of a gigantic Pleistocene bear in western New York or Pennsylvania. The story describes the purposeful investigation of fossil sites to verify the existence of a strange creature's remains, just as in the Iroquois warrior's tale of giant bison remains at Big Bone Lick (introduction). The active digging up of the buried fossil bones makes Tahadondeh's tale the earliest written reference to the deliberate *excavation* of fossils by Native North Americans.

According to Tahadondeh's story, the runner's original report was verified by the tribe and was later authenticated by modern museum excavations in the same place. Pleistocene fossils were first excavated scientifically in New York State in the 1790s. Like the Claverack bones almost a century before, these spectacles drew great crowds of onlookers, including Indians. Several Pleistocene deposits are known in western New York, and a major fossil exposure has been studied in Cattaraugus County, where Tahadondeh recounted his story. The Monster Bear remains probably belonged to the short-faced bear (*Arctodus simus*) of the Pleistocene. This gigantic bear, the biggest and swiftest carnivore of the Ice Age, was lean and rangy. Standing upright it towered eleven or twelve feet tall (a grizzly or Kodiak bear stands about eight or nine feet tall). The bear's powerful jaws had enormous, flesh-tearing canines, much larger than those of any living bear (figs. 14 and 15). *Arctodus* was an extremely fast runner, with much longer legs than heavy-bodied modern bears—an anatomical feature that the Senecas would have noticed in fossil specimens and correctly associated with great speed.[11]

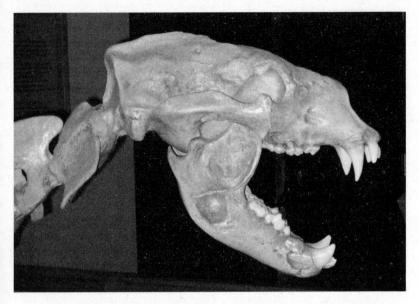

14. Fossil skull of giant short-faced bear, *Arctodus simus*. This lean, swift bear of the Pleistocene weighed about eighteen hundred pounds and stood five to six feet tall at the shoulder, towering over grizzly and polar bears, the largest living bears. Photo: Adrienne Mayor.

FOSSIL FOOTPRINTS

Bones and teeth were not the only paleontological remains that attracted attention. Fossilized footprints of mammals and dinosaurs, known to the Iroquois as *uki* prints (*uki* means sky powers, such as thunder and lightning), also drew intense interest. Near Jamestown, New York, for example, the Onondagas brought offerings to a set of foot- and handprints impressed on a rocky ledge, believed to have curative powers. In the nineteenth century, the elders explained that the prints commemorated a time when the sky spirit (translated by Europeans as Great Spirit) had descended to give advice to the chiefs. The impressions were still venerated as late as 1922, but as far as I know, their identity was never determined.

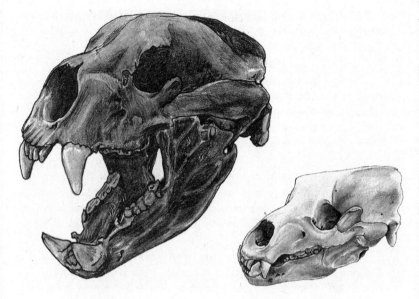

15. The skull of the extinct giant short-faced bear, *Arctodus simus* (left), compared to the skull of a present-day grizzly bear (right). Drawing © Patti Kane-Vanni 2004.

The Tuscaroras pointed out a rock near Brighton (south of Syracuse) that held the tracks of the Great Spirit *and* the Giant Mosquito Monster. According to David Cusick, this creature lived at the same time as giant bears and huge lions. The Mosquito Monster's vast wings made a loud noise as it swooped down on forts and destroyed many people in the past. The Great Mosquito was finally killed by the sky spirit at the salt lake at Onondaga, New York, *Kahyah-tak-ne-t'ke-tah keh*, "Place Where the Great Mosquito Lies." According to a version of this legend told by the Seneca chief Cornplanter (1736–1836), many Cayugas and Onondagas came to view the terrible carcass. The body was larger than a bear's and its wingspan was as long as three men. Its "talons were as long as arrows and the monstrous beak was lined with sharp teeth." The Mosquito Monster's footprints were said to be birdlike, about 20 inches long, and one could follow its trail for about 20 rods (about 330 feet).

The site of the monster's death, in a salt lake bed, and its physical description suggest that the legend might have been related to conflated observations of various fossils. Raptor birds of the Pleistocene had very large talons and wingspans from twelve to seventeen feet, but the toothy beak suggests a crocodilelike reptile, perhaps a Triassic phytosaur. Another fossil possibility is the large, "false-toothed" bird (*Pseudodontornis*) of the Pleistocene. Ancient memories of large raptor birds of the Pleistocene and Holocene may also have contributed to widespread Indian tales of flying monsters. New evidence now suggests that the range of California condors extended over the North American continent until fairly recent times. For example, in 1984 paleontologists at the Hiscock Site in New York State (occupied by paleo-Indians about ten thousand years ago) were surprised to find skeletons of California condors along with the human artifacts.

What about the footprints of the Great Spirit and the Mosquito Monster? Fossil tracks of extinct mammals, such as giant sloths or bears, can resemble oversize human prints, and dinosaur tracks sometimes resemble human hand- or footprints or bird tracks. The huge birdlike marks near Syracuse certainly sound like a trackway of a three-toed dinosaur, but that region does not have Mesozoic sediments.

However, tens of thousands of tridactyl dinosaur prints could have been observed not far away, in Connecticut and Massachusetts, and in Rockland County, southern New York. Many of these tracks are attributed to Triassic *Grallators*, a theropod dinosaur that lived about 200 million years ago. A strong possibility is that the footprints near Jamestown and Syracuse were man-made replicas of real dinosaur tracks, a common feature of rock art across the American continent. In the 1840s, the geologist Charles Lyell investigated some fossil bird and mammal tracks in Pennsylvania and found them to be petroglyphs. As noted, some of the richest sets of dinosaur tracks in the world are conspicuous in the Connecticut River Valley running through Massachusetts and Connecticut (the largest prints measure about seventeen inches long). When some of these footprints were discovered in 1802 at South Hadley by the Massachusetts farmboy Pliny Moody, they were thought to be the

tracks of Noah's raven. Later, in 1845, Edward Hitchcock identified them as *Eubrontes* dinosaur prints.

In December 2002, I examined numerous small and very large
tridactyl dinosaur tracks embedded in the dark-red sandstone slabs
on the banks of the Connecticut River near Holyoke, Massachusetts, a few miles north of Moody's famous find. I also learned of
some fascinating archaeological evidence indicating that Native
Americans were interested in these dinosaur trackways. At least a
dozen footprints (sometimes referred to as "devil's tracks") are
carved into granite outcrops across southern New England (real
fossil footprints are impossible in granite). These carvings, about
twelve inches long and five inches deep, may have been intended to
replicate the conspicuous dinosaur footprints of the Connecticut
Valley, but unfortunately their makers and their meaning are
unknown.[12]

A Delaware legend recounted by Richard Calmet Adams, a Delaware (Lenape) born in 1864, attempted to explain the presence of
dinosaur footprints embedded in rock. "When the world was
young," wrote Adams, "there lived in this country many huge
Monsters, some who dwelt in the sea, some who roved over the
land, and some who lived on land and in the water. The grandfather
of these Monsters was greater than them all. . . . He preyed upon
every living creature, and was a terror to all living things." When
this stupendous monster crossed the mountains, wrote Adams, "he
made tracks on the stones, and in many places his tracks can be
found today." According to the Delaware tradition, the monster
was trapped in a mountain pass and destroyed by lightning.

Like the Iroquois Monster Bear and footprint lore, the Delaware
paleontological legend accounts for observed fossil evidence, in this
case immense tracks left in rock by an unfamiliar animal, perhaps a
dinosaur. Theropod dinosaur tracks abound in the old Delaware
territory of New Jersey, eastern Pennsylvania, Delaware, and Maryland. And as I visited local dinosaur museums on my travels in
1998–2004, I was amused to notice how much the Delaware vision
of the "greatest monster that terrorized all other creatures," written
in 1887–1905, resembles today's popular images of the greatest
dinosaur of all, "the tyrant-king lizard." Adams would recognize

this typical description from a small-town *T. rex* display: "65 million years ago lived the greatest, most powerful predator ever to walk the Earth. The great *Tyrannosaurus rex* feared nothing."

Fossil footprints were noticed throughout the Northeast. Delaware and Iroquois women used to collect uki rocks embedded with small dinosaur tracks, which they believed were the footprints of the Little People. These rocks were distributed around the edges of crop fields as good planting medicine. At the Wyandot village of Wendake, in Quebec, the "trail of a monstrous serpent" was embedded in rock alongside the tracks of Little People, and this was taken as evidence that the Little People had hunted down and destroyed the monsters to make the world safe for early Indians. The Wyandots who traveled to the Ohio Valley pointed out the footprints of Little People on stones "all over that part of Kentucky" where the supernatural helpers had slain the Witch Buffalo (see introduction).[13]

The Wyandots were one of three northern Native groups—along with the Abenakis and Iroquois—who journeyed through the Ohio Valley and tried to explain the extensive fossil beds at Big Bone Lick. But the masses of animals emerging from salt bogs would have been a common sight for the people already living in the Ohio Valley. Big Bone Lick was picked clean by fossil collectors by 1800, but before that time, vast heaps of the bones of Pleistocene mastodons, mammoths, giant bison, and huge sloths lay exposed in the brackish mires, and for countless generations, Indians had frequented the salt licks to hunt for game and gather salt. By the mid–eighteenth century, the Natives of the Ohio Valley began to bring fossils and tusks to British forts and guided the Euro-Americans, like George Croghan, to the best bone beds, and naturalists began to ask the Shawnees and Delawares what they knew about the fossils.[14]

GRANDFATHER OF THE BUFFALO

The French naturalist Buffon (1707–1788) was the first to report that the Indians of the Ohio Valley referred to the large fossil animals as the "grandfather of the buffalo," based on accounts he received in 1748 from the French officer Fabri, who had also provided details of the Abenaki discovery of 1739 (see introduction). Later, in the mid-1800s, the French explorer Jean L'Heureux reported that the Blackfeet revered dinosaur fossils in Alberta, Canada, as "the grandfather of the buffalo."

Many Native American groups held the concept, first described by the Jesuit Paul de Jeune in Canada in 1634, that each animal species has an elder relative. This great and powerful ancestor, or "grandfather," was seen as "the beginning and origin" of a species and was always visualized as much larger than the modern-day animal. Accordingly, fossil skeletons that in some way resembled oversize versions of familiar animals were commonly identified as the "grandfather" of the bear, eagle, buffalo, and so on. For example, tales of gigantic beavers figure in Native legends from New England to Alaska. These were based on memories or on fossils of the Pleistocene beaver *Castoroides*, which was as big as a modern black bear. The Micmacs of Nova Scotia told of finding beaver teeth six inches long, and other Canadian Indians collected the big teeth of giant beavers as tools to hollow out log canoes.

The concept that giant ancestors preceded living species is not a formal expression of evolution theory, of course, but as Canadian paleontologist David Spalding points out, this "scientific interpretation by people who knew only one large animal [the buffalo]" shows that they recognized both the antiquity of the fossils and their "possible relationship to a living descendant." Among the fossils of the Ohio Valley (and across the western plains), gigantic bison skulls with very long horns stand out, and these were appreciated as "grandfathers of the buffalo" (fig. 16).

By distinguishing among specific kinds of fossils, such as giant bears and giant bison, the Natives understood that diverse faunal species were represented by fossil remains (satisfying the first two levels of Simpsonian paleontological concepts suggested by Peter Dodson, in the preface). This feature of Native American fossil traditions was noted in 1887 by the paleontologist William Berryman Scott: "The fact that the mythical animals can be distinguished apart, and referred to appropriate originals in the extinct animals of the continent, speaks strongly for the accuracy of their stories."[15]

16. Skull of giant, extinct bison of the Pleistocene, top, compared to the skull of a modern-day bison, bottom. Museum of Geology, South Dakota School of Mines and Technology, Rapid City. Photo: Adrienne Mayor.

In 1775, a Native reference to the Ohio fossils as giant *white* buffalo was recorded by the explorer Nicholas Cresswell in his journal of a visit to Big Bone Lick. "Found several bones of a Prodigious size," he noted. "What sort of animals these were is not clearly known. All the Traditionary accounts by the Indians is that they were White Buffaloes that killed themselves by drinking salt water." Cresswell's scrap of information is a garbled version of some unknown tribe's fuller tradition, now lost. But we do know that the White Buffalo is a revered motif among many Indian cultures. Albino animals are considered sacred or "medicine" animals with great spiritual powers ("medicine" can refer to something with special power or strength, as well as to a health-giving substance). When bison and other bones of extraordinary size were found, some groups imagined them as the "grandfather" of buffalo, while others identified them as sacred white buffalo. In the Tuscarora version of this belief, White Buffaloes were dangerous, mystical beasts who dwelled underground but longed to emerge from the earth into the sunlight.[16]

SHAWNEE PALEONTOLOGY

In 1756, a white woman, Mary Inglis, was captured by the Shawnees in Ohio. The narrative of her escape contains one of the earliest written records attesting to Shawnee familiarity with Big Bone Lick fossils. Mary's captors took her to the lick on one of their salt-boiling expeditions and sent her into the woods to gather wild grapes. Mary came upon three French traders who "was all sitting on One of the large Bones that was there cracking walnuts." Mary's interest was focused less on the big bone than on the traders seated upon it, one of whom gave her a tomahawk. Thus armed, Mary escaped from the Shawnees, following an old buffalo trace through the wilderness.[17]

Just a few years later, in 1762, a group of Shawnee men transported a massive molar weighing nearly seven pounds and a huge ivory tusk to the British commander at Fort Pitt on the Ohio. Curious about their find, the Philadelphia naturalist John Bartram asked his friend, a Quaker naturalist named James Wright who lived near Fort Pitt, to investigate Shawnee knowledge about the fossils. With an interpreter and gestures, Wright interviewed "two Sencible Shawanese Indians" at his farm.

The Shawnee men explained that the teeth came from a brackish meadow three miles from the river, at a crossroads of wide buffalo trails of great antiquity. This place was a landmark of long standing, distinguished by "the remains of 5 Entire sceletons" arranged in a circle with their heads pointing toward each other. The Shawnees believed that the five creatures had died at the same time, struck by lightning. Two skulls were much larger than the others—a man could barely reach around them. The Shawnees described what looked like "a long Nose" on the skulls (seen in profile, the bony structure that holds a mastodon tusk can resemble a long nose). The shoulderblade set upright reached to the men's shoulders ("and they were both tall men"). What they called the "cup" of the scapula (the socket) they compared to the size of a large bowl in Wright's house. The Shawnees had broken open a femur and it was big enough for a child to crawl inside. They estimated that when alive the animals must have been the size of Wright's small stable, and they measured the tusks, which they called "horns," at ten to twelve feet long.

Over generations, the Shawnees had observed these and many similar exposures of bones "scattered here & there . . . some upon the surface, and some Partly [buried], but all much more decay'd by time" than the five complete skeletons. Like other Europeans of the day, Wright was keen to know whether the Shawnees had "Ever seen such large Creatures living." The men assured him that no one had ever seen the creatures alive, that all the bones they found were extremely weathered and ancient. As George Gaylord Simpson remarked about this historic conversation, "These Indians clearly distinguished fact from fiction. They knew that there was no reliable testimony or memory of the animals in life."

According to Shawnee tradition, before present-day humans, these "mighty Creatures" had roamed in herds. They were hunted by "Great & Strong Men," who could sling the big carcasses over their shoulders as a hunter carries a deer on his back. Today, said the Shawnees, you could even find marks in the bedrock where some of these giant hunters had stopped to rest, impressions "like a man makes by sitting in snow."

This conversation in 1762 is the earliest documented Shawnee interpretation of Ohio fossil exposures, but the traditions had originated generations before Wright questioned the men. The Shawnee descriptions are remarkably detailed and perceptive—based on careful anatomical observations and logical deductions over time. Notably, their information not only included fossil measurements and estimates of the animals' size when they had been alive; it also attempted to account for the extinction of huge beasts and giant men in a distant era before modern humans. After the great men had died out, they said, "God had Kill'd" the mighty animals with lightning bolts, so that they could "not hurt the present race of Indians."[18]

As Barbara Mann draws out the traditional ideas in this Shawnee tale, when the giant hunters died out, "the balance of nature was disturbed and had to be reestablished, making room for humans and smaller animals." The notion that extinction was brought about by a sky spirit to make the earth safe for human beings occurs in many Native myths. The Iroquois legend of the Creator saving Indians from the Great Buffalo is another example, as are the tales of Little People and heroes like Manabozho who slew monsters to aid the Iroquois and Algonquians (introduction). Similar ideas appear in the Delaware version of Big Bone Lick, given below, and in Zuni, Navajo, and Apache myths (chapter 3). It is interesting that this same human-centered notion also appears in biblical tradition, which held that God sent the Flood to destroy evil giants and save humans. Some nineteenth-century Christian evolutionists looking for ways to reconcile the Bible and Darwin's new theories proposed that extinction was God's way of protecting early human beings from dangerous giant species.[19]

Notably, the Shawnee tradition suggested a gradual demise for the race of prehistoric giants, and a catastrophic destruction of the oversize animals. Today, in modern paleontology, similar catastrophist and gradualist extinction scenarios jockey for dominance.

Thomas Jefferson's Paleontological Inquiries

Lightning was also the agent of extinction in the Delaware traditions about mastodon fossils, as Thomas Jefferson learned a few years after Wright interviewed the Shawnee men. Jefferson amassed a great collection of Ohio bones at Monticello; he especially prized a three-foot-long femur and a molar weighing sixteen pounds. In the Academy of Natural Sciences in Philadelphia in 2001, I admired several tusks, teeth, and bones from Jefferson's personal Big Bone Lick collection, and in Paris in 2000, Pascal Tassy showed me some of the Ohio fossil specimens that Jefferson had sent to Paris. Jefferson also published a scientific paper on the discovery of a giant sloth fossil (which he mistook for a lionlike carnivore).

Jefferson was keen to learn more about the earlier big bone find at Claverack on the Hudson (in 1705, described above). In 1784, he corresponded with Ezra Stiles, president of Yale and the grandson of the Puritan poet Edward Taylor. Stiles sent his grandfather's collection of Indian lore about the Claverack giant and mentioned some other Indian "fables" to Jefferson. But Jefferson disagreed with the Indians and the Puritans who thought the Claverack creature was an extinct bipedal giant, arguing instead that it was a carnivorous elephant-type beast like those at Big Bone Lick.

Jefferson would have known of the interesting discovery described by the English botanist Mark Catesby, who studied the flora and fauna of Virginia and Carolina. In about 1725, Catesby visited Stono, a large plantation near Charleston, South Carolina, to examine several colossal teeth dug up in a swamp by slaves. The plantation owners no doubt identified the remains as a giant victim of Noah's Flood, the common interpretation in those days. But Catesby tells us that the slaves immediately recognized the shape of the teeth. In the "concurring Opinion of all the *Negroes*, native *Africans*, that saw them," wrote Catesby, these were the molars of "an Elephant," an animal of their homeland.

Catesby agreed with the slaves, since he—unlike the white masters—had recently seen African elephant teeth displayed in London. In 1806 in Paris, Georges Cuvier was also intrigued by this Stono incident, relayed to him by the colonial naturalist Benjamin Smith Barton. Cuvier translated Catesby's account into French and declared that "les nègres" had correctly recognized a fossil elephant species before any European naturalist realized that extinct mammoths were related to living elephants.

The African slaves at Stono were originally from Angola or the Congo, the habitat of living *Loxodonta* elephant species. Their identification of the molars at Stono was based on the fact that the teeth of extinct Columbian mammoths (unlike the pointed teeth of mastodons found at Claverack and Big Bone Lick) closely resemble the flat "grinders" of living African elephants. Thus, grudgingly wrote George Gaylord Simpson in 1942, "it appears that negro slaves made the first technical identification of an American fossil vertebrate—a lowly beginning for a pursuit that was to be graced by some of the most eminent men in American and scientific history."[20]

About half a century after Stono, in 1782, workmen digging in salt marshes in Virginia brought up teeth and "Bones of uncommon size." Major Arthur Campbell sent these remains to Jefferson, noting that "Several sensible Africans have seen the tooth, particularly a fellow" owned by Jefferson's neighbor, and "all . . . pronounced it an Elephant." Their identification tells us that these teeth belonged to a mammoth like the Stono find, not to a mastodon. As noted earlier, the pointed cusps of mastodon molars led Jefferson, Daubenton, and many others to believe that such remains as those at Big Bone Lick belonged to an unknown carnivorous beast rather than to an extinct species of elephant.[21]

Jefferson stubbornly clung to the hope that the creatures whose remains littered Big Bone Lick still roamed somewhere in the New World. "I understand from different quarters that the Indians believe this animal still existing in the North & North West," wrote Jefferson to Ezra Stiles at Yale, "tho' none of them pretend ever to have seen one. It is said that the bones abound on the upper Missouri." This last statement is startling. How did Jefferson come by this information about fossils on the upper Missouri River, in the western Dakotas and northeastern Montana, two decades before Lewis and Clark's expedition? Reports of immense fossil skeletons in the badlands along the upper Missouri probably filtered back to the East from Plains Indians via French traders. Barbara Mann also points out that the trails to the Rockies and the Pacific Ocean were known to eastern Natives, who sometimes made vision quests and explorations in the West, bringing back stories of what they'd seen.

Jefferson had no way of knowing that the abundant bones along the Missouri are not those of Pleistocene mastodons but remains of huge Cretaceous dinosaurs (such as *Tyrannosaurus rex*, *Triceratops*, and *Edmontosaurus*) and marine reptiles (such as mosasaurs and plesiosaurs). Jefferson's remark about large bones on the upper Missouri, overlooked by modern paleontological historians, appears to be the earliest reference to the dinosaur fossils of the Hell Creek and/or Judith River Formations of Dakota and Montana (see map 5 in chapter 5), where Ferdinand Hayden was the first scientist to collect dinosaur specimens in the 1850s.[22]

Even though Jefferson admitted that no Indians had ever claimed to have seen *live* mastodons, he based his hope that Meriwether Lewis and William Clark might discover living mastodon herds in the Northwest on the symbolic detail from Native stories about a

sole surviving bull. Neither the Shawnee nor the Iroquois traditions held out realistic hope for the discovery of relict mastodons,
however, and Jefferson knew that earlier, in 1767, Benjamin Franklin had also made inquiries among Native Americans about Ohio
tusks and had reported that *living* elephants were not "remembered
in any tradition of the Indians." In 1785, Ezra Stiles forwarded
Jefferson a letter from the Harvard-educated fossil hunter Samuel
Parsons. Parsons had explored the Ohio Valley and learned that
living elephants were "wholly Unknown to the Natives," just as
George Croghan had found no "traditionary trace" of living specimens even among the oldest Shawnees.

But Jefferson doggedly gathered tantalizing reports from other
sources. As Cuvier noted, the intriguing narrative of a certain Mr.
Stanley helped fuel Jefferson's dream. Stanley had been captured by
Indians near the confluence of the Tennessee and Ohio rivers, in the
mid-1700s. Stanley said he had been passed along among a series of
tribes and was eventually taken over the Rocky Mountains. Along
a westward-flowing river beyond the Missouri, he saw myriad
bones of strange animals, much bigger than the familiar buffalo
bones that littered the plains. According to Stanley, the Natives
there attributed the remains to great beasts that were not seen alive,
although some might still live in the Far North.

Stanley's adventure over the Rockies may have taken him along
the west-flowing Columbia River, in the territory that Lewis and
Clark would later traverse. Who were his captors? Did the huge
bones belong to large Pleistocene mammals or to much earlier Cretaceous dinosaurs or marine reptiles? About a century after Stanley,
Henry Rowe Schoolcraft, an ethnologist studying the Nez Perce
and other tribes along the Columbia River, found at the mouth of
the Deschutes River (Oregon) two enormous "flinty" thighbones,
so stony that that they actually produced fire when struck with steel.
Possibly these fossilized femurs came from bone beds similar to
those seen by Stanley. The west-flowing Salmon River is another
possibility. According to a Nez Perce elder, Otis Halfmoon, in
Idaho a great flood drowned many huge animals in the deep past,
leaving their bones along the Salmon. The bones of numerous large
mammal species (including camels, mastodons, sloths, and saber-

tooth cats) from the Pliocene era emerge from cliffs along the west-flowing Snake River. Perhaps Stanley heard the Nez Perce interpretations of the fossils. He may also have heard the Shoshone tradition about the great floods that drowned huge animals in Idaho. In fact, two vast floods occurred here in the geological past, 3 million years ago and 15,000 years ago, and fossils of the species of those epochs are now exhibited at the Hagerman Fossil Beds National Monument, on the Snake River, in Idaho (map 3, chapter 3).

When the Indians suggested to Stanley that the beasts might still survive in the Far North, the notion may have reflected the "natural harmony" of many Indian traditions. Or they could have been referring to musk oxen living west of Hudson Bay. The Philadelphia naturalist Joseph Leidy reported that travelers in Canada had seen these great animals alive as late as 1852. Unfortunately we don't know the answers to any of these questions, but as George Gaylord Simpson observed in 1942, Stanley's narrative is the earliest definite evidence we have of local Indian knowledge of the large vertebrate fossils in the Northwest.[23]

A few years before he corresponded with Ezra Stiles in 1784, Jefferson had held a council in Virginia with a delegation of Delaware leaders sometime in 1775–80. At that now-famous meeting, Jefferson asked what the Delawares knew about the Ohio *incognitum*. An elder stood up and began to orate their tradition.

"In ancient times a herd of these tremendous animals came to the Bigbone licks" and destroyed the smaller game, bear, deer, elk, buffalo, and other animals, which had been created for Indians to hunt. The "Great Man above" was "so enraged that he seized his lightning, descended on the earth, seated himself on a neighboring mountain." He "hurled his bolts . . . till the whole were slaughtered" (fig. 17). Echoing the Shawnee tale, the Delawares maintained that one could still see the impression of the Great Spirit's "seat and the print of his feet" on the rock. The elder concluded by saying that a single mighty bull, wounded in the side, had escaped by deflecting the bolts with his massive forehead, and "bounded over the Ohio, over the Wabash, the Illinois, and finally over the great lakes, where he is living at this day."

17. The Great Spirit (upper left) destroying carnivorous mastodons at
Big Bone Lick with lightning bolts; note two other dead mastodons and
the smaller game animals they have killed, a bison and a stag. Engraving,
published with a version of the Delaware tradition, in *Chatterbox*, vol.
11 (London, 1898), p 87. Courtesy of Gary Williams, *Dinosaur World
Magazine*.

Some modern commentators have suggested that the tale's conclusion shows that the Delawares were responding to Jefferson's leading questions about surviving herds of mastodons, telling their host what he wanted to hear. But as we've already seen, one or two survivors hidden away under a mountain or in some faraway land was a common motif in many other Native myths about the Great Buffalo. It reflected the ideal of balance in which no natural force could ever totally destroy another—not a belief that such creatures really still flourished on Earth.[24]

Reluctant to accept the idea of extinction, holding on to his dream that the imposing animals might yet be found in unexplored territories, Jefferson singled out the motif of the sole survivor, despite Native Americans' consistent assurances that in reality all the enormous animals had perished long ago and were never seen or even remembered alive. In contrast to Jefferson, however, Georges Cuvier in Paris took the Indians' assurances seriously, for they helped support his emerging theory of extinction.

GEORGES CUVIER'S ARCHIVES OF INDIAN PALEONTOLOGY

Cuvier (1769–1832) maintained an ongoing, active interest in Indian traditions about large vertebrate fossils of North and South America. In his house in the Jardin des Plantes in Paris, Cuvier divided his library by rooms: one for books on fishes, one for works on osteology, another for law books, another for the Greek and Latin classics, and so on. In one of these rooms he also kept the growing body of accounts of paleontological discoveries in the Americas. Many of these stories appeared in his 1806 monograph, and in 1821 Cuvier devoted more than twenty pages to a full survey of all known American vertebrate fossil discoveries in the revised edition of his *Research on Fossil Remains.*

Beginning with Cotton Mather's description of the giant bones on the Hudson in 1705, Cuvier turned to the discoveries on the Ohio initiated in 1739 when Longueuil's Indian hunters found the mastodon remains, which Cuvier noted were "still kept here in Paris." Cuvier also studied Fabri's 1748 letters reporting that Natives of Canada, Ohio, and Louisiana observed the giant bones of "père aux boeufs" ("grandfather of the buffalo"). News of enormous bones found in 1804 in Opelousa Indian lands in Louisiana had reached Cuvier, and he even examined one of the thousands of elephant teeth and bones that lay in the land of "les Indiens Osages" of Missouri, west of the Mississippi.

George Croghan's expeditions of 1765–66 were of great interest to Cuvier. Not only did he examine many actual specimens collected by Croghan, but he also pored over extracts from Croghan's journal of 1765. The fossils collected by George Morgan and Croghan in 1766, when they recorded the elderly chief's tradition about Big Bone Lick (introduction), were also known to Cuvier.

In about 1795, Cuvier received a letter from the naturalist Benjamin Smith Barton, who had been shown huge mastodon molars and pieces of a ten-foot-long tusk in a branch of the Susquehanna River by "les sauvages delawares," who called the stream *Chemung* or "Rivière de la Corne [Horn]." The name of the Chemung River in central New York also derives from the Cayuga word *chemung*, "great horn." The earliest documentation of this word and variations appeared in the mid-1700s, and *chemung* was used by the Iroquois and the Delawares to identify many other sites where big tusks eroded out of rivers. The name indicates that mastodon remains were frequently observed by eastern Indians, and indeed, remarks Cornell University geologist John Chiment, "There is no shortage of mastodons in New York state. Any glacial kettle hole or bog might have one or two. The Cayuga may have been the first mastodon paleontologists around here."[25]

Cuvier was also drawn to the Shawnee and Delaware legends surrounding the "astonishing abundance" of fossils of mastodons and other mammals at "*Bik-bone-lick*" and other "*Liks*" on the Ohio. Cuvier collected numerous Indian accounts from Rembrandt Peale, Barton, Croghan, Jefferson, and others. The landmark of five large, complete mastodon skeletons in a circle described by "les sauvages shawanais" in 1762 was of particular interest. Cuvier was impressed that the Shawnees had transported several fossil teeth and tusks to

Fort Pitt, and he noted in his writings their statements that no living specimens had ever been seen. He was especially struck by the Shawnee observation of "the long nose above the mouth" on the skulls: Cuvier compared this to an earlier discovery by the Illinois Indians, who had found a large mastodon skeleton with part of a decomposed trunk, as reported by the Swedish naturalist Peter Kalm in 1748–51. Cuvier himself examined an apparently mummified elephant foot said to have been discovered by an unnamed Indian tribe living west of the Missouri River. That find led Cuvier to ask whether some mastodons in North American bogs might be as well preserved as the frozen mammoths of Siberia (see appendix).

Cuvier also noted that after Lewis and Clark returned from their "grande expédition" to the Pacific Ocean, William Clark and his brother, George Rogers Clark, collected crates of Big Bone Lick fossils for Jefferson in 1807–8. George Rogers Clark, a naturalist like Cuvier, also had great respect for Native American oral traditions. In 1778 in Illinois, during the Revolutionary War, Clark heard Kaskaskia elders recite their oral history. In a letter to the Philadelphia Museum in 1789, he wrote, "I see no reason why [their traditions] should not be received as good History, at least as good as" much of our early European history.

In his 1806 monograph, Cuvier listed every known giant bone discovery around the world, along with the local lore, from classical antiquity up to his own day, including Spanish accounts from Mexico and Peru, discussed in the next chapter. And even after 1806, he continued to document new Native American finds of large bones. These historical and contemporary discoveries and local traditions were important to Cuvier in establishing the new science of paleontology.

No modern historian of paleontology has ever remarked on Cuvier's deep interest in Native fossil traditions. But the Native awareness that the creatures whose remains they observed must have been destroyed by violent catastrophe in the distant past contributed to his idea that the fossils represented extinct species of elephants that had died out by catastrophe in Europe, Asia, and the Americas. The Indians' accounts helped Cuvier rule out migration in explaining the disappearance of mastodons in the Americas. Alluding to the

Delaware and Shawnee fossil legends, and contradicting Jefferson's misguided hopes of finding live elephants in the North, Cuvier posed this question in 1812: "How can it be believed that the immense mastodons and gigantic megatheriums [sloths], whose bones are found underground in the two Americas, still live?" The Native American traditions "about their destruction . . . by the Great Spirit" were based on their own discoveries of the bones, he wrote. If these animals still lived, how could such enormous beasts "escape the knowledge of the nomadic peoples who move ceaselessly around the continent in all directions, and who themselves recognize that the creatures no longer exist?"[26]

REMBRANDT PEALE AND INDIAN PALEONTOLOGY

In 1802, the scientifically minded Rembrandt Peale published more Indian lore about mastodon fossils. Cuvier cited Peale in 1806 and 1821, describing his excavation of the first full skeleton of a mastodon from a farm in Orange County, New York, in 1801. That skeleton was displayed in the Peale family's Philadelphia Museum and in London, and Rembrandt's father, the artist Charles Willson Peale, illustrated the fossils collected by George Morgan in 1766, and published by Cuvier in 1806.

Pointing out that besides great mammoths and mastodons, the Ohio salt licks also contained bones of familiar species such as deer (representing the smaller game mentioned by the Delawares in their version of what happened at Big Bone Lick, above), Rembrandt Peale noted that some Indians also offered an alternative, naturalistic explanation for the death of certain animals at the licks. In a gradualist scenario, these unidentified Indians reasoned that many "sickly animals" had died while visiting the "salt morass" and their remains had accumulated over the ages.

Peale also published a sensational version of the cataclysmic extinction of the mastodon (which Peale, along with Jefferson and many other Euro-Americans, believed was a carnivorous monster). This version, attributed to the "Shawanee," related that "ten thousand moons ago," herds of colossal creatures drained lakes when they drank, crushed pine trees, devastated villages, and trampled smaller animals. The "good Spirit" destroyed these immense animals with lightning, but (echoing the Delaware version) a single wounded bull escaped the conflagration by ascending the mountain that was the source of the Monongahela River—and he may still survive in the western wilderness.

Peale tried to clarify which fossil species were being described in such tales. He noted that the skeleton of a tremendous buffalo, which stood eight to nine feet tall at the shoulder and had horn cores indicating a span of six feet, had just recently been found at Big Bone Lick, in 1803 (a living bison is five or six feet high at the shoulder; so this was probably the giant Pleistocene bison, *Bison latifrons* or *Bison antiquus*). Peale suggested that Indian traditions about the "Great Buffalo" or "grandfather of the bison" had originally referred to this extinct giant animal but later became conflated with stories about mastodon remains.[27]

Delaware Fossil Legends

In 1905, versions of the old Delaware oral legends about Ohio River fossils—stories that had fascinated Jefferson, Cuvier, and Peale—were first published by a Delaware Indian. Richard Calmet Adams (b. 1864) was an educated Lenape activist who recorded his nation's legends and history in writing. The story of the Great Bear or "grandfather of bears" in Delaware lore shares several details with the Iroquois oral tradition about collecting the fossil bones and teeth of the Monster Bear for medicine. In Adams's version of the Delaware legend, the Great Bear of the Allegheny Mountains was extremely swift and ferocious. After the Great Bear was fatally wounded in a battle with the mastodon many centuries ago, the Great Spirit advised a mighty Delaware hunter to find the bear's body and take a tooth to use as "a magic in case of sickness" or wounds.

The Great Bear, once again, refers to a Delaware discovery of the remains of the giant short-faced bear, *Arctodus simus*, which lived in the Alleghenies during the Ice Age. This fossil legend is notable for its recognition that these huge, long-legged, swift bears had coexisted with and hunted the extinct mastodon. According to Adams, the medicine tooth, several inches long, "was kept among the Delawares a great many hundred years and handed down from generation to generation, and certain of them yet have a great deal of faith in its magic power." This significant detail, published by a Delaware historian in 1905, is another early record of a specific fossil relic collected and valued as medicine centuries ago.

In old Delaware traditions, the name *Yah Qua Whee* was used for unknown monsters. In 1905, however, Adams translated *Yah Qua Whee* as "mastodon." "Long ago, in time almost forgotten, " wrote Adams, "there were mighty beasts that roamed the forests and plains. The Yah Qua Whee or mastodon," continued Adams, was intended as a beast of burden for Indians. But "this beast rebelled. It was fierce, powerful and invincible, its skin . . . so strong and hard that the sharpest spears and arrows could scarcely penetrate it. It made war against all the other animals . . . which the Great Spirit had created to be used as meat."

Adams's version portrays the Ohio Valley as a vast battleground where all the beasts of the plains and forest "arrayed themselves against the mastodon. The Indians were to take part in this decisive battle if necessary, as the Great Spirit had told them they must annihilate the mastodon." The Great Spirit "descended and sat on a rock at the top of the Alleghenies to watch the tide of battle. Great numbers of the mastodons came, and still greater numbers of the other animals," including the Great Bear. "The slaughter was terrific [and] the valleys ran in blood. The battlefield became a great mire, and many of the mastodons, by their weight, sank in the mire and were drowned." There was "a terrible loss" of the smaller game animals, too. Adams describes the Great Spirit hurling lightning bolts to destroy the mastodons. All died, except for that by-now-familiar lone bull, who "cast aside the bolts of lightning with his tusks [and] bounded across the Ohio river, over the Mississippi, swam the Great Lakes, and went to the far north where he lives to this day. Traces of that battle may yet be seen," said Adams. "The marshes and mires are still there, and in them the bones of the mastodon are still found, as well as the bones of many other animals."[28]

Adams was steeped in his people's traditions, but he was also aware of modern scientific knowledge about living and extinct elephants (note the non-Native image of the mastodon as a "beast of burden" and the way the bull deflected lightning with his *tusks* instead of his forehead, as in the older Delaware versions). Adams also knew about the variety of fossil animal species in the marshes. The detail of the Great Spirit descending as a spectator seems like a classical Greek notion, comments Barbara Mann, but she also pointed out that a war among animals is a staple of Native tradition, as is the symbolic motif that extinct creatures persist, hidden away somewhere.

Some of Adams's phrases and details recall the old Delaware tradition transcribed by Thomas Jefferson and Peale's Shawnee version of 1803. Was Adams influenced by reading those accounts? Maybe so, but the important point is that he integrated and updated Delaware lore about the Ohio fossils, using both his tradition-shaped imagination and his command of modern scientific discoveries. This educated storyteller revised the old stories just as the Iroquois historians David Cusick and Elias Johnson had added emerging scientific knowledge about mastodons to older narratives about monsters.

By a similar process, the Abenaki storyteller and historian Gerard Tsonakwa helped fill in the details of his ancestors' discovery of Ohio fossils in 1739; the old chief added new knowledge about white and black races to the Iroquois or Wyandot fossil tradition in 1766 (introduction); and the Seneca storyteller referred to modern excavations for museums (above). Living folklore about natural phenomena continually assimilates and integrates new experiences and information, so that older stories evolve in response to new knowledge, a process akin to the way scientific theories accommodate new evidence. This ability to work elements of science into the mythic narrative counters George Gaylord Simpson's characterization of Native American knowledge about fossils as static, lacking "continuous development." His perception that Native interpretations often differed from modern scientific theories was valid, but it led him to assume that the two ways of thinking must be mutually exclusive.[29]

SMOKING THE MONSTER'S BONE: AN ANCIENT DELAWARE FOSSIL LEGEND

Delaware storytellers living today still remember very old tales about the bones of monsters. In 2001, I obtained a transcript of a tradition told in 1992 by Esther Homovich, a Delaware elder living in Oklahoma, where the Delaware nation has been based since the nineteenth century. The story dates from the old days in the East and describes some hunters' discovery of the bones of a monster near present-day Philadelphia.

Long ago, in a village on the East Coast in New Jersey or eastern Pennsylvania, there was great excitement when a hunting party returned with news of finding "a piece of bone of that monster that [had] been killing people." Homovich continued, "I guess it was a prehistoric monster, and they found his bones, and they burn it." A wise man in the village urged the people to go out and find more of the monster's bones. He told the people to burn bits of the bone with tobacco in "a little clay spoon." "Put that bone in there and smoke it [and] while it's smoking, burning, . . . make a good wish for yourself." The wise man suggested some appropriate wishes, such as a good hunting expedition, a long life, or healthy children.[30]

This story exhibits no evidence of European contact. As in previous Iroquois, Wyandot, and Delaware tales, some people in a village purposely set out to find a fossil exposure discovered by hunters, in order to collect specimens for magical or curative powers. Notably, the Wyandots, who considered themselves the "uncles" of the Delawares, have a very similar tradition about hunters who find and kill strange monsters and then burn their bones to make amulets, on which they make wishes.

The concept of burning a fossil to release or transfer its powers is apparently very ancient. Indeed, this story may shed light on an "enigma" described by New Jersey archaeologists in 1973. At two paleo-Indians sites in southern New Jersey (dating to A.D. 1000–1500), the excavators found, among other artifacts, several pieces of petrified wood that had been carried some distance to the villages. The archaeologists were surprised to find that each piece of petrified wood had been deliberately charred, indicating an attempt to ignite the fossils. Surmising that the collectors recognized the Miocene fossils as pieces of wood that had wondrously turned to stone, the archaeologists proposed that a shaman may have created a "potent and moving spectacle," perhaps by demonstrating that stone wood was supernaturally fireproof. The old Delaware tradition recounted by Esther Homovich in 1992 suggests that charring the petrified wood may have been an ancient ritual to release a fossil's magical powers to grant wishes.[31]

What sort of monster bone was found by the hunters in the story? Dinosaur remains are rare on the East Coast, but the geographic setting specified in this Delaware tale is famous for yielding some of the first dinosaur fossils to be studied by naturalists in North America (*Hadrosaurus*, *Dryptosaurus*, *Coelosaurus*, and armored ankylosaurs), and it also holds the fossils of immense marine reptiles (such as Cretaceous crocodiles and the mosasaur *Tylosaurus*). The earliest written record of a dinosaur fossil in this area seems to have been in 1787, when Benjamin Franklin and other colonists examined a "large thigh bone" discovered on a farm near Woodbury, New Jersey, not far from Philadelphia. The specimen has disappeared but was probably part of a duck-billed *Hadrosaurus* dinosaur. In the 1830s, large dinosaur bones were found in a marl pit near Haddonfield, New Jersey, and in 1858 Joseph Leidy excavated part of a hadrosaur skeleton, the first dinosaur skeleton ever mounted for display (fig. 18).[32]

But the Delaware story of the monster's bone near Philadelphia must have originated long before these highly publicized dinosaur discoveries, because the Delaware nation had already left New Jersey and eastern Pennsylvania after the treaty of 1778, settling in Ohio and Indiana. In 1868 the Delawares were officially removed from there to Oklahoma Indian Territory. To determine the age of the tale, we need to look for other historical and cultural facts.

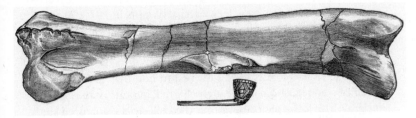

18. Femur of a *Hadrosaurus* dinosaur from New Jersey. Lenape clay pipe = about six inches long. Drawing © Patti Kane-Vanni 2004.

"The little clay spoon" is a crucial clue. To smoke the monster bone, the Delawares apparently scraped minute filings of the fossil into a pipe bowl already filled with tobacco. One would expect a modern storyteller to simply use the word "pipe," but her wording, "they had this little clay spoon," reveals the persistence of a centuries-old folk memory. I contacted Stephen Bray, a traditional clay pipemaker and historian, for further information. White clay pipes made by Indians along the Atlantic coast were first described by Europeans in the 1500s, and they were used through the late 1800s (Europeans began making copies of Indian tobacco pipes in the 1600s). Local clay for making pipes was gathered by the Delaware Indians from a well-known clay deposit in northern Delaware, just a few miles southwest of Philadelphia.

Significantly, changes in bowl shape mean that clay pipes are datable archaeological artifacts. The earliest English explorers in the 1500s described the Indian pipes as little clay ladles or spoons; by the 1600s the pipes were being made with deeper bowls (fig. 19). So the Delaware storyteller's anachronism "little clay spoon" indicates an older, shallow bowl. Accordingly, we can safely date this story to at least as early as the 1500s, and, given the lack of any European influence, it almost certainly predates European Contact.[33]

This fossil legend demonstrates the persistence of oral memory about bones of startling size. The essential details endured at least two hundred years after the Delawares were forced out of their homeland where the story had first originated. The storyteller's phrase "that monster that [had] been killing people" suggests that

19. The Delaware chief Tishcohan, with a squirrel-skin tobacco pouch and a later-style, deep-bowl clay pipe. Painting by Gustave Hesselius, 1735. Courtesy of The Historical Society of Pennsylvania Collection, Atwater Kent Museum of Philadelphia.

a much fuller tale about the monster had once circulated, woven around a discovery of extraordinary skeletal remains. The story tells us that about five hundred years ago, and probably even before

Columbus, the Delawares were already deliberately gathering fossils for special rituals. Moreover, the geographic setting of the tale suggests that besides the common mastodon fossils, the relatively rare dinosaur remains of the East Coast were also observed and collected by Native people.

The next chapter shows that pre-Columbian fossil legends existed in the Southern Hemisphere, too. More than two hundred years before European naturalists began to devise scientific theories to explain large vertebrate fossils in North America, the Spanish conquistadors in Mexico recorded the oldest American fossil legends ever preserved in writing.

2

New Spain: Bones
of Fear and Birds
of Terror

The traditions of the Incas are entirely unworthy of credit
. . . mere foolish stories obtained from the Indians by
credulous inquirers.
—*Sir Clements Markham, 1864*

The Historie and Narration of the Indians deserveth to be
received as a profitable thing.
—*Father José de Acosta, 1604*

THE Spanish conquistadors came
to the New World seeking gold and souls. They didn't expect to
find the enormous, petrified bones of giants among the treasures
of the Aztec Empire. But when Hernando Cortés and his Spanish
army first arrived in central Mexico in 1519, that's just what they
found. As I pursued my research into early European encounters
with American fossil lore, I was fascinated to learn that Aztec codices and Inca traditions, originating before the time of Columbus,
described the remains of mammoths and other immense creatures
as evidence of giant creatures from past eras.

These ancient accounts, recorded by the Spanish conquerors and missionaries in Mexico, Ecuador, and Peru, are the oldest documented American fossil legends, and some were even confirmed by deliberate excavations, the first paleontological fieldwork in America. Such reports interested the Puritan Cotton Mather, who—like the Spanish—saw them as proof of biblical giants in the New World. Later, Georges Cuvier cited them as scientific evidence of worldwide extinctions of prehistoric species. In the nineteenth and twentieth centuries, Native people of Mexico continued to collect large fossil bones for special purposes and still told tales of ancient giants and monstrous birds.

TLAXCALA, MEXICO, 1519

Soon after landing on the shores of Yucatán in 1519, Cortés acquired from the Maya people an Aztec slave who became known as La Malinche. She knew the Mayan dialects and Nahuatl, the Aztec language, and rapidly learned Spanish. La Malinche's translations and knowledge of Aztec and Mexica geography and religion were crucial for Cortés as he and his four hundred men marched on Tenochtitlan (now Mexico City), the heart of the Aztec Empire (map 2). It was La Malinche who told Cortés that many Aztecs believed he was the embodiment of their great Feathered Serpent god-king, Quetzalcoatl.

On his march west, Cortés first encountered the people of Tlaxcala (Tlascala), in the valleys and mountains east of Tenochtitlan. The Tlaxcalteca warriors, never completely subjugated by the Aztecs, readily joined the Spanish. To impress Cortés, the Tlaxcalteca chiefs brought out their most important relics, some limb bones of gigantic size. La Malinche translated the elders' explanation of the bones for the Spaniards. Bernal Diaz del Castillo, a captain in Cortés's army, described this momentous event in paleontological history, the earliest documented fossil legend in the New World.

The elders recounted a story that their ancestors had told them, a story linking the extinction of these giant creatures with the Tlaxcaltecas' own cultural history. A very long time ago, their fore-

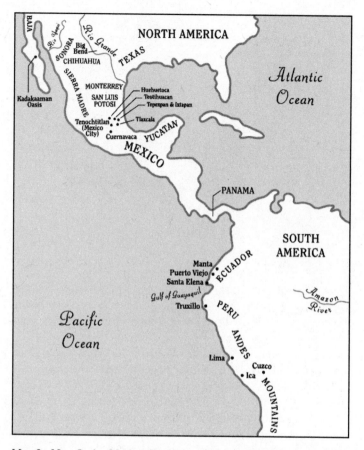

Map 2. New Spain: Mexico, Ecuador, and Peru (map by Michele Mayor Angel)

fathers found the territory inhabited "by men and women of great size, people with huge bones." The ancestors had fought and destroyed these "wicked and evil" beings—and "any of the giants who survived eventually died out." This last detail reveals that the Tlaxcaltecas understood that even if a small number of relict creatures had escaped mass destruction, they would eventually face extinction.

20. Tlaxcalteca man showing a mastodon femur to a Spanish conquistador, Mexico, 1519. The Tlaxcaltecas identified such fossils as the remains
of giants vanquished by their ancestors. Drawing © Ed Heck 2004.

So that we might see the dimensions of those giants, wrote Diaz,
"they brought a bone that had belonged to one of the giants. It
was very thick and so large that when placed upright it was as high
as an average man." It was a thighbone, recalled Diaz. "I stood next
to it and it was as tall as I am, and I'm a man of average height."
The Tlaxcaltecas brought out more bones of great size, but they
were "much rotted by the earth and consumed by time," in contrast
to "the one that I have mentioned [which] was entire." The stupendous skeletons awed the conquistadors (fig. 20). "We were all astonished to see these remains, and knew for certain that there had been
giants in that land. Cortés said that we should send the great bone
to Castile, that His Majesty might see it." And so, wrote Diaz, "we
did send it by the first ship leaving for Spain." Cortés also sent a
party of soldiers to the mountains south of Mexico City, and they
brought back many more bones of giants.[1]

Knowing that the Spanish kept records of their conquest in Mexico, I attempted to learn the fate of the femur sent to King Charles V almost five hundred years ago. The museum curators and archivists in Madrid pursued my quest with great interest. But Araceli Sánchez Garrido, curator of American ethnology at the Museo de America, could find no records of the bones sent to Charles V by Cortés, although the museum collection does include mammoth bones from Mexico sent at later dates. Begoña Sánchez Chillon, director of vertebrate paleontology at the Museo Nacional de Ciencias Naturales, noted that their collection dated to Charles III, but she was unable to locate archives for 1519–20. I did learn, however, that the Cortés Palace, the fancy residence built by Cortés in 1526–33 in Cuernavaca, Morales State, Mexico, now the Cuauhnahuac Museum, displays a roomful of fine, local mammoth fossils, just like the Tlaxcala relics that so impressed the conquistadors.[2]

Long after the Spanish Conquest, the enslavement of the Indians, and the burning of their historical chronicles, the Tlaxcaltecas still recalled their ancestors' defeat of the giants whose bones had been sent across the sea to the king of Spain. Father José de Acosta (1539–1600) traveled in Mexico fifty years after the Conquest recording Native oral histories. He preserved more details of their traditions about giants.

In ancient times, the Tlaxcaltecas told Acosta, their ancestors had come from the northwest, crossed the Sierra Madre Mountains, and conquered the original inhabitants of the region, the Chichimecas. According to the Tlaxcalteca oral historians, these were primitive giants dwelling in rock caves and armed with great clubs and wooden swords. The giants fled to the mountains and forests, where they "pulled downe trees as if they had beene stalkes of lettices." This remarkable image brings to mind the behavior of elephants. Other traditional accounts said the giants had a horrible appearance but lived on acorns and grasses. These details suggest that some aspects of the legendary giant-ogres may have originated in ancestral memories of Columbian mammoths and may have been later confirmed by discoveries of fossils.

The Tlaxcalteca ancestors decimated "all the giants, not leaving one alive." This is no fable, wrote Acosta, "for, at this day, we finde dead mens bones of an incredible bigness" in Tlaxcala. The Jesuit priest witnessed the discovery of one of these primitive giants buried on a Spanish plantation in 1586, when Native slaves brought him a tooth "as big as the fist of a man" and showed him the skeleton of "proportionable greatness." A score of other early Spanish chroniclers reported discoveries of "the bones of immense men" whenever people plowed fields, dug wells and tombs, or mined for minerals in New Spain. Other missionaries described "bones of giants discovered in Cuhuacan," a giant's thighbone "in the burial place of a temple," and bones of "truly giant men" and "immense men" in various other excavations in Mexico. The Natives' story was consistent: these were the vestiges of a giant race, now extinct owing to natural catastrophe or battles with humans of the distant past.[3]

Most of the giant bones, like the femur discovered by Tlaxcaltecas sometime before Columbus and prized as historical evidence of giants, probably belonged to the mastodon now known as *Rhynchotherium tlascalae*. Pleistocene remains of mastodons, mammoths, and giant bison and sloths are abundant around Tlaxcala and in the Valley of Mexico, the vicinity of Mexico City, and other localities in central Mexico. The femur of a mastodon or mammoth measures nearly five feet long, about the height of an average Spaniard in the sixteenth century. And it would resemble a gigantic human thighbone, leading people unfamiliar with elephants to visualize its owner as a human giant.[4]

According to George Gaylord Simpson, the Tlaxcaltecas' discovery was only a "casual find," and not a "true discovery in the historical sense." As noted earlier, Simpson asserted that Native Americans gathered fossils only as curios or magical charms, without recognizing their organic origin or speculating about their meaning. Even so, Simpson took credit in 1942 for being the first paleontologist to call attention to Bernal Diaz del Castillo's report of a vertebrate fossil discovery at "the astonishingly early date of 1519." Simpson stated that this historic event had been "overlooked by paleontological historians," but, in fact, the Princeton paleontologist William Berryman Scott had included Diaz's account in his history of American fossil myths in *Scribner's* magazine in 1887. Simpson knew that the Tlaxcaltecas had deliberately collected mastodon fossils as historic relics and recognized the bones as the organic remains of large mammals; he was well aware that they had devised an explanation for the creatures' mass destruction in a historical narrative of long standing. His refusal to acknowledge these insights, even as he recounted the facts of the historic discovery, recalls Cotton Mather's ambivalence and his abrupt rejection of Indian interpretations of the Claverack fossils (chapter 1).[5]

After the Conquest, many ships filled with New World riches—emeralds, turquoise, gorgeous parrot feathers, and the "sweat of the sun and the tears of the moon" (gold and silver)—would sail to Spain, but the giant's thighbone was placed on the very first treasure ship sent to King Charles. At that time in Europe, the fossils of very large, extinct animals were believed to be relics of giant humans who drowned in Noah's Deluge, early Christian saints, or famous personages from classical antiquity. Since Homeric and biblical times, it was a commonplace that people of past ages had been giants. By the eighteenth century, Franklin, Jefferson, and most European Americans no longer believed that giant human races still existed, although they were unsure about the idea of extinction. But in 1519, many in Europe were convinced that bizarre creatures populated the New World, and they expected explorers to discover Amazons, cannibals, weird monsters—and living giants. The colossal femur that Cortés acquired as a marvel from Mexico would have been seen as proof that giant tribes had dwelled—and perhaps *still* lived—in the Americas.

As we saw in chapter 1, however, Native American traditions about giants and immense land animals indicated that such creatures had never been seen alive in the present age, that the huge beasts had disappeared long ago—an insight of great import to Georges Cuvier. Notably, the Tlaxcaltecas, the Incas of Peru, and the Aztecs also recognized that the giant beings whose bones they found had all been destroyed or died out long before their own time.[6]

Fossil Legends of the Incas

The Incas, whose empire included what is now Ecuador and Peru, also explained colossal skeletons as the vestiges of dangerous giants of antiquity. Inca fossil lore was recorded by a Spanish explorer just a few decades after Cortés arrived in Mexico. Pedro de Cieza de Leon, born in 1519, set off at age fourteen for adventures in the New World. His *Chronicle of Peru* (1553) recounts his travels in the land of the Incas from 1532 to 1550. Cieza de Leon conversed sympathetically with the indigenous people and described the natural history of the land, as well as Inca customs and beliefs.

Remarking that more bones of giants had recently been discovered in a very ancient tomb near Mexico City and in other parts of the old Aztec kingdom, Cieza de Leon wrote that giants also came to light in the Inca kingdom. In his discussions with the Manta Indians, he heard a tradition that "had been received from their ancestors from very remote times." Ages ago, at Point Santa Elena (a barren peninsula on the north side of the Gulf of Guayaquil, Ecuador), there arrived on the coast giants "of such size" that an ordinary man was only as tall as their kneecaps. They had long hair and eyes as large as small plates, and they were covered in skins. This colony of giants put great pressure on the region's resources, consuming "more meat than fifty of the natives of the country could."

Unfortunately for us, Cieza de Leon censored the local lore, refusing to record the "various versions of the story current among the vulgar, who always exaggerate everything." And his translation displays biblical overtones. But he does tell us that because of their vile sexual habits, the giants were "detested by the natives," who made war against the invaders in vain. At last God intervened, and while the giants "were all together engaged in their accursed [words omitted], a fearsome and terrible fire came down from heaven with a great noise. At one blow, they were all killed, and the fire consumed them." This South American extinction scenario recalls the mastodons' destruction by cosmic lightning in the Ohio

Valley, which the Delawares saw as retribution for the monsters' destruction of smaller game animals (chapter 1).

After the fire, all that remained were bones and skulls of the giants, left "as a memorial of this punishment." We believe the account, declared Cieza de Leon, "because in this neighborhood the Indians have found, and still find, enormous bones," skulls, and teeth. As "witnesses to the story," the Indians showed the Spaniard an immense tooth weighing "more than half a butcher's pound," and a shinbone of marvelous size.[7]

In 1543, an event that marked an important milestone in the history of paleontology took place in Peru. The deputy governor of Truxillo (Trujillo, Peru), Juan de Olmos, undertook the first paleontological excavation on record in the New World, in order to verify the Peruvian Indian legends about extinct giants. "Hearing all these things," Olmos and his men dug pits in the valley where people said the giants had been destroyed. Besides skulls that seemed human, the workers unearthed huge thighbones, ribs and other bones, and enormous teeth so ancient they were mottled like tortoiseshell. "From that time on, the native tradition was believed."

This sixteenth-century excavation to confirm a Native tradition about large vertebrate fossils has been forgotten in modern paleontological history. But in 1712, in Massachusetts, as he compiled his "scientific" proof of the biblical Flood, Cotton Mather was fired up by the description of this Peruvian excavation, reported in 1555 by the Spanish historian Agustin de Zárate. Mather included the Peruvian account along with the examples from Mexico described by Acosta and two other Spanish historians. Anticipating the broad scientific interest of Georges Cuvier a century later (and my own research into fossil legends nearly three hundred years later), the Puritan minister sought out all available reports of giant bone discoveries, from classical antiquity to Native American legends of the sixteenth and seventeenth centuries. "I find That the *Americans* in the *Southern Regions* have Traditions of *Giants*," wrote Mather, and now "at last we dig them up in our *Northern* regions too."[8]

In 1550, more proof of the past existence of giants in Inca lands came from the City of Kings (Lima, Peru), where "certain bones of men who must have been even larger than the giants" of Santa Elena were excavated. We may gather, concluded Cieza de Leon, that since "so many persons saw and affirmed these things, these giants really did exist." About twenty years later, in 1570, Arica Indian legends about gigantic bones unearthed at Manta and Puerto Viejo (about a hundred miles north of Santa Elena) were recorded by Father José de Acosta, who said that the Indians made "great mention of certaine Giants . . . of a huge greatness." The dimensions of the bones indicated that the giants were three times the size of ordinary people. According to the Arica, "the Giants came by sea, to make warre," and for their "abominable sinnes, especially against nature" they were "consumed by fire from heaven."[9]

Native accounts of giants of "excessive size" ("exorbitant" size, in Mather's words) who committed "abominable sins against nature" strongly appealed to the pious Spanish of the sixteenth century. In popular Christian lore, the antediluvian giants had been evil savages "who overturned all laws of humanity" and nature. According to Judeo-Christian giantology, the god of the Old Testament had sent the Flood to destroy wicked primeval giants. The Native American tales of evil giants punished by the deity harmonized with the Spaniards' own cosmology and seemed to imply that the New World was included in God's divine plan.[10]

Today, the exact reasons for the extinctions of the stupendous dinosaurs, the immense early mammal species, and the Pleistocene megafaunas are debated. Many theories have been proposed to explain why gigantic species no longer rule the earth. It's interesting to compare modern scientific ideas about land creatures' shrinking body size with the pre-Darwinian extinction ideas of the Native Americans. Scientists have suggested changes in climate or landforms, depletion of food sources, "fire from heaven" in the form of an asteroid impact 65 million years ago, volcanoes, and, in the case of Ice Age megamammals, slaughter by early humans. All these modern theories have analogues in Native American traditions. No scientist today suggests that immense creatures went extinct because they deserved to for their "sins against nature," and yet even that theme finds a modern echo in the pervasive sense that animals of "excessive" dimensions were ultimately unfit to

21. Mastodon tooth (*Dibelodon bolivianus*), Pleistocene fossil from Peru, excavated by Eaton in 1912, Peabody Museum. Clay figure = 2 × 1.5 inches. Copyright © 2001 Peabody Museum of Natural History, Yale University, New Haven, Connecticut. Photo: Adrienne Mayor.

survive, that giantism somehow became unviable and was no longer smiled upon by nature.

What was the true identity of the giants destroyed by fire in Inca lands? The shoreline of the Santa Elena peninsula and the coastal deserts of Ecuador and Peru are continually eroding away, revealing the massive fossil bones of Pliocene and Pleistocene mastodons (e.g., *Dibelodon bolivianus* and the gomphothere *Cuvieronius*) and gigantic sloths the size of elephants (*Megatherium, Eremotherium*). In the fall of 2001, I visited the Peabody Museum of Natural History in New Haven, Connecticut, to photograph some impressive limb bones and teeth of these creatures. The specimens I saw were excavated by Yale paleontologists in 1869, 1912–14, and 1943 from the oil-seep deposits on the coast and in the mountains of the old Inca Empire (figs. 21, 22, 23, and 24).

Ancient observations of these huge skeletons on the desert shore gave rise to stories of a colony of invading giants from the sea.

22. Pleistocene mastodon tusk (*Dibelodon bolivianus*), excavated by Eaton in Peru in 1912, Peabody Museum. Clay figure = 2 × 1.5 inches. Copyright © 2001 Peabody Museum of Natural History, Yale University, New Haven, Connecticut. Photo: Adrienne Mayor.

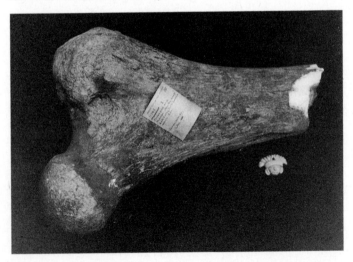

23. Femur of a *Gomphotherium*, Pliocene mastodon (*Cuvieronius andium*), from Ecuador, excavated by James Orton in 1869, Peabody Museum. Clay figure = 2 × 1.5 inches. Copyright © 2001 Peabody Museum of Natural History, Yale University, New Haven, Connecticut. Photo: Adrienne Mayor.

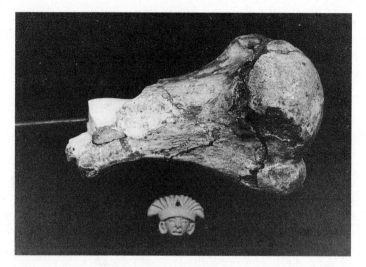

24. Giant sloth humerus (*Megatheridae*) from Cuzco, Peru, excavated by Eaton in 1914, Peabody Museum. Clay figure = 2 × 1.5 inches. Copyright © 2001 Peabody Museum of Natural History, Yale University, New Haven, Connecticut. Photo: Adrienne Mayor.

Perhaps the idea that the giants destroyed the "provisions" and game of the area arose to explain the desolate coast of Peru and Ecuador, the driest desert in the world. The notion of the giants' destruction by fire at Santa Elena may have been related to the hot tar pits there. Many of the big bones and teeth that I examined at the Peabody were blackened and look burnt, similar in appearance to the Pleistocene fossils at the La Brea tar pits of Los Angeles, California.[11]

The giant bones unearthed in 1550 in the City of Kings, the Spanish capital of Lima, may have come from the Pleistocene deposits of mastodons and giant sloths in the foothills of the Andes. But Cieza de Leon noticed that these giants were even bigger than the ones from Santa Elena. In 2001, I learned of another possibility from François Pujos, a paleontologist who excavates in Peru. He described the recent discovery of the skeleton of a Mesozoic marine reptile at Lima: such creatures grew to a length of twenty feet and might also well account for the larger giant bones described by Cieza de Leon. Pujos remarked, though, that Peruvian villagers no longer recount the old Inca stories of evil giants. "Now, they worry about living 'dinosaurs' and are generally very fearful of any discoveries of very large bones."[12]

AZTEC FOSSIL LEGENDS

In the 1520s, after the conquest of the Aztec Empire, the Spanish authorities strove to impose Christianity and erase the Aztec and other indigenous groups' historical and mythic heritage. They burned countless tomes of accumulated Native knowledge, ancient codices recorded on bark paper. Beginning in the 1530s, however, some sympathetic Spaniards, Jesuits like José de Acosta, began to salvage traditional histories in Mexico and Peru. These men learned the native languages and interviewed elders, preserving their chronicles in new codices that made their way to European monasteries and archives.

One of these priests was Father Bernardino de Sahagun, who arrived in Mexico in 1528. He learned Nahuatl so that he could converse with the Aztecs, and developed a deep fascination with their mythology and history. Sahagun's endeavor, characterized by systematic research and rapport, resembles modern ethnological fieldwork, producing in-depth interviews and learned commentaries.

From about 1530 until 1580, Sahagun met every day with a group of *tlacuilos*, artist-scribes who were the keepers of Aztec history and wisdom. He also sought out pictorial documents that had survived the burning of pagan works by the Spanish priests. Sahagun's codices translated a series of Native texts, giving a firsthand glimpse of Aztec beliefs. To the questions Sahagun posed, the tlacuilos replied in symbolic picture-writings, which he then submitted to a group of Aztec and Spanish scholars. After they interpreted the hieroglyphic paintings, yet another group of experts approved the chronicles. Only then did Sahagun commit them to writing in Nahuatl (later translating them into Spanish).

Sahagun sent his magisterial work, the manuscript of Tlateloloco, to Spain for publication. But the Church authorities suppressed its publication, fearing that it would keep paganism alive in Mexico. Sahagun's manuscript was actually lost for nearly three hundred years. It was discovered in 1830 in a crumbling convent library in Navarre, Spain. Sahagun's work is known today as the Florentine Codex.

I found two ancient Aztec legends related to fossils in the Florentine Codex. One is part of the myth of Quetzalcoatl's odysseys as the Toltec civilization was collapsing. Various Nahuatl place-names commemorated the Feathered Serpent god's journeys. On his way to Coaapan, accompanied by musicians playing flutes, Quetzalcoatl stopped to rest. This place was ever after venerated for "the marks which Quetzalcoatl left upon the stone with his hands when he rested there, when he sat down. And as he supported himself on the rock by his hands, they sank deeply; as if in mud did the palms of his hands sink down. Likewise his buttocks, as they touched the rock, sank deeply." These marks of the god's hands and seat, said the Aztec tlacuilos, "are clearly visible, so deeply are they" impressed in the bedrock. The place was named Temacpalco, which means "Impression of the Hands."

Temacpalco was two leagues from Mexico City, according to Sahagun's successor, Juan de Torquemada (a league was the equivalent of about six miles). The legend recalls the foot- and seat prints of the Great Spirit in Iroquois, Delaware, and Shawnee fossil lore (chapter 1). The prints were not illustrated in the Florentine Codex, and it's not clear what the handprints (or seat print, for that matter) of the Feathered Serpent god would look like. Would they resemble human hands? bird tracks? reptile prints? Unknown, until someone locates old Temacpalco. For now, we can only guess that the place called Impression of the Hands was a genuine tracksite of some extinct creature, or else there were carvings that resembled fossilized prints, perhaps made to illustrate or commemorate an episode in the Quetzalcoatl epic. The sediments near Mexico City are of Pleistocene date and so might hold the tracks of extinct mammals, and dinosaur footprints have been discovered in the states south and west of Mexico City, in Puebla and Michoacan.[13]

The second fossil legend in the Florentine Codex concerns the magnificent ruins of the city of Teotihuacan, about thirty miles northeast of the Aztec capital of Tenochtitlan. The origin and identity of the people of the great city, which flourished from the first century A.D. until it was destroyed by fire in about A.D. 750, were unknown to the Aztecs—and this culture remains a mystery today. In A.D. 500 the metropolis had an estimated population of 200,000 and covered more than twelve square miles. The vast Avenue of the Dead was lined with seventy-five temples, including the monumental Pyramid of the Sun (216 feet high, the tallest pyramid in Mexico) and the great Pyramid of the Moon. Painted murals and sculptures on the extant structures depict many gods familiar from later Mexican civilizations, including the Feathered Serpent god, Quetzalcoatl, whose image combined serpent, bird, jaguar, and crocodile features.

When the Aztecs arrived in Mesoamerica from the northwest (Sonora, Mexico, and the American Southwest) in about A.D. 1200, they discovered the great ruined city. They founded their own capital in 1325, and the ancient city became a place of pilgrimage for them until the Spanish Conquest. The pyramids awed the Aztecs, who believed that they had been constructed by giants. In book 10 of the Florentine Codex, Sahagun transcribed, "And they [the ancestral Teotihuacanos] built great Mounds for the Sun and Moon, as if they were mere hills. It is unbelievable that they were made by hand, but giants still lived there then." The pyramids, like mountains, with their steep, high-rise steps, were thought to be the dwellings of the giant race.[14]

Another version of this giant legend was reported by the priest-historian Juan de Torquemada (1557–1664), who drew on Sahagun's work and on Native sources for his chronicle of Mexico. He mentioned that "when the Toltecs visited the city to placate the angry gods, Teotihuacan was inhabited by monstrous giants with long, thin arms." (The Toltec civilization collapsed about the time of the arrival of the Aztecs, in the twelfth century.) From the writings of the educated Aztec prince Fernando de Alba Ixtlilxochitl, born in 1568, we learn that the Aztecs called those earth-giants *Quinames* (or *Quinametzi* or *Quinametinime*, "monstrous or deformed" giants). His history, the Ixtlilxochitl Codex, begins with creation and ends with the Spanish Conquest, and was based on oral chronicles, folk songs, and pictographic histories. According to Ixtlilxochitl, Cholula (the site of the Great Pyramid, 180 feet high, southeast of Teotihuacan) was also inhabited by Quinametinime, which were defeated by the Olmecs, thus ending the age of giants.[15]

The belief in giants was quite logical, says Dr. Leonardo López Luján of the Museo del Templo Mayor in Mexico City. He affirmed that the Aztec legends "probably originated in accidental discoveries of the colossal skeletons of mastodons and mammoths in the vicinity of Teotihuacan." The ancient city ruins are in a dry plain surrounded by distant mountains, and since the 1940s paleontologists have excavated Pleistocene mammoth remains in Tepexpan, a few miles south of the great pyramids and at nearby Ixtapan and several other sites in the old Aztec Empire. Very early obsidian and silex points are also found among the bones, which may have contributed to the Aztecs' idea that the skeletons of Columbian mammoths belonged to giant men who constructed the massive buildings as if they were piling up children's blocks. *Mammuthus columbi* stood thirteen feet high at the shoulder and weighed as much as 135 average Aztec men together. The Teotihuacanos, and later the Aztecs, collected salt from dry lake beds in the area and in the process would have uncovered massive fossils. The paleontologist Barnum Brown discovered that this was so in 1910, when he examined several mastodon skeletons that had been unearthed by salt workers at dry lakes in central Mexico. The situation recalls the Shawnee salt-gathering expeditions in the mastodon bone beds of the Ohio (chapter 1).[16]

BONES OF FEAR: FOSSIL MEDICINE IN MEXICO

In Aztec mythology, there were four previous ages of the world, each destroyed by a different cataclysm: flood, earthquake, hurricane, and fire. The first age was dominated by the earth-giants, followed by three eras of primitive humans. The Aztecs believed that inhabitants of the later worlds sometimes encountered terrifying giants who were relict survivors of the great flood and earthquakes that had destroyed the past worlds. To re-create life in the present, fifth age, the Feathered Serpent god Quetzalcoatl retrieved the scattered and broken bones of the human ancestors destroyed in the fourth age. He ground the bones to powder in a jade mortar. Mixed with blood donated by the gods, these bones produced today's humans. This mythic episode is the earliest American example of the purposeful collection of ancient bones for a mystical purpose.[17]

Did the Aztecs and other early people of Mexico collect fossil bones for medicine or power, like so many other North American Natives? The myth about Quetzalcoatl grinding the bones he collected from the fourth age is suggestive, but I did not find any references to the practice in the early Spanish accounts. However, I did come across an intriguing twentieth-century report of an ancient custom in the village of Charcas, in the state of San Luis Potosi, on the northern border of the old Aztec territory. This region is distinguished by dry gorges and caves and was famed for its mines during the Spanish Conquest. For as long as they could remember, the villagers of Charcas had collected chalky-white fossil bones of huge dimensions, which they discovered in deep *barrancas*, ravines. These *huesos de espanto*, "bones of fear," were thought to be the remains of very ancient human giants.

As recently as the 1930s—and the practice may even continue today—the people of Charcas ground the bones of these giant "ancestors" into powder, in a remarkable recapitulation of the ancient Aztec myth about Quetzalcoatl gathering the scattered bones of human ancestors from the previous age and pounding them in a mortar of jade. In Charcas, people boiled the powder of the "bones of fear" with an unknown plant and drank the concoction as an antidote against fright and panic. Notably, in the late 1800s, the explorer Karl Lumholtz observed that the people of Guerrero, Chihuahua, also made a concoction of "giants' bones" to drink as a "strengthening medicine."

I turned to a lab report from the 1930s, when a paleontologist at the University of Michigan had examined some samples of

25. Mexican workers carrying fossil elephant bones discovered at Tepexpan, Mexico, in 1946. Photo: Helmut de Terra, 1957.

"bones of fear" from Charcas and determined they were mastodon fossils (fig. 25). A few years later, in 1947, the German archaeologist Helmut de Terra explored the caves and ravines near Charcas, in San Luis Potosi, and identified the abundant remains of Ice Age mastodons, whose huge limb bones were encrusted with gypsum crystals (calcium sulfate). The giants' bones collected for medicine from the limestone of Chihuahua also turned out to be large, extinct proboscidean fossils that had crystallized inside.[18]

Collecting fossils for medicine is a widespread and very old practice. The idea that ingesting the bones of fearsome giants of antiquity could instill courage or strength is based on folk beliefs in sympathetic magic and homeopathic medicine (treating a symptom with a minute amount of whatever produces the symptom). Daring to incorporate the substance of something so frightening and powerful into one's body was thought to dispel fear and instill fortitude. In ancient Chinese medicine, "dragon-bone" powder was prescribed as a sedative, bringing to mind the calming effect of the "bones of fear" in Charcas. In the early twentieth century, paleontologists discovered that the dragon bones were really the fossilized remains of dinosaurs and extinct mammals. Dragon-bone powder is still prescribed as a tranquilizer by traditional Chinese doctors.

It may surprise many readers to know that Europeans also drank infusions and swallowed pills made of pulverized marine fossils and scrapings from the petrified bones and teeth of prehistoric elephants. When a heap of mammoth fossils came to light in 1700 in Germany, for example, apothecaries swarmed to the site to gather the teeth, while the philosophers on the scene argued over whether the skeletons belonged to Hannibal's war elephants or to a human giant drowned in Noah's Flood. European pharmacists dissolved the fine fossil powder in wine or water, or mixed it with honey or oil. Similar fossil infusions were administered to livestock. Apothecary shops in Europe sold mammoth tusk filings as an especially valuable medicine, and fossil shark teeth were used as antidotes to poisons, while crinoids and belemnites were thought to cure kidney stones and banish nightmares.

Like the Native Americans, some Europeans also wore fossil amulets to prevent disease, and they burned some fossils, such as jet (fossil coal), to release the curative powers, recalling the Delaware story of smoking the monster's bone (chapter 1). Today, one can purchase powdered fossil coral and shells as calcium supplements. Much of the old lore of fossil medicine was based on magical thinking, but in fact the calcium salts in fossil bones and shells have a nutritional "fortifying" value similar to the calcium that is derived from bonemeal or pulverized shells of living species.

From Maximo Salas, an architect and paleontological illustrator in Monterrey, Mexico, I learned that in San Luis Potosi and other places in northeastern Mexico, "Rx shops and drug stores used to sell fossil bone powder as a tonic for humans and cattle." Salas remarks that the practice was based not just on traditional mystical ideas but on observations of wild animals gnawing on fossilized Pleistocene bones to obtain mineral salts. "We are a practical people in this part of Mexico," says Salas. Pregnant and older women took the fossil powder as a calcium supplement, and farmers fed pulverized mammoth bones to their cattle.

Large fossils served other practical functions, too. Farmers in the village of Temosachic, for example, use large mastodon limb bones as the corner posts for their livestock corrals. And in Mina, near Monterrey, where the great tusk of a *Mammuthus columbi* skull poked out of a riverbank, Max Salas recalled that the villagers found it a handy place to hang up their baskets and clothing while they swam or bathed. That mammoth skull is now on display in a small museum, Museo Bernabe de Las Casas, in Mina.[19]

CUVIER'S COLLECTIONS OF CENTRAL AND SOUTH AMERICAN FOSSILS AND LORE

The legendary giant bones of Mexico and Peru first received scientific attention in Paris in about 1800. Georges Cuvier was one of the first scientists to make a comparative study of Central and South American fossils. He recounted his excitement over the large vertebrate fossils sent to him by the German naturalist Alexander von Humboldt, who explored Mexico and Peru in 1799–1804. Humboldt shipped several important specimens to Cuvier's lab at the Jardin des Plantes, including elephant fossils (along with two live axolotls for the zoological gardens).

Humboldt informed Cuvier that petrified skeletons of gigantic elephants "are found buried in the marly ground on the very ridge of the Mexican Cordilleras [mountains]." He also suggested that the series of four cataclysms depicted in Mexican codex pictographs may have derived in part from ancient attempts to explain observations of "marine petrifactions and fossil bones." (Many mammoth bones are buried in deposits of mud and lava flows from volcanic eruptions in Mexico.) Humboldt collected several large bones and teeth from Huehuetoca, an ancient site a few miles north of the old Aztec capital, Tenochtitlan. And he found more mastodon remains in Pérou, on a Spanish plantation and near the volcano of Imba-burra, in the province of Quito (now Ecuador).

Examining the fossil specimens sent by his friend, Cuvier was excited to see that a huge molar from Huehuetoca resembled the teeth of extinct mammoths from frozen Siberia. The other speci-men was a mastodon tusk from Inca lands. "I carefully placed in the Museum these two precious fossils," wrote Cuvier, "which proved that true elephants of antiquity had left their remains north and south of Panama."

Then, "to avoid neglecting any relevant information," Cuvier pre-sented some Aztec and Inca fossil legends in his scientific account. As we've seen, Cuvier maintained a strong interest in Native American traditions about large vertebrate bones. The legends demonstrated the wide distribution of elephant fossils, supporting his theory that such fossils belonged to extinct species. Here Cuvier cited the pale-ontological folklore research of Acosta and an earlier Spanish natural-ist, José Torrubia (1698–1761). After an Italian peasant girl had showed him some fossils, Torrubia traveled around the world, from China to the Americas, collecting "petrifactions." Torrubia's book on natural history was published in 1754, and his chapter on "Gigan-tologie" was translated into French in 1760. Paleontological scholars should consult that chapter, advised Cuvier, for further Aztec and Inca traditions about the bones of giants, accompanied by Torrubia's "new details and notes." Finally, Cuvier pointed out that the cusped teeth of mastodons resemble human teeth, which led Native people to think the fossils belonged to giants.[20]

DINOSAURS IN BAJA

Meanwhile, in Baja California, a Spanish Jesuit missionary had un-dertaken another early paleontological excavation to confirm a local Indian tradition about giants. At the Mission San Ignacio, founded in 1728 in the Kadakaaman Oasis south of the Volcano of the Virgins in central Baja, padre José Rotea had heard Cochimi Indian stories about giants that came from the north in ancient times.

According to the Cochimi tradition, these giants had created the now famous cave paintings of people and animals in the area, first described by the Jesuits in 1728. In his *Antiquities of Baja California* (1780), the Mexican missionary historian Javier Clavijero (b. 1731) explained how a flood at nearby San Joaquin had revealed some giant bones, in the gorge of the underground river of Kadakaaman Oasis. Padre Rotea and some Cochimi men excavated there and brought up an entire backbone with very large vertebrae, a long arm bone, a big femur (broken, but two feet long), several teeth, and part of a large cranium. Rotea's measurements of the skeleton led him to estimate that the giant had been about eleven feet tall.

What was the true identity of the giant? Dinosaur remains have been discovered by modern paleontologists further north in Baja, around El Rosario, but no modern paleontological investigations have taken place around San Ignacio. The celebrated cave paintings that the Cochimi Indians attributed to giants are in the vicinity of Rancho San Joaquin, which archaeologists recently identified as a Clovis site with fine obsidian points made eleven thousand years ago. Since the early twentieth century, the beautifully crafted, long fluted blades of the widespread Clovis culture of 9200 to 8000 B.C., named after a site first discovered in 1932 at Clovis, New Mexico, have been found along with butchered mammoth bones throughout North and Central America (see map 4, chapter 4).

It seems that the Cochimi Indians assumed that the ancient artifacts and the paintings had been created by the beings whose gigantic bones lay nearby, just as the Aztecs had linked the obsidian points and mammoth bones at Tepexpan.[21]

EXTINCT ANIMALS IN MEXICAN ART?

Are there any artistic representations of fossils or extinct creatures in Aztec or ancient Mesoamerican artwork? The examples that have been proposed are highly speculative and unverifiable, and some are fake, such as the Acambaro figures, a trove of clay statues alleged to prove the coexistence of dinosaurs with an unknown Mexican civilization, discovered north of Mexico City in 1945. When some sizable teeth turned up in association with the Acambaro figures, they were examined by the curator of the American Museum of Natural History—none other than George Gaylord Simpson. In 1955, Simpson, an expert on prehistoric horses, identified the teeth from Acambaro as those of an extinct Ice Age horse of Mexico.

Unfortunately, no records exist of Simpson's reaction to the Acambaro figurines of humans interacting with giant reptiles, but his encounter with the spurious artifacts may have reminded him of the notorious Lenape Stone, which Simpson had already discounted in 1942. Discovered in 1871 on a farm in eastern Pennsylvania, at a time when numerous fraudulent Indian artifacts were popping up across America, the incised stone allegedly depicted ancient Delaware Indians fighting mastodons. (See the appendix for the Acambaro figurines, the Lenape Stone, and other fossil-related fictions.) It's a good bet that the Lenape Stone and the Acambaro figure hoaxes contributed to Simpson's antipathy to any evidence that seemed to attribute paleontological knowledge to Native Americans.

There are, however, some credible examples of extinct creatures in Mesoamerican art. Helmut de Terra's discovery in the 1940s of mammoth kill sites in central Mexico opened up the possibility that ancient art could depict extinct elephants drawn from life, as do cave paintings in Europe. And indeed, since the time of Cuvier, Europeans in Mexico were intrigued by what appear to be representations of elephants in authentic pre-Columbian pictographs and sculptures.

Cuvier's friend Alexander von Humboldt was the first to remark on an elephantlike figure in the Codex Borgia (dating to the twelfth or thirteenth century, just before the Aztec Empire). Noting the "remarkable resemblance" to an elephant with tusks, Humboldt pointed out that the trunk was much longer than a tapir's snout. He asked, "Did their traditions reach back to the time when America was still inhabited by these gigantic animals, whose petrified skeletons are found buried" throughout Mexico? Edward Burnet Tylor took up the question of living elephants in Mexican art in

1865, when he defined "myths of observation" based on empirical evidence like fossils, and Henry Mercer discussed several examples of elephant artifacts in 1885. In 1887, paleontologist William Berryman Scott published some drawings of elephants in Mexican art, stating that the traditions and art were "irresistibly suggestive" evidence that Native Americans "knew these monstrous animals familiarly." Scott himself believed that mastodons may have survived in North America until about 1500 (on the early controversy over whether Native Americans hunted megafaunas, see the appendix). In the 1940s, A. Hyatt Verrill, an explorer-naturalist who discovered the Coclé culture in Panama and wrote extensively on Central America and Aztec mythology, also drew attention to elephantlike animals in ancient artwork.[22]

Were living elephants known to the Maya and Aztecs? Or were the images based on ancestral memories, as Humboldt suggested? Localized mammoth species (and other large Pleistocene animals and birds) may have survived to later dates in the Valley of Mexico and the southwestern United States. The Tlaxcaltecas said that the giants destroyed by their ancestors pulled down trees and ate grass, elephantlike behavior. Could the giants with "long, thin arms" in Torquemada's Aztec legend refer to a vague memory of prehensile trunks, something like the "extra arm" of the Giant Elk in Abenaki and Iroquois myth? Might the images be exaggerations of living tapirs? Another possibility is that the images were reconstructions of fossil elephant skeletons (as we saw in chapter 1, the Shawnees detected a "long nose" structure in mastodon fossils). Until we have further evidence, however, the origin of the elephant images in pre-Columbian art remains unknown.

Lured by the ancient artwork that appears to show elephants, A. Hyatt Verrill ventured into paleo-cryptozoology, proposing that other odd creatures in Aztec art could have been based on observations of the fossil remains of flying reptiles. For example, Verrill thought that pictographs of the Aztec demon Izpuzteque in the Vatican Codex were "astonishingly similar to a pterodactyl." "Possibly this demoniacal beast . . . was an invention of some . . . Aztec priest. But if so," asserted Verrill, the coincidence seems "amazing."

26. Unknown creature on ancient Coclé pottery, Panama. Drawing after Verrill 1948.

Verrill claimed that even more "realistic" images of pterodactyls appear on "the beautifully drawn . . . decorations on pottery [at] the temple site of the Coclé culture" in Panama. The Coclé civilization dated to A.D. 1330–1520 and may have influenced Aztec mythology and art. Verrill described a Coclé creature as having "beaklike jaws armed with sharp teeth [and] wings with two curved claws . . . [a] short, pointed tail, reptilian head crest or appendages, and strong hind feet with five-clawed toes on each" (fig. 26). Even if artistic imagination had led the artist to add teeth to the bird's beak and claws to the wings, argued Verrill, "he most certainly would not have given a bird feet with five toes."

Verrill proposed that such creatures were based on "accurate descriptions, or even drawings or carvings, of fossilized pterodactyls . . . handed down from generation to generation, for untold centuries." Pterosaur skeletons do have clawed wings and five toes, and some have crests and toothed beaks. But the number of toes on many other fantastic Coclé creatures varies, and the crest looks more like antlers, which also appear on other Coclé birds with no teeth and only four toes. The "wings" may be arms. Instead of a pterodactyl, the image might represent some other creature known only from fossils.

What about Aztec artwork or legends of strange winged beings? Could they have been influenced by pterosaur fossils, either the remains themselves or oral descriptions of them? Taphonomy, the study of the condition of dead bodies in the ground and their transition to fossils, is a crucial factor. For fossils to influence legends, the petrified forms must be visible enough to invite interpretation by prescientific people (who were more observant of nature and more familiar with skeletal anatomy than we moderns are). In the Great Plains of the United States, for example, complete pterosaur fossils are preserved in slabs of white limestone, and these conspicuous remains played a role in tales of Thunder Birds (chapters 4 and 5).

James Clark excavated some exquisite fossil fragments of an Early Jurassic pterosaur in northeastern Mexico in 1982. I contacted him, curious to know whether ordinary people of antiquity could have noticed such fossils. But Clark assured me that the cryptic condition of the flying reptiles would have been unlikely to attract attention in ancient times. The skeletons were broken up and folded, and encased inside very hard rock. Clark pointed out that the modern villagers who live on the Jurassic outcrops had never noticed the fossils because they do not weather out.[23]

In 1971, in southern Texas on the Mexican border, the incomplete skeleton of an ultralarge pterosaur with an estimated wingspan of forty feet was discovered at Big Bend National Park (fig. 27). Similar giant pterosaur remains exist in northern Mexico and the Southwest, although the taphonomy discourages recognition by prescientific observers. According to Aztec traditions (supported by linguistic studies), this region was Aztlan, the original Aztec homeland. Were mythic figures such as the Feathered Serpent god Quetzalcoatl influenced by pterosaur remains observed by Aztec ancestors in the Southwest, or even further north in the Great Plains? We know that traders from New Mexico transported turquoise to the Aztec capital in central Mexico—did they also bring descriptions of flying reptile fossils?

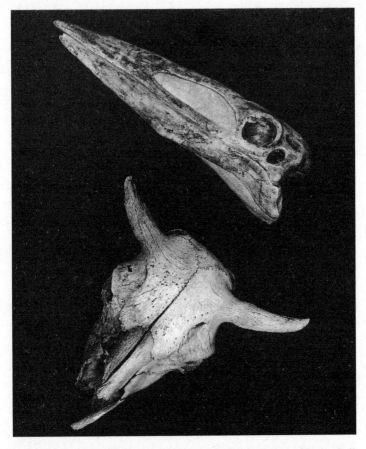

27. The enormous *Quetzalcoatlus* pterosaur skull, top, compared to the skull of a present-day bison, bottom. Early Native American discoveries of a fossil creature with a beak and wings whose skull was as large as a buffalo's would become legendary. Cast and skull in Sheridan College Geology Museum, Wyoming. Photo: James Yamada.

At this point, these questions remain unanswered. But it is amusing that in the world of paleontology, pterosaurs and Aztec myth have already been linked by scientific nomenclature. When it came time to name the giant flying reptile fossil of the Rio Grande, it was the ancient Aztec legend that influenced paleontology, rather than the other way around. The magnificent pterosaur species was called *Quetzalcoatlus* in honor of the Feathered Serpent god.[24]

BIRD OF TERROR: A YAQUI FOSSIL LEGEND

The available paleontological evidence makes it difficult to argue that the Aztecs or their neighbors were aware of the cryptic fossils of prehistoric flying reptiles trapped in stone in central Mexico. But in the Sonoran desert of northwest Mexico, the region where Aztecs said they originated, a Yaqui Indian legend about a giant bird was explicitly linked to the discovery of extraordinary bones.

As the Spanish expanded their empire north in the 1730s, they met the fierce Yaqui living in pueblos along the Rio Yaqui in Sonora. The Yaqui legend of Skeleton Mountain, a sacred site of great antiquity, tells of an enormous bird that preyed on humans "in the olden days." I found two oral versions of the old legend recounted by Yaqui elders from Sonora, Mariano Tapia, born about 1887, and Refugio Savala, born in 1904. The two versions are combined in the following account.

Long ago, men, women, and children were carried off by a giant bird of prey with huge talons that lived on the slopes of *Otam Kawi* (Skeleton Mountain), in the foothills of the Sierra Madre Occidental above the Rio Yaqui (fig. 28). In those days before pueblos, the Yaquis lived in crude shelters made of mud and branches, cowering in constant fear of the dreadful bird. Every evening someone was carried off toward Skeleton Mountain. On the hillside, villagers found great heaps of bones and skulls of the victims. The bird was impossible to kill, for it had very keen eyesight and soared very high. A young orphan decided to hunt down the fiendish raptor. An old man who lived near Skeleton Mountain advised the boy to hide near the bone piles to ambush the bird. The boy set off alone with his bow and arrows.

In Tapia's tale, the boy dug a hole in the bone field and hid. At dawn, as the bird swooped down on the pit, the boy killed it with four arrows. In Savala's version, the enormous raptor soared high

28. Skeleton Mountain (*Otam Kawi*), Yaquiland, Sonora, Mexico. Photo: David Burckhalter.

above and was brought down with three arrows. It crash-landed in a tree stump, where the boy finished it off with a club. In Tapia's version, in the era of this giant bird of prey, mammals with claws did not yet exist, although there were mammals with hooves. The feathers of the great bird were transformed into all the birds we see today, and the flesh became present-day animals and predators "of the claw."

Now, only the bones of the terrible bird remained on the hillside. The boy returned to his village with his tale. The bones are there, he said, "if they aren't you may cut my neck." The boy led a party of elders and warriors from eight villages to see the proof of the pit he had dug and the bird's skeleton. When "the men and soldiers saw the bones of the big bird, . . . they went away contented." Back in the villages there was rejoicing. We no longer have danger from above, warned the boy, but now "we must take care here below," watching out for "the animals of the claw."[25]

Here is an indigenous Mexican fossil legend that realistically portrayed Yaqui ancestors living in primitive shelters. That detail sets the tale in the time before Spanish contact, since when the Spanish arrived in the 1730s the Yaquis were already living in adobe pueblos. The early people feared predators of the air, immense raptors with terrible talons, whose death ushered in a new era characterized by dangerous land predators. The Yaqui concept of a progression of ages marked by diverse kinds of fauna (giant birds and hoofed herbivores, succeeded by large, clawed predators) is a striking element in a pre-Darwinian myth, one that might have impressed George Gaylord Simpson.

The extinction of the immense bird, and its transmutation into modern species of birds and animals, took place in hilly terrain where layers of skulls and bones were exposed. The heaps of bones and a pit dug in the hillside, and the evidence of the great bird's bones in a region now known to be fossiliferous, make this a significant paleontological legend. The verification by a party of elders guided to the site of the terror bird exposure recalls tales of Iroquois who journeyed to Big Bone Lick to confirm the warrior's discovery, and the Senecas who validated an elder's report by digging up the bones of the Great Bear in New York.

In the 1970s, Mexican and American paleontologists discovered abundant remains of Pliocene and Pleistocene elephants, bison, horses, and other creatures in the gravels along Rio Yaqui. The fossils wash down from the western slopes of the Sierra Madre and are frequently found by local people. Richard White, a paleontologist who has worked in the region, told me about a local quarry worker who discovered a large proboscidean skull (probably the gomphothere *Cuvieronius*) near Ciudad Obregon, which he advertised with a sign, "See the Giant Bones." Higher up, more complete skeletons erode out of the mountainsides, and in the Sierra Madre there may also exist patches of Jurassic-Cretaceous remains, which could include pterosaur fossils.

The Yaqui tale probably also reflects observations of giant California condors, both living and fossilized, in northwestern Mexico. Condors, with wingspans of ten feet, are known to attack prey as large as deer, and their nests are filled with bones. Strikingly, the nests of very large Ice Age condors preserved in dry caves contain the bones of mammoths, camels, bison, and horses, carried away as carrion. Familiarity with living condor behavior and chance finds of nests containing the bones of very large, extinct mammoths and bison would contribute to legends about gigantic birds that carried off humans.[26]

The huge raptors of the Ice Age, *Teratornis merriami* with a wingspan of twelve feet and *Teratornis incredibilis* with a wingspan of seventeen feet, may also play a role in tales of monster birds (fig. 29). The heavy-bodied teratorns, weighing fifty pounds or more, resembled eagles but with very long, strong hooked beaks for grabbing up prey that could include small humans. *Teratornis* remains, some as recent as eight thousand years old, have been found across the southern United States (and recently in Oregon) and northern Mexico—and the remains almost always coexist with human occupation sites.[27]

If a large, long-beaked teratorn skull and parts of the large wing structure and talons were found by the Yaquis among the Pleistocene deposits at Skeleton Mountain, it might well have inspired a legend about a monstrous bird. The nightmarish notion of enormous raptors swooping down on helpless victims occurs across Indian cultures, as we will see in the next chapter, on the fossil monsters of the American Southwest.

29. Top: Pleistocene teratorn (wingspan twelve to seventeen feet), compared
to a California condor (wingspan nine to ten feet, center), and an eagle (wingspan seven to eight feet, bottom). Drawing © Rick Spears 2004.

C H A P T E R

3

The Southwest: Fossil Fetishes

and Monster Slayers

> Even relatively savage tribes did pick up fossils on occasion
> [but] no knowledge of their organic origin is indicated.
> —*George Gaylord Simpson, 1943*

> All kinds of beings were changed to stone. We find . . . their
> forms, sometimes large like the beings themselves, sometimes
> shriveled and distorted. We often see among the rocks the
> forms of many beings that live no longer.
> —*Zuni elders, 1891*

ON THE Navajo Reservation in northeastern Arizona a few years ago, paleontologists were excavating the bizarre, five-horned skull of a *Pentaceratops*, a twenty-five-foot-long dinosaur of the Late Cretaceous with the largest skull of any land animal. An old Navajo man came up to see what they were doing. Taking one look at the creature, he uttered two words, "Monster Slayer," and walked away.[1]

The incident exemplifies the limited dialogue between paleontologists and Native Americans today about the meaning of fossils in the western United States. Paradoxically, the West has some of the richest dinosaur exposures studied by scientists, yet little is known about the traditional interpretations of the people who have observed the remains for the longest time. The lack of communication is not a new situation. As the Spanish pushed north into the American Southwest, lured by the fabled Seven Cities of Gold, they no longer inquired about fossils as they had in Mexico and Peru.

The mirage of treasure may have been based on lore about the powerful Gran Chichimeca civilization that had dominated northwestern Mexico and southern New Mexico in A.D. 1200–1425. Casas Grandes at Paquimé, the metropolitan trading center, had a population of five thousand at its peak. Among the exotic goods that passed through this vast hub were macaws from Latin America, turquoise and copper from the Southwest, and shells from the Pacific Ocean. Archaeologists even found one storeroom filled with fossils. By the time the Spanish arrived, however, the city was a ghostly ruin (map 3).

In 1540, when Francisco Vásquez de Coronado and his men reached what is now New Mexico, they encountered the Zuni pueblo dwellers. After claiming the land for Spain, the army of 350 Spaniards and about 1,000 Mexican Indian warriors continued their quest for the lost cities of gold, now guided by Turco (The Turk), a Pawnee captive they had purchased from the Apaches. Seeing a way to return home to Kansas, The Turk assured them he knew the realm of gold, and he led the Spanish across New Mexico, Texas, Oklahoma, and then north to central Kansas.

Along the way, some of the soldiers may have paused to puzzle over huge bones in the desert or great tree logs petrified by time (fig. 30). But they were seeking riches, not curious rocks. And the Franciscan missionaries in the Southwest were too busy harvesting souls to listen to old stories about old bones. Unlike the earlier priests in Mexico and Peru, the Franciscans refused to learn Native languages and cared little about the indigenous culture. The earliest written references to oral fossil traditions I know of from the Southwest and Great Basin date from the late nineteenth century, recorded by American explorers and ethnologists. But archaeological evidence from ancient pueblos like the fossil storeroom at Casas Grandes, and the oral creation myths of the Zunis, Navajos, Apaches, and others, show that conspicuous fossils, from dinosaurs

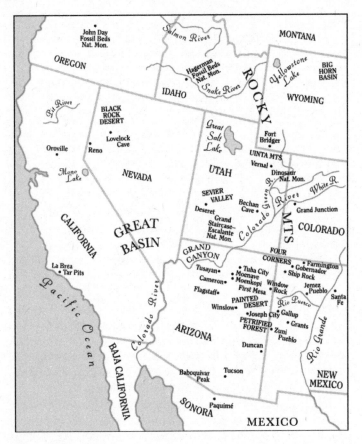

Map 3. The Southwest, Great Basin, and Rocky Mountains (map by Michele Mayor Angel)

to petrified wood, had long been significant features of the cultural landscape.[2]

The early Spanish silence on southwestern fossil lore prefigures by several centuries the closing of discussion between Euro-Americans and Native Americans. Cross-cultural conversations about fossils faded with the development of the formal sciences of geology and paleontology in the mid–nineteenth century. With the profes-

30. Sixteenth-century Spanish conquistador contemplating the fossil skull of a *Pentaceratops* dinosaur in New Mexico. Drawing © Michele Angel 2004.

sionalization of their discipline, scientists sought to "demythologize" paleontology. One of the first results of the new earth science was the realization that the earth must be extremely old, followed by the understanding that landforms and life-forms had changed drastically over vast geological ages. These were shocking ideas to Euro-Americans, but similar concepts were already deeply embedded in southwestern creation stories.

As American bone hunters and pioneer paleontologists fanned out across the West in the 1800s, snatching up fossils for museums in the East, they hired Indian scouts to guide them to bone beds and protect them from hostile tribes. But unlike the earlier bone hunters at Big Bone Lick, they no longer recorded Native fossil traditions, traditions that had helped to shape Cuvier's theory of catastrophic extinctions and anticipated other advances in scientific thinking.

In the nineteenth century, however, new conversations began in the social sciences, as ethnologists and anthropologists accompanied geological surveys in the West. One might expect that since these scholars studied Native customs and myths, stories about fossils would have been recorded. But they rarely asked about fossils. Despite the new interest in ethnology, therefore, many more complete fossil traditions were recorded in the sixteenth to eighteenth centuries, in New Spain, New France, and New England, than in the American West in the nineteenth and twentieth centuries. What little has been preserved of oral fossil lore in the West seems like tantalizing snatches of overheard conversation, compared to the vibrant dialogues of earlier times.[3]

Moreover, among traditional Indians now living in the West, secrecy veils fossil lore, and historically justified suspicion prevails about the motives of bone-hunting scientists. The systematic large-scale plunder of fossils, artifacts, and human remains by the U.S. government and museums began in the 1850s and continued with the federal seizure of the *T. rex* skeleton named Sue, found on Indian land in 1990; the controversial nine-thousand-year-old remains of Kennewick man in Washington State in 1996; and government plans, in the face of Indian protests, to excavate fossils on Pine Ridge Reservation, South Dakota, beginning in 2002. As I crisscrossed the West talking with people on reservations about dinosaur exposures on their land, I found that these historical and ongoing conflicts can make conversations about prehistoric remains oblique and difficult. Even Native Americans like Vine Deloria, Jr., the Standing Rock Sioux historian, who wish to bring more traditional natural knowledge into public light, encounter resistance to open discussions of fossils.[4]

ZUNI PALEONTOLOGY

Zuni Pueblo in New Mexico may be the oldest continuously inhabited community in America, and the Zuni creation story has very
strong ties to the volcanic mountains and deeply eroded canyons of
Arizona, Utah, Colorado, and New Mexico known as the Colorado
Plateau. In its insights about geomorphology and the succession of
diverse life-forms over deep time, Zuni mythology clearly accounts
for the fossilized remains of creatures of past ages, and with a level
of understanding that far surpasses the expectations of George Gaylord Simpson.

   Like the Aztecs and many other Native cultures, the Zunis believed that our present world had been preceded by a series of
worlds, each populated by different beings. In Zuni myth, when the
earth was new it was flooded and wracked by earthquakes. Bizarre
monsters ruled this dark, watery age. Proto-humans were sorry beings, more like cave creatures than mammals, with clammy skin,
goggle eyes, bat ears, webbed feet, and tails. Creeping along like
salamanders, they barely survived on their island of mud, preyed on
by the monsters of the deep. The Twin Children of the Sun realized
that the world needed to be dried out and solidified before the
"unfinished" humans succumbed to the monsters. Wielding a
magic shield, a rain-bow, and arrows of cosmic lightning, the Twin
Heroes ignited a tremendous conflagration. The fire raged over the
face of the earth, scorching it dry and hardening the ground. Humans emerged from their mud-cave existence into blinding sunlight
and began to evolve toward "finished" human beings.

   But now, on dry land, predatory animals multiplied. With their
powerful talons and teeth, these giant creatures devoured weaker
human beings. So the Twin Heroes stalked across the world, blasting all the land monsters—enormous mountain lions and bears and
other huge creatures—with lightning. "*Thlu!*" Instantly immolated,
these dangerous beasts were "shriveled and burnt into stone."

   The ethnologist Frank Cushing (1857–1900) lived many years
with the Zunis, learned their language, and was adopted into the
tribe. In 1881, Cushing heard this ancient epic recited by Zuni

priests. They explained that all kinds of beings were changed to stone when the earth was young. Thus "it happens that we find, here and there, throughout the world, their forms, sometimes large like the beings themselves, sometimes shriveled and distorted. And we often see among the rocks the forms of many beings that live no longer." Such finds "show us that all was different in the days of the new."

We have changed you into rock everlasting, said the Twin Heroes, as they struck the huge animals with lightning. "Now you will be good for men rather than evil." By the heart that shall endure forever within you, they vowed, the petrified creatures would become fetishes, *We-ma-we*, helpers that serve humans instead of devouring them. And so, deep within each stone beast killed by the Twins, the "hearts were kept alive, with instructions to help humankind with the magic captured in their hearts. When a Zuni finds a stone that naturally resembles an animal, he believes that it is one of these ancient stone beasts."[5]

Modern Zuni fetishes, small carved stone animals with inlaid hearts, are well known. But in the old days, the most valued personal fetishes were small rocks or fossils with a natural resemblance to an animal form that required little or no carving to bring out the likeness. The "heart power," or spirit, of the once-dangerous predator or monster remained in the fetish, even though its body had been changed to stone. We-ma-we were mostly used as hunting charms, because the heart (and breath) of a predator was believed to be the force that overpowered the hearts of game animals, and timeworn animal-shaped rocks and small fossils were handed down over generations.[6]

The Zunis also collected curious stones, minerals, and fossils whose shapes suggested that they were the body parts of monsters or the weapons of gods. Some of these amulets were concretions, hematite nodules, or basaltic forms resembling petrified organs, and others were fossilized bones, teeth, or claws, or odd marine fossils. For example, belemnites, the pointed guards of an extinct squidlike creature, have a tapered, cylindrical shape like a missile (fig. 31). Belemnites are abundant in Jurassic and Cretaceous marine outcrops, and the pointed shape made these fossils significant

31. Belemnite fossils, used for protection in battle by the Zuni. These marine fossils were called "lightning or thunder stones" by Plains Indians. These specimens were photographed in the Black Hills of South Dakota by Barnum Brown in 1941. Barnum Brown Collection, American Museum of Natural History Library.

for many tribes in the West. The Zunis identified belemnites as the weapons or the teeth of primal monsters. These belemnite fetishes, called *Shom-i-ta-k'ia*, "protective medicine of war," were kept for generations by Zuni warrior societies. Before battle, a warrior would scrape the fossil against a stone with water and anoint himself for protection against arrows.[7]

Cushing wrote that "all true fetiches [*sic*] are either actual petrifactions of the animals they represent, or were such originally." As the first anthropologist to study the Zuni practice of carving small animal fetishes as magic charms, Cushing was unaware of the possible relationship between fetishes and fossils. Writing in the late nineteenth century, several decades before the dinosaur fossils of New Mexico and Arizona became well known to science (the first dinosaur bones were collected in eastern Arizona in the 1930s), Cushing assumed that all the "petrifactions" were "mere concretions or strangely eroded rock-forms."

But today it seems obvious that when the elders spoke of finding the life-size forms of many beings that no longer live—"sometimes large like the beings themselves"—among the rocks, they were describing the skeletons of dinosaurs and other extinct creatures that continually weather out of the desert. Large animals transformed to stone were the original We-ma-we, fetishes with hearts of power, but they would be too big to carry, so smaller teeth, claws, and fossil bones were gathered as amulets, along with animal-shaped concretions and stones. Zuni carvers, aware of the connections between fossils and fetishes, have recently begun to make small fetishes in dinosaur shapes.

Extensive exposures of Cretaceous sediments lie east and south of Zuni Pueblo. Since the Zunis (like other southwestern Indians) gathered bentonite clay, salt, jet, gems, and minerals in fossiliferous areas, they would often come across the remains, trapped in rock, of large marine reptiles and dinosaurs with bizarre, horned skulls and huge teeth and talons. As the Zuni elders told Cushing, it was very good fortune to discover powerful relics from the "days of the new."[8]

"I can't believe that some of these dinosaur fossils were not recognized as 'stone beasts' by the Zuni," said Douglas Wolfe, when I met him in Mesa, Arizona, in January 2002. As the leader of the Zuni Basin Paleontology Project, Wolfe has been digging for fossils near ancestral pueblo dwellers' lands since 1996. His group has dis-

32. *Zuniceratops* skeleton, reconstructed near Springerville, Arizona, atop the Moenkopi Formation near Lyman Lake, in Zuni traditional lands. During Cretaceous times, the Moenkopi sediments were exposed in the dry uplands, with water sources and angiosperm forests. *Zuniceratops* may have walked in such a terrain. Photo courtesy of Douglas Wolfe.

covered hundreds of Early Cretaceous remains. Among the most impressive are a theropod with terrible claws heretofore found only in Mongolia and a new ceratopsian species (which Wolfe named *Zuniceratops* to honor the Zunis, fig. 32). Wolfe also finds razor-toothed raptor dinosaurs and duck-billed hadrosaurs, as well as petrified tropical trees and marine fossils.

Some 90 million years ago, these creatures and plants flourished on the fluctuating western shores of the inland sea that bisected North America, in forested wetlands teeming with prehistoric crocodiles, giant sharks, and immense marine reptiles called mosasaurs. As Wolfe points out, the era corresponds to the "days of the new" of Zuni mythology.

From desert basins to bare mountaintops, the dry climate and exposed topography make the Southwest an open textbook of geology. Millions of years of "geologic 'happenings' have left their traces for us to piece together into a coherent, albeit patchwork, history," writes one geologist. The Zunis studied these same geological and paleontological clues and accurately perceived that, eons ago, the land had been a watery place populated by strange water monsters, followed by a fiery drying period marked by gigantic land predators.

With the same logic that led the Greek natural philosopher Xenophanes in the sixth century B.C. to propose that ancient oceans must have stranded shells and other marine creatures on mountaintops and deserts far from the sea, the Zunis saw the presence of stone oysters, clams, ammonites, fish, and other marine fossils as proof that a sea had once covered the desert, further confirmed by the fossilized impressions of ripples and mud cracks on the receding shorelines.

Volcanic evidence and lava flows—and perhaps even living memories of eruptions—supported the Zuni idea of a great conflagration that dried out the young earth. According to an interesting theory proposed in 2003, the mass extinctions of virtually all marine species of the Permian period 250 million years ago may have been caused by a powerful underwater explosion of gases, which then could have been ignited by a single lightning strike to set the whole planet aflame, a scenario remarkably reminiscent of the Zuni myth. Doug Wolfe's team has discovered evidence of tremendous prehistoric fires that raged across the land, leaving burnt stumps and roots petrified in the ground, more stark evidence for the Zuni scenario. The Zuni creation story is also one of a few pre-Darwinian myths to imagine the first humans as evolving from lower life-forms. "It's all there in one elegant myth," comments Wolfe, "evolution, extinction, climate change, deep time, geology, and fossils."[9]

"It's interesting how different the Zuni approach to death is from the Navajo, who greatly fear death and its artifacts, such as fossils," Wolfe remarks. In their myth of the fetish animals, "the Zuni seem to seek some benefits from dead things, which the Navajo seem to avoid at all cost." Many paleontologists notice that traditional Navajos have negative feelings about excavating dinosaur skeletons. Recently, for example, an old Navajo woman brought some fossilized dinosaur vertebrae to a trading post in Gallup, New Mexico, but a shaman on the reservation discouraged further investigation by paleontologists.[10]

Fossils in Navajo Land

"It's not a good idea to disturb past life buried in the ground," the Navajo spiritual leader Harry Manygoats told me, when we discussed fossils in Tuba City, Arizona, in October 2002. Back in the 1930s, during construction of a dam on the reservation, Navajo workers had refused to continue after enormous bones were revealed by the horse-drawn scrapers. "*Chindee*," they whispered, "ghost." Around the same time, the San Diego geologist Baylor Brooks learned from some Navajos that the bones of immense dinosaurs and marine reptiles were considered to be the remains of *Yeitso*, a giant monster killed by the "Monster Slayer." The giant's ghost was said to haunt bone beds.

Wann Langston, Jr., in an interview in September 2003, recalled his days as an undergraduate student in the 1940s, excavating a *Pentaceratops* dinosaur with Professor Willis Stovall (University of Oklahoma). Each day, he told me, a group of Navajos would observe from a distance. At last a man named Joe approached to watch more closely. What's the Navajo name for these creatures? Professor Stovall asked Joe. Joe replied that the fossils were the "remains of the venerable ancients." Langston recalled that the word Joe used for the monster bones they were digging up sounded something like "yitso-bitso."[11]

In 1999, Mearl Kendrew, a Navajo born on the reservation in 1946, referred to the old myths when talking to me about fossils of large, extinct creatures. Her grandparents owned the roadside animal attraction on old Route 66 near Winslow in the 1940s and 1950s, with snakes, badgers, and a giant Gila monster that lived twenty-two years and grew several feet long. The poisonous Gila monster, a desert reptile whose beaded armor recalls for Navajos the flint-armored body of the monster named Yeitso, symbolizes the healing powers of medicine women and men. When I asked Mearl about dinosaur fossils, she replied, "In the story of the coming of This World, the twin Monster Slayers killed the monsters one by one. But they couldn't destroy their bodies. These are the fossils. This is a short story but I think you get the idea."[12]

To understand Merle Kendrew's laconic story, the comment made by Harry Manygoats, the Navajos' anxiety aroused by fossils, and the old man's terse reaction to the *Pentaceratops* skull at the beginning of this chapter, we need to look at the Navajo creation myth and traditional ideas about death, ghosts, and time.

In the 1930s, Gladys Reichard studied the beliefs of the Navajos (Dineh) with whom she lived. In her exhaustive book, however, she never referred to the dinosaur remains so abundant in Navajo land, perhaps because she was unaware of the first scientific collections of dinosaur species taking place at the time. Nevertheless, the ethnological work by Reichard and others in the nineteenth and twentieth centuries can give us a sense of how dinosaur skeletons were interpreted by the Dineh. When we apply a culture's ancient mythology to natural phenomena, though, it's important to keep in mind that the oral myths—often translated from their original languages by outsiders—are complex, symbolic, incompletely known, and inconsistent. The myths' origins may have nothing to do with observations of prehistoric remains, even though they might be used to account for later fossil sightings.

It's also important to appreciate the traditional reluctance to teach tribal lore to non-Indians. Many Navajos today avoid discussing fossils, even with other Native Americans. Vine Deloria tells me that he has often asked about fossil legends in the Southwest. "There *are* dinosaur stories," says Deloria, "but they are held by Navajo medicine men who won't talk about them."[13]

Based on language, scholars believe that Navajos (and Apaches) migrated from Canada and arrived in the Southwest in A.D. 1100–1400. In an argument that strains logic, some anthropologists speculate that Navajos decided to settle in the landscape that matched their mythic geography. The Navajos themselves believe that their myths originated in the Southwest, and that some bands may have migrated later to Canada. Navajo (and Apache) culture shares some mythic elements with the Pueblo peoples of the Southwest, the ancient Anasazis (who disappeared about 1300), and the Zunis and Hopis. Whatever its origins, notes one historian, the Navajo Monster Slayer myth "offers an explanation for not only the huge fossil bones and dinosaur footprints found around the Navajo reservation but also strange rock formations and other phenomena." Moreover, the myth demonstrates "an extraordinary interest" in local geography and geology. The simplified summary on the following pages shows how many features of the Monster Slayer stories reveal geological knowledge and an awareness of fossils, even though references to the physical remains themselves are indirect.[14]

The Navajos envisioned a series of past worlds that were destroyed before this world (the number varies). People escaped from each world, bringing a token from the previous era. As in the Zuni myth, the earlier, wet and muddy worlds were dominated by monsters, which were created before human beings and preyed on them. Some monsters even pursued people into successive worlds. But the Sun gave special lightning bolts to the twin sons of Changing Woman, so that they could overcome the monsters. The twins became the heroic Monster Slayers. The monsters are described below, with my speculations on their possible relationships to fossil evidence in Arizona, New Mexico, Utah, and Colorado.[15]

The Monsters

The first, most dreaded monster was Yeitso (also called Big Monster or Big Gray Monster—gray is associated with evil). Yeitso dwelled by the hot springs near Mount Taylor (near Grants, New Mexico, which has Jurassic and Cretaceous sandstones), or on Red Mesa, near Farmington, which has Cretaceous dinosaur fossils. The monster's face was striped (stripes are associated with terror), and its stupendous body was covered with scaled armor. Approaching with earthshaking footsteps, Yeitso attacked, but the Twins destroyed it with lightning. As the monster crashed to the ground, Yeitso's armor shattered, the scales scattering. Some say the scales became flint, and the streaming blood coagulated into the vast black lava flows at El Malpais and McCarty's Wash near Grants, or in the Petrified Forest of Arizona.[16]

Yeitso's bones, called *Yeitso-bitsin*, were associated with large dinosaur or marine reptile fossils (as Wann Langston heard when the Navajo named Joe identified the *Pentaceratops* as "yitso-

33. Petrified logs of immense size were identified as the bones of Yeitso, a monster of Navajo myth; or as giant arrow shafts of Shinarump, the Wolf-god of Ute myth. Petrified Forest National Park, Arizona. Photo: Adrienne Mayor.

bitso," above). Other tales identified the huge silicified logs of Petrified Forest as Yeitso's limb bones (fig. 33). Petrified wood can resemble the shape and texture of bone. In 1876, for example, fossil hunters working for Othniel Marsh of Yale University discovered some bones of a massive dinosaur in curio shops in southern Colorado and northern New Mexico. The bones were being sold as petrified wood.

Near Farmington, in 1905, one of the places where Yeitso was said to have been killed, bone hunters for the paleontologist Walter Granger investigated a "wagon load of immense bones" brought up by some Navajos digging out a spring in the Cretaceous badlands. The diggers may have thought of the fossils as Yeitso-bitsin, a possibility that is strengthened by an event a generation or so later. During the Depression Navajos working on a government dam left the site when big bones of a phytosaur, a large Triassic crocodile,

34. Phytosaur skull and teeth. The sharp, serrated teeth of these Triassic crocodilian reptiles were collected by Navajo healers as a toothache remedy. A phytosaur skull can measure two to four feet long. Here, the teeth are compared to an arrowhead about three inches long. Drawing © Rick Spears 2004.

were unearthed. This incident, mentioned earlier, was recounted by Laura Adams Armer (b. 1874), an artist who lived on the reservation in 1923–38. Armer, known to the Navajos as Hard-Working Woman, wrote that after the workers stopped digging, the foreman, a medicine man called Hasteen Akaka, explained that the "bones of one old giant Yaytso" must not be disturbed. Although the Navajos wanted water for their flocks, he said, this was not a good place for the dam, because "if the sheep drink water that flows over the bones of a giant, the sheep will die." Later, Hasteen Akaka came in the night with a flour sack to gather up the big teeth of the phytosaur (fig. 34). He explained that he would sprinkle the teeth of Yeitso with sacred pollen and use them as a toothache medicine.[17]

Yeitso was visualized as a monster covered with flinty scales, an image that recalls the distinctive remains of Triassic phytosaurs and amphibians and immense armored dinosaurs covered with bony scales or scutes. The huge Permian armored amphibian *Eryops* was also armored with bony plates, as were the dinosaurs *Ankylosaurus* and *Stegosaurus*, and *Scutellosaurus*, which had bony nodules under its skin. The Triassic aetosaur *Desmatosuchus* was fully armored and sported a collar of projecting points. Fossilized scutes or plates of these species are conspicuous objects in the desert (fig. 35). In 2001, for example, a college student fixing a flat tire in southern Arizona decided to inspect some variously colored layers in a hillside and quickly found several pieces of dermal armor from a *Nodosaurus*, another heavily armored and spiked dinosaur the size of a car.[18]

After Yeitso, the next monster was Burrowing or Horned Monster. Something like a giant misshapen elk or huge striped gopher with horns or tusks, this beast had been raised by the winds in a gully. From far off, it could be seen lying in a vast plain, and the Monster Slayers reached it by digging tunnels. As the monster plowed up the earth with its horns, they killed it with lightning arrows. A little gopher assured them the monster was dead by running out along one of its horns.

Several details hint that observations of fossils may have contributed to this myth. The monster was associated with wind in a gully: wind erosion often reveals a fossil skeleton in a depression—and the Twins found the monster by digging. The image of a large horned animal could be based on a dinosaur skull with bony projections, like that of the *Pentaceratops*. When I visited the Rainbow Forest Museum in Petrified Forest National Park, Arizona, in October 2002, I noticed another possible influence for the Burrowing Monster. The skull of *Placerias*, a large, powerful mammal-like reptile (a therapsid) of the Triassic, has large, bony tusks for digging (fig. 36). In Petrified Forest, near St. Johns, paleontologists have unearthed the remains of many of these bizarre burrowing beasts.

The Southwest also has rich exposures of Pliocene-Pleistocene mammal fossils. Mastodon skeletons of the Pleistocene may have contributed to the Burrowing Monster legend, too. Some versions

35. Armored dinosaurs covered in scutes and bony plates, whose remains are found in the southwestern deserts. Clockwise from top, *Stegosaurus*, *Scutellosaurus*, *Desmatosuchus*, *Eryops*, *Ankylosaurus*. Drawing © Rick Spears 2004.

specify four "horns," and some gomphotheres, such as *Amebelodons*, have two pairs of tusks. Mastodon and mammoth remains have been imagined as massive burrowing creatures by various cultures around the world, from Siberia to Patagonia. For example, the Yup'ik people of southwestern Alaska tell of a tusked creature

36. Skull of *Placerias*, a burrowing, mammal-like reptile with tusks. *Placerias* weighed two to three tons and flourished in the swamps and forests of the Triassic, 225 million years ago. Hundreds of these fossil creatures have been discovered near St. Johns, Arizona. Photo: Adrienne Mayor.

called *Quugaarpaq*, said to "travel underground, turning to stone when it came in contact with air. People occasionally find evidence of its existence in the mastodon tusks exposed on river banks each spring." Inuit myths described *Kilukpuk*, a monster with long, straight ivory teeth that "swam" under the earth, and similar tales were told about frozen mammoths in Siberia. In 1833 the Natives of Patagonia, Argentina, told Charles Darwin that mastodon fossils had belonged to an immense burrowing rodent.[19]

Darwin's experience reminded me that the Navajos sometimes described the Burrowing Monster as a giant horned gopher, and a small gopher had a role in the tale. Could the burrowing creature's image have originated as a folkloric exaggeration of the fossils of the unique horned rodent of the Late Miocene? About 6.5 million years ago, *Epigaulus hatcheri* was a strange burrowing "gopher" about a foot tall, with very long claws and upright horns on its head

37. Horned gopher of the Pliocene (*Epigaulus hatcheri*). Drawing by Bruce Horstall, in W. B. Scott, *History of Land Mammals in the Western Hemisphere* (1913).

for tunneling underground (fig. 37). Its distinctive fossils are found in Navajo land and the Great Basin.

Next to be killed were the Cliff Monsters (*Tse Nalyehe*), enormous birds of prey associated with alkali washes and Shiprock, the imposing geological landmark of Four Corners. As in the Yaqui tale in chapter 2, these monstrous birds would snatch people up in their talons and carry them off to feed their nestlings. According to the father of John Rustywire, a Navajo storyteller, they were "like dragons in a way." They preyed on Navajos and Zunis, smashing the victims on jagged rocks, sending their beautiful silver and turquoise necklaces "flying every which way" (fig. 38). Gladys Reichard heard that Cliff Monsters had big eyes and "something like feathers" on their shoulders. The oversize nestlings later became the eagles we see today. In one version, the monster bird resembled "a great black rock which looks like a bird," and in another it was

38. Giant raptor bird carrying off a Native American man. Painting by
Linda R. Martin, Navajo artist, to illustrate a traditional Crow story, in Joe
Medicine Crow's *Brave Wolf and the Thunderbird* (Smithsonian National
Museum of the American Indian/Abbeville Press, 1998).

transformed into Shiprock (*Tse Bit'a'i*, "Rock with Wings"). Today,
some Navajos relate the Cliff Monsters to prehistoric pterosaur fossils, but a more likely paleontological influence might be the giant
raptor bird fossils from the Pleistocene.[20]

The Gray Monsters were a variety of evil creatures of the earlier
worlds. The Monster Slayers killed some, while others were done
in by hail and windstorm. According to Navajo elders who spoke
with Father Berard Haile, who lived on the reservation in the
1930s, a great many monsters were slaughtered around Taos, New

Mexico (map 4, chapter 4). Gray Monsters "of every description exist [there, including] flying animals and quadrupeds." In those places, they said, "many enemy ghosts swarm," for "there are as many ghosts as there are stones," and rock was "all that remains of the monsters" of previous worlds. "At a place called Earth-upper-mountain-ridge, lived those who devoured [the] Earth People. Today you can see burnt earth appearing among the rocks," said the elders, marking where the Gray Ones used to roast their victims.

Since the area around Taos is volcanic, with burnt black-and-red basalt lava formations and colorful ash weathered into bizarrely shaped "hoodoos," the association of monsters with burnt earth in this landscape refers to geological formations rather than fossils. But the Navajo elders also told of other places in the desert where one could see monstrous heads "sticking out from roots of trees and stones, from springs and swamps." They said that monsters also appeared wherever there was colored earth under rocks and at the bases of colored cliffs. In fact, one Navajo name for monsters is "those who speak at the base of cliffs."[21]

Without ever referring explicitly to bones, these striking geological details convey a strong impression of the fossil-bearing strata so obvious in the Painted Desert, with the striped yellow, white, and pink cliffs of the Entrada Formation and the Chinle Formation at the cliff bases, which contains plentiful Triassic fossils of *Coelophysis* dinosaurs, phytosaurs, and large amphibians, and the colorful Morrison Formation with its large Jurassic dinosaurs. The destruction of monsters by forces of erosion (wind and hail), their grayish hue and association with different colored layers of earth, and their emergence among rocks, roots, and springs, and at the bases of cliffs—all these details paint a picture of extraordinary bones and skulls weathering out in precisely the places where modern paleontologists look for vertebrate fossils.

Big Centipede was another species of Navajo monster. This huge millipede, humped with many legs, leapt suddenly on its victims. The largest of these were slain by Monster Slayer. Zuni myth also featured a giant centipede who was shriveled by a bolt of lightning by the Twin Heroes—that's why today's centipedes look like burnt bits of fringed buckskin. These myths could be spun from fears of familiar, creepy millipedes, but the insight that many-legged insects had colossal ancient ancestors turns out to be true, as revealed by fossil impressions of gigantic centipedes that lived in Arizona about 300 million years ago. Was Big Centipede inspired by the sight of a fossil impression of *Arthropleura*, a six-foot-long centipede of the Carboniferous era? Their many-legged trails have also been fossilized in rock. Another paleontological candidate could be a large Cambrian trilobite fossil. Trilobites resemble insects with antennae, segmented bodies, and many legs, and they were collected for amulets by many western tribes.[22]

Water Monsters, born of rock in the first world, were also overcome by the Twins, but were allowed to live because they promised to keep springs and rivers flowing. Like water monsters of many other Native myths, they were imagined by the Navajos as having peculiar, elongated bodies and horns like a buffalo's. Water Monsters aroused mixed reactions—they were dangerous but could be friendly: unlike the other evil creatures destroyed by the Monster Slayers, Water Monsters were "persuadable" entities. An interesting parallel occurs in the Yaqui legend of the Snake of Nohme Hill, in Sonora, Mexico. In that story, a water monster lived in a large water hole, preying on cattle, goats, and people. A Spanish priest spoke to the monster in the Yaqui language and persuaded it to go elsewhere. The monster burrowed underground until it reached a deep aquifer under rock at the foot of Nohme Hill, where it still lives. Although unusual bones are not mentioned, once again the geological details—rocky strata and springs—correspond to the kinds of places where fossils are often seen.[23]

Several Navajo stories tell of Water Monsters' efforts to recover their kidnapped eggs or young and their pursuit of people into successive worlds. The following fossil legend was told to me in Tucson, Arizona, by Gerard Tsonakwa, who heard it from Bessie Yellowhair, daughter of Ho-tzin Yellowhair, a Navajo medicine man.

> Many of the big bones in Navajo Land belong to *Tee-hol-tso-de*, the giant Water Monster of the first world. The people of the first world so admired the monster that when they left for the next world, someone secretly took a Water Monster egg as a souvenir. But then in the

second world, the big egg began to crack open. The Water Monsters could detect the sound and went on a rampage, trying to burst into the second world to save their egg. The Navajo had to flee, taking the egg with them. In the third world, the egg hatched, and so they had to flee again. But in the fourth world, the baby monster began to cry for its parents. Fearing that the Water Monsters would hear it and break into the fourth world, the Navajo escaped into the fifth world. But then the young Water Monster grew so huge and monstrous that they left it behind, barely making it into the sixth and present world. Nowadays, when you come across big fossil bones or eggs, the ghosts of the creatures that they were in past worlds must not be aroused. Don't touch, disturb, or move them, or else the monsters might wake up and go on a rampage that could destroy our world.

This story expresses the traditional Navajo wisdom that one ought to avoid fossils, as potentially negative legacies of past worlds.[24] Was a tale like this originally based on discoveries of fossilized eggs? Nests made by giant sea turtles 110 million years ago have been discovered in the Front Range of Colorado; and in Montana, Jack Horner has found a great many clutches of eggs and hatchlings of the duck-billed dinosaur *Maiasaura*, which flourished 76 million years ago. Large theropod dinosaur eggs have been discovered in Utah and New Mexico. In eastern Arizona near Duncan, paleontologists found a different kind of big stone egg, cracked as if hatching. They identified it as the egg of a Pleistocene-era giant condor.

Dinosaur nests, eggs, and tracks are also found in Navajo land. In the 1950s, Navajo sheepherders discovered a *Dilophosaurus* nest with eggs and the footprints of babies and adults about five miles west of Tuba City, Arizona. More than sixty nests of very ancient water monsters—huge Triassic reptiles—were discovered in 1996–98 by paleontologists in Arizona's Petrified Forest. These bowl-like depressions more than a foot across and eighteen inches deep are the world's oldest reptile nests, dating to 220 million years ago, and preserved in sandstone that was once the bank of an ancient river. Superimposed over the nests are the body impressions of the ancient nest makers. So far no eggs have been found, although impressions of the eggs and claw marks are obvious in the nests.

Dug out by immense reptiles of the Triassic period, phytosaurs (primitive crocodiles), aetosaurs (armored reptiles), or giant turtles, such nests would have been easily recognized by Native observers who noticed that they evoke, on a much larger scale, the nesting behavior of modern reptiles like turtles and crocodiles. Around the ancient nests are trampled fossil tracks, and a half-mile from the nesting site there is a distinct set of phytosaur footprints. No one can say for sure whether the tradition of the Water Monster's egg was related to similar finds. But if nests like the ones near Tuba City and in Petrified Forest had been observed by Navajos in the old days, they too could have read the clues that were only recently deciphered by scientists, and may have created a story about the eggs of a ferocious water monster.[25]

Ghosts and the Thin Membrane of Time

According to Navajo myth, all the "slain monsters were beaten into the earth." But as Mearl Kendrew told me, and as Reichard wrote, "It was impossible to obliterate their carcasses. Consequently, the Navajo country is still littered with unburied remnants of their bodies." In the 1930s, as noted, the dinosaur beds of the Southwest were just beginning to receive public attention, but Reichard missed or avoided this obvious reference to fossils as the remnants of monsters littering Navajo land. She assumed, along with Cushing (above), that the belief about the unburied remnants of monsters applied only to the shapes of geological landforms. But, as we saw, Laura Adams Armer, the artist-writer who also lived with Navajos in the 1930s, was aware that some Navajos identified *Phytosaurus* fossils as the remains of the mythic monster Yeitso. The monsters whose fossils were observed in rock were believed to have played a role in forming the geological features in Navajo land, and more recent statements by Mearl Kendrew and other Navajos explicitly link paleontological evidence to the Monster Slayer myth.[26]

Traditional Navajos believed that the monsters' ghosts remained with their partially buried corpses, eternally threatening evil, and that strong rituals were needed to keep them "beaten into the ground." Elders told Father Berard Haile in the 1930s, "The monsters who formerly were powerful are gone," but without certain rites "their ghosts would devour you." In Navajo belief, "if something happened once, it can happen again." In other words, the past can suddenly burst through the membrane of time into the present, like the enraged Water Monster in Yellowhair's tale.

Traditional Navajos avoided all contact with corpses and "places where the spirits of the dead may be." Funeral practices also help explain why all kinds of bones are avoided. The dead were not deeply buried in the ground but left in the desert, which means that any bones one encounters might belong to ancestors—or monsters. Since it is hard to distinguish animal bone fragments from human, it seems best to steer clear of any skeletal remains.

Shallow human burials in the desert over the ages also help explain why paleontological excavations cause anxiety. Timothy Rowe, a University of Texas paleontologist who has permission to excavate on the Navajo Reservation, told me, "Navajos worry that fossil hunters will dig up their relatives' bones along with dinosaur remains. Explanations that we are looking only for animal bones that were buried 80 million years ago have little effect, since scientific geochronology is not meaningful to traditional people."[27]

With the vivid myths and fears in mind, it is easy to imagine how disquieting a large, fossilized dinosaur could be to a traditionalist. All dead things are supposed to decompose and become one with the earth. But mineralized bone embodies the very *opposite* of the ideal disposal of the dead. Instead of decaying away, the form of a monster's body has somehow become trapped in stone. Dinosaur skeletons—with their awesome dimensions and weird shapes—correspond to the myth of monsters of previous eras imperfectly buried, suddenly reappearing out of the earth. In the Navajo view, it would be a grave hazard to disturb these ancient enemies, for fear of breaking the spell of their entrapment.

In October 2002, I drove from Flagstaff to Tuba City on the Navajo Reservation, to talk with Harry Manygoats, a Dineh spiri-

tual leader who might be able to give me an insider's perspective
on the old accounts. It was a chilly day of constant thunderstorms
rolling across the wide, red-and-gray landscape, and the roads of
the town were awash with red mud. At the Cultural Center, I found
Manygoats in the process of moving the tribal collections to another building. When I explained my mission, to learn what dinosaur fossils mean to Navajos, he set aside stacks of boxes and pulled
up two chairs. Sketching diagrams to illustrate his words with colored markers on a whiteboard, he spent a couple of hours that
morning explaining Navajo practices and ideas about fossils.

Our present era is the fourth, white—or "glittering"—world,
said Manygoats. It was preceded by the third, yellow world; the
second, blue world; and the first, black (or red) world. Those who
"esoterically interpret the stories and watch for the signs" have noticed increasing indications over the past century of global "corrup-
tions of the environment," signaling that worldwide natural catastrophe may already be ushering in the fifth world. Everything, from
the universe to neutrinos, is "alive—nothing is inorganic or lifeless." Each era was characterized by living things specific to that
particular "time/space" (Manygoats explained that the Dineh con-
ceptualize time and space "as one"). In the first world, for example,
life was microscopic, formless except as "energies." The monsters,
dinosaurs, and other giant beings existed in the yellow (third)
world, along with small ants.

Ants, unchanged since that era, still live in our world and travel
between layers of earth and time/space. Like the monsters, ants are
unappeasable entities, and in my reading of Gladys Reichard, I had
learned that Navajo witches used the tiny smooth pebbles that ants
carry up to the surface for evil spells (notably, ants also bring up
minute fossils of extinct creatures from past worlds). But Manygoats would say only that "certain activities of ants—and other beings from previous eras—can be incorporated into harmonizing
practices," to restore balance in this world.

As Manygoats explained it, the vestiges of monsters or dinosaurs
are held by the earth within their context, their unique time and
space, and within that matrix is where they should remain. Past life
and actions never really disappear, since even time is living and ever-

changing "in accordance with each era's laws." Things of the past retain a kind of nether-life, an afterimage, a ghostly shape or echo that never changes. It is almost as though time is an energy that flows through things. For example, commented Manygoats, relics of our conversation here in this room will persist in some form in the future. And since nothing in the world is inanimate and everything is interconnected, to disturb something that was physically buried in the deep past, and bring it into the present, unravels the densely woven net of time—in effect, it breaches the barrier of time—and that will have undesirable consequences.

It is interesting to note that a breach of geochronology is the mechanism for science fiction plots in which a time warp causes humans to suddenly find themselves thrust into the Mesozoic era and coexisting with terrifying dinosaurs. The device appears in popular literature from *The Lost World* of Arthur Conan Doyle (1925) to the *Turok, Son of Stone* comic book series (1950s–60s). Spending long days in solitude laboring to release dinosaurs and extinct creatures from their rock prisons, the early fossil hunter Charles H. Sternberg was a time-traveler, too. "Whenever I awoke I was overcome with surprise," he wrote. "I could not tell whether I had awakened in eternity, or Time had turned back his dial, and carried me back to the old Cretaceous Ocean."

As a young man, George Gaylord Simpson was fascinated with the mystery of time as a human perception, as a figment of our imagination, rather than something inherent in things themselves. In his own posthumously published science fiction story, "The Dechronization of Sam Magruder" (1996), Simpson described a scientist who tries to "dissect time" and suffers a "time-slip" into the Cretaceous, where he must deal with ferocious dinosaurs of primeval New Mexico. A similar tearing of the layers of time was described in Yellowhair's Water Monster tale, and among Cheyenne and Lakota vision seekers such breaches of geochronology are known as "Medicine Holes" or "windows into time."[28]

Dissecting things in nature—taking them apart, removing them from their proper surroundings and the laws that govern them—runs counter to the holistic Navajo worldview. The monsters or dinosaurs are "alive" in suspended animation within their era, said Manygoats, and they must be respected as integral to the matter around them, never torn from the matrix that was once their world. Moreover, "Some monsters of the past could have been set forth as *negative life*," warned Manygoats, and "it is a very bad idea to kick negative nature back into life—for that could cause *history to repeat itself*."

When I asked about the activities of paleontologists, he responded that to dig up fossil bones and take them away from their matrix shows disrespect for the lives of beings in the past and courts danger because "it displaces and encroaches" on their time/space. Just as when men dig up long-buried coal, by strip-mining that rips what were once living plants from their context and pollutes the atmosphere, "it violates the natural balance for paleontologists to remove bones from the ground." Of course, explains Manygoats, "I can't tell them what to do, they must each accept responsibility for the danger themselves."

The consequences of releasing buried things from their place in the past are unknown, remarked Manygoats, but there are many ominous examples. Coal and uranium mining has had devastating effects on the reservation people's health since the 1940s, and digging and interfering with the layers of the earth can poison water and air and harm growing things. Once done, such acts can never be undone. Catastrophic mutations can result; chemical and other unknown imbalances that affect life cycles can occur. The example proposed by Manygoats gave me pause: "Ants, who once lived alongside huge monsters in the past world, might be transformed into giant ants." I was struck by the fact that, during his first peyote vision in about 1923, Lame Deer, a Lakota holy man, had experienced a terrifying image very similar to Manygoats's example. In Lame Deer's vision, a tiny ant crawling in the chinks of a log cabin suddenly grew into a monstrous attack-ant ten feet high and "all horns, shiny like a lobster."[29]

As in the Zuni story, the Navajos believe that large vertebrate fossils preserve in stone the forms of ancient monsters. But, as Reichard, Wolfe, and many others have noted, the Zunis seemed not to have the terror of the dead that many Navajos have. One explanation is that in Navajo belief, ghosts "cannot be persuaded to be helpful to man," and the hostile spirits of monsters must be overcome with rituals to keep them in the ground. Without the beneficial transformation of the slain monsters into fetish helpers as in the Zuni myth, in the darker Navajo vision the idea of dinosaurs reemerging from their time and space in the earth is a frightening one.[30]

I wondered whether Navajos and other Native people had helped the pioneer paleontologist Edward Drinker Cope locate fossil exposures when he came to northern New Mexico with the Hayden Survey in 1874 and again in 1883. The evidence is unclear. Cope wrote that Navajos and Utes often visited his camp, and that when two Ute families camped nearby, he traded tobacco for fresh meat, nuts, and berries, but he recorded no conversations about fossils. When Cope camped in Tiwa and Laguna Pueblo lands in the Rio Puerco area in 1883, he said that a local man (perhaps an Indian?) guided him to a very large "buffalo skull," which turned out to be that of an extinct rhinoceros. In the badlands west of Santa Fe, Cope learned from a Spanish American priest and from "various quarters . . . valuable information as to localities of fossils." Another man, possibly a Pueblo dweller, showed Cope some fossil teeth he had found in the badlands below the Jemez range, from an Eocene mammal, the *Bathodon*. Cope's discoveries of Eocene mammals in New Mexico were milestones in paleontological history, but he didn't record the names of any Native Americans who may have guided him there—or anywhere else in the West.[31]

Half a century after Cope, in 1942, Sam Welles, the famous bone collector for the museum of the University of California at Berkeley, heard about three huge skeletons discovered by a Navajo man two years earlier near Tuba City, Arizona. After failing to locate them himself, Welles returned to the trading post and persuaded the discoverer, Jesse Williams, to guide him to the fossils. The dinosaurs, located just a hundred meters northeast of the famous dinosaur tracksite at Moenave, were identified as the largest predator of the Jurassic, the twenty-foot-long *Dilophosaurus* (the double-crested reptile was featured in Spielberg's film *Jurassic Park* as the venom-spitting dinosaur). The bones were collected in just ten days and taken to Berkeley, where they reside today (fig. 39).

39. Restoration of a *Dilophosaurus* dinosaur, painted by a Navajo artist, at the Moenave site where Jesse Williams discovered the remains of three dilophosaurs in 1940. The artist shows the double-crested dinosaur leaving the footprints visible at the tracksite, in a tropical volcanic landscape, with a pterosaur flying in the upper left. As in fig. 38, the Native artist has given this dinosaur only two hand claws, like a *Tyrannosaurus rex*: two claws are a notable feature of Thunder Birds in some Indian traditions. Photo: Adrienne Mayor.

In his oral narration of the dig, Welles remembered that Williams "worked with a pick and shovel for a couple of days," but when the complete skeleton forms began to emerge from the sandstone and the team took up fine brushes, Williams disappeared. Welles assumed that Williams considered the detail work "beneath his dignity." But many Navajo men engage in detailed work, making intricate jewelry and delicate sand paintings. Another explanation might be that the emerging skeletons aroused some traditional anxiety in the Navajo who had discovered—but did not disturb—the

monsters in the ground. Indeed, paleontologist Wann Langston recalled a similar incident in the 1940s, when the University of Oklahoma team hired a young Navajo man to help excavate the *Pentaceratops* fossils identified as the remains of Yeitso. The young man
agreed to help shovel the overburden as long as he didn't have to
touch the bones. When only about six inches of dirt covered the
bones, he left the site.[32]

In earlier times, medicine men and women dared to gather *Phytosaurus* teeth and other fossils for medicine bundles (*jish*) used in
healing ceremonies, ritual "sings," and witchcraft spells. "I've
heard some mentions of fossils being used for spells and magic,"
said Antonio R. Garcez, an Apache writer in New Mexico who publishes oral folklore about ghosts. Garcez continued, "But it would
be very difficult to find a Navajo or Apache elder who would dis-
close such uses." When I asked Harry Manygoats about the healing
properties of fossils, he replied, "That's an interesting question. My
two brothers are healers but I don't think they use fossils." Later
in Flagstaff, Arizona, Isabelle Walker, a medicine woman who is
director of Traditional Healing in the Navajo Department of
Health and Social Services, told me that her father, Thomas Walker,
a respected medicine man on the reservation, keeps a large fossil
shark tooth as a personal amulet. The triangular shape of the tooth
is considered good for self-protection.[33]

A traditional Navajo medicine pouch, or *jish*, contained a variety
of numinous things, such as pollen, feathers, claws, crystals, turquoise, shells, and fossils. According to early anthropologists who
studied jish, the contents for one Blessingway ceremony (chanting
the Dineh creation myth) included a tiny fossil, a fossilized stone
fetish, and a "tapering stone cylinder" (a belemnite?). The jish of a
Navajo shaman in 1908 held a fossil oyster shell, and so did the jish
created in 1925 for Roman Hubbell (Navajo, b. 1904, of the family
who founded the historic Hubbell Trading Post at Ganado, Arizona, in 1878). In about 1890, the healing bundle of a Navajo
shaman named Jake contained a fossil fetish and an iridescent fossilized shell. Jake explained that he scraped flakes from the fossil fetish
to be administered to the patient and floated the iridescent shell
on top of the medicine bowl. (As with the powdered fossil bones

consumed as medicine in Mexico, the fossil shell scrapings would create a calcium-rich infusion.) The curious shapes and strange beauty, the extreme antiquity and petrified state, and the connection to mythical time—all these combined to give the fossils of once living organisms an aura of mysterious, ancient power.[34]

FOOTPRINTS OF MONSTERS

Footprints in stone are plentiful in the Southwest and Great Basin, and they too attracted attention. A dinosaur tracksite studied in the 1930s by paleontologist Barnum Brown in the Painted Desert south of Tuba City was lost until the early 1990s, when photographer Louie Psihoyos hired Floyd Stevens, a skilled Navajo tracker, to relocate the site and untangle the crisscrossing trails left by dozens of small and huge dinosaurs 180 million years ago. Stevens often helped neighbors find lost livestock. Now, using "his uncanny powers of observation," Stevens plotted out each individual trail in the maze until it disappeared under the overburden.

One sequence posed a puzzle. Three of the ten-inch-long footprints were eight feet apart, a seemingly impossible stride for such a small dinosaur. Psihoyos believed that some intervening tracks must have been obliterated. But Floyd Stevens was sure the animal had been running, even though the speed indicated by the pace—14.5 miles an hour—was astounding. Confidently measuring eight feet straight out from the last visible print, Stevens carefully chipped away a slab of sediment. Under the slab, the Navajo tracker uncovered the next print in the sequence, thereby discovering evidence of one of the fastest dinosaurs on record.[35]

Early humans were probably dinosaur trackers, in a sense, writes Martin Lockley, a Denver paleontologist specializing in dinosaur footprints. Expert trackers "must have occasionally encountered footprints on rocky pavements" and would have been "fascinated by fossil tracks of animals they could not place," impressions made as dinosaurs trudged or dashed over mud that hardened eons ago into rock. Dinosaur tracks range from small to truly stupendous, like the T. rex tracks in the Raton Basin, northeastern New Mexico.

In many places around the world, notes Lockley, Paleolithic rock art appears "right next to footprint-bearing outcrops."[36]

Theropod dinosaur tracks resemble bird tracks; petroglyphs (rock carvings) and pictographs (rock paintings) often include drawings of birds and three-toed dinosaur tracks together. As Lockley comments, the resemblance to avian prints probably led paleo-Indians to believe that the track-maker was a giant bird. A dinosaur trackway near Cameron, Arizona, for example, was known to the Navajos as the "Place with Bird Tracks." In 1999, a Navajo guide at the Moenave tracksite mentioned "old legends of giants" associated with oversize, human-looking footprints in some outcrops. In New Mexico, the name of an archaeological ruin near Jemez Pueblo (occupied A.D. 1450–1700) translates as "Place Where the Giant Man Stepped." That name may refer to fossil tracks related to the adjacent San Isidro dinosaur beds containing *Camarasaurus* and *Seismosaurus* dinosaur remains, but further information about the Jemez giant legends is kept secret.[37]

From some fossil hunters in Arizona, I learned that a petroglyph near Joseph City was inscribed between eight and fifteen hundred years ago above a slab of Moenkopi Formation rock containing Triassic *Chirotherium* dinosaur tracks. The petroglyph appears to be a schematic reproduction of the footprint. In southern Utah, pictographs appear beside a dinosaur trackway in the Chinle Formation, near Monticello (north of Four Corners). The paleo-Indians who created pictographs at the tracksite at Flag Point, Vermilion Cliffs, in the Grand Staircase-Escalante National Monument, were aware of the dinosaur trackways in the sandstone, which also contains the fossils of ceratopsids and sauropods. The ancient artists copied a tridactyl dinosaur footprint, probably a *Eubrontes* track since those are the most obvious prints, though there are also *Grallator* tracks embedded in the Kayenta Formation (Lower Jurassic). That pictograph, attributed to the Anasazi culture of the Four Corners area, was made sometime between A.D. 1000 and 1200. Several birds appear in the panel, suggesting that the Anasazi, too, associated the three-toed fossil prints with giant birds.[38]

Other dinosaur tracks may have been interpreted as the trails of giant lizards, an idea that occurred to me when Colorado rock art specialist Peter Faris showed me his photographs of petroglyphs at Cub Creek, near the Douglas/Carnegie bone beds in Dinosaur National Monument, Utah. Made during the Fremont culture, A.D. 700–1000, the petroglyphs depict lizards of various sizes, some as long as six feet, approaching the small human figure, about one foot tall. Since the region has some of the richest dinosaur bone beds ever discovered (first investigated by Othniel Marsh in 1870), Faris and I wondered whether the Fremont giant lizard petroglyphs at Cub Creek could have been related to observations of the immense fossils and conspicuous footprints in the area. In Red Fleet State Park, for example, just north of Vernal, hundreds of dinosaur and mammal-like reptile trackways have been found on the eroding shores of the new reservoir, which flooded hundreds more when it was filled in 1980. At Cub Creek itself, Martin Lockley reported a large dinosaur tracksite in 1992—it turns out to be only about two hundred yards from the giant lizard petroglyphs. Among the trackways in the region are five-toed *Brachycheirotherium* prints with tail-dragging marks, which would remind ancient observers of the trails left by living lizards.[39]

West and north of Tuba City, beyond the Navajo village of Moenave, Anasazi petroglyphs were carved on cliffs containing *Dilophosaurus* dinosaur bones. Navajo sheepherders who came across the giant reptile fossils in the area also found nests with eggs and hundreds of crisscrossing tracks impressed in hardened mud, made by the monsters that flourished before humans emerged. They call the footprints "*Naasho'illbahitsho Biikee'*," which means "big lizard tracks."

Splashing along the rutted road through another downpour as I drove toward the famous tracksite near Moenave, I recalled what Harry Manygoats had just told me about the site (fig. 40). "Before the tracks around Tuba City were exploited for tourism, Navajos used to hold ceremonies at Moenave and made offerings to the monster tracks."

When I emerged from my muddy car, Morris Chee, Jr., a laconic guide from Moenave, expressed surprise that anyone would stop in the cold rain and slog through puddles to see the footprints. But on sunny, dry days, it's hard to make out the tracks unless one pours a canteen of water into a single impression to see its shape. Today was the perfect weather for tracking dinosaurs: every footprint, big and small, was brimming with rainwater, and the wet bedrock was teeming with the traces of monsters. In fact, the trails were probably made on a rainy day like today. The tracks include rare examples of running dinosaurs, left by the huge bipedal *Dilophosaurus* as it loped with a seven-foot stride across this muddy floodplain 200 million years ago (fig. 41).

Keeping his hands in his pockets, and gazing off to the stormy horizon, Chee walked up to each track and nodded down at it to be sure I noticed it (gesturing by pointing with the finger, as well as eye contact, is avoided by traditional Navajos). In this way, he also indicated the sharp claw marks on some impressions and one large, black talon still embedded in the slick sandstone. A circle of stones marked off "the only bones we got left here. See the ribs and backbone and the jaws?" As we passed some giant cow-pie-shaped sandstone formations, Chee said they might be the droppings of dinosaurs. Looking down at some immense three-toed prints next to some dainty ones, he said, "These big ones are *Dilophosaurus*. But some people say Big Lizard or Big Bird." When I asked whether these creatures might be ones from the old stories about the Monster Slayers, he was noncommittal: "Maybe something like that."

Then Chee indicated several places where large slabs of rock with tracks had been chipped out and hauled away. "They took away all our bones, too, back in the '40s, before I was born," he said with resignation, referring to Jesse Williams's *Dilophosaurus* find now in Berkeley. "We don't ask for them back any more, that was a long time ago. Why don't they make a cast for taking away and leave the bones here? It's better to keep it in the ground right where it is. I wish we could have a museum for the bones here, then people would come to see it."[40]

More tracks are embedded in the rocks a few miles southeast of Moenave, in the Hopi village of Moenkopi. The Hopis apparently incorporated observations of dinosaur tracks into the Snake Dance, an ancient rain ritual performed with live rattlesnakes that relay the need for rain to the proper Kachina spirit, portrayed as a giant underground reptile called *Palulukon*. The Snake Dance is sur-

40. Dinosaur tracksite, Moenave, Navajo Reservation, Arizona. Photo: Adrienne Mayor.

rounded by secrecy. But as Al Look pointed out in 1981, the dancers' traditional costumes are decorated with the distinctive shapes of tridactyl dinosaur tracks, which of course are most noticeable after rain and are conspicuous in the Mesa Verde and Moenkopi areas (fig. 42). According to one version of the Hopi tradition heard in the early 1960s, the dancers themselves weave these designs into their costumes because large, three-toed fossil tracks impressed in rocks were believed to have been made by the Kachina spirit who sends the rain. Among the Indian artifacts displayed in the Museum of Northern Arizona in Flagstaff, I noticed that some Zuni figures of dancers carved about a hundred years ago also wore similar dinosaur track designs (fig. 43).[41]

In Navajo myth, the Sun god left his giant footprints on the earth, an apparent allusion to fossil trackways. Some Navajos believe that footprints retain traces of the maker and can be used in witch-

41. Morris Chee, Jr., Navajo guide from Moenave, above. Below, *Dilophosaurus* dinosaur track at Moenave. Photos: Adrienne Mayor.

42. Hopi Snake Dancers, Arizona, ca. 1900–1920. Note dinosaur track designs on the costumes; the dancer on the left has a snake in his mouth. George V. Allen Photographic Collection 1860s–1930s, National Anthropological Archives, Smithsonian Institution.

craft, but fossil footprints could also be joked about in ways that fossil bones could not. In the 1930s, for example, Roland Bird, Barnum Brown's fossil hunter in Arizona, was investigating reports of dinosaur footprints. While he was in a trading post examining a slab with a peculiar, oversize footprint, an obvious fake, the Navajo men in the store joked that the big foot impression had been made by a barefoot Zuni.[42]

A couple of decades later, a trickster played a practical joke on scientists who had just become aware of fossil footprints long known to the Navajos and Hopis. In 1929–30, Barnum Brown and L. I. Price had photographed some dinosaur tracks next to a Hopi house in Moenkopi (fig. 44). By 1942, the dinosaur trackways in the red Kayenta Formation at Moenkopi were being publicized, and the government had placed a fence around the site. In about 1950, a geology student came to study rocks near Moenkopi and Moenave, in an area of joint use by Hopis and Navajos (the Hopi Reservation lies within the Navajo Reservation). One day, he came

43. Wooden Kachina figure wearing a costume with dinosaur track designs, Zuni, about one hundred years old. Snake Dance figures are rarely depicted by Native artists today. Photo: Adrienne Mayor.

44. Hopi men pointing out dinosaur fossil sites to AMNH paleontologist L. I. Price, above First Mesa, near Cameron, Arizona, in 1930. Not far from here, Price and Barnum Brown investigated dinosaur tracks at Moenkopi Pueblo, a Hopi village south of Tuba City, Arizona. Photo: Barnum Brown. American Museum of Natural History Library.

upon a sharply defined dinosaur footprint. He summoned his geology professors, and the next day the party followed the trail across bare rock for a quarter-mile. The prints ended abruptly.

After hours of searching for more tracks, the scientists returned to the last print. Then they noticed that an Indian had carved his name beside the impression. Suddenly, the curiously unweathered appearance of the tracks made sense. With all the excitement over dinosaur footprints, the artist knew that his bogus trail would eventually be found; he didn't need to witness the discovery to enjoy imagining the temporary confusion of the scientists. When I told Morris Chee, the guide at Moenave, about the trick, he just smiled.

Those tracks were carved as a practical joke, but replicating dinosaur tracks and hand- and footprints is an ancient practice. Examples in Connecticut were mentioned in chapter 1; in the Southwest and Great Basin, dinosaur tracks appear in ancient rock art near real dinosaur trackways; and in the Great Plains, hand- and footprints were carved on large boulders. The makers' motives are unknown, although among the Navajos and Plains Indians, human handprints carved in stone were places where "people prayed with their hands pressed into handprint impressions in a rock." Carved foot- or handprints and replicas of dinosaur tracks could also mark sacred sites or meeting places, call attention to genuine dinosaur tracks in the vicinity, or illustrate a creation story.[43]

CALIFORNIA CREATION STORIES: EXILED

QWILLA MONSTERS

The creation story of the Pit River nation (Achumawi) of California is another example of how concepts of deep time and successive faunas were expressed in mythic language.

In about 1908, the elder Istet Woiche (b. 1840s) narrated the "History of the Universe." The First People, he said, were "neither animal nor man, but curious beings who lived on the earth for thousands of years before real people came." Real humans appeared only after the "Great Change," an extinction and evolutionary event ushered in by a great flood. Many First People were drowned, but others were transformed into modern mammals, reptiles, birds, fish, and insects. These retained some characteristics of their primal ancestors.

Pit River people collected stone acorns called *Nachil*, said to come from before the Great Change—these were fossilized acorns from Tertiary white oak trees, *Quercus hiholensis*. Other relics of the earlier time were footprints in rock said to have been made by Coy-ote-man (*Ja-mul*) and other First People. Istet Woiche pointed out *Ja-mul dok-im-choi*, "Coyote-man's track," on the south side of Big Bend on Pit River, just east of Hot Springs. The large boulder in the gravel channel has a noticeable depression, about eight inches long, shaped like a man's footprint. This region is mostly volcanic and fossil-free, but it is possible for early human footprints to have been preserved in hardened lava flows. A natural foot-shaped depression is another possibility, or the track could have been carved by a shaman.

The first creatures included "many terrible water animals" and a Giant Water Dragon (*Himnimtsooke*) that was something like an enormous salamander. That dragon was finally killed, its body parts scattered in the sea. Another species of dragon, the *Qwilla* monsters, were transformed at the Great Change into the small alligator lizards of California, a rough-scaled reptile up to twenty-two inches long, which resembles a miniature alligator.[44]

Frank Day, a Maidu artist-storyteller born in 1902, painted a picture of giant lizards based on the stories he heard elders recite in their native tongue when he was a boy in central California. Day claimed that the Maidu people had observed petrified giant lizards from "many 1000s of years ago" in the hills above Oroville. Dinosaur fossils are rare in California, but, interestingly enough, some remains of Cretaceous marine reptiles were recently discovered a few miles north of Oroville. In the Pit River area, the rare *Shastasaurus* ("Shasta lizard," an ichthyosaur), a few diapsid reptile fossils of the Triassic, and the shinbone and toes of one small Cretaceous dinosaur have been found in recent years, but it's doubtful that such fragmentary fossils would have been recognizable enough to contribute to the old Achumawi or Maidu myths of giant lizards.[45]

Darryl Babe Wilson, an Achumawi born in 1939, also recalled listening to the "old ones" recite myths. One elder, born in about 1876, told how the voracious lizard monsters preyed on First People. The monsters were killed or driven out before the Great Change. Originally, Qwilla monsters were described as giant lizards, but after the term "dinosaur" entered popular knowledge, Pit River storytellers began to identify Qwillas as huge alligatorlike dinosaurs. In another elder's version, for example, the "king of the Qwillas" was slain south of Fall River Valley. Then the Creator "ordered the rest of the Qwillas to the south land forever. *That is why there are no dinosaurs or alligators in [our] land.*"

This extraordinary narrative is unique among fossil traditions because it explains the notable *absence* of large dinosaur fossils visible to ordinary observers in northern California. As already noted, dinosaur remains are extremely rare there because the region was underwater during the Cretaceous. The Achumawi not only correctly envisioned a great flood in the deep past, but they came up with the logical idea that most of the mythic monsters must have been exiled to the southwestern deserts, which have conspicuous dinosaur remains.

The Qwilla legend reminds us that myths of giant monsters can flourish in the absence of conspicuous vertebrate fossils. Many dragon images around the world were based on folk knowledge or exaggerations of living reptiles, such as Komodo dragons, Gila monsters, iguanas, alligators, or, in California, alligator lizards. But the elder's conclusion also indicates that northern California tribes knew about the impressive bones of giant reptiles in the Southwest. Indeed, since the Pit River people originally came from the Southwest, they may have wondered why there were no giant lizard remains in their new territory. The story suggests that people came to *expect* to find big bones where mythical monsters had been destroyed, and it also shows how the new term "dinosaur" and new observations and zoological knowledge were introduced into a preexisting tradition. A striking parallel is evident among the Dene people of northwestern Canada, where dinosaur fossils are unknown. Yet recent versions of Dene myths include dinosaurs among the giant monsters that once roamed the earth but were destroyed by the culture hero Yamoria.

The Pit River creation story emphasizes the great length of time it took for the world to come into being, and the vast span between the first life-forms and the appearance of "real" humans. In the beginning, there was only water and darkness. After "ten summers and ten winters" (a metaphor for cosmic seasons, like the symbolic "six days" in the book of Genesis), ocean foam eventually condensed into a bit of land. An elder known as Uncle Ramsey, born in the late nineteenth century, recounted the story of the earth's formation by alternating forces of creation and change. "More than a million years" passed before mist emerged from nothingness, he said, and "another million years" later the mist finally jelled into land.

When young Wilson asked an elder how long it took the universe to be formulated, the old man replied, "A very long time, maybe longer than the mind could imagine." Then, "with his old hand, worn by time and burned very dark by the sun, he smoothed out a place on the earth and with a crooked finger wrote 10^{10} in the dust." With this powerful image, Wilson shows how an elderly storyteller interpreted the meaning of "ten summers and ten winters" in the ancient oral myth by applying the modern mathematical concept of 10 to the power of 10 (10 billion).

In 1880, about the time of Uncle Ramsey's birth, America's foremost geologist (James Dwight Dana of Yale) had announced the new scientific discovery that the earth was very old indeed (far older than Bishop Ussher's seventeenth-century calculation of six thousand years; see appendix) and that, in fact, "Time is long—very long." Today's scientists are more precise, estimating that the Big Bang occurred about 12 billion years ago, so the elder's guess of 10 billion was not far off. After Earth was formed about 4–6 billion years ago, there was a long, lifeless period, the Azoic era, which corresponds to the very long era of "nothingness" in Uncle Ramsey's account. All life lived in water until about 400 million years ago, and the first vertebrates appeared about 500 million years ago. The traditional Pit River "History of the Universe" fits remarkably well with modern scientific geochronology.

Indeed, Wilson recalled that when he and other Pit River children encountered fundamentalist Christian teachers at school, there was a "head-on clash" with the "six-day-world-maker." "What a magician this God was [that] he nonchalantly created the heavens and the earth in six days!" The pinched vision of instant creation seemed intuitively improbable to the Pit River people—it offered such a stingy view of the complex wonders and extreme antiquity of the world.[46]

George Gaylord Simpson would have been struck, I think, by the sense of deep time expressed in the Pit River, Zuni, and Navajo creation stories. As Simpson once wrote, in the study of paleontology "there is an almost painfully epic sweep to the vastness of geologic ages." Contemplating geological time and grasping its immensity could be profoundly frightening, Simpson noted, even for scientific thinkers. Acknowledging that fear and awe of vast time scales was not confined to the naive or unsophisticated but was also felt by scientists, Simpson surmised that the reaction was related to the brevity of human life and dread of death. Simpson was startled to find that uneducated Patagonians in Argentina concurred with his opinion that the world was many millions of years old. To his surprise, he wrote, "they agreed heartily. They were sure, for instance, that the fossil wood so common here could not turn to stone in less than millions of years."[47]

PAIUTE AND UTE FOSSIL KNOWLEDGE IN THE GREAT BASIN

In eastern California, Mono Lake was a legendary place for the Paiutes of the Great Basin. Along the shore of the lake, with its weird salt pillars and rock formations, the Paiutes revered footprints left by the First Woman as she searched for the First Man. During her search, she killed a terrible giant, and its body was turned to stone at Mono Lake.

Although the Mono Lake tale of giants is related to landforms, not fossils, paleontological evidence that pointed to the former existence of giants or unknown creatures in Paiute territory can be found in the hills and deserts north of Mono Lake, in northwestern Nevada. According to Paiute tradition, a race of redheaded cannibals called *Si-Te-Cahs* once dwelled in the area around Lovelock, north of Reno, until the Paiute ancestors exterminated them with fire and smoke in Lovelock Cave. The Paiute Sarah Winnemucca recounted this tradition in 1929; she owned a clump of the cannibals' red hair and an ancient dress trimmed with red hair, relics that had been passed down from her fifth great-grandfather.

A combination of archaeological, natural, and paleontological evidence—and, later, white showmanship—appears to have contributed to the Paiute legend as we now have it. Lovelock Cave contains artifacts and human mummies with red hair from two thousand years ago, and fossils of mammoths and cave bears lie in the desert to the north of the cave (see appendix for the full story).[48]

In Nevada, Utah, Colorado, and northern Arizona, Ute and Paiute people were also aware of dinosaur footprints. At the dinosaur
tracksite in Cactus Park, near Grand Junction, Colorado, a big pon-
derosa pine long known as the Ute Council Tree stands just a few
yards from Jurassic theropod dinosaur tracks (ranging from very
large to turkey-size). The conspicuous tracks may have figured in a
Ute fossil legend, now lost, which made the place an important
meeting point.[49]

Other, smaller fossils captured attention in western Utah. West
of Deseret and east of Antelope Spring in the House Range, very
fine specimens of the Cambrian trilobite *Elrathia kingii* are found
in abundance. These small, black invertebrate fossils from 530 million years ago weather out of the shale matrix and are popular with
modern rock hounds (fig. 45). The trilobite locality first came to
the attention of geologists in the 1860s, but the local Indians, the
Pahvant Utes of the nearby Sevier Valley, had long collected the
fossils as protective charms.

In the early 1900s, an amateur natural historian named Frank
Beckwith roamed the area scanning for fossils and artifacts. One
day he came across an ancient Indian burial site and noticed a trilobite amulet that had been worn around the neck of the long-dead
Native (since then, drilled trilobites have turned up in many burial
sites in the Great Basin). Beckwith asked his Ute friends, Joseph
and Tedford Pickyavit, about his find. The brothers told him the
traditional name for the fossil was *Timpe khanitza pachavee*, "little
water bug in stone."

Beckwith asked Joseph Pickyavit what the *weenoonse*, Ute elders,
believed about the trilobites. The fossils were "body defendancies,
Beckwith; help diphtheria, sore throat, lots of sickness. Old-timers
wore 'em in necklace—no get shot while have 'em on—at least it
work for a time." In the late 1800s, Mormon pioneers reported
that groups of Utes often came to gather trilobites from the outcrops near Antelope Spring "to keep them from being hurt by the
white man's bullets." In exchange for $2.50, Tedford Pickyavit
made a necklace for Beckwith in the traditional style, thirteen trilobites of ascending size strung on a rawhide thong, with green, red,
and brown clay beads and two horsehair tassels.

45. Trilobite (*Elrathia kingii*, Middle Cambrian), collected by Utes for protective purposes. Digital scan of actual specimen, with penny for scale, reproduced with permission of Roger Kaesler, University of Kansas Paleontological Institute; photo provided by Kansas Geological Society.

The discovery of normally vulnerable creatures something like water bugs mysteriously encased in stony armor may have given rise to the idea that wearing the trilobites might magically protect against arrows or bullets. In fact, as one paleontologist remarked to me, large necklaces or gorgets made of overlapping trilobites or ammonites might well deflect arrowheads or bullets. Geologists Michael Taylor and Richard Robison pointed out in 1976 that the Ute name for the trilobites in matrix clearly shows that "the Indians recognized the organic origin of the fossils." Before the land was drained by white farmers, the Sevier Valley had been a swampy area, where Pahvant Utes would have had "ample opportunity to observe aquatic insects." The resemblance between living water bugs and the Cambrian-age aquatic trilobites "could have been the impetus" for the name *little water bug in stone.*[50]

In summer of 1870, Othniel Marsh and his Yale students were the first scientists to explore the Green and White rivers on the border of Utah and Colorado, the land of the Uintah Utes. "Indians and hunters had brought back stories of valleys strewn with giant petrified bones," recalled one of the students, Charles Betts.

Intrigued by tales of huge bones during their stay at Fort Bridger (Wyoming), Marsh hired a Mexican guide named Joe Talemans. After crossing the Uintah plateau, wrote Betts, "We stood upon the brink of a vast basin so desolate, wild, and broken, so lifeless and silent, that it seemed like the ruins of the world." But Talemans did not know the area ahead. Noticing the smoke from a campfire of a hunting party of Uintah Utes, he rode out and hired one of the hunters to guide the party to the White River. Then, at Fort Uintah, Utah, Marsh hired a Shoshone guide from Wyoming to lead them through the Uintah Mountains.

It's frustrating that the Yale crew preserved no details of the Ute or Shoshone ideas about the fabulously productive Eocene mammal and Mesozoic dinosaur bone beds of what is now Dinosaur National Monument. But this was typical of the pioneer paleontologists, desperately competing with rival bone hunters for fossil treasures in the West. Marsh, Cope, and others relied on local guides to find deposits, but we can only imagine the stories they heard around campfires and in the forts. Unlike the time of Jefferson and Cuvier, this era showed little interest in recording Indian traditions about fossil remains. Marsh's attitude was an exception: he conversed with Native Americans about his work; he befriended the Sioux chief Red Cloud and argued his tribe's case in Washington, DC. But most of the early bone hunters seem to have regarded Native Americans as an inconvenient, faintly amusing part of the exotic wildlife of the West (Cope, for example, facetiously referred to the Cheyennes as "dangerous beasts").[51]

Native customs and beliefs were left to the ethnologists, who for their part were not curious about Indian views on geology or paleontology. The Uintah Ute fossil lore may be lost, but their name was given to the major fossil of their landscape, a bizarre, lumbering rhinolike Eocene creature with tusks and knobs on its massive skull, which was nearly four feet long. In 1872, Joseph Leidy (the father of American vertebrate paleontology) named the new species *Uintatherium*, "Beast of the Uintahs."

The railroads were pushing west at this time, and railroad workers frequently unearthed fossils that were passed along to Marsh, Cope, and others. Since so many of the railroad workers were Chinese immigrants, I could not help wondering about their reactions to the extraordinary skeletons. Did they recognize them as "dragon bones," the large vertebrate fossils used for medicine in China? When I raised the question at the San Diego Chinese Historical Museum in 2001, the curator pointed out that the Chinese workers endeavored to maintain their cultural traditions in America. He guessed that if railroad workers found any giant bones, they would have powdered them for medicine. If so, they were unknowingly recapitulating the practices of Native Americans who also ingested fossil medicine.[52]

HOPI AND PUEBLO FOSSIL COLLECTORS

At least two types of fossils were collected by the inhabitants of the ancient Homol'ovi ruins (occupied in A.D. 1280–1400), near Winslow, west of Petrified Forest, Arizona. Archaeologists noticed that crinoids (the segmented hollow stems of sea lilies) were used for beads, as in countless other paleo-Indian sites across America, and numerous tabular pieces of petrified wood had been brought to the pueblo from the Chinle Formation deposits of the Painted Desert and Petrified Forest.

The archaeologists discussed these fossil collections with Hopi elders, who said that their ancient ancestors related the fossils to myths about the worlds that existed before this, the fourth, world. Like the other cultures considered in this chapter, the Hopis perceived that the desert had been under water in the beginning, before the seas began to recede to the east and west, a picture that accurately describes the ancient inland sea that bisected the continent. The land of the Hopis and earlier pueblo dwellers was once the western shore of this sea. As for the fossilized wood in the ruins, the Hopis believe that it comes from the trees of the third world and contains guardian spirits or Kachinas.[53]

From the mesas near Tusayan, south of the Grand Canyon, the Hopis collected beautiful cephalopod fossils, ammonites that they called *koaitcoko*. These fossils with iridescent nacre were included in medicine bundles, proof that they were "highly venerated," wrote the archaeologist-anthropologist Jesse Fewkes in 1895. "As a natural object with a definite form," the fossilized ammonites were "regarded as a fetish." Personal fetishes and tribal bundles of Hopis found at Sikyatki, an enormous village abandoned in about A.D. 1500, on the east flank of First Mesa, also consisted of fossils. But the Hopis are very secretive about sacred things. Fewkes, one of the few anthropologists to ask about fossils, was able to learn only that fossils were regarded as evil by "the uninitiated," while the shamans, "the knowing ones," looked upon fossils with reverence. Fewkes admitted that he failed to find out how the Hopis regarded large animal fossils.[54]

More than a century after Fewkes, I too had to admit that I had no luck in eliciting Hopi ideas about the meaning of large vertebrate fossils. But I did learn of two unusual types of fossils sought out by traditional Hopis. The first, known as *moqui* marbles, are unique rock spheres found at the base of Navajo Sandstone Formations in Arizona and Utah, encasing pink sand from the Cretaceous inland sea. These were long thought by scientists to be mere iron concretions, but recent studies have revealed their true origin: mollusks trapped in a great flood of sand about 130 million years ago. As the mollusks decomposed, their internal juices were drawn out, leaving hollow centers, and as water filtered through the outer shell over the ages, fine sand filled the centers and iron deposits formed around the outer shell, along with phosphorus and lime from the mollusks' shells.

The Hopi word *moqui* means "dearly departed ones," and according to legend, Hopi ancestors descend from heaven in the evening, bringing the marbles to play games. At dawn, the ancestors return to heaven, leaving the marbles behind to reassure their relatives that they are happy. Hopi people gather the moqui marbles and keep them in their homes to welcome the spirits of departed relatives.[55]

I also discovered that Hopi and Pueblo potters made special expeditions to collect trace fossils associated with dinosaurs. Hopi and Pueblo pottery is burnished with smooth stones to achieve the highly polished surface that is especially notable in the glossy black Santa Clara pottery. The stones were often selected from riverbeds, but for some traditional potters, the best burnishing stones came from within dinosaur skeletons (fig. 46). These "dinosaur stones" were passed down over generations of craftspeople. Potters describe going out with elders to areas where dinosaur bones are found, to search for rounded, smooth pebbles inside the rib cages. (When I mentioned this Hopi and Pueblo practice to Tony Semallie, a Navajo who sells new and antique pottery in the Cameron Trading Post, he said that the potters he knew used white quartz or river rocks. "No Navajo would take anything from a dinosaur skeleton—our people, we don't even talk about such things!")

The special stones sought by Hopi and Pueblo potters are gastroliths, or gizzard stones, that were swallowed by dinosaurs and large marine reptiles, possibly as aids to digestion or as ballast. A large quantity of smooth, multicolored stones—up to two hundred stones in some cases—can be found within large fossil skeletons, along the backbone and ribs. The rounded quartzite, granite, or basalt stones have a polished or waxy patina from churning in the huge creature's stomach millions of years ago. The piles of stones are very noticeable because of their rock-tumbled surface, and because they are not local rocks, having been ingested hundreds of miles away from where the body ended up.

The purposeful selection of gastroliths from fossil exposures as special tools is an extremely ancient practice in America. At a mammoth kill site in the Big Horn Basin, Wyoming, for example, Clovis people who lived eleven thousand years ago gathered gastroliths

46. Archaeoceramicist Gregory Wood of Colorado collects gastroliths (dinosaur stomach stones) from Utah. Here he uses a gastrolith to burnish an Anazasi-type Pueblo pottery replica. Photo courtesy of Gregory Wood, ArchaeoCeramics™, AncientArts.org.

from Jurassic Morrison Formation dinosaur exposures to use as hammer stones. Another Clovis site recently discovered in west-central Montana near some large dinosaur exposures also reveals that the paleo-Indians purposefully selected gastroliths for stone tools.[56]

Petrified Wood

Petrified wood occurs throughout the West, but Arizona's Petrified Forest and the Painted Desert have the largest and most colorful concentration in one area, more than ninety thousand acres with tens of thousands of tons of logs from forests that grew 225 million years ago.

As I drove and hiked through the high badlands of the Petrified Forest in October 2002, I tried to imagine how the First Americans reacted to the awesome sight of so many gigantic trees turned to stone. In the Triassic period, these two-hundred-foot-tall conifers flourished in the tropical plain until the entire forest was felled by a great flood, followed by a volcanic eruption (a succession that corresponds to Zuni myth). Looking like colossal Technicolor Tootsie Rolls, the segmented tree trunks (mostly *Araucarioxylon*), preserved by mud and ash, are over two feet in diameter (see fig. 33).

Petroglyphs, potsherds, and pueblo dwellings show that humans occupied the area for ten thousand years, living amid the huge stone logs and constantly eroding fossils of Triassic ferns and fish and large marine reptiles and dinosaurs. When the ethnologist-geologist John Wesley Powell surveyed the Petrified Forest in the late 1800s, he reported that the Indians chipped out arrowheads and axes from the fossilized wood. Many different groups made special trips to the area to gather chunks of the tree trunks, and petrified wood of Arizona was traded over long distances, as shown by finds in distant archaeological sites. Paleo-Indians built their dwellings out of blocks of the petrified wood. An example is Agate House, near the south entrance of Petrified Forest National Park, a partial reconstruction of an eight-room pueblo built of petrified wood logs sealed with mud mortar. Archaeologists believe the original pueblo was built between A.D. 1050 and 1300.

The Paiutes told Powell that the stone logs were the enormous shafts of arrows unleashed by the Wolf-Thunder god, Shinarav, or Shinarump, an important force in the Ute origin myth (fig. 47). Pikes Peak, for example, was created when Shinarump hurled gigantic rocks down to Earth, and many of his great battles occurred in the Petrified Forest. The Paiute Wolf god has given its name to a unit of the Chinle Formation that is famed for its petrified wood: Shinarump Conglomerate.[57]

In 1878 near Navajo Springs, when army Lieutenant J. Hegewald and his soldiers were loading two mule-drawn wagons with huge petrified logs to be shipped to the Smithsonian Institution, they met some Navajo shepherds, curious about their activities. Hege-

160

CHAPTER 3

47. Ute chief Tau-Gu talking with John Wesley Powell, on horseback, in Arizona, 1873. National Anthropological Archives, Smithsonian Institution.

wald explained that the "Great Father in Washington needed the specimens," and recorded the Navajos' "mystified" reaction: "Why would he want the bones of the Great Giant that their forefathers had killed years ago when taking possession of the country?" Along with this allusion to the Yeitso fossil legend, the Navajos told Hegewald that the "surrounding lava beds were the remains of the blood that ran from the giant's wounds."

As Paul Apodaca, a Navajo-Mixtec scholar, has pointed out, many Native fossil legends functioned as a way of claiming territory. The Iroquois fossil legend about the Ohio Valley fossils, narrated to English traders in 1766 (introduction), was an explicit example of this use of conspicuous fossil remains as evidence of land "deeds." In this case, it seems likely that the Navajos were more angry than mystified about the U.S. Army's removing important relics from their mythic landscape.[58]

APACHE FOSSIL LEGENDS

The Apaches also speculated on the meaning of petrified wood. Several versions of myths describing the origin of fire and petrified wood were recorded in the late nineteenth and early twentieth centuries among the Jicarilla Apaches of northern New Mexico.

Coyote, the trickster figure of Amerindian lore, brought fire to the First People. Until then, trees had been fireproof, so there was no fuel and the people had to live without fire. In Apache myth, Coyote tied a torch to his tail and ran around the world, deliberately igniting entire forests. Everything was "afire and burning, it was burned black everywhere." His blazing tail touched trees but not rocks, which explains why stones can't burn and how wood became so flammable. "Now, you can make a fire with a drill from all kinds of trees," said the storyteller. Except for one kind of tree. Coyote intended to touch every kind of tree with his tail, but he missed some. Now those trees are fireproof like stone and "will not burn if they are put in the fire."[59]

This legend about fireproof wood harks back to the mystery of the deliberately charred petrified wood found by archaeologists in New Jersey (chapter 1). The paleo-Indians may have marveled at the "miraculous" immunity to fire of something that had obviously once been wood but somehow became fireproof stone. The Apache myth also suggests that ritual demonstrations of petrified wood's immunity to fire may have helped to illustrate the etiological tale.

In 1898, the Jicarilla Apache storyteller Laforia told a version of the killing of the Giant Elk and the Giant Eagle. The account has many parallels to the Navajo myths of the Burrowing and Cliff Monsters, with one significant difference. The Apache version of 1898 *directly* linked the destruction of the giant raptor to remarkable skeletal remains in the desert.

In the early days, animals and birds of monstrous size preyed upon people, the story began. The Giant Elk, the Giant Eagle, and other monsters devoured men, women, and children, so Jonayaiyin, a brave youth, set forth to battle these enemies. The Giant Elk he found lying in the desert far south of Jicarilla territory. After killing it, he took one of the dead monster's horns as a weapon and sought out the Giant Eagle in the west, at an inaccessible rock. Suddenly the mother bird snatched him up in her talons and dropped him to her nestlings on a ledge. But when the raptor parents reappeared during a thunderstorm, the youth clubbed them with the great horn, and the huge birds plummeted to the earth.

The Apache storyteller verified the myth by referring to fossil evidence. The wing of the male monster bird "was of enormous size [with] bones as large as a man's arm." In fact, said the storyteller, "fragments of this wing are still preserved at Taos." Just as the Yaqui elders traveled to see the skeleton of a ravaging bird on Skeleton Mountain (chapter 2), the Apaches authenticated their giant bird story by reference to an extraordinarily large wing that could be seen and touched at Taos.[60]

It has been suggested that monster bird tales of the West might have been inspired by Mesozoic pterosaur fossils. But pterosaur bones were hollow and lightweight, which did not favor fossilization, and recognizable pterosaur skeletons laid out in rock slabs are not known in the Southwest. As discussed in chapter 2, a more probable inspiration in the Southwest would be the great birds of prey that coexisted with early humans in the Pleistocene and Holocene, such as giant condors or teratorns with wingspans of twelve to seventeen feet. According to teratorn expert Kenneth Campbell, these predator birds grabbed up large prey in their long beaks, rather than with their talons as eagles do. It is not known exactly when these enormous birds went extinct (some remains are only eight thousand years old), and some may have persisted in

Mexico and the Southwest and other isolated locales until relatively recent times.

The giant bird wing displayed at Taos may have been a naturally mummified specimen from a dry cave. Raptors from 12,500 years ago have been preserved in desert caves littered with fresh-looking dung pellets and the bones of extinct mammoths, horses, and camels. According to Pleistocene bird specialist Tommy Tyrberg, a *Teratornis* fossil preserved in a dry desert cave could have cartilage and feathers. "Even a wing of *Gymnogyps (californianus) amplus*, the large Pleistocene subspecies of the California condor, could be described as having man-sized bones. Remains of this bird have been found in at least six New Mexico caves." Several very well-preserved *Teratornis merriami* remains have also been discovered in Dry Cave, Eddy County, and other caves in southern New Mexico, and teratorn skeletons have turned up in southern California, Nevada, Oregon, and Florida. A Native American fossil story that circulated on the Internet in 2002 claimed that a black-and-white feather, nearly sixty inches long with a quill the diameter of a stick of blackboard chalk, was made into an amulet by an old shaman in southern New Mexico. Whether or not that story is true, a feather of that size could be plucked from the remains of a mummified teratorn in a dry cave.[61]

Arizona paleontologist Paul Martin told me about certain caves rich in fossils that attracted prehistoric human visitors, who left offerings of twig figures and grass bundles. As Martin wrote in 1999, the "elegant preservation of the fossils, their apparent association with late prehistoric artifacts, and historic" sightings of living condors and teratorns might make it hard for later observers in the caves to "escape a haunting feeling that the animals must still be alive."[62]

With the images of teratorns in mind, on a windy October day in 2002 I sought out a petroglyph in the ruins of Puerco Pueblo in Petrified Forest National Park. Alone at the site, I spotted the image chiseled into the rust-colored desert varnish on a sandstone boulder below the ruins. The petroglyph, made between six hundred and a thousand years ago by the Puebloan ancestors of the Hopis, perhaps the Anasazis, shows a large bird carrying what appears to be a small,

48. Petroglyph of a large bird holding a struggling man in its long beak, chiseled on a sandstone boulder at Puerco Village ruins, 650–1,000 years ago. The dots below the man may represent eggs in a nest. Petrified Forest National Park, Arizona. Photo: Adrienne Mayor.

struggling man in its long beak (fig. 48). Later, when I asked people about the petroglyph, I learned that a Hopi elder had discussed the image with park ranger Hallie Larsen. A long time ago, he said, a giant bird used to swoop down on the pueblos and fly away with their children.[63]

Archaeological Evidence of Ancient Fossil Collecting

In New Mexico, between Taos and Shiprock, lie the Gobernador ruins, settlement sites of ancient pueblo dwellers and early Apaches and Navajos. Ironically, it was the skeptical George Gaylord Simpson who announced the discovery here of "the first known vertebrate fossils to be collected by human beings in the Western Hemisphere."

In 1941, a colleague of Simpson's, the anthropologist E. T. Hall, excavated the ruins of a dwelling occupied between A.D. 700 and 900 and found two fossil jawbones of mammals that lived about 45 million years ago. Paleo-Indians had brought these fossils to the dwelling more than a thousand years ago from the Eocene outcrops in the nearby San José Formation, with its weird mushroom pillars. Ten centuries later, in 1874, Cope would rediscover these important fossil beds. One of Cope's prize finds was a *Phenacodus primaevus* skeleton, a relative of the "dawn horse."

One of the jaw fragments in the ancient Gobernador dwelling, with three teeth still embedded, belonged to *Phenacodus*. The other fossil, part of a lower jaw of a large carnivore of the Early Eocene, had been ground smooth on two sides and coated with red ocher pigment widely used by Indians for sacred objects. Red pigment would have been obtained from deposits in the Chinle Formation and Petrified Forest, but we can only speculate about the meaning the fossils held for the owners. The mystery deepened when I heard about another fossil find in the area.[64]

In the late 1980s, another fossil jawbone turned up near the Gobernador ruins. Spencer Lucas, the paleontologist who examined the bone, was surprised to find that it belonged to an Oligo-cene mammal (38–24 million years ago) found only in the South Dakota Badlands. The discovery indicates that sometime in the past someone carried the bone from its original site in South Dakota to New Mexico, a distance of about eight hundred miles.

The Blackfeet of the northern plains made regular forays into the land of the "Many Bracelets People" (the Navajos) and the vanished Cliff Dweller people of the Southwest and Mexico, to make war, to raid Spanish horses, to trade, and to obtain Spanish "shirts of mail, and big-knives" (Spanish swords). Was the Badlands fossil a trade item from the North, perhaps exchanged for a local fossil jawbone like the two Eocene specimens described above? Did jawbones in particular have a special significance? Were jawbones of various mystery creatures collected for comparison? Did traveling storytell-ers from the northern plains use the bone as a prop to dramatize a story of strange monsters in their lands?

"We have no monopoly on curiosity about the past," remarked the archaeologist Jack T. Hughes in 2000. Hughes found evidence of fossil collecting by paleo-Indians in Texas, and in 1996 he helped authenticate a farmer's exciting discovery of a chain-mail glove and other Spanish artifacts that established the route of Coronado's long-lost trail through Texas in 1540–41. "People of the past were just as interested in gigantic bones and tusks as modern visitors to museums. Without the distractions of our artificial environment, people who spent their entire lives outdoors were fully aware of every rock and bush and creature around them. When they found something beyond their ken—such as bones ten times bigger than those of the animals they hunted and butchered—they took notice. And sometimes they took samples, collecting to whatever extent their limited transport permitted."[65]

Native people traveled great distances to view impressive skele-tons in the ground, and in the East they brought mastodon teeth and tusks to their villages and to European forts. People in perma-nent settlements, such as the Tlaxcaltecas in Mexico, kept collec-tions of very large fossil limb bones. But most Indians of the prairies and plains were nomadic, and their possessions were transportable necessities. Trilobites, shells, crinoids, belemnites, teeth, scutes, claws, and bits of bone were portable fossil amulets for people on the move. Yet even in the prairies, some Plains Indians found it worthwhile to transport heavy, mineralized bones and skulls over long distances and pass them down over generations. The next chapter begins with the story of a massive fossil collected by the Pawnees, who were first encountered by Coronado in 1541.

CHAPTER

4

The Prairies: Fossil Medicine
and Spirit Animals

In Kansas, some Indians passed Fort Dodge with large
mastodon bones lashed on their ponies, taking them to a
medicine-lodge to be ground up into good medicine.
—*William E. Webb, 1872*

These finds have a great sentimental and literary interest,
but . . . the temptation to consider them in more detail
must be resisted.
—*George Gaylord Simpson, 1943*

IN 1541, the Pawnee scout known as The Turk led Coronado up from Texas into central Kansas, to the Pawnee town of Quivira. Expecting to enter a fabulous city of gold, the Spanish conquistadors were disgusted to find only earth lodges and wealth measured in buffalo robes. After The Turk confessed that he had deliberately misled Coronado, the Spanish executed him and at last gave up their search for gold treasure in the plains.

Some two hundred years later, a very different sort of treasure discovered in Kansas territory was prized by the Pawnees. Neither gold nor Spanish silver, the object was a great fossil bone of stone.

As America's first paleontology professor, Othniel Marsh, declared in 1877, such bones of long extinct animals "guarded faithfully by savage superstition" were "treasures more rare than bronze or gold." This chapter traces the earliest documented knowledge and special uses of fossil remains by the Pawnees, Kiowas, Comanches, Osages, Yuchis, and Cheyennes in the Great Plains.[1]

The Stone Medicine Bone, Pawnee Territory

In about 1855, a Pawnee known as Young Bull (Ari-Wa-Kis) asked an old medicine man to teach him the mysteries of the Stone Medicine Bone Lodge. Young Bull (also known as White Hawk, and later as Captain Jim) of the Pitahawirata band lived at Wild Licorice Creek, a large Pawnee community on the Loup River (near Genoa, Nebraska; see map 4). Young Bull was born in about 1835 and died in 1916, leaving descendants among the Pawnees today (fig. 49). In 1902, Young Bull was interviewed by Young Eagle, better known as James R. Murie, a Pawnee who was collecting his people's tales for the anthropologist George Dorsey of the Field Museum, Chicago. Young Bull told Murie that he was the last of the fossil bone doctors.[2]

The medicine men who belonged to this society have all died, said Young Bull, and now "the whole ceremony and everything connected with it are lost," including the precious medicine bundle containing the fossil bone itself. In 1832, the tribe had numbered between 10,000 and 20,000. By 1874, only 2,000 Pawnees were left to be removed to Oklahoma, and by 1902, only 500 Pawnee people were alive. Murie and Dorsey were collecting traditions from the 39 surviving Pawnee storytellers. Like many traditions about medicine power, Young Bull's story was his personal possession, never told except in exchange for something of value (Murie probably gave him the standard gift of tobacco).

Young Bull told of the creation of a medicine society based on a large fossilized bone that was deliberately excavated in western Kansas or Nebraska and transported many miles to a Pawnee village, and then venerated for more than a century. His narrative is unique

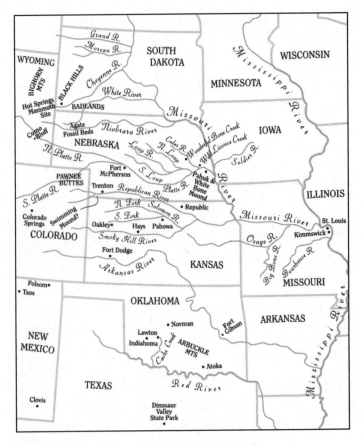

Map 4: The Prairies (map by Michele Mayor Angel)

in Native American fossil lore, yet, remarkably, this detailed and carefully recorded account of Pawnee fossil medicine has been overlooked by modern scholars. Perhaps that is because all other known Pawnee medicine lodges were based on healing arts obtained by communing with "spirit animals," whereas this lodge was based on a fossil bone whose powers were taught by a giant man.[3]

During summer buffalo hunts the Pawnees camped in tipis, but the rest of the year they lived in earth lodges, large domed buildings

49. Young Bull, Pawnee fossil bone doctor, photographed in 1913, when he was about seventy-eight years old. Wanamaker Collection, William Hammond Mathers Museum, Indiana University.

with log frames covered with willow branches and sod. Each lodge had an altar at the back with a buffalo skull and a sacred medicine bundle. An important medicine lodge could be a permanent structure, like the immense deserted medicine lodge in southern Kansas described by George Armstrong Custer in 1868. Inside, Custer saw a raised altar, with herb and other offerings, trophies of war and hunting, horns and skins of animals beautifully decorated in "fantastic styles." We can imagine that the altar of the Stone Medicine Bone Lodge was similarly arranged.[4]

In fall 2002, near Republic, Kansas, I entered a spacious, reconstructed earth lodge, nearly fifty feet in diameter, at the archaeological site of a Pawnee community on a hill above the Republican River where it crosses from Nebraska into Kansas. The fortified town, burnt in about 1830, was home to two thousand Pawnees when it was visited by mountain man Jedediah Smith in 1826. Dimly illuminated and suspended over the altar area was an old sacred bundle, about three feet long, wrapped in red ocher-stained buffalo hide. What it contains is a mystery, for this bundle has not been opened since 1873, when it was saved by a five-year-old girl named Sadie who survived the last battle between the Sioux and Pawnees. In August of that year, about 350 Pawnee hunters and their families were camped in a draw near a bluff on the Republican River in western Nebraska (near Trenton in Hitchcock County), bringing back meat and hides from what would be their last buffalo hunt. Suddenly, nearly 1,000 Sioux with rifles surprised the Pawnees, who were armed with only bows and arrows. In the heat of the battle, Sadie's father lashed his medicine bundle to her back and sent her off on his horse. She was one of the few to escape. Her descendants donated the bundle to the Pawnee Indian Village Museum.[5]

As Young Bull entered the earth lodge with the elder in about 1855, in the smoky gloom he could just make out the large white stone displayed on the altar. To the ordinary Pawnee people it seemed to be a big rock, but, "when I was taken into the lodge to be taught the mysteries of these medicine-men, I found it different," recalled Young Bull as an old man in 1902. "As I approached the altar, . . . I found out that instead of a stone it was a bone [and] I saw the pictures" carved on it. The old medicine man told him the following story.

"Many, many years ago, when our people lived upon the Republican River, we used to go hunting in the western part of what is now Kansas [and Nebraska]. Upon our journey, we stopped near a place where there was a big mound known as the Swimming-Mound." That day, one man climbed the hill and walked into the timber. "There he wandered until he became tired [and] lay down upon this high mound."

He dreamed that a giant person was standing near him. "My son, I have come to you. Many of my people were drowned here at this place, and here our bones rest. . . . The people make light of our bones when they find them. I will now tell you that when you find some of these old bones they have curative powers. On the south side of the hill you will find a bone. . . . one of my thighs. Take it, wrap it up, and my spirit will be with that bone. I will be with you and will give you my great power." The Pawnee hunter awoke and went around the hill and found what looked like a long white rock sticking out of the cliff. He dug out the object and recognized it as the thighbone of a giant, turned to stone.

"The man took the giant bone home with him and placed it in a buffalo robe and hung it up in his tipi." That winter he took the heavy fossil back to his village and placed it in his earth lodge. Over the following years, the giant reappeared in his dreams and taught him the rituals and songs about the stone bone. At last, the keeper of the fossil invited several other medicine men to learn the new healing ceremony. The bone was later wrapped in calico cloth inside a buffalo-calf hide and kept in the doctors' lodge. Only the initiates of the lodge knew that the large white stone was really a giant bone. Inscribed on the petrified femur were carvings of a woman and a man, a human skull, a bow and arrows, and stars and a moon. A sunburst design was carved around the joint (fig. 50).

The original fossil finder became a great warrior and medicine man. He had the strength of a giant on the warpath; he could kill a buffalo with one arrow and carry all the meat home on his back. In his doctoring, he "took dust from the bone" to make a tea that cured the sick. When smallpox arrived on the Great Plains, re-

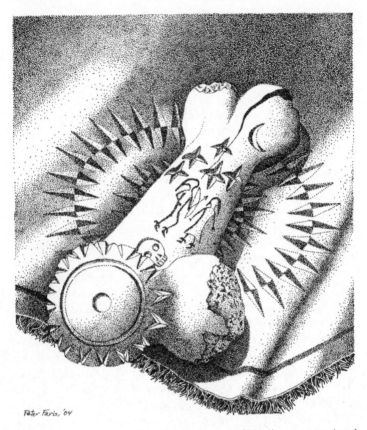

50. Artist's conception of the Pawnee fossil medicine bone on a painted buffalo hide. As described by Young Bull, the bone was carved with stars and the moon, a bow and arrow, a man and a woman, a skull, and a sun around the joint. Drawing © Peter Faris 2004.

counted Young Bull, the bone helped the Pawnees. Although the people never realized the true identity of the "wonderful stone," anyone who touched the giant bone did not fall sick, and those who took sick and drank the fossil-bone tea survived.

As a little boy in about 1840, Young Bull heard from his grandmother about giant beings who had drowned long ago, "before we lived upon this earth." These "wonderful human beings" lived "where the Swimming Mound is in Kansas." There a great flood occurred, "so deep that it killed these wonderful beings." She told Young Bull that the Pawnees found many giant bones "upon the sides of the hill of Swimming Mound."

Dorsey and Murie collected another version of this tradition from a Pawnee storyteller named Buffalo in 1906. Buffalo stated that as the giant creatures drowned, some were stranded on steep banks and high hills, while others sank down into the muddy earth and their bones lodged in riverbanks. Some of their great powers remained with their bodies, "so that their remains would become medicine" for humans. The Creator "promised that the small people [of current times] should find these bones and that the bones should contain curative power for the sick," said Buffalo. The Pawnee fossil medicine tradition reflects the widespread Amerindian belief that one could somehow tap into the strength and vital forces of such obviously powerful, unknown creatures whose bones had hardened into rock in the deep past.[6]

How long ago was the giant medicine bone discovered at Swimming Mound? Young Bull's grandmother's story indicates that when she was born, in the late 1700s, Swimming Mound was already well known for its bones of great size, and a story already existed to explain them. Young Bull said that the people "made light" of fossil bones on the plains until the giant femur was deliberately dug out at Swimming Mound and used for medicine, and that detail tells us that the Pawnees had long been aware of the remains of large, unfamiliar creatures in Kansas and Nebraska.

In about 1750, for example, the Pawnees called Spring Creek, a tributary between the North Loup and Cedar River north of Grand Island, Nebraska, *Paruksti Kisu Kitsu*, Wonderful Bone Creek, because of enormous bones discovered along the banks. The Pawnees were also intensely interested in other remarkable objects that stood out on the surface of the windswept prairies, such as meteorites and marine fossils of striking appearance. An example of the latter is a fine point, made between five hundred and a thousand years ago by a toolmaker who was attracted by the curious spiral fossil fusulinids embedded in stones from the Flint Hills of Kansas (fig. 51).[7]

51. This point contains distinctive single-celled marine fossil fusulinids from about 300 million years ago (Upper Pennsylvanian *Triticites*), embedded in chert from the Flint Hills of southeastern Kansas. The patterned stone attracted the attention of a toolmaker between five hundred and a thousand years ago. The finely crafted point, a little over an inch long, was discovered in 1972 on a sandbar in Cowskin Creek, south-central Kansas. Photo: Mike Everhart.

Young Bull was in his late sixties in 1902. He probably learned the stone bone ceremony in his twenties, in about 1855, from an elder who had been initiated into the lodge as a young man, say around 1780, by doctors who had themselves been initiated decades earlier. Young Bull's band had lived along the Republican River "a very long time ago," according to the elderly Pawnee Fighting Chief quoted in 1870. Pawnees dwelled along the Republican River from at least 1300 onward, according to historian Henry Hyde. Historical records place Young Bull's band in Kansas in the mid-1700s, and a British map of 1755 shows many Pawnee villages along the Republican River, which flows across southwest Nebraska, crossing into Kansas at the Pawnee Village Museum at Republic.

We also know that the stone bone was found sometime before the appearance of smallpox, because it was used to cure the new disease. Smallpox reportedly arrived among the Pawnees from the Southwest in about 1800, striking again in 1832—though it may have arrived with the Spanish in 1741. Furthermore, the bone was originally wrapped in bison skin, and later in calico cloth, a European trade item that first appeared in the early 1700s. Based on the historical and traditional evidence, then, it seems likely that the giant medicine bone was discovered around 1700, perhaps even earlier.[8]

What kind of animal did the fossil belong to? That depends on the exact location of Swimming Mound, no longer known. Another Pawnee storyteller, a woman named Good-Food-in-Kettle, interviewed by Murie and Dorsey in 1902, also located Swimming Mound on the Republican River. The name Swimming Mound, *Pahua*, means "hill swimming on water," so it was apparently a timbered hill-island in braided water or a bluff at the fork of a creek entering the river.

Swimming Mound was one of several sacred hills in Nebraska and Kansas where mysterious spirit animals called *nahurac* resided. Good-Food-in-Kettle told of a medicine man who had once tunneled inside Swimming Mound to confer with the spirit animals. That doctor's encounter with extraordinary creatures at Swimming Mound, the same place where Pawnees had found many giant bones, strongly suggests that at least some nahurac or spirit mounds were places where Pawnees observed the remains of extinct animals (this possibility is discussed later).[9]

So Swimming Mound was a forested hill where fossils weathered out conspicuously, somewhere along the Republican River floodplain of western Nebraska or Kansas, once prime buffalo hunting grounds for the Pawnees, Sioux, Cheyennes, and Osages. I spent some time searching for the site during my research trip of October 2002, driving from Bozeman, Montana, on two-lane roads through South Dakota, Nebraska, and Kansas (ending up thirty-five hundred miles later in Princeton, New Jersey). On an overcast, warm autumn day, I first followed a lonely dirt road west for some forty miles along the South Fork of the Republican in the northwestern corner of Kansas, looking for a prominence along the banks. I got out several times to scan the horizon and scuffed through the yellow loess, prehistoric windblown and alluvial silt from the young Rocky Mountains. The clay is easily carved by rain and wind and often contains Ice Age mammal fossils. But the landscape here is flat and the cut banks of the wide South Fork had no notable hills, ruling out that locale for Swimming Mound.

Over the next few days, I drove east along the Republican River from western Nebraska to its confluence with the Solomon and Smoky Hill rivers in central Kansas, also prime fossil territory. I made a special trip to the Fick Fossil Museum (Oakley, Kansas), where I admired a large *Pteranodon* wing from the Niobrara chalk mounted by the famous bone hunter Charles H. Sternberg (*Pteranodons* were huge flying reptiles of the Late Cretaceous). I also examined the huge skull of *Tylosaurus*, a marine reptile, and the thighbone of an eighteen-foot-tall mammoth, perhaps something like the bone discovered at Swimming Mound.

The rolling terrain of Kansas and Nebraska was covered by the great inland sea during the Cretaceous period (144–65 million years ago). In the distinctive chalk bluffs of the Niobrara Formation along the Solomon and Smoky Hill rivers and their tributaries in Kansas are the petrified remains of many kinds of marine creatures, enormous eel-like mosasaurs, long-necked plesiosaurs, huge sea turtles, palm-size shark teeth, and countless seashells.

The first photographs of a mosasaur skeleton were taken in this area by the Topeka land surveyor William Webb, in 1868 (he sent the photos to the naturalist Joseph Leidy of Philadelphia). Othniel Marsh, exploring the Smoky Hill drainage in the 1870s, found the skeletons of giant, toothed diving birds, such as *Hesperornis*, and pterosaurs with wingspans of twenty feet, the first flying reptiles discovered in America, twenty times the size of European specimens. In 1884, John Bell Hatcher, the "king of the bone collectors," shipped thousands of fossils from western Kansas to Marsh at Yale. Dinosaurs are rare in Kansas, but some remains of armored and duck-billed dinosaurs were recently found in the ancient seabed.

Skeletons of marine creatures and flying reptiles in the Kansas-Nebraska chalk beds certainly contributed to Plains Indian myths about Thunder Birds and Water Monsters, but it is unlikely that these creatures' limb bones would have been mistaken by the Pawnees for those of giant humans. When I described the discovery at Swimming Mound to paleontologists Mike Everhart and Greg Liggett at the Sternberg Museum in Hays, Kansas, they pointed out that since the femur was thought to be that of a giant man, it almost certainly belonged to some very large extinct mammal, such as a

Miocene or Pleistocene elephant or rhinoceros. A mammoth femur three or four feet long resembles a human femur in form. It would make a hefty medicine bundle, somewhat larger than the bundle I saw displayed at the Pawnee Indian Village Museum.[10]

Overlying alluvial Miocene to Pleistocene mammal deposits dot western Kansas and Nebraska. Bones of mammoths, mastodons like *Stegomastodon* and four-tusked *Amebelodons*, rhinoceros and camel species, and giant sloths continually erode out of bluffs along stream banks. At the Long Island (Kansas) site in the Republican River floodplain in 1882, for example, Charles H. Sternberg discovered numerous mastodon and hundreds of Pliocene *Teleoceras fossiger* (rhinoceros) bones. The Ladder Creek fork of the Smoky Hill in western Kansas yielded a "super bison" skull with straight horns measuring six feet from tip to tip, along with camel and elephant remains, and similar giant bison skulls are found on the Solomon. In 1908, eight skeletons of extinct giant bison were found on the Smoky Hill, along with flint arrowheads. It's easy to imagine how similar finds of immense bison skulls accompanied by ancient arrowheads would have fostered the Pawnee image of giant men hunting giant buffalo.

As I continued to search for Swimming Mound, I learned of a major fossil find in 1996, near Trenton, Hitchcock County, Nebraska, a few miles from the site of the 1873 Sioux massacre of Pawnee families, mentioned above. A rancher had spotted some big bleached bones emerging from a mound; they turned out to belong to a *Stegomastodon*, a primitive gomphothere that lived 1.3 million years ago. Many other significant Late Miocene and Pleistocene fossils have been found along the Republican River in Hitchcock County, for example at Oak Canyon fossil beds near Culbertson and at the Hazard Homestead Quarry. In the 1930s, the enormous thighbone of *Mammuthus imperator* was on display in the Trenton Hardware Store. Robert Hunt, a paleontologist at the University of Nebraska State Museum, explained that in the upper Republican drainage, Pleistocene mammoth bones would be found in the terraces above the river valley, and the river cuts through Ogallala Formation bedrock, which contains the bones of earlier species of Miocene mastodons and rhinos.

The abundance of large mammal remains makes Hitchcock County the most promising locale for Swimming Mound. The Pawnee group attacked by the Sioux in 1873 had traveled to the same summer buffalo grazing area where the much earlier hunting party had originally discovered the medicine bone at Swimming Mound. Guessing that hunting parties routinely camped at the familiar landmark known as Swimming Mound, I concluded that the so-called mound must be the bluff that rises eighty feet above the riverbed where Massacre Canyon Creek flows into the Republican River. My theory is supported by archaeological studies in the 1930s revealing that this bluff area had been repeatedly occupied as a summer hunting campsite over a great many years.[11]

The Pawnee tradition did not attribute the demise of the giants to lightning, as in so many other Native myths about large vertebrate fossils. In areas with sparse vegetation like the dry plains and southwestern desert, where geology and paleontology reveal the obvious evidence of former seas, Native observers correctly visualized ancient oceans or floods. The Pawnee insight that giant beings had drowned long ago was logical, and it suggests that they were aware of petrified clams, fish, and other out-of-place sea creatures scattered across the landscape. Notably, however, the medicine bone was recognized as that of a large drowned mammal, not a sea creature.

Vivid evidence of Indians' collecting large fossil bones to make medicine powder a couple of decades after Young Bull's initiation comes from the memoir of William Webb, the surveyor who escorted Edward Drinker Cope on a paleontological expedition in 1871. Webb created a literary character who was a hybrid of Cope and Marsh, and he also quoted Cope directly and discussed the geology and paleontology of the plains. During their time in Kansas, wrote Webb in 1872, a hunter directed them to an immense fossil skeleton that had weathered out of the ground. But when Webb's party arrived at the site, only a single vertebra of a mastodon remained.

Back at Fort Dodge, on the Arkansas River in southwestern Kansas, Webb's party learned the fate of the mastodon remains. It "transpired that, shortly before our trip, some Indians had passed

52. Indian pony with a travois loaded with mastodon bones, as described by William Webb in 1872. Drawing © Ed Heck 2004.

[the fort] with the large bones lashed on their ponies." They were taking them to a "medicine-lodge on the Arkansas, to be ground up into good medicine" (fig. 52). The soldiers at the fort recalled that the Indians (perhaps Pawnees, Cheyennes, or Wichitas) said the bones belonged to "one of the big buffaloes" that roamed the plains in the time of their ancestors. In that distant time, said the Indian fossil hunters, the Happy Hunting Ground was on Earth, but it had been "removed beyond the clouds by the Great Spirit, to punish his children for bad conduct."

Webb's story, despite its Euro-American spin and probable exaggeration, shows that he was aware of the Plains Indian practice of gathering fossil bones for medicine. The account given by the Indians has parallels to Iroquois and Delaware traditions identifying mastodons as super-buffalo of the past, but with one significant difference. In those earlier tales, the giant buffalo were destroyed because they endangered smaller game and early humans. In this more recent Kansas tale of 1872, the Indians viewed the giant buffalo nostalgically, as evidence of once-plentiful game. In fact, the buffalo of the Great Plains had nearly disappeared by the 1870s: Charles Sternberg saw the last Kansas herd in 1877. As early as 1852, Joseph Leidy remarked that the great bison herds were vanishing "in advance of the migrating column of the white race of man. . . . To find [them] now in large numbers," wrote Leidy, "it is necessary to travel to the foot of the Rocky Mountains, and the day is not far distant when [bison] will become quite extinct." By 1882, only about a thousand bison remained of herds that had once blackened the plains as far as the eye could see.[12]

OTHNIEL MARSH AND THE PAWNEE SCOUTS

Othniel Marsh and his team of Yale students arrived in Nebraska in 1870. They met Buffalo Bill Cody at Fort McPherson, near North Platte, and he served briefly as a scout for Marsh. Cody recalled, "Marsh had heard of the big bone which had been found by the Pawnees in the Niobrara [chalk hills]." Unfortunately, we have no more details of this conversation between Marsh and the Pawnees about fossil localities, but a large bone embedded in Niobrara chalk would belong to some Cretaceous creature; perhaps it was a dinosaur femur or a mosasaur spine. In July 1870, Marsh hired a troop of soldiers and two of Major Frank North's renowned Pawnee Scouts to escort his party to the Niobrara chalk bone beds on the Loup Fork.

The Pawnee Scouts worked as official allies of the U.S. Army. The situation was dangerous at that time, as Sioux and Cheyenne warriors (longtime enemies of the Pawnees) were aggressively defending their lands against white incursions. The greenhorn Yale students rode horses that the Pawnees had captured from the Cheyennes the previous fall, while the two scouts rode a mile in advance and crept up each high bluff, parting the bunchgrass to scan for Sioux or Cheyennes.

Marsh's student Charles Betts preserved some Pawnee ideas about fossils in 1870–73, and we actually have the names of the two Pawnee Scouts, recorded by Betts and by another Yale student,

George Bird Grinnell. The older man, Tucky-tee-lous (Duellist) was renowned as a warrior, and the younger man, La-hoor-a-sac (Best One of All), was a celebrated hunter. Both men had long, neat braids decorated with colored cloth and feathers, and were "clothed simply with moccasins, breech clouts and a blanket," recalled Grinnell. They had been issued full cavalry uniforms, but as soon as they got away from the fort, the scouts carefully packed these away until they returned to the fort. Grinnell described them as "jolly fellows" who entertained the soldiers and students with Pawnee songs and dances.

I attempted to learn more about these two men in the muster rolls of 1865–66 and 1876 of North's Pawnee Scouts, kept in the Nebraska State Historical Society. But their names, as Marsh and his men knew them, do not appear in the records. That's not surprising, for it was Pawnee custom for names to change several times over a lifetime (at least three names were recorded for Young Bull, above).

The badland ravines and sandhills between the Loup Fork and the Platte were littered with fossils on the surface: ancestral rhinos, camels, and horses, mosasaurs, flying reptiles, peculiar toothed birds, and other creatures new to science. Some of the soldiers helped the students collect bones, but Betts reported that the "superstition of the Pawnees deterred them for a time from scientific pursuits." Believing that "the petrified bones of their country are the remains of an extinct race of giants," Duellist and Best One of All "refused to collect until the professor, picking up the fossil jaw of a horse, showed how it corresponded with their own horses' mouths." Quickly absorbing this new paleontological knowledge, from that day on the Pawnee Scouts rarely returned to camp without bringing fossils for the "Bone Medicine Man."

The scouts' reference to extinct giants reflects the traditions recounted by Young Bull, and told by his grandmother and by the storyteller Buffalo. The men's nickname for Marsh, Bone Medicine Man, seems to give him status similar to that of the Pawnee medicine men associated with the Stone Medicine Bone Lodge. (The scouts also gave the professor another, less dignified nickname, Heap Whoa Man, for his nervous habit of constantly harrumphing and muttering to himself, which confused his poor horse). As the Pawnee scholar Roger Echo-Hawk points out, the scouts were probably "reluctant to disturb the spirits of extinct giants, thought to be ancient humans. One should only handle such remains if authorized by a dream," like the original finder of the medicine bone at Swimming Mound. But when they "learned that these were the bones of animals, the two Pawnees might then have felt free to help in collecting."[13]

George Bird Grinnell and the Pawnees

One of the Yale students in Marsh's crew, George Bird Grinnell (1849–1938), later went on to become an eminent ethnologist and naturalist. After collecting fossils in Nebraska, Kansas, Wyoming, and Utah, Grinnell became Marsh's assistant at the Peabody Museum. In 1874, Marsh sent Grinnell to join General George Custer's gold-seeking military expedition in the Black Hills of South Dakota, sacred to the Sioux.

Grinnell's task was to find fossils, and Custer recorded that as his Sioux guides led them south through the valleys of the Little Missouri, Grinnell located a huge dinosaur bone four feet long and two giant turtles in the Cretaceous Hell Creek Formation of northwestern South Dakota. This was a fossil-rich landscape. A few years later, in 1881, the paleontologist J. L. Wortman collected one of the most perfectly preserved dinosaur skeletons in that area (the huge sauropod *Atlantosaurus copei*) for the American Museum of Natural History in New York. And in 1892, in bluffs along the Moreau River, Cope was guided by a Standing Rock Sioux boy to a prolific dinosaur bone bed where Cope identified more than twenty different dinosaur species, including an enormous skeleton that he dubbed *Manospondylus gigas* (see chapter 5). A century later, in 1990, the splendidly preserved *T. rex* named Sue was found in the same region.

When Grinnell was riding with Custer in 1874, he probably received help in locating fossils from Custer's two Hunkpapa Sioux guides, Cold Hand and Maga ("Goose," a renowned medicine man), both from Standing Rock Reservation. Guides were important not only because they knew the best and safest routes; they also provided water and game—and they knew where extraordinary bones weathered out of the ground. A couple of weeks later, Grinnell's fossil foray into the Cheyenne River Badlands of South Dakota *without* any Indian guides was a disaster. He and his companions attempted to ride straight up and down the steep ravines, so weakening their horses that most of them died. Their provisions and water nearly ran out, and after four days the men straggled back, with only one small scrap of a rhinoceros bone from the fossil-laden badlands.[14]

White land claims, gold prospecting, and broken treaties across the Great Plains had created a very tense atmosphere at this time, alluded to in the writings of the early paleontologists Grinnell, Ferdinand Hayden, Charles Sternberg, Marsh, and Cope. Hostilities climaxed in 1876, when Custer's Seventh Cavalry was annihilated by Sioux and Cheyenne warriors on the Little Bighorn River (Montana). George Bird Grinnell would have died with Custer that day, but his paleontological work for Marsh at the Peabody had prevented him from accepting Custer's invitation to join the 1876 expedition.

After collecting more dinosaur fossils on the Judith River in Montana and at Como Bluff, Wyoming, Grinnell earned a Ph.D. in paleontology in 1880 under Marsh (who named a fossil after his student, *Crocodilus grinnelli*). But Grinnell's real loves were ethnology and conservation. He returned to the West, where he was adopted by the Pawnees (they called him White Wolf), and began his well-known studies of Plains Indians.

In 1889 Grinnell published some Pawnee beliefs that help clarify their ideas about fossils. It's curious, however, that after his paleontological work in the area, Grinnell failed to connect the fossil legends with conspicuous bone deposits. For example, Grinnell described in detail the Pawnee notion that certain mounds or hills were the lodges of nahurac, "spirit animals," without ever acknowledging that these mounds were located in fossil-bearing chalk and loess hills that he himself had excavated with Marsh.[15]

53. The famous spirit animal mound known to the Pawnee as Pahowa and to the Sioux as Waconda. Note bison skeleton at foot of hill. The sacred mound is now submerged under Lake Waconda, Kansas. Engraving by Henry Worrall, in Webb 1872. Photo: Princeton University Library, Rare Books.

Spirit Animal Mounds

Grinnell named six spirit animal mounds known to the Pawnees. In Nebraska there were Pahuk (Hill Island or Mound on Water) near Fremont and Dark Island near Central City, both on the Platte River; White Bank on the Loup River; Pahur near Guide Rock; and Swimming Mound farther west on the Republic. In Kansas, the spirit mound Pahowa on the Solomon River (near Glen Elder) was a curious limestone formation about forty feet high with a spring-fed mineral pool on top. Pahowa was a sacred place for many tribes, but white settlers claimed it in the 1870s; William Webb published an engraving of Pahowa in 1872 (fig. 53).

Pahowa became a popular spa in the early 1900s, known as Waconda, Great Spirit Spring, after a Sioux legend. In the 1960s, despite the landmark's designation as a unique historical and geological site (natural artesian springs are extremely rare in Kansas), it was declared a "mud hole" by the Army Corps of Engineers. They piled debris from the old spa into Pahowa's sacred pool and, in 1968, submerged the mound under the newly created Waconda Lake. Now a highway marker is the only memorial.

If one reads Grinnell's accounts now with a paleontological folk-lorist's eye, it seems obvious that some nahurac mounds were considered spirit animal sites because they contained the peculiar fossil remains of extinct creatures. A story told by White Eagle, an old Pawnee interviewed in 1914, lends credence to this idea. White Eagle described a medicine man who had received powers at a mound called *Nakiskat* (White Bone), on a creek west of Pahuk mound. This spirit lodge was marked by a large white bone, bringing to mind the fossils protruding from Swimming Mound and Wonderful Bone Creek on the Loup. Grinnell mentioned that a great medicine man had received his healing powers by communing with spirit animals inside Pahuk (also known as Mound where Spirit Animals Sleep), a cut bank about two hundred feet high on the Platte. Another Pawnee story tells of a medicine man who entered a nahurac lodge on the Missouri River where he saw a water monster and many different kinds of spirit animals (fig. 54).[16]

Pahuk and White Bone mounds were located a few miles west of a cavern near the confluence of the Missouri and Soldier rivers, in western Iowa, the site of a paleontological mystery. In the cave, in 1804, Lewis and Clark discovered the petrified jawbone of some large, unknown creature. That fossil, kept in the Philadelphia Academy of Natural Sciences, has now been identified as *Saurocephalus lanciformis*, an enormous lizard-headed fish of the Cretaceous epoch. But the specimen could have come only from Niobrara chalk of western Nebraska or Kansas, since such fossils do not exist in the Soldier River area.

This fact has made Lewis and Clark's discovery of the fossil a puzzle for paleontologists ever since George Gaylord Simpson wrote about it in 1942. The simple solution, so far unmentioned by any commentators, is that the fossil must originally have been found by a Native American in western Nebraska or Kansas and taken to the cave in Iowa, which may have been a Pawnee nahurac

54. Artist's conception of a vision quest in a spirit animal mound. The medicine man is shown swimming among plesiosaurs, large marine reptiles of the Cretaceous whose fossil remains are common in traditional Pawnee lands. Artwork by Pete Von Sholly.

site. Paleontologist David Parris agreed with my theory: "I think it's virtually certain that an Indian put the Cretaceous fish fossil in the cave, since the basic geology of the Soldier River is Pleistocene loess hills."[17]

Carrying fossils long distances was not unusual for Native Americans, as we have seen. Petrified wood from Arizona was traded long distances, and someone carried a fossil jawbone from South Dakota to New Mexico (chapter 3). But much larger fossils were also transported. Eastern Indians brought heavy mastodon teeth and tusks to French and English forts in the colonial era (chapter 1); William Webb described Kansas Indians lashing large mammoth bones to their horses, and Young Bull told of the large fossil femur from the western Republican River transported to central Nebraska near the Loup River.

On the Loup, White Bank spirit mound mentioned by Grinnell has been identified as the steep loess bluff at the confluence with the Cedar River north of Fullerton, Nebraska, an area that holds Pleistocene fossils. Pahowa (Waconda) mound on the Solomon was formed of travertine and thus contained no fossils, but mysterious bones in the surrounding area would have enhanced the idea that Pahowa was a spirit animal lodge. Cretaceous shale fossil beds exist not far away, along the Republican River, and also north and south of the mound. Just a few miles to the southeast, for example, the skeleton of an armored dinosaur, the ten-foot-long *Silvisaurus*, was discovered in 1955. The Solomon River floodplain also has plentiful deposits of fossils dating to 85 million years ago, including nearly complete skeletons of large flying reptiles, like the *Pteranodon* discovered by Mike Everhart's team in 1996. The reddish-brown bones weather to blue-gray and stand out in the light chalk hills, and the beaked and crested skull and even the fragile wing parts were easily removed from the soft earth (figs. 55 and 56).[18]

Cretaceous creatures may have influenced some Pawnee legends of giant birds and water monsters. *Hu-huk* (or *Hoh-hoq*) was a huge raptor said to swoop down and devour hunters, and a Pawnee ceremony involved making life-size models of giant water monsters with "feelers" (recalling the antlers or horns of other water monsters), which were thought to confer healing powers on medicine

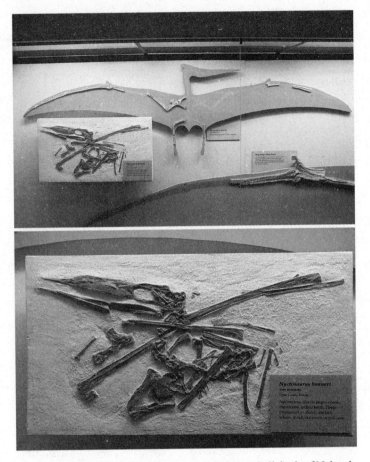

55. Pterosaur fossils are common in the Niobrara chalk beds of Nebraska and Kansas. Top, a large pterosaur fossil skeleton reconstruction; bottom, close-up of the pterosaur skeleton. Sternberg Museum of Natural History, Hays, Kansas.

men. Water monster eggs were also featured in a Pawnee tradition of two warriors who traveled a long time ago to the lands far north of Nebraska where they discovered some very large, "strange eggs," unlike any they had ever seen. These turned out to be the eggs of

56. Loess bluff on the South Fork of the Republican River, northwestern Kansas. Large vertebrate fossils from the Pleistocene, Miocene, and Cretaceous erode out of bluffs and riverbanks of Kansas and Nebraska. Photo: John Charlton, Kansas Geological Survey.

a water serpent. Was this tale influenced by the discovery of dinosaur eggs in Cretaceous sediments of eastern Montana, where Jack Horner has discovered so many *Maiasaurus* nests?

The imagery of water monsters in the Great Plains may have been related to observations of the undulating skeletons of mosasaurs, so common in the hilly terrain from Kansas north to the Dakotas and Montana. Seated on his horse in the badlands one day, Othniel Marsh marveled that he could count "the remains of five huge monsters spread upon the plain." The serpentine spines of the great marine reptiles resemble colossal snakes embedded in stone, and even Marsh and his students could not resist referring to these immense creatures as sea serpents and dragons. The tendency to identify the huge marine creatures as snakes or serpents actually anticipates the latest scientific thinking. As I learned from paleontologist Greg Liggett at the Sternberg Museum in Kansas, mosasaur skulls and vertebrae are very snakelike, and the most advanced theories now propose that mosasaurs were ancestors of snakes rather than relatives of varanid lizards, as was previously assumed.[19]

Among the Kiowas, neighbors of the Pawnees in the southern plains, water monster images demonstrate affinities with mosasaur remains. Sketches of *Tenocouny* (or *Zemoguani*), the giant horned water monster of Kiowa myth, by the artist Silverhorn in 1887 and 1891–94 showed a long, scaly serpent with a toothy crocodilian head, much like a mosasaur skull, with the addition of branching antlers. Another representation of Tenocouny was painted on a Kiowa tipi in 1904: it shows a many finned, straight-horned toothy serpent with antennae or "feelers" and a forked tail (fig. 57).[20]

Drowned Giants in Pawnee Lands

Grinnell also recorded a complete Pawnee narrative about the giants who had drowned long before the time of present-day people, a story consistent with the traditions recounted by Young Bull and other Pawnees.

"The first men who lived on earth were very large Indians," the Pawnee elders told Grinnell. These giants were "very big and very strong [and] used to hunt the buffalo on foot. They were so swift and strong that a man could run down a buffalo, and kill it with a great stone, or a club, or even with his flint knife." A giant could throw a bull buffalo over his back as a hunter today carries an antelope, and he would tuck a yearling in his belt like a rabbit. But these giants did not believe in Tirawa, the Creator. Nowadays, remarked the elders, "all people, wherever they live—all Indians, all white men, all Mexicans and all black men—speak to [Tirawa] and ask that he will give them the right kind of a mind, and that he will bless them."

But the giants of the old days did not respect the Creator. Thinking that "nothing could overcome them, they grew worse and worse." At last, Tirawa got angry and made the waters rise. The ground became soppy mud. "These great people sank down in the mud and were drowned. The great bones found on the prairie are

57. Top: water monster by the Kiowa artist Silverhorn, ledger book drawing 1891–94. National Anthropological Archives, Smithsonian Institution. Center: water monster painted on a Kiowa tipi, 1904; drawing by Michele Angel. Some water monster images may have been influenced by observations of large marine reptiles such as mosasaurs. Bottom: mosasaur skull; photo by Adrienne Mayor.

the bones of these people." We have been in deep canyons and have seen big bones underground, the elders told Grinnell, and they "convince us that these [giants] did sink into the soft ground." "After the destruction of the race of giants, Tirawa created a new race of men, small, like those of today."

The notion of giants preceding humans on Earth has parallels to the Shawnee legend of giant hunters of antiquity who could sling mastodons over their shoulders like deer (chapter 1). In Young Bull's tradition, the hunter who discovered the giant bone at Swimming Mound acquired the strength of these ancient giants, able to kill a buffalo with one arrow and carry all the meat home on his back. The giants' extinction was retribution for bad behavior, as in several legends in previous chapters. But the flood and massive creatures sinking into the mud are original Pawnee ideas that accurately envision the vast, shallow sea of the Cretaceous era, with the skeletons of huge creatures trapped in once muddy shores.[21]

The elders' realistic imagery of giant beings sinking into mud and drowning came to mind when I visited Hot Springs Mammoth Site in southwestern South Dakota. The mineral springs there were frequented by Indians for their curative powers. In the sediment, where hundreds of Pleistocene animal skeletons have been preserved, modern paleontologists discovered violent swirling patterns, created by the feet of cumbersome beasts struggling in sucking mud. Similar patterns can be seen at the Miocene-era water holes at Agate Fossil Beds, Nebraska.

George Bird Grinnell was present when the two Pawnee Scouts told Othniel Marsh that large vertebrate fossils had belonged to a race of giants, but Grinnell did not relate the scouts' explanation to the story he collected later when he lived with the Pawnees. Unlike the ethnologists Cushing and Reichard, who neglected to ask the Zunis and Navajos about fossils out of ignorance (chapter 3), Grinnell actually *knew* both sides of the story. With his early experience of fossil collecting with Marsh's Pawnee Scouts and his later familiarity with Pawnee traditions about spirit animals in mounds and giants' bones in ravines, Grinnell was in a perfect position to point out the obvious relationship between the legends and fossils.

As an ethnologist with a degree in paleontology, why didn't Grinnell acknowledge the paleontological aspects of the traditions?

Pawnee historian Roger Echo-Hawk has studied Grinnell's papers, manuscripts, and correspondence. He suggests that Grinnell considered the oral material he gathered to be "imagined events or pseudo-history" created by an intellectually inferior culture, the accepted anthropological attitude of his day. Because Grinnell "did not give very deep credence to oral literature as a form of record-keeping that could preserve sophisticated knowledge about ancient history and nature," he rejected any relationship between the stories he recorded and the physical evidence of prehistoric remains. Whatever the motivation, Grinnell exemplified the emerging development of separate scientific disciplines of the late nineteenth century. Just as paleontologists of his day no longer solicited fossil traditions, leaving folklore to the ethnologists, so the ethnologists left paleontological topics out of their conversations with Native Americans.[22]

COMANCHE FOSSIL MEDICINE IN OKLAHOMA

Like the Pawnees, the Comanches also collected fossil bones for medicine. Comanches, related to the Utes and Shoshones, had migrated from the Great Basin to Oklahoma and Texas in about 1650. According to anthropologists writing in the 1930s, Comanche people gathered white, chalky fossils for medicine from "certain deposits known to the Indians" in southern Oklahoma near Indiahoma (Comanche County). They called this fossil bone powder *tsoapitsitsuhni*, "ghost-creature bone," and mixed it with water to treat sprains and broken bones. If the fossilized bones were infilled with gypsum crystal (calcium sulphate), the powder would have formed a sort of plaster cast when mixed with water.[23]

A wide variety of fossils exists in Comanche territory. Early Permian "red beds" dominate Comanche County, and in the eastern part of the county, north of Lawton, is Richards Spur, the source of the most Permian vertebrate fossil specimens ever found in Oklahoma. Similar outcrops occur near Frederick, Cache, and Snyder

counties, not far from Indiahoma, with fossils of reptiles and amphibians (such as *Captorhinus*). To the east, the Arbuckle Mountains also have clearly exposed Permian fossils. Some of these fossils
may have been the "ghost-creature" bones collected by Comanches, but impressive Jurassic-Cretaceous dinosaur fossils are also
found in Oklahoma, including the immense *Saurophaganax* and
Apatosaurus (previously known as *Brontosaurus*). In 1990, a nearly
complete skeleton of a very large theropod dinosaur came to light
in Atoka County, and in 1994, a twelve-foot-long rib and a five-
foot-long vertebra on the grounds of a prison yard led to the discovery of a new species of sauropod, the stupendous *Sauroposeidon*.
With a thirty-nine-foot neck and a height of sixty feet, it may be the
tallest dinosaur on record. In 2001, the most perfectly preserved
Tenontosaurus skeleton (about twenty feet long) was also unearthed
from the prison yard.

Rich deposits of Pleistocene mammals occur throughout Oklahoma, too, and these conspicuous, bleached bones were also gathered for medicine. The remains of Columbian mammoths, mastodons, giant bison, bears, camels, and glyptodonts have been
discovered near Lawton, in sites a few miles north of Indiahoma,
and in Blaine, Caddo, and Kiowa counties, north of Lawton. According to ethnologists writing in the 1950s, the Comanches
referred to small pieces of mammoth leg bone as "madstone or
medicine bone." When placed over an affected spot, the medicine
bone was supposed to "draw out the poison [of] wounds, infec-
tions, boils, and pains." Indeed, fossil bone is porous and exerts a
capillary action that draws away moisture, thereby drying up sores
and infected wounds.[24]

As I investigated Comanche lore surrounding fossils, I learned
that large, white fossil bones were said to belong to *Piamupits* or
Mu pitz, a cannibal monster. According to anthropologist Daniel
Gelo, Piamupits or Mu pitz was a terrifying, cave-dwelling ogre,
sometimes visualized as a giant owl-man with a beak, who preyed
on humans, especially children. Gelo pointed out that large owls
were a "source of fascination and dread among Comanche traditionalists. Owls' nocturnal stealth contributes to the idea that they
are really ghosts." The earliest reference in writing that I could find

was from 1895, when a trader among the Comanches reported that Mu pitz was "an evil spirit" about twelve feet tall and covered with hair. In 1972, the Comanche medicine woman Sanapia described Mu pitz as a very tall, hairy giant with big feet. She said she collected the "big, old giant" bones to make a powder to use as salve or applied a bit of moistened bone to strengthen bones or treat sprains.

I asked Juanita Pahdopony and Harry Mithlo, Comanche storytellers, about this tradition. They grew up near Lawton, Oklahoma, along Cache Creek where large Pleistocene remains are found, and as children they learned about Mu pitz and fossil medicine from their parents and medicine men and women. They explained that Mu pitz was a bogeyman figure used to scare children into good behavior in the tipis at night. Juanita Pahdopony pointed out that some bands thought of Mu pitz as a cannibal owl-man, but to others—like her father, Sam Pahdopony (b. 1919)—Mu pitz was a "huge, foul-smelling, fur-covered man" something like Big Foot or Sasquatch. Everyone was aware of Mu pitz bones all around the countryside. Sam Pahdopony has donated several Mu pitz specimens (mammoth teeth) to the local museum and keeps one in his home. Some elders say that the ghostly Mu pitz still roams Oklahoma creek beds in fall and winter, and migrates to the forests of the Pacific Northwest during spring and summer. Some people even put out food for Mu pitz. Pahdopony noted that Mu pitz was thought of not as evil but as part of the natural balance of nature, and therefore the huge bones aroused mixed emotions of fear and respect.

Harry Mithlo heard Mu pitz stories from his mother and grandmothers. He remembers searching for the bones of the scary monster as a boy on the west bank of Cache Creek. One grandmother, an elder relative named Mable Mahseet, used to send Harry and two other boys to "go out and look for the bones of a giant to make a special medicine." Grandmother Mahseet told the kids exactly what to look for and how to test the bones' "drawing out" power. "Look for the bones of Mu pitz in steep and deep ravines," she said. "When you find some bones that are sticking out of the sides of the bank, put your tongue to the bone. If it grabs your tongue, then that's it!"

Intrigued, I made inquiries among a score of paleontologists about this old Comanche fossil bone test. Their replies revealed that many modern fossil hunters frequently lick specimens in the field as a quick and easy test for fossil bone. Fossil bone absorbs moisture, as mentioned above, causing it to cling to one's tongue. And I learned that the technique is still surrounded by oral lore. Some paleontologists use the tongue test to distinguish fragments of fossil bone from petrified wood. Others attribute the strength of the hydrophilic effect to the level of calcium salts or kaolinite clay in the fossil. Some said that the test does not work on invertebrate fossils or teeth, or on bones that have been mineralized with agate or opal. One fossil hunter told me that dinosaur bone adheres to the tongue, while another claimed that younger fossil bones, such as mastodon, stick more readily than very ancient dinosaur bones.

Contemporary Comanches still use Mu pitz fossils to treat sprains and bone problems. "Some of our medicines are sacred knowledge," says Juanita Pahdopony, "but this example has been published before—although not many people outside our culture know of the bones' medicinal value. I have a fossil medicine bone that I keep in a special glass cabinet at home. Its value is not monetary, but it is priceless to those who need it and precious for the preservation of our culture. I have given some of the bone to Comanches who requested it."[25]

The Ox Bone Throne

The bones of extinct creatures in Oklahoma were collected for other practical and ritual purposes, besides medicine. Sometime before 1852, a man named Thomas Kite visited an Indian's "hut" near Fort Gibson, in eastern Oklahoma, and noticed that the owner was using a large fossil skull with down-turned horns as a seat. The Indian told Kite he had brought the skull to his home from a gravel bluff on the Arkansas River. Recognizing that the big skull was not that of a living buffalo, Kite obtained the fossil (it is not clear how Kite got it—did he steal or buy it?), and brought the skull to Joseph Leidy in Philadelphia (fig. 58). Leidy was acquiring a burgeoning

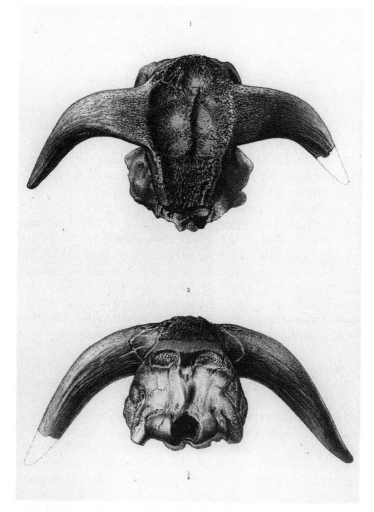

58. Skull of the Pleistocene musk ox (*Bootherium cavifrons*) that was used by an Osage Indian as a special seat. The fossil was obtained by Joseph Leidy in about 1850. Engraving in Leidy 1852.

collection of western fossils, from huge titanotheres to giant tortoises, sent to him by fur traders and explorers. By 1869, he had received nearly four tons of western fossils, many of which had originally been obtained from Indians.

In 1852, Leidy identified the Indian's fossil seat as the cranium of a new species of large, extinct musk ox of the Pleistocene, *Bootherium cavifrons*. Leidy noticed that the skull had been infiltrated with red oxide of iron. That may have occurred naturally, since iron oxide deposits can occur in fossil sediments. Earlier, in 1821, Georges Cuvier in Paris had examined fossils from this region and suggested that the iron oxide stain indicated that they had been buried for many thousands of years.

But the red pigment may also have been applied by the owner. As we now know from many examples of fossils collected by Native Americans (such as the red-tinted *Phenacodus* jaw in the New Mexico ruins; chapter 3), red ocher was rubbed on sacred objects. The owner may have venerated the large ox skull as the remains of a giant buffalo of past ages. The Indian who found the fossil was not identified, but he was probably an Osage living in an earth lodge. And the Osage Indians of eastern Oklahoma and Missouri had their own legends to account for colossal bones on the prairie.[26]

Osage Fossil Lore: Battles of Monsters in Missouri

At a certain time in the past, according to an Osage Indian tradition published in 1840, long before white settlers arrived from the East, many monstrous animals came from the East, advancing along the Missouri and Mississippi rivers. The animals already occupying the land of Missouri became so "enraged and infuriated by reason of these intrusions, that the red man durst not venture out to hunt any more." In the valley below a bluff called Rocky Ridge, the invading monsters and the native animals assembled, and a "terrible battle ensued, in which many on both sides were killed. The remainder of the monsters resumed their march toward the setting sun."

Other battles of monsters occurred along the Big Bone River (now renamed the Pomme de Terre River in Benton County) and the Osage River. After the battles, the Osages "gathered together many of the slaughtered animals, and offered them on the spot as a burnt-sacrifice to the Great Spirit," while many other immense carcasses were buried by the Great Spirit in the Osage and Big Bone rivers. Every year the Osages gave thank-offerings at a table rock overlooking Big Bone River.

At some point, continued the legend, a white homesteader from the East disrupted these ancient ceremonies by settling at the table rock and farming in the Big Bone River valley. The infuriated Osages drove him off. But after a time, more white farmers returned. The Osages protested, but the settlers with much "perseverance gained their good opinion" by promising not to disturb the ancient ceremonies of the sacred place, and so they were permitted to farm there. But when some old Osage chiefs returned after a long absence, they "were exasperated to madness on seeing the violation of the sacred ground of their forefathers by the encroachment of the white man." The settlers were driven away again and "from that time this spot remained in the hands [of the Osages] until they were removed by the government."[27]

The legend can be connected with historical events. In the early 1800s, at Big Bone River, white settlers digging out a spring discovered some huge bones, which they linked to the local Osage lore about the Battle of the Monsters. In 1806, Georges Cuvier received news of the bones of mastodons in Osage lands; he even acquired a mastodon molar from Big Bone River, sent to Paris by the American naturalist Benjamin Smith Barton, who obtained it from an "intelligent *voyageur*." There were thousands of mastodon bones along the "rivière des *Indiens Osages*," wrote Barton: many of the skeletons were buried in a standing position, and many were well preserved in peaty bogs. The single molar sent by Barton was the first specimen in Cuvier's collection of American fossils to come from west of the Mississippi River. Two hundred years later, in 2003, Pascal Tassy told me that he had located the upper right molar from Osage territory in the cellars of the Museum of Natural History in Paris.[28]

Osage lands proved to be a rich source of fossils for early American paleontology. In 1838, Albert Koch of the St. Louis Museum

59. After hearing Osage legends about battles of monsters, Albert Koch
(pointing, on right) excavated mammoth fossils at Kimmswick, Missouri,
1839. Detail of panoramic painting by John J. Egan, ca. 1850, Saint Louis
Art Museum, Eliza McMillan Fund.

unearthed the remains of a huge clawed monster (later identified
as the giant ground sloth *Mylodon*) east of the Osage River, and in
1839, further digging along Big Bone River produced more large
bones and teeth. Over the next decade, Joseph Leidy acquired many
fossils of mastodons and oxen from Benton County, Missouri.
Meanwhile, Albert Koch, spurred on by the Osage legend and the
settlers' finds, continued to dig along Big Bone River and other
sites on the Bourbeuse River and south of St. Louis at Kimmswick
(figs. 59 and 60). Koch amassed hundreds of teeth and tusks and
discovered several enormous skeletons, including a well-preserved
Mastodon americanus. The entrepreneurial Koch dubbed one of the
immense skeletons the "Missourium" and exhibited it (misassem-
bled, with extra bones), along with a printed version of the Osage
tradition, in Philadelphia, Dublin, and London (fig. 61).[29]

The Osage tradition, published by Koch in 1840, is striking on
many levels. The concentration of so many large, unfamiliar bones
of mastodons, giant beavers, oxen, horses, and giant sloths in the
river valleys was explained through the narrative of a great war
among competing animals. The scenario shows that the Osages dis-

60. Mastodon skeleton, excavated and reconstructed by Albert Koch, showing an Osage Indian relating the story of the Battle of Monsters to a white man. In the background, note another monster (far left) swimming toward canoeing Indians (right). A present-day Indian elephant is placed under the skeleton to emphasize the grand scale of the fossil creature. "Missouri Leviathan," engraving by G. Tyler, published by Lefevre, London, 1842. Missouri Historical Society, St. Louis.

tinguished the remains of several different species of animals of a past era, a paleontological perception that might have piqued the interest of George Gaylord Simpson. The Osages also noticed that some of the fossils were burnt, while others were sunk in the riverbed: hence the legend's specifications that the Indians of the old days had burnt some carcasses and the Great Spirit buried others in the river. And in fact, the bones of a *Mastodon giganteus* discovered in one of Koch's sites were charred by fire and mixed with ashes, while many other bones were blackened by lignite, which makes them look burnt.

Missourium *Theristrocaulodon,*

OR LEVIATHAN MISSOURIENSIS
OPEN FOR EXHIBITION, IN THE
Saloon at the rere of Tommey's Hotel,
ENTRANCE IN GREAT BRITAIN-STREET,
(Opposite the Lying-in-Hospital.)

PARTICULAR DESCRIPTION and EXPLANATIONS GIVEN EVERY DAY AT 3 o'C. BY Mr. A. KOCH.

This unparalled Gigantic remains, when its huge frame was clad with its peculiar fibrous integuments, and when moved by its appropriate muscles, was Monarch over all the Animal Creation; the Mammoth, and even the mighty Iguanodon may easily have crept between his legs, and now is universally acknowledged by all the European and American Men of Science, to be the greatest Phenomenon ever discovered in natural history. On viewing this vast relic, which after lying prostrate in the bosom of the Earth for Thousands of Years, now standing erect in all its grandeur, the beholder will be lost in wonder and astonishment, at its immensity and perfect preservation.

The MISSOURIUM was disinterred in 1840, after Five Months labour, in N. lat. 40., W. long. 95.

ITS LENGTH IS THIRTY FEET. ITS HEIGHT NEAR FIFTEEN FEET.
From Point to Point of the Tusks 21 Feet.

There will also be exhibited Specimens of THREE SPECIES OF GENUS TETRACAULODON, With Microscopical Sections of their Tusks, also Three species of the Genus MASTODON,

From the great applause this Unique Collection has already received in London and other large Cities in England, during the last 18 Months, and the Attraction it has already created being so well known the Proprietor considers further remarks unnecessary.

Mr. A. KOCH, the discoverer of this Collection is present to give explanations of the specimens, and will also show, and make statements, which bear indisputable evidence, that the human race existed cooval or contemporary with the above animals.

ADMISSION, - - - - ONE SHILLING.

Pamphlets containing a description of the Mis-ourium, with its supposed habits, Indian tradition concerning it &c., &c., can be had at the Door or Saloon.

Doors open from Half-past 9 in the Morning, 'til 10 in the Evening.

C. CROOKES, PRINTER 87, CAPEL-STREET. DUBLIN.

61. Osage Indian standing under a mastodon skeleton, on a broadside advertising Albert Koch's exhibit in Dublin, about 1843. A pamphlet recounting a version of the Osage tradition of the Battle of the Monsters accompanied Koch's fossil skeleton displays. American Philosophical Society, Philadelphia, Pennsylvania.

Albert Koch's efforts have been derided by paleontological historians who follow George Gaylord Simpson's sarcastic dismissal of him in 1942. But scholarly reevaluations of Koch's discoveries now focus on their scientific value in their historical context. In the 1960s, in anticipation of extensive flooding by a new dam, a team of Missouri paleontologists and archaeologists began to study various sites excavated by Koch and found new evidence confirming Koch's once-discredited early work. For example, in 1839 Koch claimed to have unearthed arrowheads with mammoth bones in several Missouri sites, and it was this startling discovery that sparked the great nineteenth-century scientific debate about whether Native Americans had hunted elephants (see appendix). Now Koch's Kimmswick site has been positively identified as a genuine Clovis mammoth kill site, with weapons dating to ten thousand years ago. Though the scientific team did not refer to the Osage legend published by Koch, their findings (published in 1976) support the topographical and paleontological elements of the tradition. For example, the table rock where the Osages commemorated the Battle of the Monsters is the "singular rock" shaped like a table atop a pillar, a landmark located a few yards from a fossiliferous spring on the Big Bone River.[30]

The Osage chiefs returning to Missouri after a long absence is a realistic detail in the legend, since the Osages often traveled to hunt buffalo as far as western Kansas. Another interesting detail, pointed out by Sioux historian Vine Deloria, is that the Great Spirit and "humans are strictly observers and not actors" in the interspecies conflict (in contrast to the Delaware tale of Indians participating in the battle of beasts on the Ohio; chapter 1). Deloria suggests that the story might preserve ancient memories of packs of large, frightening predators fighting over territory in the Late Pleistocene era.

According to an Osage traditionalist named Shirley, the "Battle of the Monsters" is still told among the Osage people and regarded as an oral history of real events in the deep past. Koch's version has many inaccuracies, remarked Shirley; for example, "monsters" is a mistranslation of the Osage word for "the large hairy animals with horns," suggesting that the original legend concerned the disappearance of Ice Age mammoths. Similar linguistic evidence for ancestral memories has been noted, by Vine Deloria, in the ancient Sioux name for a constellation of stars: "Hairy Elephant."[31]

The Osage story describes how one group of animals, defending their territory, drove off invading beasts from the East. The time frame of this tale, told to whites in the early 1800s, is a dramatic example of how an old fossil legend could be used to justify territorial claims. Like the Iroquois Big Bone Lick tradition recounted to encroaching whites in 1766 (introduction), the Osage legend was told as a parable, giving the Osages the right to resist the white intruders from the East, just as the native animals of Missouri once repelled monsters from the East.

How old is the original story of the Battle of Monsters at Big Bone River? It may date to the time when the Osages migrated to central Missouri (mid-1600s), since the rituals commemorating the battle predated the first white homesteaders. The moral message may have been added to the old tale later, in response to the inexorable pressure of westward expansion. The version we have from the early 1800s describes in metaphor the very real escalating conflicts over land appropriations, following the typical pattern: initial accommodation to the first settlers and treaties, followed by anger and rising hostilities at broken treaties and the rapid expansion of land-grabbing homesteaders, and finally government land seizures and military removals of the Indians. Pioneers began crossing the Mississippi after the Louisiana Purchase in 1803, but the Osages were granted a federal land claim to Missouri in 1810. Despite the grant, however, by the 1820s waves of land-hungry settlers began arriving, and the Osages were forced to cede their territory in 1825–30.

By the 1830s, when Koch's version was circulating, U.S. troops were forcibly driving the Indians of the East, most famously the Cherokees in 1838–39, and including the Osages, to Indian Territory (Kansas and Oklahoma). My own family legend exemplifies the collision of white and Indian cultures in Missouri in that era. My great-*grandfather's* father came by covered wagon from New York State to homestead in Missouri in 1858. A couple of decades earlier, in 1839, my great-*grandmother's* father had been born to a young Indian woman, one of the tens of thousands of displaced Native Americans crossing the Mississippi that winter into Missouri, on what became known as the Trail of Tears.[32]

Even though no mention was made of the poignant Osage legend by the scientists who studied the paleontological and archaeological evidence first discovered by Koch in 1838–40, a sense of loss pervades their 1976 report. They knew that all the historic sites in the Big Bone (Pomme de Terre) Valley were doomed to disappear beneath the waters of the new dam, completed by the Army Corps of Engineers in 1979.[33]

LIZARDS AND DINOSAURS IN YUCHI FOSSIL LEGENDS

In Norman, Oklahoma, in spring 2001, I heard a fascinating contemporary version of an old Yuchi legend about a giant lizard. Originally from Tennessee, the Yuchis have been in Oklahoma since the early 1800s; many also have Shawnee ancestry. The story was told to me by Jason Jackson, a folklorist who had been invited by the Yuchis to witness the annual Lizard Dance in 1993. An elder named Jimmie Skeeter recounted the sacred narrative of the ceremony's origin.

Long ago, a medicine man chose three boys for training in medicine knowledge and took them far from the village. While they made camp in the unfamiliar land, the medicine man scouted the site and discovered a big tree with a large hole in it. Warning them to stay away from the hollow tree, he sent two of the boys to get wood. A huge lizard emerged when one boy tried to chop down the hollow tree. It seized him and dragged him into the hole. The medicine man made a trap for the lizard by preparing a special medicine. Attracted by the medicine, that night the monster lizard approached. It died after tasting the poison. They cut off the monster's head and took it back to the village.

Jackson interviewed Norman Littlebear, a Yuchi-Shawnee elder, about the monster lizard story in 1996. Littlebear pointed out that some details in the ceremony dated to the Civil War era, but noted that the basic story is much older, harking back to "what modern books call it prehistoric times, the time of the big giant lizards or dinosaurs. Our people didn't know the word for dinosaur," he commented, but "small lizards . . . they had names for them. But these [dinosaurs] were giant lizards and . . . when they roamed the earth . . . they were so huge that they shook the earth." Littlebear then told another giant lizard story about "dinosaurs or giant lizards [that] roamed this earth." In that tale two giant lizards, one from water and one from land, had a great battle that shook the earth. These traditions suggest that Yuchi medicine men may have sought visions west of the Mississippi and encountered Cretaceous fossils of giant reptiles.

Jackson pointed out how each generation in an oral culture gives new readings to inherited material. The Yuchis show a "strong willingness to make new inquiries," and to "extrapolate deeper interpretations based on further consideration and new evidence," in order to constantly supplement old legends, as shown by the elders' references to modern knowledge of dinosaurs when they talk about the lizard monster. Indeed, when Jackson watched the 1993 ceremony—which took place after the Hollywood film *Jurassic Park* was released that year—the phrase "monster lizard" in the old story was replaced for the first time by the word "dinosaur." And seven years later, when Jackson invited Yuchi tribal members to the grand opening of the Oklahoma Natural History Museum in 2000, the group clustered before the display of the immense predatory dinosaur *Saurophaganax*, exclaiming, "That's it. That's the monster lizard!" They recognized their traditional giant lizard story as a fossil legend about dinosaur remains (figs. 62 and 63).[34]

The evolving imagery of reptilian monsters into dinosaurs was evident in the previous chapter, in the Pit River traditions, and in chapter 2 we saw how Iroquois and Delaware historians incorporated new paleontological knowledge of mammoths into their retellings of old traditions about monsters. A similar process can be seen in Kiowa artists' representations of mythical monsters. The traditional Kiowa homeland lay between the Missouri and Yellowstone rivers in Montana, but in about 1790 they migrated south and became allies of the Comanches in Oklahoma. In 1975,

62. *Saurophaganax maximus*. This allosaurid dinosaur, found only in Oklahoma, was a fearsome predator in the Jurassic. The fossil reptile skeleton was identified by the Yuchis as the Giant Lizard featured in their traditions. Sam Noble Oklahoma Museum of Natural History, University of Oklahoma. Photo by Patrick Fisher.

when the Kiowa artist Barthell Littlechief illustrated the traditional tale of the "Ancient Evil Beast," he depicted the monster as a *Triceratops* dinosaur, a common fossil in the old Kiowa territory of Montana.[35]

CHEYENNE FOSSIL KNOWLEDGE

A battle between two prehistoric monsters is a widespread motif in Amerindian mythology. For Plains Indians, for example, the Water Monster and the Thunder Bird were eternal enemies. George Bird Grinnell (known to the Cheyennes as Wikis, "Bird," because he came and went with the seasons) recorded myths about these warring creatures among the Cheyennes of western Nebraska and Kansas in the 1890s.

"Thunder often appears as a great bird, somewhat like an eagle, but much larger," wrote Grinnell. Thunder Birds shoot arrows of

63. Indian confronting an *Allosaurus*, a giant meat-eating reptile, as in Yuchi traditions. Artwork by Pete Von Sholly.

lightning, which can kill people and animals. Sometimes, noted Grinnell, the Cheyennes find "stone arrowpoints, which some people think is the head of the Thunderbird's arrow." These stone objects may have been fossil belemnites, whose resemblance to pointed missiles made them valuable fetishes for the Zunis and other nations (chapter 3).

Many stories refer to battles between sky or thunder beings and water monsters. In the Great Plains, the idea of primal conflicts between water monsters and giant birds was influenced by discoveries of the striking remains of huge flying reptiles, *Pteranodons* whose wings spanned twenty feet, lying in the ground near the skeletons of thirty-foot-long marine creatures such as mosasaurs. As noted above, these bluish-gray fossils are often well articulated in the Niobrara white chalk beds of Nebraska and Kansas. Skeletons of the great diving bird, the toothed *Hesperornis,* have even been found inside skeletons of mosasaurs and long-necked elasmosaurs and plesiosaurs. Such finds would further animate the idea of hostility between gigantic birds and water serpents.

The Cheyennes told Grinnell that several different kinds of water monsters dwelled in springs, lakes, and rivers, and inhabited certain hills and high bluffs. The location of water monsters in these places is suggestive, since Cretaceous marine reptiles, as well as scatterings of shells and shark teeth, often weather out of ridges and hilltops, or emerge along streambeds and other places where water cuts through sediments. "Water monsters were of various sorts, and whether harmful or not, they were alarming," wrote Grinnell in 1889. They could swallow humans and overturn canoes. In 2002, I was informed that even today many traditional Cheyennes avoid spending the night near springs, for fear of water monsters.[36]

One type of water monster was the *mihn,* described as a very large lizard, an image that suggests the forms of large Cretaceous reptiles. Some Cheyennes claimed that mihnio had one or two horns and were covered with hair; this may have been partially based on first-hand observations of mammoth tusks and reports of well-preserved hairy elephant remains trapped in ice—or even ancient memories of living mammoths. As Grinnell commented, horned water monsters with hair appear in Sioux traditions, too (chapter 5). No Cheyennes claimed to have seen a mihn alive, yet Grinnell refrained from relating the monsters to the conspicuous fossils in Cheyenne lands.

Ahke was another kind of monster, found in streams or on land. Despite their association with water, the Cheyennes visualized ah-kiyo as four-legged beasts that walked on land, something like a giant buffalo. And here Grinnell makes one of his very rare refer-

ences to fossils, necessitated by his Cheyenne informants' definition
of the word *ahk*, which means "of stone," or "petrified." In this
case, the Cheyennes must have actually shown Grinnell the remains
of ahke monsters turned to stone, for he explained that "large fossil
bones sometimes found along streams or on the prairie are said to
belong to *ahk*." As Grinnell well knew, these skeletons belonged to
huge mastodons or to *Titanotheriums*, colossal Oligocene rhinoceroses that Grinnell had helped excavate only a few years earlier in
western Nebraska and South Dakota, or to Cretaceous skeletons of
Tyrannosaurus and *Triceratops* dinosaurs in the Hell Creek Formation of western South Dakota, eastern Montana, and the Lance
Creek Formation of eastern Wyoming.

Grinnell did not report any uses of ahke bones, but the Cheyennes, like their allies the Sioux and their enemies the Pawnees,
also collected fossils for medicine. Their other allies, the Arapahos,
gathered fossil oyster shells for the sick to hold in their hands while
they slept, according to anthropologist Albert Kroeber in 1907.
They also gathered "the bones of large mammals or reptiles, found
especially on river-banks," said to belong to *Hiintcbiit*, water monsters. As the Comanches discovered with Mu pitz bones, the porous
bones of the monsters could be applied to wounds or sores to draw
out infection.[37]

The Cheyennes identified yet another extinct monster of great
power, found on land. The Shoshones of Wyoming were reputed
to be the last people to have seen this beast alive, and "in some way
they killed it." The *Hi stowunini hotua*, "double-toothed bull," was
like a buffalo with a blunt snout and small, sharp, polished horns
like those of a mountain goat. It was said to eat people, and its
outstanding feature was a set of large upper and lower incisors. No
living animals in North America have both horns and fangs, but all
large mammals known to the Cheyennes have either one or the
other. So was this double-fanged monster purely imaginary? Or did
it combine the features of extinct and living species?

Might the image have been influenced by Shoshone tales based
on ancestral memories of the giant short-faced bear (*Arctodus
simus*), a frightening predator of the Pleistocene-Holocene? The
short-faced bear's snout is blunt, with huge upper and lower ca-

nines, and the species may have persisted in the Big Horn or Rocky Mountains into the present era: their fossils are found in the region. Dinosaur skulls from the Lance Creek and Hell Creek formations may also have played a role in the story of this monster. The Cheyennes would also have been aware of unusual skulls in the Oligocene-Miocene exposures of western Nebraska, South Dakota, and eastern Wyoming—for example, the queer horned and fanged ruminant *Proceras* (a type of ancestral deer); or oreodons, a sheeplike animal with large upper and lower incisors in the White River Badlands; and other Tertiary fossils of *Creodonts* (early carnivores), rhinoceroses, giant canids, and saber-tooth cats.

In October 2002, I visited the museum at Agate Fossil Beds National Monument in northwestern Nebraska, traditional Cheyenne and Sioux territory, looking for fossil skulls that might match the man-eating "double-toothed" monster of Cheyenne lore. The massive, lumpy skull of a giant piglike beast, the entelodont *Dinohyus*, immediately captured my attention. This carnivore, nearly six feet tall at the shoulder, lived twenty million years ago: its powerful skull, almost three feet long, has bone-crushing jaws with upper and lower incisors as thick as a man's wrist (fig. 64). Paleontologists have nicknamed entelodonts "Terminator Pigs." Bite marks on the limb bones of chalicotheres, large bizarre ruminants with claws that were also found in the Agate Fossil Beds, were made by the double fangs of the terrible entelodonts.

A week later, in Hays, Kansas, I described the "double-toothed" monster of Cheyenne myth to Greg Liggett at the Sternberg Museum. The first image to leap to his mind was that of the entelodont, whose remains are also abundant in the South Dakota Badlands and the Pawnee Buttes area of northeastern Colorado.[38]

Except for his remark about the ahke monsters, Grinnell did not refer to prehistoric remains in his recounting of Cheyenne Thunder Bird or Water Monster myths, despite his years of collecting the fossils with Othniel Marsh and Custer. As noted earlier, Marsh himself often referred to the great water creatures as sea serpents, and he frequently described pterodactyls as "ancient flying dragons." Edward Drinker Cope named the mosasaur *Pythonomorpha*, after the giant serpent in Greek myth. The sky and water monsters of

64. Entelodont skeletons, the carnivorous "Terminator Pig" of the Miocene. A possible candidate for the double-fanged bull of Cheyenne myth? Agate Fossil Beds Museum, Nebraska. Photo: Adrienne Mayor.

prehistoric times were competing for the same ocean prey, and Cope imagined the giant pterodactyls flapping "their leathery wings over the waves" and plunging amid the "combats of the powerful saurians of the sea" (fig. 65).

Perhaps Cope had witnessed timeless scenes of large sea birds plunging into violently churning waves to snatch food from schools of great fish and sharks preying on smaller fish in the coastal waters of the Atlantic Ocean. In the company of William Webb, Cope had seen "the bones of an immense snake, all turned to stone," in western Kansas. That huge mosasaur fossil, said Webb, "lay exposed upon a bed of slate, looking very much like a 70-foot serpent carved in stone." The jaws were over six feet long, with sharp, "cone-shaped teeth still very perfect." Webb, who was steeped in Plains

65. Cope's vision of "flying dragons" and "water monsters" of the ancient Cretaceous sea. Henry Worrall's engraving of pterodactyl and plesiosaur fossils in Kansas and Nebraska, titled *The Sea Which Once Covered the Plains*, was apparently based on Cope's illustrations of fossil reptiles, 1869. Webb 1872. Photo: Princeton University Library, Rare Books.

Indian lore, also remarked on the "fierce conflicts" among the creatures of the ancient inland sea and the winged reptiles of the air, "more hideous than any creation of the imagination."[39]

Ironically, while the paleontologists indulged in mythic language to describe their sensational fossil discoveries on the plains, the paleontologist-turned-ethnologist Grinnell refrained from linking Cheyenne myths to indigenous fossil discoveries, except for his description of ahke bones and a horn coral fossil with buffalo-calling power. But what is so striking about the fragments Grinnell did preserve is that the Cheyennes distinguished the ahke and double-toothed monsters as quadruped land monsters, different from the reptilian mihn water monsters. This shows that they recognized a variety of land and marine creatures by their fossil remains. These distinctions fit Peter Dodson's second category of legend types (recognition of multiple faunas), which would suit George Gaylord Simpson's definition of a true paleontological insight.

A Cheyenne born in 1884, John Stands In Timber, used the evoc-
ative phrase "the blue vision" for the vast blue-shadowed distances
"familiar to all travelers on the Plains." I think the image also cap-
tures the sense of distant time in Native American narratives. As a
boy, Stands In Timber listened to stories about the creation and
the first Cheyennes told by two old women, White Necklace (b. ca.
1820) and the renowned female warrior Yellow Haired Woman.
These elders explained how the early Cheyennes had hunted giant
animals and tried to avoid large, fierce predators. Other elders used
to point to the high branches of cottonwoods to indicate the size
of the animals of long ago.

The "stone bones of great animals" from those days were collected by Cheyenne medicine men and ground to a powder to
make paints with protective powers. This unique practice was
undertaken by the medicine man White Bull (b. 1834), who used
fossil bones to create war paint to protect the famed Cheyenne warrior Roman Nose from lightning and enemy weapons. George Bird
Grinnell described how White Bull gathered many different colored stones, black and yellow earth, charcoal from a lightning-
blasted tree, plants frozen inside hailstones, "as well as powdered
stone bones of great animals," which he mixed with clay to make
the special paint.

Just as petrified bones were often discovered by Native Americans gathering salt at Big Bone Lick and the salt beds in Mexico,
so Indians in the West searching for colored earth such as red ocher
(hematite, iron oxide) and other minerals for paint would often
come across fossil bones. For example, in the Chinle Formation and
the Painted Desert in Arizona, deep red ocher deposits are associated with Triassic vertebrate marine and dinosaur fossils, and the
Pleistocene bone beds of Missouri also have ocher deposits. In Wyoming and Montana, the intense red-clay sediment of Unit VII of
the Cloverly Formation was traditionally mined for paint by the
Crow Indians, who would have encountered dinosaur fossils as they
prospected. White Bull, searching out colored sediments for pigments, would certainly have found the fossilized remains of unfamiliar creatures, including dinosaurs and early mammals.

White Bull also collected smaller fossils—baculites—for amulets. Baculites are cylindrical marine fossils of cephalopods that drifted in vast numbers in the great inland sea of the Cretaceous period. These distinctive fossils are found throughout the Great Plains and range from finger to forearm size. The glossy, sometimes iridescent surface is marked by beautiful, complex pearly white suture lines that resemble fractals, and crystals sometimes fill the interior sections. The intricate sutures and interior structures seem to form faces or animal shapes. The Cheyennes (and many other tribes) invested baculite fossils with a kind of living essence and special powers. Cheyennes used them to indicate the location of enemies or to bring rain to efface one's tracks in hostile territory.

White Bull's personal war charm was a baculite wrapped in beads and ermine tails. When he abandoned war for peace, he spoke to his fossil helper, "telling it that he had now given up fighting and killing people, and from this time forward the stone would be obliged to live as best it could, and that he was going to war no more. Then he put it away in his house."[40]

Ant Power

I discussed the traditional Cheyenne interest in the powers and meanings of fossils with Nita Manning, a Northern Cheyenne in the Black Hills, South Dakota. Nita's daughter loved to collect fossils as a child in the Badlands, and she studied geology in college; Nita herself remembers hearing Cheyenne stories about creation and water beings as a girl in the 1950s. But they were fragmentary "because people were not so open about their traditions then. It was against the law to practice our religions, so everything was secret. That's probably why so many of the old stories have been lost."

"Long ago I heard something about fossils from a Cheyenne holy man that has always stayed with me. When a young man was to make a vision quest, the rattle maker for the ceremony would find anthills on the prairie. He would gather 405 little fossils brought up by ants for the rattle. For some reason, ants push up little fossils.

I have seen that myself. The creatures whose fossils the ants bring to the surface were living back when ants were first created. Ants lived at the same time as dinosaurs! I find it fascinating to ponder the mysteries and stories the fossils have to tell us. In the sacred circle of life, maybe the ants honor their old relatives by bringing up their fossils. In a way," Nita muses, "I suppose the ants were the first fossil gatherers, since they were here long before we were. I wonder if anyone else ever heard of this?"

As I had learned from talking with Harry Manygoats in Arizona, Navajos also recognized that ants had originated in the same era as the dinosaurs. This prescientific perception of the great antiquity of ants, which in fact first evolved in the Cretaceous and have survived unchanged over the millennia, surprises many paleontologists. The allies of the Cheyennes, the Sioux, respected "ant power," too, and collected tiny fossils and pebbles brought to the surface by helper ants. On his vision quest, the Sioux holy man Lame Deer shook a rawhide rattle filled with 405 little fossils gathered from an ant heap: the sound was "soothing, like rain falling on rock." In northern Montana, an Assiniboine spiritual leader told me that a medicine man could request ants to "please mine white quartz" and could return a week later to gather the white pebbles; these were valued because they produce flashes of light in the dark, an important feature of the *yuwipi* (stone power) ceremony.[41]

Another group of keen natural observers—paleontologists—also consider ants as their allies. The ingenious "ant hill method of collecting minute fossils" was perfected in 1886 by one of the most original and successful bone hunters of that era, John Bell Hatcher. Noticing that anthills in the Nebraska-Dakota badlands yielded a "goodly number of mammal teeth," Hatcher used a baker's flour sifter to sort piles of anthill sand. By this method, he wrote, "I frequently secured from 200 to 300 teeth and jaws from one ant hill." Hatcher even began transporting shovelfuls of sand and ants to other Cretaceous mammal localities that he had discovered. After two years he would return to the site to harvest the ants' "efficient service in collecting . . . small fossils." By 1888, Hatcher was scooping up entire ant mounds on the prairie and packing them into crates addressed to Professor O. C. Marsh at

Yale, where they were sifted in the Peabody lab for minuscule fossils of the earliest mammals.

Now, of course, it has become standard paleontological practice to examine anthills for microfossils. One Cretaceous mammal deposit in eastern Montana is known as the Bug Creek Anthills site, after paleontologists gritted their teeth and braved the stinging red harvester ants to collect an astonishing 130 tiny mammal teeth in just ten minutes. In 1965, fossil hunters found five thousand fossil traces of more than twenty-five species in a hundred anthills in the Badlands of South Dakota.

Prospectors and archaeologists also examine anthills for minerals and artifacts. As early as 1872 in Kansas, William Webb described a paleontologist (most likely Edward Drinker Cope) watching ants bring up, not fossils, but tiny blue beads, indicating that an ancient Indian burial lay beneath the anthill. Wyoming paleontologist Michael Flynn told me that when he looked for small mammal teeth in an anthill near Pompey's Pillar on the Yellowstone River in Montana, he found multicolored glass trade beads from the early 1800s among the grains. As Nita Manning jokes, "Maybe the Natives knew something back then, about the power of ants, that scientists are learning now."[42]

CHAPTER

5

The High Plains:

Thunder Birds, Water Monsters, and

Buffalo-Calling Stones

The abundant occurrence of fossil bones in North America
was not widely known among the Indians and not a common
subject of remark by them.
—*George Gaylord Simpson, 1942*

What you people can fossils, these too are used by us. Deep
in the Badlands we find the bones of the water monster,
which lived long before human beings appeared.
—*Lame Deer, Lakota holy man, born 1902*

CROW CREEK SIOUX RESERVATION,

SOUTH DAKOTA, SUMMER 2000

I PITCHED my tent on the east
bank of the Missouri River. It was late afternoon, the last day of
July, my first day at the paleontological field camp on the Crow
Creek Sioux Reservation. I hurried to pound in the tent stakes.
The western horizon was black with a fast-approaching storm—the

Sioux would have said that Thunder Beings were striking the ground with lightning and beating up strong winds. Under the towering clouds, a tornado was gathering force over the High Plains. By midnight it would pass over the roiling river and touch down east of our camp, twisting metal highway signs, uprooting cottonwoods, and demolishing barns.[1]

Holed up in my tent that night as lightning flashed and thunder cracked, I thought about the wars between the Thunder Birds and the Water Monsters. According to the Sioux creation myth, the first creatures were insects and reptiles, under the domain of *Unktehi*, the Water Monster. In the days before humans, there were many kinds of reptiles, those with legs and tails, those without legs, and those with armored shells, and many varieties of each kind. All became cold-blooded, ravenous monsters, devouring every living thing on land and in water, and finally had to be destroyed for natural balance to be restored. In the first of the four great ages—the age of Rock—the Water Monsters were blasted into stone by Thunder Birds' bolts of lightning. The earthly bodies of Thunder Beings, like the Unktehi, were also buried in the ground (fig. 66).

The awesome bones of these ancient enemies were strewn over the plains. Many paleontologists working today remember an illustration in a popular children's book of the 1950s, depicting a band of Sioux warriors discovering a *Pteranodon* skeleton after a lightning storm (fig. 67). The remains of those huge flying creatures are often found together with the skeletons of marine reptiles in Cretaceous sediments. Such a discovery would provide strong physical evidence to confirm the idea of hostility between Thunder Birds and Water Monsters.[2]

When he was a boy on the Rosebud Reservation in the early 1900s, Lame Deer, a Lakota Sioux holy man, had been caught in a storm that recapitulated one of those cosmic battles. Tracking lost horses in the Badlands (*Mako Sica*, "Land Difficult to Travel"), the boy was surprised by a sudden storm, pitch-black with constant thunder and lightning. Fearing a flash flood, he looked for high ground. The air crackled with *wakangeli*, electricity. Hair standing on end, Lame Deer scrambled up the steep side of a gulch and clung to the top of the hogback ridge.

66. Artist's conception of how fossils may have influenced traditional Plains Indian tales about Thunder Birds and Water Monsters. In this badlands scene, a pair of Native Americans imagine the battle that resulted in the fossil skeletons of the *Pteranodon* and mosasaur turned to stone, below. Artwork by Pete Von Sholly.

67. Artist's impression of Sioux warriors discovering a *Pteranodon* fossil (note that saguaro cactus, normally found in the Sonoran desert, does not exist in the Niobrara chalk beds containing pterosaur fossils). From *Dinosaurs and Other Prehistoric Animals* by Darlene Geis, illustrated by Russell F. Peterson, copyright © 1959 by Grosset & Dunlap. Renewed © 1987 by Putnam Publishing Group. Used by permission of Grosset & Dunlap, A Division of Penguin Young Readers Group, A Member of Penguin Group (USA) Inc., 345 Hudson St., New York NY 10014. All rights reserved.

As he inched along the ridge, clods of earth crumbled under the driving hail, and flashes of lightning revealed how precarious his position was. Teeth chattering, shivering, hearing the powerful voices of the *Wakinyan*, Thunder Birds, in every thunderclap, the boy gripped that ridge till dawn. Stiff with cold, he waited for the sun to warm him up. Then, "I saw that I was straddling a long row of petrified bones, the biggest I had ever seen. I had been moving along the spine of the Great Unktehi." The Water Monster's backbone lay "right along the spine of the mound. Riding the ridge like a horse was spooky, like riding the monster."

"It scared me when I was on that ridge, for I felt Unktehi . . . moving beneath me, wanting to topple me." Lame Deer searched many times for the ridge "deep in the Badlands that formed Unktehi's spine. I wanted to show it to my friends." Exposed to the weather, that particular fossil would have disintegrated away, but Lame Deer found other ridges where "you can see vertebrae sticking out in a great row of red and yellow rocks." Petrified seashells and turtles are scattered about, noted Lame Deer, proving that "all this land around here was once a vast ocean."[3]

Lame Deer's boyhood memory recalls the experience of the fossil hunter Arthur Lakes, searching for bones atop the sandstone ridge known as the Hogback, near Morrison, Colorado, in 1877. Along the crest some seven hundred feet high, Lakes came upon the "monstrous" spine of a gigantic creature in sharp relief. The bones' purplish hue contrasted with the yellow-brown-gray of the Morrison Formation, and each vertebra was an astounding thirty-three inches around. Lakes had the impression that the entire hogback ridge might be the remains of the monster.[4]

Lakes loaded the giant bones into wagons and sent them by rail to the Peabody Museum at Yale, where Othniel Marsh named the eighty-foot-long Jurassic dinosaur *Titanosaurus* (now *Atlantosaurus*). Since this early episode in Marsh and Cope's "Bone Wars" in the late nineteenth and early twentieth centuries, fossil hunters in the Dakotas, Nebraska, Wyoming, Colorado, Montana, and Alberta, Canada, have continued to unearth the skeletons of *Triceratops*, *T. rex*, mosasaurs, and pterodactyls, as well as the remains of the earthshaking mammals of the Tertiary (see map 5). In the summer of 2000, I had come to the ancient battlegrounds of the Thunder Birds and Water Monsters, where American paleontology came of age, to learn how the Sioux, Crow, Blackfeet, and other people of the northern plains had viewed these extraordinary remains, and to see for myself how the bones of Unktehi looked as they emerged from the earth.[5]

Back in 1804, when Lewis and Clark followed the Missouri River to its headwaters, dinosaurs were unknown to science. But on an island just a few miles south of our dig site in South Dakota, Lewis and Clark had unearthed a forty-five-foot-long backbone and ribs of what is now thought to have been a plesiosaur. Did Lewis and Clark ask the local Yankton Sioux their opinion of the strange creature? There is no record of such conversations, but their French-Sioux interpreter, Pierre Dorion, had lived among the Yanktons

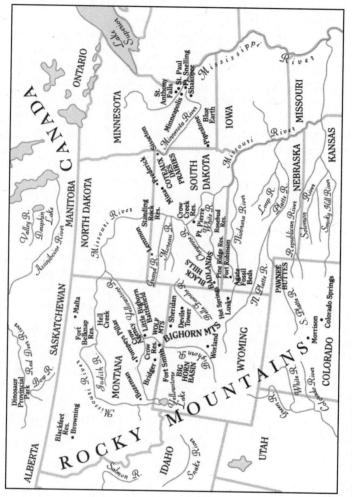

Map 5: The High Plains (map by Michele Mayor Angel)

since the 1780s and could have told the explorers water monster tales, some of which, recounted below, were first recorded by French missionaries.

On the return trip, in 1806, near Pompey's Pillar in Montana, William Clark excavated a large rib from a big skeleton in a cliff above the Yellowstone River. Having seen whale carcasses beached on the Pacific coast, he concluded that the skeleton was some colossal fish, but it was more likely a duck-billed dinosaur, a *Triceratops*, or a *T. rex* from the Hell Creek Formation there. Half a century would pass before Ferdinand Hayden's discoveries in the 1850s brought the dinosaur and early mammal fossil beds west of the Missouri to the attention of scientists like Joseph Leidy, Marsh, and Cope.[6]

Early in the morning after the tornado, I got my tools and canteens ready. Today we would begin prospecting for fossils exposed by the storm in the badlands above the Missouri River, searching for the skeletons of plesiosaurs and mosasaurs, so abundant in the somber black-and-gray Pierre shale deposits that were once the floor of the great inland sea (fig. 68). Many of the major mosasaur sites on the reservation were first shown to David Parris, the co-leader of our dig, in 1993 by an avid fossil collector named Lee Azure, a member of the Crow Creek tribe. Azure's "unusual perception" allowed him to locate subtle three-dimensional fish and other fossils overlooked by experienced paleontologists. "Rather than wrenching fossils from their context and regarding them as curiosities," wrote Parris, Azure remembered the location of each specimen he found in the field, frequently finding "more specimens over the winter than our field expedition could collect in the summer." One of Azure's discoveries, credited to him in the 1994 *Journal of Vertebrate Paleontology*, was a "spectacular but poorly-exposed" rare species, *Mosasaurus dekayi*.[7]

Buffalo-Calling Stones

On that first day at Crow Creek, my boots crunched over glinting expanses of fossil shells, pearly spirals now turned to stone, opalescent sea-worm tubes, coiled and straight ammonites, rippled clam

68. Fossil-rich badlands and ravines along the Missouri River, painting by George Catlin, 1832. "Three Domes, Clay Bluffs, Fifteen Miles above the Mandan Village." Smithsonian American Art Museum, Gift of Mrs. Joseph Harrison, Jr.

and oyster shells, and other marine fossils on the ridge tops. I examined some cylindrical fossils with complex fractal patterns—baculites. Because the internal structure and patterns of these cephalopod marine fossils sometimes resemble bison shapes, the Blackfeet, Cheyenne, and other Plains tribes invested baculites with an ability to summon buffalo herds. Buffalo-calling stones, known as *Iniskim* among the Blackfeet bands of northern Montana and Alberta, have also turned up in archaeological sites across the Dakotas, Montana, and Canada, indicating that the Iniskim tradition goes back at least a thousand years (fig. 69).

According to Blackfeet legend, the sacred power of the fossil with the form of a buffalo was first discovered long ago by Weasel Woman, who was picking berries at a constantly eroding cut bank called "Falling off without Excuse," probably the big fossil deposit

69. Baculite fossil, above, collected by Blackfeet and other Indian groups as buffalo-calling stones. Below: as the marine fossil erodes, the isolated sections resemble bisonlike shapes.

on the Bow River in Alberta now known to rock hounds as "Baculite Beach." After she taught the ritual of the curiously shaped stone to her husband, Chief Speaking, Blackfeet and other northern tribes began to collect the fossils, which they rubbed with red ocher and placed in medicine bundles. Iniskim were used to draw buffalo herds over cliffs before the arrival of horses. As Chandler Good Strike—a Gros Ventre artist at Fort Belknap Reservation, Montana—told me later that summer, "We used to collect the fossils to call the buffalo each spring." People also kept personal Iniskim fossils for luck, healing, and other powers. Charlie Crow Eagle, a Piegan (Blackfeet band of Canada), owned an interesting buffalo-skin

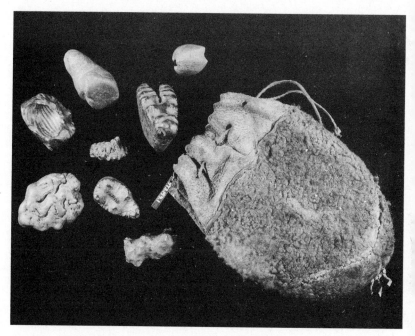

70. Medicine pouch made of buffalo hide, owned by Charlie Crow Eagle, a Piegan of Alberta. It contains several Iniskim or buffalo-calling stones, fossil ammonites and bivalves from Cretaceous shales, and a fossil horn coral of the Carboniferous. The pouch was purchased by paleontologist Loris Russell in 1965. With permission of the Royal Ontario Museum © ROM. Photo: David Rudkin.

medicine pouch in about 1880 (fig. 70). It originally held nine Iniskim: two *Baculites compressus*, four *Placenticeras* ammonites, an *Acanthoscaphites* ammonite, a Paleozoic coral, and a *Corbicula* clamshell, all coated in red pigment.[8]

The Indians who collected fossil shells on the plains recognized them as water organisms and correctly concluded that, in the words of Bull's Dry Bones, an Assiniboine (Sioux) holy man, "The whole surface of the earth was at a time covered with water." Indeed, the plentiful shells in the hills I was traversing along the Missouri River made it easy to imagine a vast sea teeming with immense sharks, enormous carnivorous reptiles, giant turtles, and myriad smaller sea creatures. Edward Drinker Cope, searching for mosasaurs in a similar landscape in Kansas, amid an expanse of huge oyster shells—some more than two feet across and many of them open—thought the debris looked like the "half-finished meal of some titanic race."

Riding across the same hills in 1835, the artist George Catlin had the same thought, and he recorded an amusing anecdote in his memoirs. Amazed at the lifelike quality of the heaps of stony oysters, Catlin filled his portmanteaus with several pounds of the fossils, intending to fool his seafood-loving friends back East. After several weeks, however, exhausted by the weight of his treasure, Catlin tossed the oysters away, only to gather up loads of other intriguing fossils further on, which were also discarded and re-placed in turn, and so on across the wide prairie. An Assiniboine fossil hunter in Montana told me a similar story about the problems of transporting heavy fossils. In about 1840, on the border between Alberta and Montana, Father Pierre De Smet had found a petrified "red" skull of an extinct giant bison. He attempted to pack the skull out on a mule but finally had to leave it along the trail. The fossil hunter hoped that by carefully reading De Smet's journals, he might someday locate that giant bison skull, obviously a ceremonial relic since it had been tinted with red paint.[9]

Remembering how John Bell Hatcher used to check anthills for fossils, I stopped to examine them too. Sure enough, among the small grains of quartz were bits of white bone and shell, yuwipi gathered by Cheyenne and Sioux medicine men for power in seeking visions. As I walked up and down the hills, each and every rock seemed alive with potential, full of secrets of nature's past. And over the following days, as I worked to help release the backbones of sea serpents trapped in stone for millions of years, I felt closer to comprehending some facets of the great mystery of Sioux belief, that Rock, *Inyan*, was the origin of life, and that rocks still hold the essence and record of early life on Earth.

By the end of our first day on the Crow Creek Reservation, each prospector—even those who had never seen fossils in the ground before—had discovered pieces of mosasaur jaws, teeth, and back-bone. Our hours in the field were dusty and hot, with fierce sun and angry rattlesnakes, but in four days we found six mosasaurs and a giant turtle (*Archelon*). By week's end, using trowels, awls, and brushes (simple tools much like those available to early Indians: knife, awl, bone picks, scraper, rock hammer, and feathers), we had exposed long rows of vertebrae, shoulderblades, limb bones, skulls, and paddles of the huge reptiles. Many lay along ridge tops, just like the Unktehi backbone ridden by Lame Deer during the storm.

WATER MONSTERS AND THUNDER BIRDS ON THE PRAIRIE AND IN THE BADLANDS

Some Sioux imagined that the large boulders on the northern prairies were the spent ballistics of the Water Monsters, hurled up at the Thunder Birds who struck back with lightning. Lame Deer remarked that in places where the bones of the Thunderers and Water Monsters were very thick, you could find "many *kangi tame*, bolts of lightning which have turned into black stones shaped like spear points." Pointed belemnite fossils, common in the Badlands, do resemble blackened stone missiles, and they are abundant in the sediments where mosasaurs are found. And of course, a severe thunderstorm would wash away soil, revealing fossils that were not visible before: hence the common association of fossils with Thunder Beings.[10]

I had heard that Thunder Bird footprints were impressed on certain big rocks in the eastern Dakotas and Minnesota, so, in July 2000 before setting up camp on the Missouri River, I searched out several of these sacred boulders in the Coteau des Prairies in northeastern South Dakota. This is where the midwestern prairie begins to slope upward into the High Plains. Looking west from these grassy hills, one can appreciate what the Cheyenne elder John Stands In Timber called the "blue vision" of distant time and space. In the words of George Catlin, the Coteau des Prairies offered "the most unbounded and sublime views of—nothing at all—save the blue and boundless ocean of prairies that vanish into azure in the distance."[11]

This tall-grass prairie is dotted with great boulders, glacial errat-
ics that traveled south from Manitoba, Canada, during the Ice Age.
Similar landscapes exist further west, too, in northwestern Montana, for example, where scientists note that "every rock, without
exception, moved east . . . miles from where it formed." Geologists
developed the theory of glacial transport of erratic boulders and
moraine gravels in the 1870s, but the reality of traveling boulders
and stones was already acknowledged in ancient Sioux belief. The
concept was first recorded in writing in 1834 by the missionary
Samuel Pond in Minnesota. Some granite boulders were thought
by the Sioux to "possess the power of locomotion," even to be capable of leaving tracks or furrows.[12]

In the 1830s, the French explorer Joseph Nicollet recorded Dakota Sioux legends about Thunder Birds. Their original *nesting*
ground was said to be the Coteau des Prairies, but their *dwelling*
place was the Black Hills (thunderstorms here typically arrive from
the west, and large birds often soar on thermal updrafts in front of
approaching storms). I visited the three Thunder Bird track and
nest sites marked on Nicollet's old maps. Reading Catlin's memoirs, I learned that when he visited a mound called Thunder's Nest
in the Coteau des Prairies in 1832, Sioux medicine men told him
the Thunder brood was hatching whenever "the skies are rent with
bolts of thunder." The Thunder Bird's gigantic nest was said to be
a pile of serpent bones, and the hatchlings were often "destroyed
by a great serpent."

Catlin also viewed some deeply impressed footsteps in solid rock,
identified as the tracks of a huge bird that—long before the creation
of man—had devoured the first buffaloes. Some Sioux believed that
the great bisons' blood had stained the red catlinite rocks (named
after Catlin, commonly known as pipestone) quarried at a sacred
site in southwestern Minnesota (other legends said pipestone was
red with the blood of primal human ancestors).[13]

I talked with Clifford Canku, a teacher of Dakota Sioux culture
at Sisseton-Wahpeton College (South Dakota), about the ancient
prints on the boulders I had come to see. Canku referred to them
as "dinosaur tracks," and he identified the Unktehi monsters as "di-
nosaurlike reptiles." Since fossil dinosaur footprints are geologi-

cally unlikely in this area, these tracks were carved on granite boulders by medicine men, perhaps to illustrate tales of Thunder Birds. The petroglyphs may have represented the three-toed dinosaur footprints observed further west in the Lakota Formation near the Black Hills, the dwelling place of Thunder Birds. Moreover, fairly well preserved *Pteranodons* lie in the Pierre Shale Formation around the Black Hills and would have bolstered tales of Thunder Birds in the Black Hills.[14]

Sky and water/earth spirits, whose conflicts symbolized nature's struggle for harmony in Amerindian myths, were personified by Thunder Birds with their lightning and Water Monsters who caused floods (see fig. 71). Reflecting on the science of thunderstorms, one realizes that the myths symbolize the dynamic collision of natural forces in actual storm phenomena.

The updraft formation of towering cumulus clouds causes radical imbalances in the electrical charges between the sky's atmosphere and the earth. To restore the balance, nature equalizes the negative and positive charges through explosive bolts of lightning (which appear to strike the ground but actually surge upward). Lightning is incredibly powerful. Each bolt strikes with *several hundred million* volts of electrical energy and is hotter than the surface of the sun, nearly 50,000 degrees Fahrenheit. Lame Deer compared lightning power to a colossal atomic welding torch. Lightning is indeed a sky "weapon" of violent force, matched in deadly destruction only by floods on Earth. In fact, lightning and flooding are the major causes of weather-related deaths, and their powers are most awe-inspiring on the open plains of the American West.[15]

The earliest written reference to oral tales about Unktehi, Water Monsters, comes from Father Hennepin, a French Franciscan who was captured by the Dakota Sioux in Minnesota in about 1680. Hennepin observed the Dakotas making offerings at St. Anthony Falls (on the Mississippi River between Minneapolis and St. Paul) to "the great deity called *Oanktayhee*." Oanktayhee, or Unktehi, was said to live under the falls, and to manifest itself as a gigantic buffalo. Almost two hundred years after Father Hennepin wrote this, in 1874, mammoth teeth and tusks were recovered from St. Anthony Falls.[16]

In 1834, Samuel and Gideon Pond, missionary brothers who recorded the beliefs of the Dakotas in Minnesota, were shown many
large bones of the "chief object of respect, *Unkteri*." The Ponds
recognized these as mammoth bones, whose remains far exceeded
the largest creatures known to the Sioux. But since the beast was
never seen on land, wrote Samuel Pond, "and their bones were
found in low and wet places, they concluded that their dwelling
was in water."[17]

Similar logic accounts for the Potawatomi legend about the
bones of generations of water monsters submerged in Lake Manitou, Indiana (now called Devil's Lake; *manitou* means mysterious,
powerful spirit). The legend was first recorded by white settlers in
1828, and in 1905 the complete skeleton of a Columbian mammoth (now mounted in the American Museum of Natural History)
was discovered nearby; similar bones also lie in Lake Manitou. Tales
of water monsters arose in other areas rich in Ice Age elephant
fossils. For example, in the northern Yukon, which has the most
prolific beds of Pleistocene megafaunas in Canada, paleontologist
C. Richard Harington investigated Native Dene folklore about a
"monster" that suddenly emerged in the Whitestone River in the
1980s. He found a nearly complete woolly mammoth skeleton at
the site.[18]

In Minnesota, the Dakotas collected pieces of mastodon bones
for their medicine bags. Pond wrote that the bones were "highly
prized for magical powers, perhaps as valuable to them as relics of
a saint are to a devout Catholic." An irresistible, "mighty *wakan*
influence," which the Sioux compared to the trajectories of magical
arrows, was thought to issue from the bodies of Unktehi. Wakan is
a concept similar to manitou: it signifies anything mysterious or
incomprehensible, and the more inexplicable a phenomenon is, the
more wakan it is.

In 1859, Edward Neill of the Minnesota Historical Society described a Sioux initiation ceremony in which a holy man chewed a
piece of the bone of "Oanktayhee, the patron of medicine men."
Near Fort Snelling above the Minnesota River, the Indians pointed
out a mound said to contain Unktehi bones, and a Dakota man
told Samuel Pond that he had discovered Unktehi bones in the lake
at Shakopee, an Indian village south of Minneapolis on the Minne-

sota River. The man had tried without success to drag the heavy fossils up into his canoe.[19]

"The fossil bones of the Mastodon, which are sometimes found by the Dakotahs, they confidently believe to be the bones of *Onkteri*," wrote Henry Rowe Schoolcraft in Minnesota in the early 1800s. Schoolcraft (1793–1864), a geologist and Indian agent who married an Ojibwe woman, wrote extensively on Native American tribes. The bones of Unktehi, noted Schoolcraft, are preserved by the Indians "most sacredly, and are universally esteemed for their *wakan* qualities, being used with wonderful effect as a sanative medicine." Schoolcraft heard that Unktehi was something like an ox but much larger; its horns could extend to the skies and its body could swell to cause floods or whirlpools. Schoolcraft reproduced drawings of several types of Unktehi monsters on birchbark by an Ojibwe named Chingwauk (or Shingvauk) sometime before 1850 (fig. 71).[20]

Because the Dakotas were "well acquainted with comparative anatomy," noted the Ponds, they knew that the animal whose bones they found was an immense quadruped, which resembled in some ways an enormous buffalo or ox. The Dakota-English dictionary of 1852 defined *Unktehi* (*Oanktayhee, Onkteri, Unkteri*, etc.) as "a fabled monster of the deep . . . an extinct animal, the bones of which are said to be sometimes found by the Indians, probably the mastodon." The related term *Unlicegila* (*Uncegila, Unktegila*) was also defined as "the mastodon, or other large animal, whose petrified remains are found in Dakota Territory," and such bones were called *unlicegilanhu*.[21]

As these early documents show, when the Sioux resided in the Great Lakes area they visualized Unktehi as a large underwater mammal, based on the Pleistocene mammoth and mastodon remains that eroded out of lakes and rivers. In the mid-1700s, however, some Sioux bands acquired horses and began to move west from the Great Lakes to Dakota Territory (South and North Dakota, Nebraska, and eastern Wyoming and Montana). The Dakota Sioux remained along the Mississippi River, while the Nakota (Assiniboine Sioux) moved along the Upper Missouri in Montana, and the Lakota and Oglala Sioux traveled to the Black Hills–Badlands regions of South Dakota, Nebraska, and Wyoming.

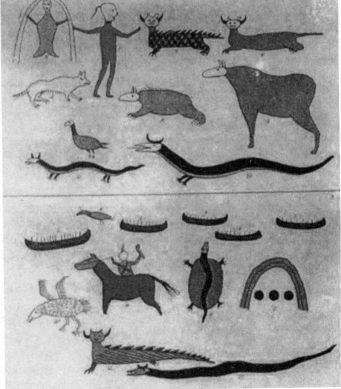

As Sioux people migrated west along the Missouri River and into the badlands terrain, they began to encounter the fossil skeletons of large marine reptiles—true water monsters from the era of dinosaurs—very different from the Ice Age mammal remains of Minnesota. Mammoth and mosasaur skeletons overlap in South Dakota. For example, at Wetonka, near Mina, about seventy-five miles west of the Minnesota border, a mammoth with twelve-foot-long tusks was found in glacial debris, and just thirty miles north of that site, near Frederick, a nearly complete mosasaur skeleton recently came to light.[22]

As the Sioux encountered different types of paleontological exposures, their ideas about Thunder Birds and Water Monsters evolved to match the changing physical evidence of fossils. I imagine that George Gaylord Simpson would have been interested in this progression of observation and interpretation. In the West, the image of Unktehi retained horns, but it was no longer compared to a giant buffalo. Instead Unktehi and its relatives came to be visualized as immense reptiles or serpents with legs. By the 1890s, when ethnologists began to interview the Oglala-Lakotas of the Badlands and western Dakotas, holy men explained that Unktehi was "shaped like a giant scaly snake with feet," an image that matches the appearance of long, snaky mosasaur skeletons with four short appendages. The Unktehi had a notched backbone or crest like a "giant saw," a graphic reference to the jagged outline of the backbone of a dinosaur or marine reptile emerging from the ground. By 1976, when the Lakota historian-storyteller James LaPointe recounted the legends of his people, he identified "*Unkche Ghila*, the huge animal whom no human being has ever seen alive," as a dinosaur.[23]

71 (opposite). Top: Thunder Birds in rock art. Upper left: Pipestone, Minnesota, traced in 1889; lower left, along the Minnesota River, traced in 1911. Center: Iowa, traced 1885. Upper right: Nebraska, traced 1889; lower right, Minnesota, traced 1885. Sources: Winchell 1911, Callahan 2000–. Bottom: Birchbark pictographs by Chingwauk, in about 1850, based on rock art describing a war party of five canoes that encountered various creatures while crossing Lake Superior, including types of Water Monsters. Sources: Schoolcraft 1884, Dewdney and Kidd 1967.

Other attributes of Unktehi included a heavy spiked tail, scales or shaggy red hair, and a crystallized stone heart. The scales may have been extrapolated from living reptiles, or perhaps this detail was related to rare observations of mummified dinosaur skin. The red hair could be a traditional detail based on the discovery in caves or ice of well-preserved bodies of extinct sloths and mammoths, whose dark hair lightens to red over time (see the appendix). The notion of a stone heart brings to mind the recent, controversial discovery of a red "stone heart" in the chest cavity of a dinosaur skeleton found in western South Dakota in 1993. Some paleontologists identify the object as a heart-shaped iron concretion, while others maintain that the concretion formed around the actual heart of the dinosaur. Did a similar discovery lead to Sioux stories of stone Unktehi hearts? Another possible inspiration for the notion might have been the find of a special gastrolith within a dinosaur skeleton.[24]

Unktehi's foes, the Thunder Birds, Wakinyan, were divided into four types, according to the lore recorded in the mid-1800s by Schoolcraft, the Ponds, and others in Minnesota (see fig. 71). All Thunder Birds had "terrific proportions," but one type was black with a very long toothed beak, enormous claws, and four-jointed wings. Another was yellow with four joints in each great wing but only six quills. The third was scarlet, with extremely long, large wings, each with eight joints. The fourth type was blue or white, and amorphous, often shown in rock art as a wide U with two zigzag lightning bolts. Lightning, with its power to "destroy life and shiver the oak to atoms," was the weapon of Thunder Birds.[25]

The Sioux pointed out collapsed river bluffs, very common along the Missouri River, as places where Thunder Birds had swooped down to attack Unktehi and its relatives. Clifford Canku's father had shown him mounds that had been split open by Thunder Birds' attacks on Unktehi, and Canku told me that the cloudy yellow Buffalo Lake had turned sour because a Water Monster had been blasted there. "Many stories are told of these beings and their mortal combats," wrote Gideon Pond in the 1830s. And in turn, Thunder Beings were "often surprised and killed by the Unktehi." A Sioux man told Pond he'd found the body of a Thunder Bird along the Blue Earth River (southern Minnesota), with a wingspan of

"25–30 yards" (perhaps a typo for "feet"). In 1859, Edward Neill reported that some Sioux had found a Thunder Bird skeleton near Kaposia (a Dakota village of 1750–1830, now South St. Paul), with a beak like an eagle's and wings with four joints that zigzagged like lightning.[26]

Now much of the lore about the four types of Thunder Birds was symbolic, and some of the stories may have combined living memories of very large, extinct raptors of the Ice Age with the storytelling imagination. But discoveries of large skeletons that were identified as Thunder Birds reported in the 1800s suggest that the actual fossils of winged or beaked creatures also played a role in the mythology. Giant condors' range extended over North America until about 1800, and their remains, along with those of Ice Age teratorns (with wingspans of between twelve and seventeen feet) could exist in the Midwest. The geology of Minnesota precludes any Mesozoic fossils of flying reptiles, but Sioux who traveled in the Dakotas and Nebraska could have encountered large *Pteranodons*, or the giant bird *Hesperornis*, in Cretaceous chalk and shale beds.

Another possible fossil influence on big bird legends in the West could be the giant *Diatryma*, a monstrous predatory land bird of the Eocene that weighed over 350 pounds and stood six feet tall, with strong legs, vestigial wings, and a massive beaked skull. A complete skeleton of *Diatryma* was discovered in Wyoming in 1916. The beaked skull or the leg and foot of such a huge fossil bird might have contributed to legends. The Yakima Indians of the Northwest, for example, tell of an immense ground-dwelling bird, the *Pach-an-a-ho*, that left huge three-toed tracks (the name means "crooked beak/rough-looking bird"). Recently, some Yakima people noted a similarity between their vision of the Pach-an-a-ho and a reconstructed model of a *Diatryma* in a museum.[27]

OTHNIEL MARSH AND THE SIOUX THUNDER BEASTS

Thunder *Beings* existed before Thunder *Birds*, noted Lame Deer, and they became stone just like the Water Monsters, so their bones are also scattered throughout the Badlands. The fossils of large Tertiary mammals with odd skull projections or claws, such as the elephant-size titanotheres and ponderous chalicotheres, were identified by the Lakota Sioux as "Thunder" Beings or Beasts. "Thunder" referred to the wakan nature of the mysterious animals, and their bones were found after heavy thunderstorms. Black Elk, the great Oglala holy man who recounted his life story to John Neihardt in 1930 at Manderson, Pine Ridge Reservation, referred to Thunder Beings as something like giant horses accompanied by thunder and lightning.

In about 1875, Othniel Marsh heard about Thunder Beast remains in the Badlands from James Cook, a trapper-scout who had spent years among the Sioux. Cook's friends Red Cloud, Little Wound, and American Horse described the "bones of strange creatures that had once lived in the land of the Sioux—bones now turned to stone." They led Cook to the tipi of Young Man Afraid of His Horses to see an immense jawbone with a big molar some three inches across. American Horse explained that it had belonged to a Thunder Horse that had lived "away back" in time, but sometimes during thunderstorms they lived again to "chase the buffalo, striking and killing some of them with their great hoofs." Some Sioux likened lightning flashes to the way sparks were thrown up by the hooves of bison as they thundered over rocks on the dry plains.

American Horse recounted an old tradition handed down from the time *before* the Sioux obtained horses in the late 1600s. Thunder Beasts had once saved a band from starvation by driving a herd of buffalo right into their camp, where the men were able to kill them with lances and arrows. Another Lakota legend described a hellish scene of giants mounted on huge white Thunder Horses slaughtering an entire herd of bison with lightning. Masses of twisted bison bones lay around the Black Hills, and it was said that one could see embedded in stone the tracks of the Thunder Horses (perhaps the dinosaur tracks in the area). In Pine Ridge Reservation and in sites around the Black Hills, bison bone beds from ten thousand years ago are not far from—and often overlie—fossil deposits of large, unusual creatures that died many millions of years ago. As Edward Drinker Cope remarked in Kansas, living buffalo "now range over a surface strewn with the remains of monsters." In eastern Montana, Jack Horner pointed out accumulations of modern buffalo bones of centuries past scattered around a big *Triceratops* skull eroding out of the Hell Creek Formation. These are good examples of the kind of evidence that might have inspired the mythic notion of Thunder Beasts stampeding herds of bison.[28]

Cook showed the tooth and jawbone collected by Afraid of His Horses to Othniel Marsh and persuaded the wary Sioux leaders that Marsh was seeking not gold but the "stone bones" of Thunder Beasts. Cook introduced Marsh to Red Cloud, and the two men became lifelong friends. Marsh's Sioux nickname was Wicasa Pahi Hohu, Man That Picks Up Bones, and in 1874, his Sioux escort in the Badlands called him Big Bone Chief. In 1877, a Sioux hunter brought the Big Bone Chief an amulet that he'd kept in his tobacco pouch, another great molar of a Thunder Horse.

In honor of the Sioux legends, Marsh named the fourteen-foot-long rhinoceroslike titanothere (an early relative of the horse) the *Brontotherium*, "Thunder Beast" (fig. 72). And he dubbed the tremendous, sixty-foot-long sauropod dinosaur *Brontosaurus*, "Thunder Reptile." Ironically, although no human being ever heard the sound, the *Brontosaurus* (later renamed *Apatosaurus*) may literally have been capable of creating thunderous sonic booms with its long, whiplike tail, according to a theory proposed in 1997.[29]

LAKOTA FOSSIL KNOWLEDGE IN THE BADLANDS
AND BLACK HILLS

In 1887, some twelve years after introducing Marsh to Red Cloud, Cook bought Agate Springs Ranch, in western Nebraska on the Niobrara River, and invited his Oglala and Lakota friends to camp each summer on the land that had once been theirs. Cook climbed the two conical buttes dominating the ranch landscape and noticed a proliferation of bones glittering with calcite crystals. He assumed that they were the remains of "an Indian brave . . . laid to his last long rest" with his favorite ponies.

Some years later, in 1892, a University of Nebraska geologist recognized the bones as those of Miocene mammals, and soon rival

SCIENTIFIC NOMENCLATURE DERIVED FROM NATIVE AMERICAN LANGUAGES

Marsh's way of honoring the Sioux myth made me curious about whether Native American languages and lore had found their way into scientific nomenclature for fossils. In fact, numerous species have been given names based on Native words. For example, the name of the doglike carnivore *Sunkahetanka* is Sioux for "dog with large teeth," and the primate *Ekgmowechashala* is Sioux for "monkey" or "little cat man": both were discovered near Wounded Knee, on Pine Ridge Reservation. In 1873, Joseph Leidy named a fossil carnivore *Sinopa*, the Blackfeet word for "small fox."

Quetzalcoatlus, the giant pterosaur of Texas, is named for the Aztec Feathered Serpent god, as noted in chapter 2. The pterosaurs *Tupuxuara* and *Tapejara* ("Old Spirit") are names derived from the language of the Tupis, indigenous inhabitants of Brazil. The name of the theropod *Ilokelesia* comes from the Mapuche (Natives of southern Chile) words *ilo* (flesh) and *kelesio* (lizard). The trivial nomen of *Megaraptor namunhuaiquii* is Mapuche for "foot lance."

Sioux words are well represented in fossil species. There are, for example, *Iguanodon lakotaensis* (an Early Cretaceous dinosaur); *Manitsha tanka* Simpson (a giant rodent); the aplodontid rodent *Campestrallomys siouxensis*, the anthracothere *Kukusepasutanka*, the fossil mammal *Ekgmoiteplecela* and the florentiamyid genus *Hitonkala*. J. Reid MacDonald of South Dakota bestowed Lakota designations on several Oligocene mammals, such as *Sunkahetanka*, from the White River Badlands. A new species of apatosaur from the Jurassic Morrison Formation in southern Wyoming, the first sauropod dinosaur found with a complete set of "belly ribs," was named *Yahnahpin* in 1994. During the excavation, the paleontologists (Filla and Redman, 1994) noticed that the in-place gastralia bore a striking resemblance to the ceremonial hair pipe breastplates worn by the Lakotas, who had hunted in the area. In the Sioux language, the breastplate is called *mah-koo yah-nah-pin* ("breast necklace"). In keeping with other three-syllable apatosaur names, however, only the latter half was used for the species.

Zuniceratops christopheri, a horned dinosaur discovered by Douglas Wolfe, was named to honor the Zunis. An Early Cretaceous marsupial of the Southwest is named *Kokopelia juddi*, after the familiar flute-player of rock art. The hadrosaur dinosaurs of the San Juan Basin, New Mexico, *Naashoibitosaurus ostromi* and *Anasazisaurus horneri* are part of the taxonomic nomenclature associated with *Kritosaurus navajovius* named by Barnum Brown in 1910.

The taxon of a very well preserved small reptile of the Early Cenozoic recently found in Wyoming will combine the Shoshone word for ghost, *tso'ape*, and Greek for the genus. The Crow words for "ancient thunder" were given to a new sauropod by Jerry Harris and Peter Dodson in 2004, as noted in chapter 5.

One of the petalodontiform chondrichthyians from the Upper Mississippian Bear Gulch limestone, in Montana, was named *Siksika ottae* by R. Lund in 1989. *Siksika*, literally "black foot," is the name for the Blackfeet nation, including the Piegan and Blood tribes.

The source of a mosasaur species, *Tylosaurus nepaeolicus*, can be traced to a local Indian name. The type specimen of "*Liodon*" *nepaeolicus* was described by Edward Drinker Cope in 1874 from material discovered by Professor Benjamin F. Mudge (1817–79) in the "gray shale of the Niobrara Cretaceous, a half mile south of the Solomon River," in north-central Kansas. The species name comes from *Nepaholla*, the old Indian (Pawnee?) name for the Solomon River meaning "water on a hill." In 1871, Cope had described the origin of material in the Mudge collection as "from the yellow chalk of the upper cretaceous [*sic*] of Kansas on the Solomon or Nepaholla River."*

* Thanks to Kenneth Carpenter, Michael Bell, Sean Bell, Craig Scott, Jack Conrad, Dave Lovelace, Mike Everhart, Ben Creisler, Thomas Holtz, André J. Veldmeijer, Jerry Harris, Peter Dodson, and many other paleontologists who supplied examples of Indian languages preserved in fossil species' scientific names.

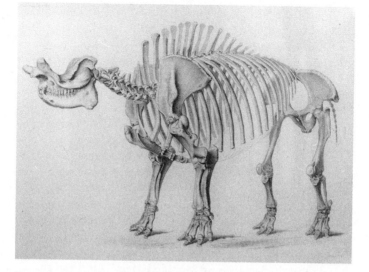

72. Othniel Marsh's Thunder Beast of the Badlands, the *Brontotherium*, a colossal rhinoceroslike creature of the Miocene (also called *Titano-therium*). Brontothere or titanothere remains, known as Thunder Horses to the Sioux, are common in western South Dakota and Nebraska.

paleontologists began arriving in droves from the East. From 1904 on, Carnegie and University Hills produced many tons of significant Tertiary mammal fossils, excavated by the Carnegie Museum, Yale, Princeton, and the American Museum of Natural History.

It was a mild autumn afternoon with scudding clouds in 2002 when I drove south from Pine Ridge Reservation, South Dakota, stopping at Red Cloud Agency (now Fort Robinson) to see the place where Marsh had met the famous chief. I continued southwest through a spare and beautiful landscape to Cook's old ranch, now the Agate Fossil Beds National Monument. I was the only visitor at the isolated site. First, I climbed Carnegie and University Hills to see the quarries—now gaping, empty scars—where so many tons of ancient mammal fossils had been wrested from the earth a century ago and dispersed to big museums. Then I viewed the dioramas and reconstructed skeletons of the peculiar species that lived here 20 million years ago: the grotesquely proportioned *Moropus*, a grazing chalicothere with huge claws, surprised by a pack of hulking entelodonts, ferocious brutes with fang-filled three-foot-long skulls (see fig. 64 in chapter 4).

Beginning in 1892, James Cook's ranch on the Niobrara River had been a gathering place for both Indians and paleontologists every summer for over two decades. One might expect such a cross-cultural haven to offer a unique opportunity for the two groups to exchange ideas about prehistoric fossils in the heady early days of American paleontology. But the promise that seems so obvious now went unfulfilled. Cook's sole comment is maddeningly laconic: "I heard a great deal of the Indian side regarding bone-hunting." Except for the well-known friendship of Marsh and Red Cloud, I found no records of communication about fossils among the Lakotas and the paleontologists from the ten major institutions who dug at Cook's ranch. Meanwhile, however, whites disputed the meaning of the fossils among themselves. One circuit-riding preacher declared that the "great mass of petrified bones" were dead animals heaved overboard by Noah as the ark floated over Nebraska, and another minister deplored the fossils as "toys of the devil."[30]

Today, the superintendent of the museum, Ruthann Knudson, maintains a positive relationship with the Sioux who have long-standing ties to the land. A buffalo-hide calendar painted in 1997 by Dawn Little Sky, a Lakota artist in Pine Ridge, is displayed in the museum entry (fig. 73). Traditional Plains Indian calendars, called winter counts, begin with a crucial event in the center and spiral outward with pictographs representing memorable events for each year. Dawn Little Sky began with the formation of Earth (a spinning symbol for earth, fire, and water), the age of dinosaurs (a stegosaur), and the extinction of giant animals (a pile of fossils under an arc, the Lakota sign for "gone under"). Her chronology continues through the Spanish Contact and the Indian Wars, up to the arrival of scientific fossil hunters at Cook's Agate Springs Ranch in 1892–1920s, and the 1965 bill creating the National Monument (fig. 74).

In 2001, Knudson commissioned a traditional cultural evaluation of Agate Springs Fossil Beds for the National Park Service. That winter, Sebastian (Bronco) LeBeau of the Cheyenne River Sioux tribe undertook a scientific and cultural pilgrimage to the fossil site to prepare the report. After consulting with elders at Pine

73. Traditional calendar made for the Agate Fossil Beds Museum, Nebraska, by Lakota artist Dawn Little Sky, Pine Ridge Reservation, in 1997. The calendar, painted on buffalo hide, begins with Earth's creation in the center and continues with events including the death of James Cook in 1942. Photo: Adrienne Mayor.

Ridge, Rosebud, Cheyenne River, and Spirit Lake Sioux reservations about the oral history of the area, Bronco LeBeau walked over the landscape, surveying the archaeological and geological features and describing their spiritual significance for the Lakotas.

Bad Medicine: Stinging Fossils

Agate Springs on the Niobrara River had been a traditional place for gathering food, finding special stones and other items for medicine bundles, and making offerings. Long before paleontologists flocked to Carnegie Hill, which entombs thousands of ancient mammal fos-

74. Paleontological events in Dawn Little Sky's calendar. Top: creation of Earth, rise of dinosaurs, and extinction of dinosaurs and early mammals. Left: paleontologist O. A. Peterson of the Carnegie Museum, Pittsburgh, begins excavations at Carnegie Hill, Agate Springs ranch, 1904. Right: President Lyndon Johnson signs bill establishing Agate Fossil Beds National Monument in 1965 (cannons represent the escalation of the Vietnam War). Photos: Adrienne Mayor.

sils, the Lakotas knew the hill as *A'bekiya Wama'kaskan s'e,* "Animal Bones Brutally Scattered About." It was a wakan place because of the bones, said to belong to Unktehi monsters destroyed by Thunder Beings. Young men came here seeking visions, and men and women gathered petrified bones for medicine (fig. 75).

But the startling revelation in LeBeau's report is that at Agate Springs the fossils were collected expressly for the purpose of *harm-*

75. Carnegie Hill, right, known as "Animal Bones Brutally Scattered About" to the Lakotas. (University Hill is on the left.) The masses of Miocene fossil animals were identified as the remains of Unktehi, malevolent monsters destroyed by Thunder Beings, according to Lakota traditions. Agate Fossil Beds National Monument. Photo: Adrienne Mayor.

ing ("stinging") others, not for healing or good. According to Lakota myth, the stinging fossil (*H'mun'ga*) ceremony originated at Carnegie Hill, taught by the malevolent mythic figure of *Gnaski*, Crazy Buffalo (Gnaski was the son of Unktehi, the Water Monster). Long ago, goes the story, Gnaski came upon a band of the First People traveling west along the Niobrara River to the springs. As they passed Carnegie Hill, Gnaski "grabbed up a piece of bone from the long-dead Unkte'gi monsters that laid buried there" and magically projected it into the body of a young man. Then he showed the man how to use the fossils to make powerful medicine.

Back among his people, the young man stung by the fossil bone began behaving frantically and violently, like a crazed bull. The first Lakota medicine man, Wata, managed to cure him and removed the fossil splinter from his body. Wata warned the people not to follow Gnaski's stinging ceremony, in which a wizard could "enchant, bewitch, or cause sickness" by ritually shooting a sliver of fossil bone into another person.

In the old days, LeBeau said, the Lakotas had avoided Carnegie Hill "because the fossils were considered *wakan sica* (bad medicine), and exposing oneself to the danger they represented was regarded as foolish." During his survey in 2001, LeBeau located ancient stone markers that had enabled people to avoid the forbidden area around Carnegie Hill.

"Unfortunately," said LeBeau, "people did visit Carnegie Hill to perform ceremonies and to gather fossil remains to make bad medicine." Collecting the bones and fasting for a fossil-power vision on Carnegie Hill were "easy ways" to obtain malignant spiritual power. On the summit of the hill, LeBeau found archaeological evidence of vision quest sites, the quests undertaken by those who wished to become a *H'mun'ga Wicasa* (Stinging Man). From the elders he had interviewed, LeBeau had heard many stories about H'mun'ga Wicasa traveling to the Agate area to gather fossils and make altars to Gnaski. LeBeau experienced an unsettling sense of anxiety and foreboding while on Carnegie Hill.[31]

Agate Springs was the place where the ritual for using fossils for evil sorcery first originated, but, as Sioux historian Vine Deloria remarks, fossils can be picked up throughout the plains. "There are many stories of medicine men using old bones and even giant skulls for rituals, but using them for an evil spell would be considered improper, as it is said that it comes back on you if you try to hurt someone else." Some Lakota healers still warn people not to touch any fossil bones, because they "possess very strong medicine powers." The stinging fossil idea is related to the early Sioux belief that claws, shells, and bones could be aimed and magically shot at an enemy, as recorded by early ethnographers in Minnesota and alluded to by Lame Deer. It also brings to mind the "irresistible *wakan* influence" issuing like magic arrows from Unktehi bones, first described in Minnesota by the Ponds.[32]

The legend about the evil use of fossils, published for the first time in LeBeau's report of 2001, sheds light on the oft-cited Sioux attitudes toward Ferdinand Hayden, the first white fossil hunter the Sioux encountered, in 1853. Histories of paleontology typically state that Hayden was thought to be a harmless lunatic, mentally ill, a crazy white mystic, or a holy man. His "madness" was thought to render him "safe from the wrath of the Great Spirit which smote any man in his right senses who became so inadvised as to disturb the great bones of the 'Thunder Horse,' " wrote Henry Fairfield Osborn. When the Sioux had dwelled in Minnesota, they collected bits of mammoth fossils for good medicine; and in the Badlands, too, a Sioux might keep a special fossil shell, tooth, or bone as a protective amulet. But those Sioux who also knew about the evil potential of fossils may have viewed the white man's obsessive bone collecting as more than just a sign of insanity or foolishness—it could signal malicious intent. No wonder many Indians gave a wide berth to the black-bearded, sunburnt "Man Who Picks Up Stones Running," who dashed across the badlands frantically filling his knapsack with fossils.[33]

The uncanny spectacle of the carcasses of so many species of extraordinary creatures emerging from the dinosaur graveyards and mammal bone beds evoked disquieting emotions in observers. As Vine Deloria commented, the incredible profusion and variety in the animal burial grounds certainly "suggested a major catastrophe." Modern paleontologists use the phrase "the mark of death upon the land" to describe the great disaster that resulted in the variety of fossil species so brutally scattered about at Agate Springs. Deloria cites paleontologist Richard Lull's figures for a single slab from the Agate beds, with remains so densely packed "as to form a veritable pavement of interlacing bones." A block measuring five by eight feet contains nearly five thousand bones.

In South Dakota in 1892, Edward Drinker Cope used morbid words to describe how, in the flickering light of a lightning storm, "I beheld the . . . skull" of a dinosaur in a mound shaped like a grave, in "an eerie-looking place with a poisonous alkaline pool just below." Ferdinand Hayden described his first view of the White River Badlands in terms of a vast cemetery: "All around us were naked, whitened walls, with now and then a conical pyramid standing alone." His party stood in a sepulchre, he wrote, for at the bases of the walls and pyramids were the skulls and scattered bones of long-gone creatures laid open by the "denuding power of water." The nature writer David Rains Wallace, who retraced Hayden's path in 1997, found the fossil hunter's vision fittingly "macabre and ghoulish," and somehow "prophetic of the bison bones and human corpses that soon would litter the plains." As Wallace walked along the same "tortured slopes" robbed of their bones over a century of collecting, he recalled the vivid Agate Springs diorama of vultures circling above hideous predator skeletons squabbling over a rhino carcass as a "gruesome . . . evolutionary *danse macabre*."[34]

The Race for Survival

Not only are the Black Hills surrounded by masses of vanished creatures from many eras, from dinosaurs to mammoths, but a curious geological depression also encircles these hills, a broad valley of red siltstone eroded through the greenish Morrison Formation sediments just inside a steep ring of Cretaceous hogback ridges. The racecourse-like landform rimmed with abundant fossil bone beds was noticed by the Lakotas, who created the myth of the "Big Race" to explain the conspicuous geological feature and layers of bones.

The Lakota storyteller James LaPointe recounts the tale. In the chaotic "first sunrise of time," before the existence of the Black

Hills, all the immense and strange creatures, including the "*Unkche Ghila*, dinosaurs," were summoned for a great race to bring order to the violent world. LaPointe's version of the Lakota tradition suggests a concept of evolution as a pitiless race whose results would sort out the species and decide which would survive.

"The land was covered with a seething mass of animals." At the shout, Your fate is at hand! the earth trembled under the impact of the beasts, and the sky was thick with circling birds. Around and around the racers sped, and, amid the groans and cries and roars of weaker creatures being trampled, the earth beneath the runners began to "sink crazily under their weight" while a huge mound began to bulge in the center. The rising mountain burst and spewed fire and rocks, mixing with the clouds of dust thrown up by the feet of the desperate racers. The animals were felled by flying rocks and smothered in ashes and debris. Now, say the Lakotas, the remains of the great racecourse are still visible in the Red Valley around the Black Hills, and the bones of mammoths, dinosaurs, birds, and other extinct beasts lie buried where they fell.[35]

In fact, during the Cretaceous and into the Miocene, intense volcanic activity and tectonic forces violently uplifted a seventy-five-hundred-foot dome of granite rock in the Black Hills region, and then rapid erosion ate away the ash and soil atop and all around the dome. The insights of myths like the one recounted above, had he known of them, might have led George Gaylord Simpson to revise his dismissive assumptions about Native observations and speculations about Earth's deep past. In the Lakota legend of the racetrack, one sees how observation and mythic explanation can yield surprisingly accurate perceptions, in anticipation of modern geological and paleontological knowledge.

Beaver Lodges at Agate Springs

One of the Lakota traditions about Agate Springs recorded by Bronco LeBeau is striking in its understanding of an enigmatic fossil that confounded the early paleontologists. Large corkscrew formations averaging 6.5 feet deep are visible in eroding cliffs in great numbers—"like a forest," wrote one paleontologist. These odd trace fossils have also been found as far west as Lusk, Wyoming, and eastward to Eagle Nest Butte, South Dakota. They were named "Devil's corkscrews" (*Daemonelix*) in 1892 by scientists who thought they had been left by the giant taproots of some monstrous, unknown plant. Even though fossilized *Palaeocastor* beaver skeletons were frequently found at the bottom of the structures, not until about thirty years later, in the 1920s, did paleontologists grasp that the burrowing rodents had made the corkscrews (fig. 76).

Yet the paleontologists staying at Cook's ranch each summer since the 1890s could have learned the truth from the Lakotas camped there. Observing the very same fossil evidence, the Lakotas had recognized the burrows of ancient beavers, and the formations were traditionally called *Ca'pa el ti*, "Beavers' Lodges."

The lodges and bones of the ancient beaver were of great importance to the Lakotas. According to the stinging fossils myth, even in death the stony remains of the monsters buried around Agate Springs posed grave peril to humans. To balance that threat, the Thunder Beings asked the animals whether any species would sacrifice themselves and become stone too, to counteract the negative medicine of the Unktehi bones. The Beavers volunteered, and that is why their fossilized bones and spiral burrows are now "always on hand to protect the people" from evil fossil power. It seems that the presence of a recognizable, benevolent species—the beaver—served as a comforting antidote to the spells that could be cast with the Unktehi bones. LeBeau noted that a Ca'pa el ti formation is visible from Carnegie Hill, to remind vision seekers of the ominous path they were choosing.

The protective power attributed to extinct beaver fossils helps account for the giant beaver tooth amulet worn by a Sioux friend of the father of writer Mari Sandoz, whose pioneer family ranched in western Nebraska in the nineteenth century. The beaver tooth was "four or five times as large as those of the beaver skull nailed up outside our house," Sandoz recalled. (The amulet tooth would have come from a Pleistocene giant beaver skull in overlying loess deposits, rather than from the smaller Miocene species at Agate.)

76. Top: Dawn Little Sky's painting of paleontologist Erwin Barbour discovering a "Devil's Corkscrew" in 1892 at Agate Springs. These trace fossils of the burrows of extinct beavers were known to the Lakotas as "Beavers Lodges." Below: park ranger next to a Devil's Corkscrew, *Daemohelix*. Agate Fossil Beds National Monument.

Familiarity with animal anatomy allowed Native Americans to recognize some large, extinct fossil species as ancestral to smaller, familiar creatures of the present day. C. Richard Harington, for example, was impressed by the ability of his field assistant Peter Lord, a Vuntut Gwitchin trapper from Old Crow, Yukon, to immediately recognize the limb bones of the Pleistocene *Castoroides* as those of a beaver, even though the skeleton was the size of a bear.[36]

At Agate Springs, the Lakotas identified the terrestrial Miocene *Palaeocastor* fossils as ancestral beavers despite the difference in appearance and behavior from modern aquatic beavers. Modern beavers make their lodges with sticks along rivers, but the Lakotas understood that the "grandfather of the beaver" had made the corkscrew burrows, demonstrating once again how accurate geological and paleontological knowledge can be expressed mythically.

PINE RIDGE RESERVATION, SOUTH DAKOTA

Early in October of 2002, I set out from Bozeman, Montana, for Pine Ridge Reservation to talk with Oglala-Lakota people about fossil legends. At Wounded Knee, the site of the massacre in 1890, I spoke with Eldon Little Moon. He remarked that "most people won't travel in the Badlands at night. They say there are some strange animals, like none you see anywhere else, maybe still alive from dinosaur days. Snakes as big as telephone poles. Sometimes you see them at night going across the road."

In 1906 the ethnologist James Owen Dorsey recorded the Lakota belief that the bones of "enormous serpents" in the Badlands could strike a person blind, crazy, or dead, a belief reiterated by Lame Deer in the 1970s. I noticed that Little Moon, like many other Native people, referred to fossil bones as vestiges of gigantic snakes or lizards. The petrified remains of large marine reptiles common in South Dakota do have snakelike bodies and skulls, but there are other logical reasons for the common association of all sorts of fossil remains with snakes or lizards of incredible size. In popular thinking, reptiles are associated with primeval times, and snakes burrow underground where fossils are found. Moreover, to

77. Spine of *Brontosaurus*, "Thunder Lizard," a stupendous sauropod (now called *Apatosaurus*) exposed at Bone Cabin Quarry, Como Bluff, Wyoming. Photo by Menke, Barnum Brown Collection, American Museum of Natural History Library.

an ordinary observer, the spine of any immense, unfamiliar creature partially eroded out of the earth resembles the backbone of a huge serpent (fig. 77).

I stopped at Bette's Kitchen in Manderson for lunch, where Bette O'Rourke fries hamburgers for customers in her home, on the site where Black Elk told Neihardt his life story. When I mentioned fossils, Bette and her husband urged me to seek out their most respected elder and historian, Johnson Holy Rock.[37]

After some searching, I finally find the dirt road winding uphill to the little trailer-home ranch, overlooking a prairie dog village guarded by a very large, limping German shepherd, friendly as a puppy. Johnson Holy Rock opens the door, a slim, cheerful man of eighty-four with tousled gray hair, wearing jeans, a blue-and-white striped cowboy shirt, and boots. I introduce myself, offering a box of wild plums from my backyard in Bozeman, and explain that I'm looking for the Oglala historian. He invites me in to sit at the tiny kitchen table, stacked with books and papers. "You heard I'm a historian? Well, that depends on what you want to know!"

Holy Rock moves aside some of the books and copies of treaties, court decisions, and the U.S. Constitution piled everywhere—the former tribal chairman is still very active in politics—and tells me about his people, originally from the Powder River in Wyoming and Montana. He speaks of the illustrious "diehards" Gall and Rain-in-the-Face, and his grandfathers, the chiefs Holy Bull and Holy Bald Eagle, who had a falling out with Crazy Horse. His father, Big Gall (Jonas Holy Rock), was about ten when he hid with the women and children during the Battle of the Little Bighorn (June 25, 1876), on the day General Custer and his army were rubbed out by the warriors led by Crazy Horse, Gall, and Sitting Bull. The afternoon flies by as Holy Rock recounts stories about the Lakota hero Crazy Horse and his assassination in 1878 at Fort Robinson, not long after Red Cloud met with Marsh at the fort.

Our conversation turned to Thunder legends. Johnson Holy Rock's father always believed that he would be killed by the Thunder Birds' lightning for disobeying their wishes when he was a young man. So whenever a big electric storm approached, his father would set all his horses free and go off to wait for the fatal lightning strike. Terrified, Holy Rock's mother would send the kids to find their father, hoping that their innocent presence would protect her husband from the Thunderers' anger. But their father would order them back to the log house, and they would obey, only to have their mother order them out again. "It's dangerous, making us run around in these pourdowns," young Holy Rock would complain, "We could be struck by lightning!" Throughout their childhood they had to run back and forth in the worst storms, dodging lightning and never understanding the fears of their parents until they grew up.

"These stories about the big bones of Water Monsters killed by lightning were before my time," remarked Holy Rock. "And anyway I was always more interested in historical events—treaties and wars." He chuckled when I told him about Dave Bald Eagle's similar response to my request for old fossil stories a couple of years earlier. Bald Eagle, a Miniconjou chief and tribal historian (b. 1920) of the Cheyenne River Sioux Reservation in South Dakota, had replied, "There are old stories about big lizards, big snakes, and monsters, but I don't know them. I'm not an anthropologist, I'm a historian. I'm interested in *history*, what really happened—I don't care about fairy tales!"

"We always knew this whole area was under water once," said Holy Rock; "there are plenty of fossils that show it. I remember one old story. These things were told from one generation to the next for centuries. We didn't write them down, we told them over and over. This story came from the time just before the [white] immigrants began to cross over the Missouri River."

A Lakota hunting party traveled down by where Colorado Springs is now. In those days, people traveled a very long way to hunt and explore and to get horses even further south than Colorado. These hunters camped in a high meadow one night, and there was a strong storm with thunder and lightning striking over and over below on the plain. Why was the Thunder so violent there, they wondered, what were the Thunder Birds trying to kill there? In the morning, they said, Let's go see why the Thunder Birds were so angry. They went down to the lower elevation where the lightning had been striking. They found a very large animal carcass like nothing they knew. They had never seen an animal like that. It was really big, and it had a strange, big, or maybe a long nose—so strange that they wondered how it managed to eat.

Looking at a map later, I saw that the hunters, traveling at a time before whites arrived in the West, had headed south through the Pawnee Buttes corner of northeastern Colorado, once excellent grazing land for antelope, elk, and bison. Pawnee Buttes is also one of the most productive vertebrate fossil sites in the world; "Bones Galore" is the name of one of the well-known quarries (most of the fossils are now in the Denver Museum). In 1870, Othniel Marsh discovered troves of giraffe-camels, entelodonts, bear-dogs, primitive tapirs, and immense brontotheres (titanotheres) in Pawnee Buttes.

When I told David Parris of Holy Rock's story, he suggested three possibilities for bizarre skeletons that would command attention. After the heavy rain, the hunters may have found an Oligocene titanothere or brontothere, the elephant-size, rhinoceroslike beast with a large, forked horn extending from its snout. Or they may have seen a Miocene entelodont with its odd, lumpy skull. Perhaps the animal was a Pliocene or Pleistocene elephant. Holy Rock himself leaned toward identifying the large, lightning-struck Unktehi found by the hunters as some sort of elephant or giant tapir.[38]

In northeastern Wyoming, *Mato Tipi*, "Bear's Lodge," was a sacred landmark to the Sioux and many other tribes, observed Holy Rock, who is involved in the movement to restore the Indian name. "Mato Tipi" appeared on the first army map of 1857, and the name continued to be used on army maps into the 1890s. But in 1876, the unique geological formation was dubbed "Devil's Tower" by white settlers. Whites tended to rename any mysterious—or wakan—natural phenomena the "Devil's" this or that—as in "Devil's corkscrews," and so on. The countless "Devil's lakes" on U.S. maps today were once known as "Manitou," "Wakan," or "Spirit" lakes, often because of their mysterious fossil associations.

The Indian mythology of Devil's Tower involves a monster bear whose claws created the distinctive vertical grooves of the volcanic column. The Kiowa "still tell of how they once found the ivory claws of this great bear lying at the base" of the tower. The nearby Belle Fourche River has Quaternary alluvial deposits, so ivory mammoth tusks could account for the huge ivory claws. Claw-shaped belemnite fossils in the Sundance Formation might be another possibility. Bill Matteson, paleontology student at Sheridan College, Wyoming, remarked, "With all the immense claws of dinosaurs that one can pick up in eastern Wyoming, the legend of the Devil's Tower scored by the claws of a monster bear makes sense." He pointed out that the surrounding land has exposed areas of Morrison Formation, which yields *Camarasaurus*, *Apatosaurus*, *Allosaurus*, *Stegosaurus*, and *Diplodocus* dinosaur fossils with very large talons (fig. 78).[39]

I showed Johnson Holy Rock the painting by Pete Von Sholly, showing a Thunder Bird battling a Water Monster (fig. 66). "Ah. Ah, yes, the setting of the old stories was something like this," he

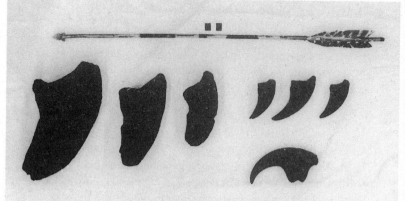

78. Dinosaur claws found in Morrison Formation rocks in Wyoming. Talons like these may have inspired legends that Devil's Tower had been scored by gigantic claws. Left: three hind foot claws of *Camarasaurus*, a sixty-foot-long, twenty-ton dinosaur. Right: three hind foot claws and one hand claw of *Allosaurus*, a thirty-nine-foot-long carnosaur. Arrow = twenty-four inches long. Sheridan College Geology Museum, Wyoming. Photo: James Yamada.

said. Pointing at the *Pteranodon*'s sorry little tail, Holy Rock laughed: "I always wondered how those creatures could fly with no tail for a rudder. Maybe the head was the rudder," he said, gesturing at the large head counterbalanced with a massive crest. "There was some natural animosity between these two animals. They were never peaceful, they were always enemies."

"When I was a boy, I used to ride my horse bareback up to Red Shirt Table, across the badlands, taking note of the landmarks so I could find my way back at night. On those rides I would see strange things, things I'd never seen before. I'd stop my horse and be curious and look more closely, rock formations, crystals, big stone turtle shells, big teeth and bones. Up on Red Shirt Table, an old man, a relative of Silas Fills the Pipe, used to tell me stories about the Badlands."

I knew that Silas Fills the Pipe of Red Shirt Table had been a friend of Black Elk's in 1896–1916, helping Jesuit missionaries on the reservation. There is a story that the two friends celebrated baptisms with war whoops and victory songs. In 1925–27, when Holy Rock was a boy, Silas Fills the Pipe was helping the Princeton paleontologists Glenn Jepson and William Sinclair, and other fossil seekers, on excavations with the South Dakota School of Mines. Several photographs of Fills the Pipe are included in the records of the expeditions (fig. 79).[40]

INDIAN FOSSIL SCOUTS

The contribution of Silas Fills the Pipe sent me combing through published sources and field books for evidence that other Native guides had helped earlier paleontologists find fossil exposures in the West. I learned that the fur trader Albert Culbertson collected fossils in the White River Badlands with his Blackfeet wife, Medicine Snake Woman, in the 1840s. One of their fossils, a *Titanotherium* jaw, was obtained by Hiram Prout, a doctor in St. Louis, in 1843 and sent to Joseph Leidy in Philadelphia, who wrote that the great stone skulls and other conspicuous fossils strewn across the Badlands "excited the wonder of the Indian." The first geologist to survey Badlands fossils, John Evans, set out from Fort Pierre on the Missouri River in 1849 with five voyageurs, an Indian guide, and an interpreter. They helped him find an eighteen-foot *Titanotherium* skeleton in perfect condition, with teeth as brilliant as polished steel. Evans's successor, Ferdinand Hayden, wrote in 1855 that he left Fort Pierre with "an Indian as a guide, one voyageur and a boy." Evans's and Hayden's guides from Fort Pierre were probably Sioux.

Othniel Marsh, as noted, had the help of two Pawnee Scouts and conversed with Red Cloud and others about Thunder Horse lore. To the Sioux chief Spotted Tail, Marsh explained that he "wanted very much to learn about the . . . great animals, which used to range [over Sioux lands, and] find their bones." Negotiating with the chiefs Sitting Bull, White Tail, and other prominent leaders, Marsh agreed to pay the Sioux warriors who accompanied him $1.50 a day (Sitting Bull had suggested $5.00). In 1874, for his first Badlands sortie, Marsh hired, through Red Cloud Agency, a party of guides and warriors led by Red Cloud's son, Sword.[41]

79. Silas Fills the Pipe, a Lakota elder of Red Shirt Table, Pine Ridge Reservation, holding a Badlands fossil (perhaps a canid skull), ca. 1925. Fills the Pipe guided and participated in several fossil excavations undertaken by groups from Princeton and the South Dakota School of Mines. Photo courtesy of David Parris, New Jersey State Museum, Trenton.

Cope's Young Indian Guide

What about Marsh's rival? Two anecdotes about Edward Drinker Cope's encounters with Indians have been widely reported: he astonished a group of Crow and Assiniboine men in the Judith River

Badlands, Montana, by removing his false teeth, and he suffered a choking fit during an attempt to share a peace pipe with the Cheyenne chief White Wolf in Kansas. As far as I know, however, only one reference to a Native fossil guide emerges from Cope's correspondence. Cope, as one historian remarked, generally "steered clear of Indian territory" and seems to have had little exchange about prehistoric bones with Native Americans. He was careful to avoid encounters with the Sioux in South Dakota because he recognized that they were "angered by trespassers on their reservation . . . and suspicion of white people who want to go on their land." Another reason may lie in Cope's Quaker pacifism. Unlike Marsh, who hired Indian warriors as scouts and bodyguards, Cope usually refused to ride with armed escorts. A couple of months after the Battle of the Little Big Horn in 1876, for example, Cope was warned not to explore without escorts along the Missouri River, but he and Charles Sternberg went anyway, despite the danger. The one time that Cope did rely on an Indian guide, his helper was a young boy.[42]

In July 1892, Cope visited Little Eagle, a settlement in Standing Rock Reservation straddling South and North Dakota. He dined with the YMCA missionaries Miss Collins and Miss Pratt, who assured him that the Sioux had long known the locations of impressive dinosaur bone beds. In his letters home, Cope related what the teachers had said about Sioux beliefs. The bones "belonged to evil monsters, which were slain by lightning," he wrote, and the Sioux refuse to touch the bones "for fear a like fate would befall them." Lightning is "always trying to find and kill" the huge serpents that burrow in the earth, and the ravaged badlands had been formed by lightning's efforts to destroy the monsters.

The teachers arranged for a Sioux boy to lead Cope to a particularly rich dinosaur exposure known to the Standing Rock Sioux. The next morning the pair set off and reached the spot between the Grand and Moreau river valleys at dusk. As "lightning played across the sky in forked streams [and] blinding bolts," recalled Cope, the "Sioux boy motioned me to him and showed me" a low clay hill filled with "numerous bones of giants nearly entire." We "could hardly walk without stepping on them. [And] so it was all around

. . . bones everywhere." The flashing lightning revealed a skull, over three feet long, of a duck-billed dinosaur. After eating supper with his guide, Cope went to bed to "dream of Dinosaurs," awakening before dawn to dig up the skull of the *Edmontosaurus annectens*. Over the next three days, Cope and the unnamed Sioux youth collected fossils from twenty-one different dinosaur species.[43]

Dinosaur fossils in that arid terrain were readily noticed by early white settlers, too. In the Grand River Museum in Lemmon, South Dakota, in June 2002, I saw *Edmontosaurus* and *Triceratops* skulls that had been dug up by a rancher in his pasture on the Grand River. He dug there because of a story in his family that, as a boy in about 1900, the rancher's grandfather had repeatedly told his parents he'd seen "a monster" in the pasture. In the winter of 1999, another rancher, Bucky Derflinger, investigated some "different-colored rock" on a bank of the Moreau River and realized he was looking at a very large dinosaur skull. He contacted Peter Larson of the Black Hills Institute of Geological Research in Hill City, South Dakota. Larson's team excavated the site in 2000.

The find turned out to be the ribs, vertebrae, and parts of the jaw and skull of a forty-foot-long *Tyrannosaurus rex*. But the paleontologists were puzzled when they came across scraps of old metal at the site, perhaps pieces of a wagon wheel. Stranger yet, the bones appeared to be stacked in an organized manner. Lichen growth indicated that the bones had been piled on the spot about a century earlier. Since the find was in the general area that Cope had explored in 1892, Larson surmised that the skeleton may originally have been discovered by Cope and then reburied. That year Cope had reported finding a big dinosaur that he called *Manospondylus gigas* ("giant, thin vertebra"), but the bones were too massive to transport back East, and so Cope's name for the specimen never became official.

If the fossil is actually the same one discovered by Cope in the area shown to him by the Sioux boy in 1892, the implications are far-reaching. The find occurred ten years before Barnum Brown's 1902 Montana discovery of the skeleton that was designated *Tyrannosaurus rex* by Henry Fairfield Osborn in 1905. The publicity surrounding Larson's idea that the *T. rex* on Derflinger's ranch was

Cope's specimen focused on whether the name of the most famous dinosaur in the world should be changed to the insipid appellation *Manospondylus* to register Cope's priority. Trace element testing was suggested in 2000, to determine whether the specimen matched the small *Manospondylus* fragments Cope sent to the AMNH in New York, but the Black Hills Institute has not pursued the tests. As Peter Larson's brother Neal Larson told me in 2003, "We are not in too big of a hurry to do that—it would be a shame to have to change the name of *Tyrannosaurus rex*."

Cope was not the only pioneer paleontologist to explore that area, however. As we saw in chapter 4, on the Custer Expedition in 1874, two Standing Rock guides named Goose and Cold Hand helped George Bird Grinnell locate fossil beds in the same terrain. Custer reported that Grinnell found a very large bone, four feet long, in the Hell Creek Formation of the Grand-Moreau drainage. Grinnell did not collect any specimens on that trip but only recorded their existence. Perhaps he was the one who stacked the bones of the *T. rex*? Paleontologist J. L. Wortman excavated dinosaurs in the same region in 1881. The identity of the person who first dug up the bones and reburied them may never be determined, but if it was either Cope or Grinnell, it would mean that Standing Rock Sioux guides were directly involved in the first scientific discovery of *Tyrannosaurus rex*.[44]

William Berryman Scott's Lakota and Crow Guides

Inspired by Othniel Marsh, William Berryman Scott of Princeton led several expeditions to the Badlands and Wyoming and Montana. I was able to recover the names of three of his scouts and found photos of two.

In 1882 at Pine Ridge, Scott hired a "half-breed" Lakota named Joe Richards. Scott, who admired the "value of oral tradition among people that cannot write," says he tried to learn fossil myths from Richards. The scout mentioned something about big animals occasionally coming to life to hunt with a mystical weapon that never failed to kill. Lakotas searched for this magic weapon in the

Badlands, said Richards, to rub on their guns as a charm. Could this be a reference, misunderstood by Scott, to bullet-shaped belemnites? Or was Richards alluding to the magical "shooting" power of fossils?

Scott's student Cornelius Agnew kept the logbook of the Princeton expedition of 1890 led by Scott and John Bell Hatcher the summer before the Wounded Knee Massacre. At Fort Robinson, the team hired Alick Mousseau, a Lakota scout of about twenty-five, probably a relative of the owner of the Mousseau Store shown on maps of Wounded Knee in 1890. Stout and muscular, "with black silky hair and beautiful eyes, Alick's appearance is most striking," wrote Agnew, who pasted two photos of Alick in the expedition album (fig. 80).

Alick was "extremely popular" with the students, and although he was illiterate, his knowledge of the terrain and Lakota history was "unlimitable." But the Princeton undergraduates, who crated up in sawdust nearly seven hundred pounds of White River fossils that season, were more keen to hear accounts of Alick's experiences in exciting Sioux battles with the U.S. Army than old stories about fossils. A few months after the Princeton team left, U.S. troops massacred 150 men, women, and children at Wounded Knee (December 29, 1890), thus ending the Indian Wars. I was unable to determine the fate of Alick Mousseau.[45]

In 1884 at Fort Custer, Montana, Scott engaged White Bear, a scout from Crow Agency, near the Little Bighorn Battleground where Custer's forces had been wiped out eight years earlier. White Bear could read maps and knew a "right smart of English," although Scott's brother (an army officer known to the Crows as Captain Metal Eyes because of his spectacles) "conversed fluently with him in sign language." White Bear guided the group to the Bighorn Basin, Wyoming, to look for Eocene fossils (the area also has Jurassic *Stegosaurus*, *Diplodocus*, and *Allosaurus* remains, as well as dinosaur trackways). For a week the fossil hunters survived on nothing but the "disagreeable" meat of a grizzly bear. But White Bear nearly starved because he could not eat his totem animal. Finally, the arrival of an old bull buffalo saved the guide's life (fig. 81).

80. Alick Mousseau, Lakota fossil guide for the paleontologists William Berryman Scott and John Bell Hatcher, South Dakota Badlands, 1890. Princeton Scientific Expeditions student photo album, Box 6, 1890, University Archives, courtesy of Department of Rare Books and Special Collections, Princeton University Library.

"We came to like White Bear extremely," recalled Scott. "With us he was always joking and playing tricks, but among strangers he became taciturn." White Bear led them west past the petrified forest above the Lamar River (Yellowstone Park) and found a flint arrowhead on the beach of Lake Yellowstone. Although some Crows be-

81. White Bear, Crow fossil guide who led William Berryman Scott's expedition in Wyoming in 1884. National Anthropological Archives, Smithsonian Institution.

lieved that supernatural Little People had made these ancient stone arrow points, White Bear explained that before horses and guns and iron, people had hunted buffalo with points like these. If Scott asked White Bear any questions about Crow knowledge of the large prehistoric remains in Bighorn Basin, however, they went unrecorded. Three years later, in 1887, when Scott published his survey of American fossil legends, he included no oral lore from tribes he met west of the Mississippi.[46]

CROW FOSSIL COLLECTORS

It was a sunny, cool afternoon on October 12, 2002, when I arrived at Crow Agency and parked by some painted tipis at the Custer Trading Post, a few miles west of Little Bighorn Battlefield. Putt Thompson, the owner, had promised to show me his unusually large rock medicine bundle, owned by a Crow in the 1860s.

Upstairs in his home above the trading post, we sat on the floor as Thompson reverently unwrapped the bundle, a process that revealed the age of the relic. The outer layers of fabric were fairly new, bright brocades, followed by a succession of older and more worn cloth, until we reached the last piece of faded, red-checked trade calico, more than 150 years old. There lay a gleaming ammonite, almost completely encased in fringed buffalo calfskin with light-blue metallic beads surrounding the opening where the fossil peeped out, glossy from rubbing. Attached to the bundle (about seven inches across, weighing about four pounds) were many other beads and small buckskin packets, plus the tiny hoof of an unborn colt. "My Crow friends say this old bundle should bring me good luck—but if it doesn't, they say get rid of it," said Thompson, who has many other rock medicine bundles made for him by medicine people on the reservation.

A new medicine bundle was always tested for effectiveness, and the number of attachments and beads indicated its successes in hunting, granting wishes, curing sickness, breeding horses, or protecting the owner. Beads and wrapping cloths were given as "offerings" to the bundle and could absorb some of the power of the "rock medicine." Rock medicine of the Crows and their traditional enemies, the Sioux, often included unusual fossils, especially ammonites and baculites.

82. Crow ammonite fossil necklace, ca. 1850, on rawhide string with blue trade beads. The iridescent ammonite is about 3.5 inches in diameter. Washakie Museum, Worland, Wyoming. Photo: Adrienne Mayor.

In July 2003, I drove to the Washakie Museum in Worland, in Wyoming's Bighorn Basin, to see another old Crow amulet dating to about 1850. The large coiled ammonite was covered with ocher paint and strung on a strip of rawhide with blue trade beads (fig. 82). The curators and I wore white cotton gloves to admire the way the rose-colored pigment brought out the rainbow fractals in the fossil.[47]

In November 2001 I had taken the train from Princeton to New Haven to view several old fossil medicine bundles stored in the collections of the Peabody Museum of Natural History. The first item on my list was a small ammonite "worn by a medicine man," acquired by Othniel Marsh in the 1870s in the Black Hills or the Bighorn Basin. To my surprise, however, the historical amulet is not kept with the other medicine bundles in the Peabody's anthropological collections. Instead it is stored with ordinary shell specimens in the drawers of invertebrate fossils in the Yale geology collections, in a different building. When the geology student working in the lab unceremoniously handed the ammonite to me, I noticed that the dark coils of the fossil had been rubbed with red ocher by the medicine man who once depended on its powers (fig. 83).

Back in the basement of the Peabody Museum, Roger Colten, the anthropology collections manager, carefully brought out a medicine amulet worn by the famous Sioux chief Gall (b. 1840), one of Johnson Holy Rock's ancestors who helped defeat Custer at the Little Bighorn. Gall's medicine necklace was purchased in 1902 from a soldier at Standing Rock Reservation where Gall had been a prisoner of war (Gall died in 1894). The necklace was a large ammonite mostly covered in hide like Putt Thompson's Crow bundle, and covered with numerous beads and valuable dentalia (or "tusk") shells testifying to its power.

Dentalia shells from living Pacific Ocean species were exotic trade items from the Northwest coast, and they are found in ancient archaeological sites across the plains. A recent analysis by paleontologist Jim Martin surprised some South Dakota archaeologists, however. A good proportion of the decorative shell artifacts from occupation sites of about A.D. 1000 in South Dakota turned out to be fossilized Cretaceous forms of the rare living species. It seems that people "in the hinterlands" copied the fashion for expensive, imported Pacific shells by using fossilized versions, locally available stone dentalia shells that they picked up from the Pierre shale.

Colten also showed me the "head and tooth medicine" bundle once owned by a Crow named Runs Away. The contents were kept next to the buckskin bag: a small white animal paw, a baculite, human teeth, and a large ammonite necklace encased in ocher-stained hide with heavily beaded fringe. Another medicine bag containing a marine fossil was painted red, brown, green, and black, adorned with red and white wool fringe and many beads: it belonged to White Man Runs Him, one of Custer's most famous Crow soldiers at the Little Bighorn battle. A similar Crow rock medicine bundle owned by Pretty Coyote was acquired in 1921 by the Museum of the American Indian in New York City. It is decorated with ermine tails, Pacific abalone and dentalia shells,

83. Ammonite fossil amulet from the Cretaceous Niobrara Formation, rubbed with red ocher. According to the original label, Othniel Marsh acquired the amulet from a medicine man near the Black Hills, South Dakota, or in the Big Horn Basin, Wyoming, in about 1870. Photo by William Sacco. Copyright © Peabody Museum of Natural History, Yale University, New Haven, Connecticut.

and nine scalp-locks, and inside—wrapped in twenty-one pieces of different colored calicos—are an ammonite and a baculite, both daubed with red.[48]

The Crows believed that curiously shaped stones and fossils were invested with *baaxpee* (*baxbe*, *maxpe*, mystical powers), and they imagined that sacred rocks and fossils, called *bacoritse*, could grow and multiply as though alive. "They were light in weight early in spring, but grew heavier by summer [and] in the coldest winter there would be frost on them, for they breathed," a Crow told anthropologist Robert Lowie, who lived with the tribe beginning in 1907. Gray Bull showed Lowie several of his bacoritse, kept in cloth wrappers inside a rawhide case. Bacoritse were often sewn into buckskin coverings and decorated with beads, teeth, and ermine tails, like the ones I'd seen in the Peabody. Two Crow elders, Big Medicine Rock and Spine, claimed that their bacoritse could summon bison, like the baculite buffalo-calling stones treasured by the Blackfeet, discussed above.[49]

Plenty Coups, the renowned Crow chief born in 1848, explained that a medicine bundle contains the spiritual power and talismans of the owner, and he commented that they could be quite large and cumbersome. The medicine bundle of the Blackfeet warrior Many Tail Feathers (b. 1835), for example, contained buffalo-calling stones along with many other heavy items, perhaps fossil bones. "It made a bundle that was a load for a horse!" recalled his friend Bear Head. Plenty Coups himself kept a buffalo skull from his vision quest for more than seventy years, although he was relieved that the spirits advised him that he was not "obliged to carry a heavy medicine bundle."[50]

Archaeological sites of Clovis and other cultures going back twelve thousand years exist throughout traditional Crow territory. This means that Jurassic and Cretaceous dinosaur deposits around the Big Horn, Pryor, and Wolf Mountains in north-central Wyoming and south-central Montana were known to Native observers for thousands of years before Barnum Brown's excavations of dinosaurs on the Crow reservation in 1903–4 and the 1930s, and John Ostrom's important fossil discoveries in 1962–66. In the scorched red, blue, and gray Cloverly Formation near Bridger, Montana, Ostrom's finds included a pack of *Deinonychus* dinosaurs with terrible sickle-shaped claws, and their massive prey, the two-thousand-pound ornithopod (bird-footed) reptile *Tenontosaurus*. The Crow people and their ancient predecessors frequented these same Cloverly sediments to obtain the intensely red minerals for paint. As noted by Desmond Maxwell, a paleontologist familiar with the area, the red pigment is most prominent in the dinosaurian layers, so it is highly likely that generations of Indians came across the remains of *Tenontosaurus*, *Deinonychus*, and *Sauropelta*.

Archaeologists discovered evidence that early cultures camped in the fossil-bearing area to gather pine nuts each fall. Maxwell studied an ancient occupation site in the Cloverly which demonstrated that the hunter-gatherers had deliberately collected the large, bony scutes of the armored nodosaur *Sauropelta* to use as hearths for the slow roasting of limber pine cones. They selected the fossil scutes instead of the more common sandstone rocks because the fossils provided a flat surface and—unlike the friable sandstone, which crumbles in fire—the scutes could withstand the very high heat needed to open the cones and roast the nuts.

Dinosaur fossils were collected by paleo-Indians in the Morrison Formation too. At ancient dwelling sites between St. Xavier and Pryor on the Crow Reservation, archaeologists were interested to find that large dinosaur bones had been used to line the walls of fire-pits. These and Maxwell's discoveries reminded me of archaeologist Michael Fosha's finds in paleo-sites in western South Dakota, where wood is rare. Here people cooked by heating large stones placed in hide bags. Fosha's evidence showed that in several prehistoric sites people had deliberately selected large dinosaur bones instead of rocks for cooking.[51]

On July 11, 2000, I camped in the Pryor Mountains on the Crow Reservation not far from Ostrom's famous *Deinonychus* site, on my way to visit Peter Dodson's team from the University of Pennsylvania. The team was excavating dinosaurs in the Morrison Formation on Bureau of Land Management rangeland near Warren, Montana, south of Bridger on the Wyoming border. The next morning dawned hot and dry, and when I arrived at Rattlesnake Ridge the temperature was over 100. I helped clear a Jurassic theropod skele-

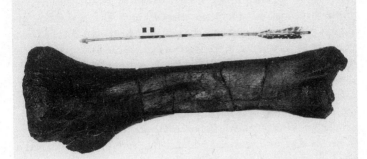

84. Shinbone (tibia) of *Diplodocus*, a huge sauropod dinosaur. Arrow = twenty-four inches long. Sheridan College Geology Museum, Wyoming. Photo: James Yamada.

ton with an awl and brush, and Dodson showed me some other dinosaur fossils weathering out in a gully nearby. That exposure turned out to be a diplodocoid sauropod (fig. 84). In homage to Marsh's "Thunder Lizard" appellation for sauropods, Dodson's student Jerry Harris named the dinosaur *Suuwassea*, Crow for "ancient thunder."

It was a much cooler day in October later that year when I called on paleontologist Michael Flynn and his student Bill Matteson at Sheridan College, Sheridan, Wyoming. They showed me specimens of Jurassic sauropods and other dinosaurs from their digs on private land between the eastern slopes of the Bighorn Mountains and the western slopes of the Chetish (Wolf) Mountains. (The Crow Reservation lands in this region and in the Pryor Mountains to the west are designated holy grounds by the Crows and are off-limits to paleontological surveys; see conclusion.) The paleontological wealth of the region convinced me that the Crows must have been aware of the remarkable remains in the hills where they sought visions.[52]

According to Crow historians, their name, *Absarokee*, meant a large bird with a big beak (or a forked tail) that had disappeared long ago, a possible allusion to an extinct raptor, such as a teratorn or condor. Crow people also told stories of "the familiar feud between Thunderbirds and a water-dragon," wrote Lowie in 1907, and ethnologist Frank Linderman heard many Crow references to water monsters and "alligators" in the 1930s.

That the Crows had a word for *alligator* had been noted in the nineteenth century, and it has been taken to indicate that they were familiar with fauna of the Deep South. But it could also have a fossil-related meaning. In about 1880, Chief Medicine Crow (1848–1920) made drawings of four quadruped reptiles, including an alligator that he called the "Big snake with legs." Notably, the skulls of large, extinct marine reptiles, crocodilians and mosasaurs, found in Crow territory do resemble those of living alligators. The ethnologist Ella Clark reported that Crow people told of alligatorlike monsters in the Tongue, Rosebud, and Little Bighorn rivers. Such reports may refer to observations of fossil skeletons of gigantic prehistoric reptiles eroding out of riverbanks.

It was frustrating that the early anthropologists never asked the Crows about finding fossil bones. But in 2003, I learned that modern historians and archaeologists digging with shovels and backhoes to recover the bodies of soldiers and horses at the Little Bighorn Battlefield often exhumed very large, prehistoric animal bones. One historian told me that he had spotted an enormous bone sticking out near the bottom of a ten-foot-high bank on Little Bighorn River. Large fossils like these help account for the stories of water monsters in Crow country. In 2004, Marvin Stewart, a Crow elder born in 1936, told me that his father, Francis Stewart (great-grandson of Sees the Living Bull), used to entertain his children at night with stories about Old Man Coyote and what Marvin now calls "the old dinosaur days." The Little Bighorn River was especially "treacherous due to alligators," he recalled. "We often find big alligator teeth," said Stewart, although he and most people he knew were more interested in finding ancient weapons, stone points made by paleo-Indians.[53]

On a stifling day in August 2003, the air hazy and choking with smoke from wildfires raging across Montana, I drove from Bozeman to Fort Smith on the Crow Reservation to talk with the medicine woman Alma Hogan Snell (b. 1923) and her husband Bill Snell, an Assiniboine from Fort Belknap, Montana. We talked about the various water monsters believed to lurk in deep river pools, and we discussed Chief Plenty Coups's close call, in the Missouri River in about 1870, with a water monster, a *Bulukse'e* ("large meat-eater," sometimes called *Buruksám Wurukcé* and sometimes translated as "giant lizard or alligator"). Nowadays the word can also refer to giant snapping turtles, which are known to drag cows into rivers. "I've seen giant turtles, as big as a table, and many big bones along the rivers," said Alma, who remarked that the Crow word for ordinary small turtles is *Ba-sha-re*, but *Dáa-ko* is used for giant turtles. Gigantic turtleshells are common Cretaceous fossils in the region: *Archelon* species can measure between ten and fifteen feet across.

Alma thinks that observations of immense fossil bones along riverbanks had something to do with traditional Crow images of water monsters. It's interesting to note that the Crow Reservation Head Start program recently coined a word for "giant dinosaurs" that incorporates the traditional Crow words for "very large flesh-eating animal" or giant alligator: *Bulukseeisee*.[54]

The eminent Crow historian Joe Medicine Crow (b. 1913) published a tale in 1998 about a Thunder Bird, *Sua'dagagay*, striking a water monster, Buruksám Wurukcé, with lightning, and he has spoken of the spiritual power of fossilized dinosaur eggs, which the Crows found in eastern Montana. Describing a Thunder Bird painted on a Crow shield cover that I saw in the Gustave Heye Collection in New York in 2000, Medicine Crow pointed out the two claws. "That's how you can tell it's a Thunder Bird and not an eagle. The Crow believe that the Thunder Bird has only two claws." In his 1998 book, the Thunder Bird is illustrated with only two claws. I reflected on this detail a year later, in the Field Museum in Chicago, as I gazed at the monumental skeleton of the *T. rex* named Sue; it occurred to me that a distinctive feature of *Tyrannosaurus rex* is that each arm has only two clawed fingers. Someone who discovered a tyrannosaurid forelimb with its peculiar pair of claws, and perhaps with the elongated, birdlike shoulderblade, might well have identified the fossils as part of the skeleton of some mysterious bird.[55]

The Mysterious Medicine Bundle of Goes Ahead

Alma Snell's account of the medicine bundle of her grandfather, the Crow scout and medicine man Goes Ahead (Basáakoosh, 1850–1919), captured my attention as a possible fossil find (fig. 85). Alma knew the details of his vision quest from her father and her grandmother, the medicine woman Pretty Shield, Goes Ahead's wife. Goes Ahead fasted for a vision as a young man (about 1870) in the sacred Wolf Mountains, and Alma mentioned that the rock circle of his vision quest place could still be seen there.

After a time, Goes Ahead noticed what he thought was a bird flying very awkwardly, unbalanced, as though the body was too heavy for its wings. It fell twisted at his feet, and he saw that although it had wings, it was not a bird, but more like a serpent—"lizardlike," said Alma. The body was long and heavy, "serpentine," with wings something like a dragonfly's and a tail. Goes Ahead picked up the strange creature, took it home, encased it in beadwork, and wrapped it up. This became his main medicine.

Goes Ahead always carried that bundle with him or hung it on a tripod by his tipi, and he took it along as he scouted for Custer before the Battle of the Little Bighorn. As the battle loomed, Goes Ahead and the other Crow scouts agreed among themselves that Custer was already a dead man, since he ignored their warnings about the multitudes of Sioux and Cheyennes massing for the battle. On that morning in 1876, Goes Ahead and his companions hid their shirts and leggings and medicine bundles in the side of a hill, tucked eagle down in their braids "so they could float onto the other world easier," and rode into battle prepared to die.

But Goes Ahead survived. After the battle, he went up to a pine-covered ridge, Squaw Butte, about three miles east of the battlefield. He climbed a tree and carved "his mark," an image of the mysterious creature in his medicine bundle. Alma's father often pointed out the ridge visible from the battleground, though he never searched for the "blaze" himself. Nearly a hundred years after the battle, in 1973, Alma happened to meet a historian named William Boyes at the battlefield. Boyes had a particular interest in

85. Goes Ahead, Crow medicine man, 1908. Edward S. Curtis photograph. McCormick Library of Special Collections, Northwestern University Library.

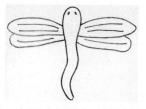

86. Image, about eighteen inches long, carved on a pine tree by Goes Ahead in 1876, after he survived the Battle of the Little Bighorn. It depicts the mysterious creature, possibly a fossil, that Goes Ahead found on his vision quest in about 1870 and placed in his medicine bundle. William Boyes, sketch from memory, 2003.

Goes Ahead, so Alma told him about the carving her grandfather had made (she did not mention Goes Ahead's vision or medicine bundle). Boyes went to the ridge and began to climb trees. He located the carving, about six to ten feet up the trunk of an old pine. Boyes took a Polaroid photo of it, and he sent Alma a map, the photo, and a sketch of what he called the "winged serpent."[56]

During my visit in 2003, Alma and Bill Snell were unable to locate the old photo, but I was able to track down William Boyes, age seventy-five, in Maryland. Boyes recollected that the image was not a crude trailblaze as he had expected, but "a careful carving about 15–18 inches long that must have taken hours to make." Since Boyes had no knowledge of Goes Ahead's vision or medicine bundle, I was very interested to hear his objective description of the image. "The body was a flying animal, like a lizard with no legs or a thick, blunt snake," he recalled, "but there were 2 wings on each side like what we used to call a Darning Needle [dragonfly]." Boyes sent me a rough sketch from memory in 2003 (fig. 86).[57]

This account and the sketch illustrate the serious difficulties of trying to interpret pre-Darwinian descriptions of potentially pale-ontological evidence expressed in mythological language. A vision quest involves hallucinatory experiences brought about by fasting. The combination of insect and reptilian features in the creature described by Goes Ahead poses a puzzle obscured by the passage of time and the metamorphoses of language and folklore. Interest-

ingly, the drawings of reptiles made in about 1880 by Chief Medicine Crow, mentioned earlier, included a "snake with wings."

One might simply say that the creature was imaginary, except
that Goes Ahead picked up whatever it was and took it home. The
fact that he brought back the physical body of a cryptic creature
from an area known to have fossiliferous sediments suggests that
he may have found unidentifiable petrified remains of some sort and
then experienced a vision of the flying, dying creature to explain the
find. Alma Snell agrees. "It could have been something prehistoric.
It was dried out, complete. Over in the Big Horn Mountains, people find other things like that—strange giants with big heads and
little bodies petrified, like they were freeze-dried!"

Paleontologists I consulted about Goes Ahead's discovery were
intrigued but mystified. The Smithsonian's fossil insect specialist,
Conrad Labandeira, has found Late Jurassic insect wings preserved
in the Morrison Formation, and Jeff Hecht remembered observing
a small, detailed insect impression in the Moenkopi Formation's
Triassic red rock in Utah. Triassic red beds and Morrison Formation sediments occur south of Bridger, Montana, near the Crow
Reservation. Many fossil insects do have long, heavy bodies with
dragonflylike wings, commented insect expert Cary Easterday,
but he also brought up the possibility that Goes Ahead may have
misinterpreted part of an unusual vertebrate spine with four ribs
outstretched, or he could have found part of a naturally mummified bird or animal. A piece of mummified dinosaur skin might be
another explanation. Jerry Harris noted that some plant fossils
have veined or meshlike textures that might resemble insect wings.
Another possibility might be a small, folded pterosaur or bat
fossil, remarked Jeff Hecht. The oldest known bats come from
the Green River Formation of western Wyoming. Michael Flynn,
a paleontologist familiar with the Crow Reservation lands, thought
Goes Ahead may have found part of a dinosaur or crocodilian
skeleton.[58]

Goes Ahead's medicine bundle may or may not have contained
a fossil. And we will never know, because in about 1900 he tossed
his medicine bundle into the Little Bighorn River, swollen with the

March thaw. As the women in the tribe wailed, he threw it away, along with all his other sacred possessions of bygone days, when he was baptized as a Christian.[59]

Pretty Shield and the Medicine Skull

A clear report of a genuine fossil find comes from Alma's grandmother, Goes Ahead's wife, the medicine woman Pretty Shield (1856–1944), although once again the details are meager. A childhood discovery in about 1866 persuaded Pretty Shield that "a tribe of giants once lived on this world," she told Frank Linderman, her biographer in 1931. The following account is based on what Pretty Shield told Linderman in sign language and through an interpreter, supplemented by the recollections of Alma Shell in 2003, who heard her grandmother tell the story many times (fig. 87).

"When our village was at The-place-where-we-eat-bear-meat," said Pretty Shield, "several of us girls walked up to The-dry-cliff" to play ball and other games till dusk. This cliff, an ancient buffalo jump, was a haunted place for Pretty Shield, where the accumulated bones of bison "told a bad story." She knew that before horses her people had driven buffalo herds over bluffs, and you could see the long V of stones that funneled the bison over the precipice (such Vs are a notable archaeological feature in Montana). At the base of the cliff lay "bones, many, many bones," but Pretty Shield could not take her eyes off a dark, burnt looking streak in the cliff face.

As the sun slanted into late afternoon, Pretty Shield, Hail that Shows, Shows the Lizard, and the other girls were playing "house" with the old buffalo bones, arranging them into tipi rings, when someone decided to dig at the dark soil at the base of the cliff. Suddenly, Shows the Lizard came upon a skull that was not a buffalo's. Further digging unearthed a huge skull—twice the size of a man's and with massive neck bones. The girls thought it was a giant's skull—even though it was nothing like ours, said Pretty Shield. "I noticed that the seam ran from front to back, straight, with no divisions."

87. Pretty Shield, Crow medicine woman, ca. 1895. This portrait was taken by Richard Throssel (1882–1933), a French-Cree photographer who was adopted by the Crow tribe in 1905 as Esh Quondupahs (Kills Inside Camp). Photo courtesy of Richard Throssel Collection, American Heritage Center, University of Wyoming.

Frightened, the girls ran home. As with numerous Native discoveries described in this book, the fossil find was verified. Pretty Shield told her father, a medicine man named Crazy Sister-in-Law (b. 1828), about the giant skull. He took up a piece of calico and a fine tanned buffalo hide from his tipi, and the girls led him back to the skull. At the base of the Dry Cliff, he told them to wait a little distance away while he smoked tobacco with the skull, taking a puff and then holding the pipe out to the giant. Pretty Shield could hear her father talking with the skull, explaining that the girls were only playing and had not meant to disturb the giant. Then he called the girls over to watch as he wrapped the powerful "medicine skull" in the calico cloth and rolled it up in the buffalo robe and reburied it.

Pretty Shield recalled that Shows the Lizard, the girl who actually dug up the skull, seemed to have no fear of it, and she suffered ill fortune in later life. The idea that removing ancient bones out of their burial places can bring bad luck is a recurrent theme, as we saw with the Navajo fears of fossils and Sioux traditions of evil spells associated with Agate Springs. Another striking example of this superstition appears in an Indian legend (probably Modoc) recorded in Oregon in 1900, about the bones of a water monster slain in primal times by Coyote near the ghost town of Bethel on the Willamette River, a locale where Pleistocene megafauna fossils often emerge. The Indians expected "evil to come upon the paleface who dug out and carried away its remains." The accursed paleface may have been none other than Edward Drinker Cope, who excavated fossils in Oregon in 1889. Cope reportedly also dug up the skulls of Modoc Indians who had been hanged after the Modoc War of 1873.[60]

The extraordinary giant skull found by Pretty Shield and her friends did not resemble a human skull or the bison skulls at the foot of the cliff, or any large animal, such as bear, known to the Crow people, a strong indication that it belonged to some species of dinosaur or extinct mammal. The exact location of the "Bear Meat" village was not known to Linderman, who speculated that it was near Headgate, the stone irrigation headgate built by Crow workers in the early 1900s. That would be along the irrigation canals on the east side of the Yellowtail Dam constructed on the Bighorn River in the 1960s. When I visited in July 2003, the Old Headgate Hiking Trail was closed owing to the U.S. government's fears of terrorism.

In August, however, I returned to Fort Smith and asked Alma Snell about the location of Pretty Shield's village and discovery. Alma said she herself had camped in the vicinity of the Bear Meat village, a campsite often used by the tribe in the old buffalo days. Commenting that the village site would be evident by the number of tipi rings (circles of stones used to hold down the bottom edges of tipis), she gave me directions to the Dry Cliff buffalo jump. As I drove west from St. Xavier toward Pryor, I saw an imposing cliff in the distance off to the south, a few miles west of the dam.

Later, in 2004, I learned more from Alma's nephew, Marvin Stewart, who used to do surveying work for the Bureau of Indian Affairs on the reservation. His late friend Wallace Red Star had told him in Crow that the Bear Meat camp was along Bear Coulee, a few miles from Dryhead Cliff. Linderman had translated "Dry Cliff" from Pretty Shield's sign language. It refers to the famous Crow buffalo jump once called "Place of Many Dry Buffalo Heads" or Dryhead Cliff, at the confluence of the Hoodoo and Dryhead creeks overlooking Bighorn Canyon. According to Joe Medicine Crow, this jump was distinguished by a vast accumulation of bison skulls and bones deliberately piled up at its base.

Dryhead Cliff lies within an extensive wedge of Triassic and Jurassic sandstone surrounded by Paleozoic limestone between the Bighorn River and the Pryor Mountains, which could account for the burnt looking streak that held the peculiar skull, as noted by Pretty Shield. The fossil may have belonged to a Mesozoic creature. The straight seam on the big cranium could refer to the more prominent suture dividing the skull of reptiles. The only sure way to learn the identity of the giant was suggested by Alma Snell, who asked whether paleontologists had ever investigated the Dry Cliff area.

"They would have to get permission," she remarked, but she was sure that if the scientists dug down about three or four feet, they would come to the great skull that Pretty Shield's father had wrapped in calico and a buffalo robe. "And I bet they would find some more giants' bones there," said Alma.[61]

"There were other things in the Crow country like that big skull, that told of people who came before us," observed Pretty Shield. For example, a Crow named Three Wolves had once taken the tribe to see a very large cache of ancient stone weapons in the mountains. Pretty Shield never forgot the sight of the beautiful red-flint arrow points, some long and slim and others very tiny, in a pile about fourteen inches high.

Ancient caches of prehistoric weapons and tools, made by Clovis and other paleo-Indians and well known to archaeologists, were discovered by other tribes, too. The Sioux attributed the weapon caches to the mythic trickster Iktomi, who liked to pile stones and arrowheads in round heaps. Pretty Shield explained that in one Crow myth, the first female, Red Woman, had bones of stone that were shattered by fire into myriad chips, and these accounted for the old stone arrowheads scattered everywhere.

The "medicine pile" of ancient arrow points was left alone, but people often kept loose flint arrows or stray fossils they found on the ground, observed Pretty Shield. For tribes in western dinosaur-rich terrains, a similar tendency seems to have governed discoveries of fossils recognized as the remains of large, unknown creatures. As Alma Snell commented, "The people *want to see* the large bones and skeletons, but there is the problem of superstition." A small fossil shell, a piece of petrified wood, or an isolated fossil bone, tooth, or claw could be safely picked up for various uses, but actively digging up large vertebrate fossil remains embedded in the earth or disturbing partially eroded skeletons seemed disrespectful and dangerous.[62]

Assiniboine and Blackfeet Fossil Knowledge
in Montana and Canada

"We won't leave this place until you find your own stone arrow-head," declared Wayne Archambault, who had already spotted five. I finally found a few just as the sun was setting. We were at the base of an ancient buffalo jump in northern Montana, searching among the old bones for tiny arrow points dated by archaeologists to about A.D. 800. The previous day we had searched for fossils, clambering up and down the ravines of Timber Ridge, south of Cow Creek above the Missouri in the Judith River Badlands (fig. 88). Many large pearly ammonites stood out, along with some big slabs of mica and a few worked stone artifacts, showing that paleo-Indians had frequented this fossil-rich ridge. Baculites—buffalo-calling stones—were especially thick there (see fig. 69).

I'd been introduced to Wayne Archambault by Chandler Good Strike, a Gros Ventre artist who paints drums and bison hides with earth pigments, in the summer of 2000. Wayne, an Assiniboine (Nakota Sioux) born in 1936, now retired, loves to explore the badlands for fossils and arrowheads after heavy rains. A well-read world traveler, he is also a photographer and maker of old-style lances for pow-wow dancers. In his modest house decorated with a fine collection of southwestern Indian pottery and museum reproductions of classical Greek vases, we sat on the floor to look at old photo albums. Wayne's father was born in Little Eagle, Standing Rock Reservation, where the Sioux boy had taken Cope fossil hunting in 1892. A photograph from about 1920 showed Wayne's grandfather, Tall Youth, and a friend, Rustler, with Coming Day, an old Assiniboine holy man (fig. 89). Wayne recalled that Coming Day, whose face was always painted red, was feared for his powers. Bill Snell, Alma Hogan Snell's husband, who also grew up in Fort Belknap, remembered Coming Day as "Little Red Man."

I asked Wayne about Assiniboine explanations of dinosaur fossils. "Well, when Coyote first created the world, there were a lot of mistakes," said Wayne. "Animals in the wrong terrain and eating the wrong things, like buffalo up in the mountains instead of the plains, and carnivorous buffalo, and so on. There was a lot of experimentation until nature got it right. The old myths say this all happened before humans." There were lots of old stories about how monsters, or "dinosaurs," were destroyed by Thunder Birds, Wayne recalled.

The Assiniboines who came to the Northwest in the late 1500s knew from their observations of vertebrate fossils that animals of immense size had once existed in Montana, according to the

88. Wayne Archambault, Assiniboine fossil collector, holding an ammonite that he discovered in the Missouri River badlands, Fort Belknap Reservation, Montana. Photo: Adrienne Mayor.

89. Left: Coming Day, Assiniboine medicine man, Fort Belknap Reservation, Montana, ca. 1920. Coming Day recounted an old tradition about a giant lizard in about 1930. On the right is Rustler, the first Assiniboine reservation policeman. Photo courtesy of Wayne Archambault.

ethnologist Edwin Denig in the 1920s. One Assiniboine name for bones of monstrous size was *Wau-wau-kah*. This was a "half-spirit, half-animal" imagined as a great river monster with long black hair, scales, and horns like trees. Myth tells of its violent death by the impact of a "thunder stone," a black projectile that came whistling out of the west with "terrible velocity," deafening noise, and a bright flash—a scenario that seems akin to the modern theory of an asteroid impact 65 million years ago. "My bones may be found," warned the Water Monster Wau-wau-kah, but unless the Assiniboines made offerings to its spirit, the monster vowed to create disastrous floods and block their trails with its colossal bones. At Fort Belknap Reservation, one Assiniboine told me that many traditional people still avoid traveling wherever fossil bones are obvious.[63]

A tale of the antagonism between Thunder and Water Monsters was recounted by an unnamed Assiniboine storyteller (perhaps Coming Day?) in 1909 at Fort Belknap. Long ago, some Sioux and Assiniboines camping at a big lake witnessed a battle between a Thunder Bird and a Water Monster on an island in the lake. The storyteller's grandmother had told him that as the Thunder Bird drew the writhing monster up from the island, the Indians' hair and their horses' manes stood on end from the electricity. The Thunder Bird's lightning ignited raging forest fires; then a long, terrible blizzard followed; and still later that lake dried up and many kinds of animals perished there.

The storyteller said that he had traveled to the dry lakebed to verify his grandmother's tale. He found an enormous turtle skeleton as big as a man and the remains of strange "horned animals." It seems likely that the tradition was a way of accounting for Tertiary fossil exposures weathering out of a dry lakebed, perhaps discovered by some Assiniboine and Sioux people after a fierce storm. The succession of natural disasters and climatic changes over time in the story—storms, fire, ice, and drought—helped explain observed geological phenomena.

Based on his own observations on a driving trip west, Wayne Archambault thought that volcanism may have caused a more gradual destruction of the dinosaurs. "All that lava in Oregon, Washing-

ton, and Idaho—that got me thinking about volcanoes and dinosaurs," said Wayne. "Maybe the eruptions blotched out the sun so
bad that the plants died, then the plant eaters, and finally the predators." Indeed, many of the dinosaur fossils in Montana are buried
in volcanic ash. I was interested to hear Wayne's alternative to the
catastrophic asteroid hypothesis. According to the most recent scientific theories, the mass extinction of dinosaurs was brought about
by a series of calamities that gradually shut down photosynthesis by
plants: multiple asteroid impacts, widespread volcanic eruptions,
and global wildfires, resulting in a dark, cold earth, a "fire and ice"
scenario that combines Archambault's speculations and the old Assiniboine story.[64]

Blackfeet and Ojibwe Fossil Discoveries

The Blackfeet bands in Montana and Alberta, Canada, were also
very aware of the bones of enormous creatures. Traditional painted
designs on tipis, handed down over generations, included images of
giant lizards that resemble dinosaurs, according to Blackfeet tribal
councilman Jim Kennedy in Browning, Montana. Kennedy believes
that the images may have been influenced by his people's observations of fossil skeletons of pterodactyls, mosasaurs, and dinosaurs.

The Canadian Blackfeet storyteller Percy Bullchild recounted his
tribe's traditional explanation in 1985. The first creatures were
many kinds of snakes, some with legs. These reptiles abounded and
"became overgrown," says Bullchild, "big, big in their form. Tall
and long." These creatures were dinosaurs, he added, updating the
old tradition. Great floods caused the massive dinosaurs to sink
"down into the soft mud-mire" while others took refuge on hard-
surfaced places, but even those places tipped the animals into the
mud. The great reptiles were covered with mud "so fast . . . that
they are found, in these days, intact." Bullchild's traditional explanation closely parallels the fossilization process along Cretaceous
lakeshores described by scientists.

The earliest documented discovery by Canadian Natives of large
vertebrate fossils occurred in the early 1800s. For many years, Indi-

ans (probably Ojibwes) had told of "Great Bones" in a landslide on the Shell, a branch of the Assiniboine River. Henry Hind explored Manitoba in 1858, writing in 1860 that the Natives "had long regarded these ancient relics as the bones of Manitou." Hind assumed the bones must have belonged to a whale, and he traveled well out of his way to examine some of them. The Indians had burnt and/or reburied the big skeleton, but some Métis (French-Indian) hunters brought a tooth and a scapula to Fort Ellice (or to Fort Pelly; the record is muddy) in 1854, and eventually the Great Bones were shipped to the British Museum, where they were identified as those of *Mammut americanum*.

Another early Ojibwe account appears in Hind's memoirs. Accompanied by his Métis guide, he met with Ta-wa-pit, an elder camped at Dauphin Lake. His tribe often collected salt on the Valley River where there were gigantic petrified bones. Hind's guide translated while the elder expounded at length on the appearance and healing virtues of the bones, which were ground up for medicine. Ta-wa-pit made a rough sketch of the skeletons and teeth in the sand, which indicated that these too were prehistoric elephants. As the Canadian paleontologist Edward Kindle pointed out in 1935, these early records of the First Nations fossil finds preceded Joseph Tyrrell's first scientific dinosaur discoveries in the Red Deer Valley, Alberta, in 1884—and it turns out that those Cretaceous fossils were also well known to local tribes long before Europeans arrived.

In some places in Alberta, there were so many bones of dinosaurs you couldn't help stepping on them, exclaimed one early fossil hunter. Jean L'Heureux, a Frenchman who lived with the Piegan (Blackfeet) bands in Alberta in 1860–90, wrote a survey of the geography and Indian customs. The Piegans collected iron oxide pigments near drifts of fossil shells in the Red Deer River and Bow River valleys, the same area where the Blackfeet tradition said the first Iniskim baculite or buffalo-calling stone was discovered (above). The Piegans also frequented Flint Knife Hill for its hot springs, lignite and other minerals, and numerous fossil remains.

L'Heureux accompanied his Piegan friends to an ancient lakebed and a three-hundred-foot-high coulee near the Red Deer River, where the Indians came to honor earth spirits. Among the tumbled rocks, they showed him many great bones of a "powerful animal," whose enormous vertebrae measured twenty inches in diameter. This fossil site was marked with numerous offerings of cloth and tobacco, and the Natives told the Frenchman that the "grandfather of the buffalo" lay buried here.

Like the Shawnees and Delawares who called mastodon remains "the grandfather of the buffalo," the Piegans associated the curious bones with the largest animal they knew. Their interest was spiritual, notes Canadian paleontologist David Spalding, but their interpretation was "scientific" in that they recognized the fossil animal's "antiquity and possible relationship to a living descendant," an insight that might have gained George Gaylord Simpson's approval. In this case, the massive bones visited over centuries by the Piegans belonged to huge dinosaurs, the ceratopsians, duck-billed hadrosaurs, ankylosaurs, and theropods first scientifically collected by William Dawson in 1874. Dawson was followed by Tyrrell, Charles Sternberg, and many others in what is one of the most productive dinosaur locales ever studied; the Red Deer River Canyon is now Dinosaur Provincial Park. In the park, archaeologists have found a Piegan vision quest site and an effigy figure overlooking the fossil-laden valley.[65]

In the Hell Creek and Judith River formations of Montana, dinosaur species include the thirty-foot-long tyrannosaurid *Albertosaurus*, the seventeen-foot-long ceratopsian *Chasmosaurus*, *Tyrannosaurus rex*, hadrosaurs, and other gigantic reptiles. In 1995, on the Blackfeet Reservation in the Two Medicine area, a Blackfeet fossil hunter discovered a baby *T. rex*, one of the youngest and best-preserved dinosaur fossils ever found (see conclusion). As I drove from Bozeman to the Fort Belknap Reservation, just north of the Missouri and Judith River Badlands where Hayden, Charles Sternberg, and Cope had discovered troves of dinosaur fossils, I stopped for a view of the Little Rocky Mountains, where the Blackfeet, Assiniboines, Crees, and Gros Ventres came to seek visions. Bill Snell, an Assiniboine of Fort Belknap who knows that area, told me that his tribe used to collect fossils near a warm spring on a bare hill covered with shells. A terrible water monster called *Bax'aa* was fabled to lurk at a spring there.

I wondered whether the creature was inspired by observations of the petrified reptiles that I saw displayed in the Blaine County Museum in Chinook and the Phillips County Museum at Malta. The curator at Malta, Nate Murphy, showed me some splendid theropod dinosaur specimens. Murphy's spectacular find in the summer of 2000 jolted the paleontological world. It was a nearly complete, naturally mummified reptile over twenty feet long, still covered in its scaly hide.[66]

Battling Giant Lizards in the Badlands

"No one has ever asked us these questions before," said John Allen, Jr., when I explained my research into Native American fossil traditions. "If only you had started your project a generation ago, when oral stories were still strong." I had arranged to meet Allen, an Assiniboine spiritual leader, at Fort Belknap Reservation on a windswept September day in 2000. Allen (b. 1953) grew up here, playing ancient Greeks and Romans (instead of cowboys and Indians) on horseback with bows and blunt arrows and wooden swords fashioned from snow fence slats. He loved the stories of Indian heroes battling dinosaurs in the *Turok* comic books, which he used to get at the store in Lodge Pole by trading in pop bottles.

As a boy, Allen often heard old hunters describe their discoveries of remarkable bones, and, whenever they set off to hunt, his father and uncle always mentioned a sacred site where there was a Big Lizard, in the badlands west of Fort Belknap. In 1990, said Allen, the Big Lizard bones at the sacred site were identified as those of a dinosaur. Recently, some tribal members found a giant bison skull in the Missouri breaks. It was worth five hundred dollars to a fossil dealer, said Allen, but after observing and marveling at the breadth of its horns, they left the skull undisturbed, preferring to regale people with the tale of their discovery.

In anticipation of my visit, Allen asked his mother, the storyteller-poet Minerva Allen, whether she knew any old fossil stories from her childhood. She remembered a story she had heard the old medicine man Coming Day tell to her grandfather Henry Chopwood in the 1930s (fig. 89). John Allen recounted her tale, with some asides that I have bracketed and identified as his.

A long time ago some warriors in a war party traveled a long distance to unfamiliar lands and [saw] some large lizards. The warriors held a council and discussed what they knew about those strange creatures. [They called these creatures *She X On*, meaning demon, bad medicine, or unholy—John Allen]. They decided that those big lizards were bad medicine and should be left alone. However, one warrior who wanted more war honors said that he was not afraid of those animals and would kill one. He took his lance [a very old weapon used before horses—John Allen] and charged one of the large lizard-type animals and tried to kill it. But he had trouble sticking his lance in the creature's hide and during the battle he himself was killed and eaten.

Like Johnson Holy Rock's story, this is a stripped-down, compressed summary of what was once an exciting narrative tradition, recounted by elders to the tribe on long winter nights. The tale was told to explain the giant lizard skeletons that littered Assiniboine lands. Allen and I agreed that Coming Day's story seemed to date to the time before horses (since the warriors carried lances), and that it appeared to be an elaborated account by hunters describing their discovery of a very large petrified dinosaur skeleton—maybe even a mummified reptile like Nate Murphy's recent find a few miles east of the reservation. The detail that the men had traveled a long way to unfamiliar lands suggests that the warriors may have been an advance party of Assiniboines as they migrated northwest into Montana in about 1600.

For me, the story of an attack on a terrifying, gigantic reptile to win war honors also brought to mind Cope's account of his discovery of a giant mosasaur skeleton during the Bone Wars. Describing the scene as if he were "battling that ancient creature" with jaws full of gleaming teeth, Cope exulted, "We attacked it with picks and knives!"

"What is it that urges a man to risk his life in these precipitous fossil beds?" mused Charles Sternberg, the famous fossil hunter with a mystical streak, in 1909. Sternberg thought the motive must be the deeply implanted hunting instinct, but taken beyond the simple "desire to destroy life." George Gaylord Simpson concurred, when he wrote that "the fossil hunter does not kill; he resurrects." Simpson and Sternberg were talking about the overwhelming desire to find and observe exotic, wild creatures "in their natural environments," even if—*especially* if—that meant observing the skeletons of long vanished, bizarre species trapped in stone. Sternberg always visualized those creatures as vividly alive. "The monster . . . before me now [had] glistening teeth as perfect as in the days when they dripped with the blood of its victims," he wrote after coming upon an immense marine reptile. "They are never dead to me," he declared, for "my imagination breathes life into 'the valley of dry bones,' and not only do the living forms of the animals stand before me, but the [lands] which they inhabited rise for me through the mists of ages."[67]

Coming Day's old tale, even in its condensed form, reflects the awe and respect that were accorded extraordinary creatures turned to stone in the earth, and it underscores the narrative value of the fossil record embedded in its geohistorical context. "Indians would have noticed such unusual bones in their lands for sure," Allen said. "They would stop and examine a dinosaur skeleton without disturbing it, and then they would mark the place so it could be located again."

It is the storytelling about the discovery that gives meaning to the extraordinary bones of animals from the deep past. "There is no need to possess the remains, except as a story," said John Allen. "And it makes a great story."

CONCLUSION

Common Ground

> We should be astonished by the existence of fossils and treat
> them with the respectful awe reserved for the very old.
> —*Fossils on Federal and Indian Lands*, 2000

NATIVE Americans observed, collected, and attempted to explain the remains of extinct invertebrate and vertebrate species long before contact with Europeans, and their cultural connection with fossils continues today. Their explanations, expressed in mythic language, were based on repeated, careful observations of geological evidence over generations. Search parties traveled long distances to verify reports of fossil beds, and some remains were deliberately excavated to confirm old traditions and to obtain fossils for special uses. Discoveries of fossil traces resulted in etiological stories imbued with a sense of deep time. Earth's history was visualized as a series of ages marked by different landforms, climates, and a succession of different faunas no longer alive today. The Native observers envisioned the extinct creatures' appearance, behavior, and habitat, as well as the cause of their disappearance, proposing gradual and catastrophic extinction scenarios. Some animals and plants observed only in fossil form were identified as ancestors or relatives of living species. Not only did many of the insights about Earth's past anticipate modern scientific theories, but some traditional narratives were revised to integrate new scientific knowledge. All these activities evince the stirrings of scientific inquiry in pre-Darwinian cultures. And as

European and Euro-American naturalists became aware of the significance of fossils in the New World, Native knowledge and guides actively contributed to the development of paleontological science.

In expanding the definitions of paleontological discovery and inquiry, this book takes up the tapestry begun by Cotton Mather, Thomas Jefferson, Georges Cuvier, and Edward Kindle. I have endeavored to gather enough dramatic evidence, backed up by rigorous documentation, to persuade even George Gaylord Simpson, were he still alive, to relax his stance as a sentinel of hard science and give in to the "temptation" to contemplate First American fossil discoveries and insights as something more than simply a "diffuse awareness of fossils." Would Simpson be convinced that Native American discoveries and interpretations deserve a place in the history of paleontology? That's debatable—by all accounts he was an "irascible man and very firm in his convictions"—yet I feel that this new evidence would encourage Simpson to reconsider his judgment. As Michael Novacek, curator of paleontology at the American Museum of Natural History, remarked to me in 1998, when I first began writing about the earliest recorded discoveries and interpretations of fossils in classical antiquity and among Native Americans, "It is important to uncover any inklings of the facts that fossilized creatures were indeed from the distant past, are now extinct, and have some connection with living creatures," ideas usually credited to Nicolaus Steno in the seventeenth century. "Any foreshadowings of these scientific concepts would be fascinating."[1]

But as Allison Dussias observed in her 1996 article tracing the legal ramifications of fossils on reservation lands, traditional beliefs "about land, stones, and fossils are not simply of historical interest." Because many of the traditions about land, stones, and fossils survive in the living culture of Native Americans today, they influence tribal members' interactions, for good or ill, with paleontologists who work on Indian lands. Native American fossil knowledge once enjoyed a mutually informing relationship with Euro-American science, but nowadays the two cultures often have clashing views of paleontology, especially in the American West, where conflicts over land and fossils are most recent and raw.

On my research trip to Pine Ridge Reservation in 2002, it seemed ironic that I arrived on Columbus Day, which arouses no celebratory feeling among First Americans. But then I learned that in South Dakota, a state with a long history of rancor between Indian people and the descendants of white homesteaders, October 11 has been officially declared Native American Day and is devoted to reconciliation. In that spirit, this conclusion explains some of the cultural and historical reasons for tensions over fossil resources on Indian lands. Two worst-case examples of fossil disputes are followed by several examples of how other paleontologists have forged good working relationships. The final section suggests that despite real cultural differences about the meaning and fate of fossils, there are also some surprising points of consilience between traditional Native views and paleontological science.[2]

CULTURAL AND HISTORICAL CONFLICTS

The chief disagreement between traditional Native Americans and paleontologists centers on the proper treatment of ancient animal remains that weather out of the earth where they have lain for ages. Both groups hold passionate ideas about the fossils. For many traditionalists, digging into the ground and removing such things as rocks and bones violates the integrity of the earth, the source of life. As the Sioux medicine man Lame Deer maintained, loose fossils and pebbles may be collected for special uses, but embedded fossils and stones should not be dug up. Even a medicine man "finds his stones on the surface of high buttes," said Lame Deer.

In the Indian worldview, the land and all the things that compose it, including stones and fossils, are hallowed, vital entities. Wovoka, a Paiute holy man, expressed this reverence in powerful language in about 1890: "You ask me to plow the ground! Shall I take a knife and tear my Mother's bosom? Then when I die, she will not take me to her bosom to rest. You ask me to dig for stones! Shall I dig under her skin for her bones?" Custer's Crow scout, Curly, voiced similar sentiments in 1907: "The soil you can see is not ordinary soil—it is the dust of the blood, the flesh, and the bones" of our ancestors and relations.

The sense that the earthly remains of past life-forms should be respected by being left in place was evident in each Native culture discussed in this book. People took notice of fossil bone beds, marked their locations, revisited the sites, and speculated on their identity and meaning, but generally refrained from taking away large bones except in special cases. This core belief was expressed by the Oglala leader Johnson Holy Rock in 2002: "Fossil bones should be left in the ground as they were found. It is not good to take them away and put them in a museum. If we want to understand them, shouldn't we go to see the animals where they lived and died?" Clifford Canku, a Dakota teacher, declared, "It is madness to take a dead creature from the earth and set up its bones in a building as if it were still alive!" The Navajo spiritual leader Harry Manygoats warned that it courts environmental catastrophe to tear fossils out of the realm where they now "live" in a kind of suspended animation.[3]

And yet, despite strong feelings that large petrified bones should remain undisturbed, there are, of course, many Native Americans who collect fossils for their natural beauty and interest, like my Assiniboine friend in Montana who dreams of finding a perfect pearly ammonite. In Oklahoma, traditional Comanches still gather mammoth and dinosaur bones for their medicinal qualities. Around Rosebud Reservation, stone turtles and hatching turtle eggs are treasured finds. Moreover, as the preceding chapters show, there were also numerous historical and legendary accounts of indigenous people who deliberately gathered fossils, sometimes even excavating partially embedded bones of great size. In the old days, these relics were obtained for special uses, such as healing, personal power or protection, trade, or historical evidence of past life. As Roger Echo-Hawk points out, however, a dream or vision frequently authorized the collection of a large vertebrate fossil, and the quantity taken was minimal. In contrast, many paleontologists today believe that scientific inquiry authorizes them to remove massive quantities of fossils for education and to preserve them from loss to weather and commercialization.

The fact that weathering causes mineralized bones to disintegrate is not disturbing to traditional cultures, for that seems good and natural, a way of returning a life-form's energy to nature's "hoop." This holistic worldview, with its nonlinear idea of time and appreciation of the sacred nature of the earth, differs profoundly from the Euro-American approach to science. Many paleontologists regard Native misgivings about sundering animal fossils from the earth as superstition and ignorance, and they wince to think of exposed fossil skeletons crumbling away uncollected and unstudied. Yet in the case of common species already well described in the literature, how many more plaster-jacketed specimens are really needed to further science? Numerous historical examples can be found of compulsive overcollecting in numbers that far exceed what is justified for scientific study. One notorious example is Fossil Cycad National Monument (1922–57), the only national park that actually had to be abolished owing to total depletion of the natural resource it was supposed to protect.

The 320-acre forest of fossil cycads in the southern Black Hills was one of the world's largest concentrations of well-preserved Jurassic-Cretaceous trees. In Sioux mythology, the petrified forests and the barren badlands were evidence of a great catastrophe in deep time, raging forest fires caused when Thunder Beings fought Water Monsters with lightning. The "forest of solid stone at the head waters of the Chayenne River," first described in 1811 by the Hunt Expediton in Dakota Territory, enchanted Edgar Allan Poe, who described it in one of his stories. In the 1890s, however, George Wieland, a colleague of Othniel Marsh, developed "an extreme interest" in the fossil forest and built a special railroad spur to haul away seven hundred logs to the Yale Peabody Museum. When the site was later established as a national monument in 1922, scientists acknowledged that the petrified forest had already been denuded of all visible specimens. Finally recognizing that most of the trees from the national monument were actually in New Haven, Connecticut, Congress legislated the park out of existence in 1957. Although the stripping of fossils on public lands is commonly blamed on souvenir hunters, amateur fossil collectors, and commercial dealers, pillaging on a grand scale was done in the late nineteenth and early twentieth centuries by professional collectors for famous museums, a practice now euphemistically referred to as "unchallenged research collecting" by "misguided researchers."[4]

Today, the National Park Service (NPS) cites the Fossil Cycad National Monument as a unique case of paleontological mismanagement. In fact, though, the impressive numbers of animal fossils that awed early observers at historic boneyards like Como Bluff, Wyoming, and Pawnee Buttes, Colorado, were also placed in museums; and substantial fossils are no longer visible to the public even in the sites set aside as national or state parks, such as Agate Fossil Beds National Monument, John Day Fossil Beds (Oregon), the Badlands National Park, and the birthplace of American paleontology, Big Bone Lick State Park. The spectacular vistas of remarkable, long-extinct creatures weathering out of the earth have vanished. Gone are the days when Marsh, scanning the plains while astride his horse, could count the skeletons of five colossal mosasaurs strewn around him.[5] Marsh's experience gives us a fleeting sense of what the great fossil exposures must have looked like to the First Americans before the arrival of white settlers and the unchecked collection of every large bone in sight. Science has been advanced, to be sure, but who can say something grand has not been lost as well?

The cultural disinclination to unearth creatures long dead is only one factor in the tensions over fossils. Compelling historical reasons underlie Native Americans' distrust of paleontological work.

Paleontologists commonly complain that Indians tend to conflate archaeology and paleontology, and worry that human ancestors will be dug up along with dinosaurs. But these fears are neither irrational nor unfounded. "The Indians connect paleontology with archaeology," explains Michael Flynn, a paleontologist who works on the Crow Reservation, "because they have had bad experiences with archaeologists who took human bones." Beginning in 1868, U.S. soldiers were ordered to collect Indian skulls for "science," and over the next decades, more than four thousand heads were removed and taken from battlefields, fresh graves, burial scaffolds, hospitals, mission cemeteries, and abandoned villages struck by smallpox and starvation. This deplorable episode in the history of science continued into the twentieth century, as the

skulls of Native men, women, and children were amassed by archaeologists and anthropologists—*and* paleontologists. Othniel Marsh,
George Bird Grinnell, and Edward Drinker Cope each collected
Native American remains as a matter of course during fossil-hunting expeditions.[6]

Marsh's Yale students described in popular magazine articles how
they removed skulls from burial scaffolds, and even included a
sketch of the activity. In Montana in 1876, Cope collected "a number of skulls and skeletons of Sioux" and attempted to load them
onto the river steamer that was transporting his seventeen hundred
pounds of fossil specimens. But this created "an uproar among the
poor white" passengers, wrote Cope, and the captain ordered him
to return the dead to their gravesites. Cope was indignant: "It is
not a nice job, taking dirty skulls from skeletons . . . and it is done
at some risk to life." Although he had to leave this load of human
bones behind, he was able to sneak out about a dozen other skulls
that he had packed in among the animal fossils. (Cope left his own
skull to science. Ironically, in the 1990s it was taken by paleontologists as a prank to numerous fossil sites across the United States.)[7]

The sheer number of Native American skulls and bones, amassed
for scientific study of now-discredited racial theories and still stored
in museums across the United States, strains credibility. In response
to that situation, legislation known as NAGPRA (Native American
Graves Protection and Repatriation Act) was passed in 1990, en-
abling tribes to recover human remains and artifacts from agencies
and museums that receive federal grants.[8]

Field paleontologists today repeatedly assure Native people that
they are interested only in animal bones millions of years old, not
in recent human remains. But some Native Americans, such as the
Shoshones and Bannocks, believe that ancient animals buried in
the earth should be accorded the same respect as human ancestors.
Others, like the Navajos, fear that dinosaur excavations might inter-
fere with ancestors' bones. Scientists often attribute such concerns
to ignorance of geochronology. But, beyond the fact that the early
paleontologists saw little difference between robbing fresh human
graves and excavating fossilized dinosaur specimens, burial customs
are another reason for anxiety about paleontology. In the arid land-

scapes where the most abundant large vertebrate fossils lie, the dead
were left exposed in the desert. Plains Indians traditionally placed
their dead on scaffolds, in trees, or on rock ledges, "where the wind
and the air, the sun and the snow could take good care of them."
This means that, just as the dry bones of buffalo herds from centuries past were scattered over much more ancient fossil exposures, so
human remains and artifacts from past centuries can overlie fossiliferous sediments millions of years old.[9]

A third reason for distrust of paleontological activity is the systematic removal of significant animal fossils from Indian lands without consent, often facilitated by the government despite treaty obligations. The legal ramifications of that history in the American
West was summarized by Allison Dussias, who points out that many
outstanding fossils now displayed in museums were taken from reservations beginning in the nineteenth century, often surreptitiously
and "with as little contact as possible with the region's native inhabitants, except when such contact, as with [Marsh's] Pawnee guides,
was advantageous." Her study of documented cases through the
1990s reveals that "high-handed attitudes toward tribes and disregard [of] tribal sovereignty" were not confined to the nineteenth
century but continue today.[10]

Recently, in 2001 in Morelos, Mexico, a dispute arose over possession of gigantic bones of Columbian mammoths found by villagers in a cavern long known as the "Enchanted Cave" near Chimala-
catlan. The discoverers carried the huge bones to the village for
public display on concrete benches in the plaza and refused to give
them up to government or museum officials. "Before, people came
from outside and took the bones," explained Aureliano Flores,
hoisting a huge femur onto his shoulder. "We are not going to sell
them. We want to build a museum for them here." Meanwhile, in
Nebraska, the Santee Sioux tribe requested that the University of
Nebraska State Museum acknowledge that the skeleton of a long-
necked plesiosaur excavated by university paleontologists in 2003
rightfully belongs to the tribe. The Santees did not ask for possession of the fossil but hoped for a label in the museum stating that
the marine reptile was displayed on their behalf. The university displayed the find on the museum Web site but argues that the bones

were on disputed land and that budget constraints rule out exhibiting the plesiosaur in the museum.[11]

In the early twentieth century, paleontologists often told Indians that fossils had no real value and accused Indians of greed when they protested their removal. The attitude is evident in a popular article of 1926 by Chester Reeds, associate curator of invertebrate paleontology at the American Museum of Natural History. Collecting Silurian-Devonian fossils in the Arbuckle Mountains of Oklahoma, Reeds was working on land that had been allotted by treaty to the displaced Choctaw and Chickasaw nations, and then taken away in the Oklahoma Land Run of 1889 and statehood in 1907. In 1909, Reeds was interrupted as he attempted to haul away "several hundred" specimens of the rare, spherical echinoderm *Camarocrinus* from an Indian's property. The land, noted Reeds, was good fossil-hunting ground because it had been grazed by Indian herds. "A full-blood Indian ride[s] upon the scene and say[s] 'If there is money in these rocks me want it.' You tell him," wrote Reeds, "that you are collecting them for a school, an academy. Your driver [apparently a local Indian] tells him that you are from the Great White Father and that you are taking the specimens with you and will acknowledge John Seeley, Indian from Coal Creek, as donor of the specimens." But for the record, I learned that it was Reeds who profited from the fossils. He sold the collection of 1,665 fossils to the AMNH for three hundred dollars in 1918. The AMNH archives contain no record of John Seeley of Coal Creek as the donor of the specimens, as promised by Reeds.[12]

As I gathered information for this book, some paleontologists who work in the West expressed fears that publishing the extensive evidence for Native fossil traditions not only would encourage tribes to ban fossil hunting on their lands but also might inspire tribes to use NAGPRA to request the return of fossils now in museums. "The days of the wild and free-roaming paleontologists are over," one Bureau of Land Management (BLM) paleontologist lamented. Traditional Native folklore about fossils may be an interesting subject, I was told, but it has ominous implications for the discipline of paleontology.[13]

Currently, NAGPRA does not apply to fossils, although "it is conceivable that a particular fossil might fit the definition of a 'sacred object' " or cultural item, writes Dussias, who suggests that NAGPRA might serve as a model for "the regulation of paleontological resources on reservation lands." According to the Archaeological Resources Protection Act (ARPA) of 1979, paleontological specimens are not considered archaeological resources or artifacts unless they are found in an "archaeological context." Deliberately collected and worked fossils like the Tertiary mammal jawbones, filed and painted with red ocher, found in ancient dwelling sites in New Mexico (chapter 3), might fall into this category, as would medicine bundles containing fossils. Dussias argues that since "prehistoric animals and their fossil remains play a role in the myths and healing practices of a number of tribes," paleontological resources ought to be recognized as cultural items like human remains and artifacts.[14]

In the course of my research, I noticed that some paleontologists are critical when Native people show scant interest in fossils, while others find fault when keen interest is evident. Several paleontologists told me that Native people they meet in the field show little curiosity about fossils. But that reaction could have a cultural basis. Among many traditional Indians, silence shows respect for sacred, wakan phenomena. This trait helps explain the Sioux chief Red Cloud's lack of response in 1883, when Othniel Marsh proudly showed off his fossil collection in the Peabody Museum. Red Cloud's apparent indifference to the bones—in contrast to his wide grin at the Winchester rifle factory—was much remarked on by the press at the time and by later historians. "The treasure of fossils in the Peabody Museum apparently made no impression on [Red Cloud]," wrote one. But rifles, unlike the bones of mysterious vanished creatures, were not sacred to Red Cloud. The cultural meanings of silence might account for what some paleontologists perceive as Native disinterest in fossils.

On the other hand, many scientists are under the impression that Indian interest in fossils is a brand-new phenomenon, driven by desire for profit. "Fossils have suddenly been incorporated into their religion," a BLM paleontologist told me. A historian of the Indian

Wars expressed the same opinion: "Indians are now claiming that fossils are of spiritual significance to them." It is true that the market for fossils has sent prices soaring in recent years, and some Indian people sell fossils from their reservations. But, as the traditional and historical accounts in this book amply demonstrate, the remains of extinct creatures were already an important feature of the cultural and natural landscape long before European contact.[15]

Another cultural difference, referred to above, is the natural weathering of fossils. The process evokes anxiety among paleontologists, as exposure to wind, rain, and ice means that some prehistoric evidence will be lost forever to science. Of all the organisms that ever lived, only a small proportion have been preserved in stone. The discovery of a complete fossil skeleton is a "remarkable intersection of fate lines," a unique and rare event, explains one historian of paleontology. In the first place, the chances that any animal of the deep past would achieve "paleontological immortality are exceedingly remote." And if the bones of an animal, say a tyrannosaur, do happen to mineralize and are preserved intact by burial over millions of years, that dinosaur will be found only if erosion brings the skeleton back into the sunlight. And then the ancient bones inevitably begin to crumble away upon exposure to the elements. To collect the specimen, the fossil hunter must act at the "instant of geological time between the exposure of the remains and their final disintegration." The window of opportunity to learn about past species is slim and ephemeral. As one South Dakota fossil hunter put it, even if every rock hound "went out and pounded every fossil in sight into powder one day, they couldn't hope to equal the devastation wreaked by a few hard freezes and a couple of good gully-washers." Refraining from collecting fossils only "saves them for the wind." "Nature is the greatest vandal," agrees paleontologist Bob Bakker. "There are specimens literally rotting in the ground as we speak."[16]

But perhaps most galling for many academic (and often underfunded) paleontologists is the possibility that amateur or commercial collectors will unearth fossils on reservations, with or without permission, destroying valuable contextual data in the process and placing the most scientifically desirable fossils in the hands of wealthy connoisseurs, thus making them inaccessible to science and the public. The popularization of dinosaurs and sensational fossil sales have drummed up a thriving market for fossils. On impoverished reservations—land once thought to lack any valuable resources—fossils can bring dollars.

Unfortunately, the tangled skein of treaties, antiquities laws, overlapping and conflicting jurisdictions, tribal sovereignty, and legal precedents has produced no clear set of rules to govern fossils on either public or Indian lands. Anyone can dig fossils on private land with permission, but fossil hunting on federal lands depends on many factors, such as the type of fossil, commercial value, purpose of collecting, which government agency has priority, and the research qualifications of the collector. Reservations are lands "held in trust" for Native Americans, but each tribe has a different treaty relationship with the government, which has differing obligations and restrictions on the land use. The nineteenth-century treaties focused on potential revenue resources, like forests and mineral rights, but fossils were never considered.

Technically, fossils on reservations belong to the tribe or individual landowners, and Indians may use their fossil assets for economic profit. But fossils with commercial value are deemed "fossil trust resources," and selling them to dealers transfers property rights. When actual ownership of fossils is transferred, the transaction must be approved by the government as benefiting the Indian landowner. Scientists who wish to excavate fossils on Indian lands must negotiate directly with the tribe (or individual Indian landowner) to secure permission to dig, and the tribe can impose special conditions. Legally, those fossils must be conserved under proper conditions and be available for exhibit, research, and public education, and the tribe can also repossess fossils held in trust at their discretion. Because the fossils remain the property of the tribe and the paleontologists are not claiming possession, government review is not required.[17]

In 2000, Congress requested an interagency report on how to manage America's paleontological heritage, entitled *Fossils on Federal and Indian Lands*. The report set out principles for future legislation but made "no recommendations concerning the management of fossils on Indian lands, since this should be . . . addressed by tribal governments." The government agencies and members of the Society of Vertebrate Paleontology (SVP) who contributed to the report advocate a uniform policy restricting the collection of all vertebrate fossils on federal lands to qualified scientists, with the fossils remaining forever in federal ownership as a collective national treasure. So far, however, court decisions about the custody and commercial value of fossils on Indian reservations have not clarified the issues. Allison Dussias reasonably argues that, given the trail of broken treaties and the long-standing importance of fossils in traditional cultures, each tribe should have independent control of paleontological resources on their reservation.[18]

Cultural, legal, and emotional conflicts over who should possess prehistoric remains and who has the right to interpret them recently came to a head in two complex fossil disputes, both in South Dakota. This pair of worst-case debacles shows how nearly everyone can wind up losing in the crosscutting tensions. Until some uniform agreement is reached about the stewardship of America's nonrenewable paleontological heritage, similar issues are bound to crop up between paleontologists and Native Americans on reservations with rich fossil exposures.

In 1990, the largest and most complete *Tyrannosaurus rex* skeleton was discovered on a ranch owned by Maurice Williams, a member of the Cheyenne River Sioux tribe. The find took place in the same region where the young Sioux boy led Edward Drinker Cope to find over twenty species of dinosaurs, creatures the Plains Indians identified as primeval water monsters killed by lightning. The 1990 find was sensational because so few *T. rex* specimens were known, but it was the legal decision on the ownership of the fossil that sent shock waves through the paleontological world.

Fossil dealer–paleontologist Peter Larson of Black Hills Institute of Geological Research (BHIGR) in Hill City paid Williams $5,000 for the tyrannosaur nicknamed Sue. The custody of the skeleton was immediately challenged, because the ranch land was held in trust by the U.S. government for benefit of the Indian landowner, and the government claimed that Larson's removal of the fossil from federal lands without permission from the tribe or the Interior

Department violated the 1906 Antiquities Act. In an early morning raid in May 1992, FBI agents, NPS rangers, and the National Guard seized the dinosaur bones from the BHIGR, "as if they were crates of cocaine," in the words of one reporter.

After four federal court decisions, it was determined that Larson had not committed any crime in digging up the dinosaur without permission of the tribe or federal agencies, but the courts decided that the rightful owner was still Maurice Williams, who should receive a fair market price. So Sue was auctioned off on his behalf in 1997 by Sotheby's. Within ten minutes it sold for $8.3 million, to the Field Museum in Chicago, which unveiled the reconstructed reptile in 2000.

The confiscation polarized the paleontological world. Bob Bakker called it an "academic jihad" against amateur fossil hunters, dealers, and private collectors. Douglas Wolfe commented that "no good—and less wisdom or precedent—emerged from that debacle." Academic paleontologists regarded the bidding frenzy for Sue as the worst thing that could happen to their discipline, fearing that Indian landowners would sell fossils to the highest bidders, and that profiteers would steal fossils from public and reservation lands. Meanwhile, legal representatives for Native Americans pointed out that the removal of Sue from Indian-allotted land without notification of the tribe was "simply the most recent example of paleontologists' historic failure to respect tribal sovereignty."[19]

The courts' opinions about Sue did not take into account Sioux traditions concerning fossils (the name *Sue* and its homonym *Sioux* is just one more ironic feature of this case). And yet one important aspect of the court decision is worth noting here, because of its inadvertent agreement with the Native concept that the sacred nature of the earth extends to the rocks and fossils found within it. The court defined any dinosaur bones embedded in the ground as "land." Both the courts and the Sioux agree that the *T. rex* dinosaur was an "ingredient composing the solid material of the earth," just like soil and rocks and the organic remains of any other creatures that turned to stone millions of years ago.[20]

Another paleontological crisis erupted in 2002 over the fossiliferous Stronghold (South) Unit of the Badlands National Park. Because it lies within Pine Ridge Reservation, the Stronghold Unit is held in trust for and jointly managed by the NPS with the Lakota-Oglala Sioux tribe. Without consulting the tribe, however, the NPS announced that excavations of Oligocene mammals in the Stronghold Unit would be conducted over the next three years by paleontologists from the Denver Museum and the South Dakota School of Mines. The fossils to be removed were titanotheres, also called brontotheres, the huge creatures traditionally known to the Sioux as Thunder Beasts. Accusations flew, and the Stronghold Table, an inaccessible, grassy mesa saturated in sacred history and bloodshed, was occupied by members of the tribe. The Oglalas accused the NPS of desecrating a sacred site that contains human graves, and of taking fossils from reservation land illegally held by the NPS. The NPS claimed that their excavations were the only way to halt poaching on federal land and prevent precious fossils from weathering away.

As of this writing, the standoff was unresolved. In 2003, Rachel Benton, the park paleontologist, echoing statements by other officials, dismissed tribal objections that the area contains human remains or artifacts, and suggested that the tribe jumped to the wrong conclusion because they misunderstood the NPS "nickname" for the fossil bed, "Titanothere Graveyard." Benton wrote in the official Badlands Park newspaper, "Since the fossil bed is over 34 million years old, it lacks human remains and is considered a fossil site, not a cultural site." She also mentioned that because of the "enormous economic interest in poaching fossils from the [Stronghold] Unit, it is very possible that this motivation is generating some of the controversy."[21]

According to NPS cultural resource specialists, no human remains or cultural resources exist at the Titanothere Graveyard. The park superintendent stated that "the NPS has no knowledge of any human remains in the South [Stronghold] Unit of Badlands National Park." But there is no doubt that human bones and artifacts exist in the area, as acknowledged in the official Badlands Park literature stating that the Stronghold is "steeped in history," holding "the stories of the earliest Plains hunters, the paleo-Indians, as well as the present-day Lakota nation." According to the park newspaper in 2003, the Stronghold Unit "contains many sites sacred to the Oglala Lakota and other American Indian cultures," and archaeologists have found artifactual evidence that paleo-Indian big game hunters of 11,500 years ago camped regularly in the Stronghold. Moreover, a tribal member was convicted under the Archaeological Resource Protection Act "for selling shell beads found near 800-year-old human remains" in the Stronghold Unit. As the NPS cultural resource specialist Marianne Mills pointed out at a meeting with reservation representatives in 1999, geo-archaeological surveys of the Badlands show that flat areas throughout the park are likely to have archaeological evidence of human occupation, while eroded areas constantly reveal the underlying fossils of extinct animals. Under the Executive Order on Sacred Sites of 1996, fossil collecting must not affect the physical integrity of sacred sites, and for the Sioux the entire Stronghold Unit is sacred ground.[22]

The area was called the "Stronghold" because it was said the guerrilla warrior Crazy Horse hid out there during the Indian Wars, and the area is sometimes mentioned as the site of his secret grave. In 1890 the Stronghold Table was the stage for the mystical Ghost Dances, the last hope of desperate people being forced from their land. That winter, many Ghost Dancers and their families gathered at the Stronghold. Fearing an uprising, the U.S. Seventh Cavalry cut down a peaceful band of Ghost Dance followers, 120 men and 230 women and children, an act now universally deplored as the Wounded Knee Massacre. The survivors escaped to the Stronghold Table, where they were slaughtered, according to the Oglalas, who say they have found human skeletons scattered at the base of the butte. The claim is supported by white militiamen's boasts that they killed as many as 75 Ghost Dancers at the Stronghold.[23]

Badlands National Monument was established in 1939, outside of the reservation boundary. But in 1976, the park's size was doubled by the controversial addition of the Stronghold Unit, even though it is part of the Pine Ridge Reservation (given by treaty to the Sioux in 1868). Park literature explains how that happened. During World War II, the U.S. Air Force took over more than 300,000 acres of the reservation and "cleared it of human occupation," driving 125 families from their homes. From 1942 through 1968, the Stronghold area was used as a huge aerial bombing range.

Old wrecked cars were painted bright yellow and scattered throughout the badlands as targets, and gigantic bull's-eyes 250 feet across were plowed into the prairie mesas.

But the favorite bombing targets were the bleached bones of huge mammals eroding out of the Stronghold cliffsides. According to the official NPS literature on the Stronghold Unit, the skeletons of the largest fossils in the Badlands, the elephant-size brontotheres, "gleaming bright white from the air . . . were commonly targeted by the bombers." In a grotesque travesty of the sacred Sioux traditions of Thunder Birds blasting with lightning immense creatures burrowing underground, the Air Force and National Guard gunners deliberately blew to smithereens the fragile bones of great animals that had roamed the earth 40 million years ago. "Hundreds of fossil resources were destroyed in the bombing efforts," according to the park information sheet.

The Sioux awaited the promised return of their ravaged land, but instead, in 1968, the Gunnery Range was designated the Stronghold Unit of Badlands National Park. The appropriation of this sacred area within the reservation remains a flashpoint for the Sioux. As Lame Deer observed in 1972, "The only use you have made of this land since you took it from us was to blow it up. You have . . . despoiled the earth [and] the rocks, which you call 'dead' but which are very much alive." Indeed, the entire Stronghold Unit is littered with dangerous live ammunition, from machine gun bullets to very large unexploded bombs, buried in the dirt and continually eroding out of cliffs along with the fossils. Park officials warn that "unexploded ordnance (UXO) of all shapes and sizes" poses a grave hazard throughout the Stronghold Unit and could detonate at any time.

Some Oglala protesters believe that the titanothere excavation plan is an excuse to collect not just fossils but also human remains, artifacts, and minerals from sacred land. For their part, the Badlands and NPS spokespeople seem unable to avoid making contradictory statements. To the media, for example, the fossil bed is described as a buried treasure that will help paleontologists understand evolution. But we're only excavating because we "have to," an NPS director explained to the protesters, "not because the paleontologists are interested. That's not it at all." When we remove the fossils and store them in Rapid City in trust for the tribe, stated another Badlands official, it is "just exactly as if they were still in the ground." That same official also claimed that Indians protest the NPS plan because they want dig up the fossils and sell them. But Oglala fossil collectors explain that they don't have the means to excavate such huge, heavy items as brontothere skulls; they sell only small, common fossils for meager amounts. The NPS considers this "poaching," while the Oglalas consider the Stronghold Unit part of their reservation and the fossils theirs to manage.[24]

The history of Stronghold Table is so fraught with violence and government-sponsored destruction that the NPS project seems remarkably ill-advised. The Denver Museum and the South Dakota School of Mines withdrew from the project in 2002. In 2003 the Badlands paleontologist stated that the NPS is "negotiating with the Oglala Sioux Tribe to complete the excavation." And in summer of 2004, the park superintendent, William Supernaugh, told me he was "optimistic" that the dispute would be resolved to allow scientific collection of the fossils. It's difficult to see how the chain of violence and broken promises—not to mention the government's own past destruction of the fossil resources—can ever be set right now, except through an acknowledgment that the tribe controls the cultural and paleontological resources in the Stronghold Unit inside their reservation.

Thankfully, few fossil sites have a legacy as bitter as the Stronghold, where "outrage and accusations flow like acid rain."[25] Other paleontologists, working with permission and goodwill on other reservations throughout the West, realize that trust, compromise, education, and tangible benefits are the keys to paleontological partnerships on reservations.

PALEONTOLOGICAL RAPPORT

In my research I came across several examples of positive interactions between modern paleontology and traditional views, beginning with my experience of excavating marine reptiles on the Crow

Creek Sioux Reservation in South Dakota. Since the 1980s, the co-leaders of the field camp, Jim Martin (Museum of Geology, South Dakota School of Mines) and David Parris (curator of natural history, New Jersey State Museum), have had a working agreement with the Crow Creek tribe about removing Cretaceous mosasaur, plesiosaur, turtle, fish, and pterosaur fossils to Rapid City for study (the fossils remain the property of the tribe).

In 1995, the Outreach Committee of the Society of Vertebrate Paleontology initiated an offer of cooperation and partnership with Native American groups. The SVP paleontologists agreed to provide amateur Indian fossil collectors with historical and scientific information about identifying and preserving fossils and advice about establishing museums or interpretive centers on reservations, which would showcase fossils for tourists and create jobs. As a member of the Outreach Committee, David Parris has broadened the effort to assist tribes that hope to create museums for fossils on reservations. Parris sent out public notices of the SVP's offer of assistance to local media and tribal members. "Where tradition permits, [fossils] may be major attractions in tribal museums and should be regarded as important scientific resources. Discoveries of fossils frequently are made by amateurs," he wrote. For example, "Lee Azure of the Crow Creek Tribe has found hundreds of important specimens, which are being studied by many scientists and which have brought great recognition to the Crow Creek people."

Building accredited museums with facilities for fossil conservation is expensive, of course, and currently no funding support exists for establishing them on reservations. Parris suggests that reservations apply for grants and try to attract philanthropy, but he also pointed out that tribal colleges and visitor centers may already have rooms suitable for preserving and displaying fossils. Such centers for fossil education and tourists would bring economic benefits, says Parris, and tribal members could also create and control sales of replicas, casts, and photographs of fossils.

These SVP proposals assume that Native Americans have full rights to manage fossils on their lands and are motivated to retain fossils as rare antiquities of natural, cultural, and scientific significance, instead of selling them to high bidders. But the rewards of partnerships with academic paleontologists must be substantial and tangible. "It is no secret that offers of mutual friendship and assistance to the various tribes historically were often more theoretical than real," acknowledges Parris, with the "benefits typically lopsided" in favor of the scientists.[26]

I spoke with Michael Flynn, at Sheridan College (Sheridan, Wyoming), about his relationship with the Crow tribal council, whose reservation contains significant dinosaur fossils. Flynn's connection with the tribe began in about 1980 and grew out the fact that Crow students majoring in geology attend Sheridan College. His "science" agreement with the tribal council, which is renegotiated every three years or so, specifies that Flynn may take students on field surveys on the reservation, but under strict conditions. "We can measure and examine the geology, but are forbidden to make maps of fossil locations. We cannot pick up any fossils, not even common seashells and not even rocks," says Flynn, because "the land and everything on it is Crow heritage." Moreover, Flynn must not enter the "holy areas," the eastern slopes of the northern Bighorn Mountains and the Wolf Mountains, where the medicine man Goes Ahead found a strange creature, possibly a fossil, during his vision quest (chapter 5). Flynn points out that the Hell Creek formations in the eastern, off-limits parts of the reservation probably contain abundant large vertebrate fossils. Even though he cannot map or collect, Flynn feels that his students gain valuable field experience during the time spent on the reservation.[27]

In Arizona, Timothy Rowe excavates dinosaur fossils with the permission of the Navajo nation and holds them in trust in the University of Texas lab in Austin, until the tribe has "the capability to conserve and display them." To give something in return for the Navajos' contributions to science, Rowe offers scholarships to Navajo students to study paleontology at the University of Texas, and he posts photos and information about Navajo land dinosaurs on the Web.

Rowe also enlisted the help of a teen group, the Navajo Eco-Scouts, who located and excavated dinosaur fossils with the Texas paleontologists in cliffs southeast of Jesse Williams's *Dilophosaurus* site and the Moenave dinosaur tracksite. The Eco-Scouts, excited about Hollywood movies featuring dinosaurs, such as the *Jurassic Park* series, "were motivated by similarities to their traditional Monster Slayer myths to find monsters killed by the Monster Slayers in their own backyards."

Rowe is sympathetic to the Navajo holistic worldview and traditions, and has discussed his excavations with the spiritual leader Harry Manygoats. Despite his feeling that digging up fossils is not right, Manygoats understands that paleontological discoveries help make Navajo land important in the modern world, and hopes that Rowe's scientific and educational outreach will help Navajo youth see why their land and its resources are worth conserving and understanding.

According to Rowe, it would violate the requirements of his Navajo permits and the Antiquities Act to return the excavated skeletons before they could be properly cared for in a museum, something he often explains to Navajos who ask why he is transporting their fossils to Texas. In 1974, when the *Pentaceratops* dinosaur, described at the beginning of chapter 3 (fig. 30), was excavated by the Museum of Northern Arizona, some Navajos wanted the twenty-five-foot "monster" to be kept at the Burnham Trading Post, but the skeleton would have been exposed to the elements outside under a tin roof. "That is why the Navajo Nation paleontology collection is housed in Flagstaff, Berkeley, Denver, Austin, Texas, and New York," says Rowe. "I wish the situation were simpler. Although the fossils are not physically kept on tribal lands, at least the tribal collections are being cared for and are available for study."[28]

Controversy as to who has the right to display fossils from Indian lands is a complex, unresolved issue. Resentment over Sam Welles's appropriation of the *Dilophosaurus* flared up in 1998, when the Arizona state senate attempted to name the *Dilophosaurus* the state dinosaur. The Navajo nation contends that the *Dilophosaurus* skeletons were taken illegally by Sam Welles to the University of California Museum at Berkeley (fig. 39). "Designation of this specimen would constitute de facto approval by the Legislature . . . of the illegal act of removing the specimen," protested Bessie Yellowhair on behalf of the tribe.[29]

From Timothy Rowe, who had worked with Sam Welles, I learned a forgotten piece of history about the contested dinosaur: Welles had given a cast of the *Dilophosaurus* skeleton to the Navajo nation as a gesture of goodwill. "It was a beautiful display," recalls Rowe, and he often went to see it in the old tribal museum at Window Rock. But after the new multimillion-dollar museum was opened in Window Rock in 1997, Rowe noticed that the dinosaur cast was not on display.

Eager to find out what had happened to the historic cast, I contacted archivists at Berkeley. After the fossil's arrival in Berkeley in 1942, graduate student Wann Langston, Jr. (now a University of Texas paleontologist emeritus), prepared a bas relief wall mount of the original *Dilophosaurus* skeleton and two plaster casts. Decades later, in 1970, the University of California Museum curator wrote to the Navajo tribal chairman, acknowledging the "strong feeling among the Navajo Tribe that this dinosaur should be returned to their custody." The letter was intended to smooth the way for further excavations by Sam Welles on the reservation.

Since 1955, the Navajos had required that all specimens must be returned to the tribal museum after study by scientists, but the curator argued that scientific study was perpetual and that it was impossible to transport the fragile dinosaur fossil back to Arizona. Instead, he offered a fiberglass or plaster cast of Wann Langston's wall mount, along with all the scientific reports of Welles's excavation and a drawing of the double-crested *Dilophosaurus* as it appeared in life by an artist at the California Academy of Sciences. He also offered a replica skull of a phytosaur, the large crocodile-like reptile whose fossils were identified by traditional Navajos as those of the monster Yeitso and whose teeth were collected for medicine (fig. 34).[30]

The Navajo tribe received the *Dilophosaurus* cast in June 1970 and placed it in the old tribal museum, a quonset hut at the fairgrounds in Window Rock. Had it been misplaced in the move to the new museum in 1997? In 2003, I contacted the curator of the new Navajo Nation Museum, Clarenda Begay. She was not aware of any large dinosaur casts in the museum collections. "The old tribal museum collection in the quonset hut was put together by an Anglo," she pointed out, "and he mixed fossil bones and artifacts together. The new museum is arranged in the Navajo way, and we don't display any fossils." Then, suddenly, she remembered something. "Is that cast *really big*?" she asked. I told her the dinosaur was about twenty feet long. "Then I know where it is! It's in the museum gift shop. It used to hang on the wall there but now it's on the floor, leaning against the wall."

The museum's director, Geoffrey Brown, gave me the full story in 2004. Shortly after his arrival in 1999, he brought the cast out of storage and, for want of space, placed it on display in the gift shop. There was a lot of curiosity about the dinosaur and its history, but the story of its original discovery was not generally known. Brown intends to add the important *Dilophosaurus* cast to the museum's catalog, and he hopes to create an exhibit of paleontology at the museum someday, using casts of dinosaurs discovered on the reservation.[31]

A true fossil homecoming was celebrated recently on the Blackfeet Reservation in Montana, where significant dinosaur specimens had been collected by the AMNH, the Smithsonian, and the Royal Tyrrell Museum in Canada, beginning in about 1910. In 1995, a Blackfeet rancher named Dale Fenner had discovered a nearly complete dinosaur skeleton. Jack Horner, curator of the Museum of the Rockies in Bozeman, identified it as the smallest, youngest tyrannosaur fossil ever found, "an absolutely exquisite specimen that every museum in the world would love to have."

The creature was about two years old when it died and was covered with mud in a stream flowing from the fledgling Rocky Mountains about 74 million years ago, a scenario that matches the Blackfeet storyteller Percy Bullchild's traditional story about giant reptiles sinking into mud so fast that their whole skeletons are found (chapter 5).

In 1998, the tribe sent the baby dinosaur to the Museum of the Rockies to be prepared, with the understanding that it would be returned to the Blackfeet Reservation. As Horner told me in early 2003, the Blackfeet tribe "could request possession of the skeleton at any time and they may decide to sell it to the highest bidder."

That would be regrettable for science, observed Horner, but as "part of their cultural heritage, it is their right to dispose of it as they wish." As many others have pointed out, however, Indians who choose to sell important fossil assets disregard their own cultural heritage, but in this case, the Blackfeet are eager to build a museum for the prize specimen.

Horner's staff worked for three years to partially release the skeleton from extremely hard rock, and in September 2003 the baby dinosaur curled in its plaster cradle was returned to the reservation. The return was viewed as "a victory by the Blackfeet, who saw past treasure-seekers plunder their rich fossil cache." Blackfeet schoolchildren named the little *T. rex* Cameron, and the tribe takes great pride in their fossil. In a reversal of the *Dilophosaurus* story, the actual specimen is now on display in the Blackfeet Heritage Center in Browning, while the Museum of the Rockies retains a cast. "If you want to see that baby dinosaur, you're going to have to go to Browning," said Horner, who hopes the Blackfeet will be able to fulfill their dream of a museum. "I think it's very important to keep the fossil on the reservation."[32]

As I noted in the introduction, natural history museums typically make no connection between local Indian culture and local fossil resources. Agate Fossil Beds National Monument, Nebraska, is a notable exception. "We are always in search of traditions that relate to the fossils," says superintendent Ruthann Knudson, an anthropologist and NPS land manager. "We consult with 31 tribes that are culturally affiliated with our landscape." The Lakota cultural evaluation of the fossil beds, commissioned by the NPS from Bronco LeBeau of the Cheyenne River Sioux tribe in 2001, was described in chapter 5, as was the work of Lakota artist Dawn Little Sky. In 1997, Little Sky painted a history of Agate Fossil Beds on a traditional buffalo hide calendar, in which significant chronological events for the Lakotas and for paleontologists are represented by pictographs. Several paintings show the fossils known to the Lakotas as the bones of Water Monsters killed by lightning (figs. 73, 74). The calendar is prominently displayed in the museum entry with an information sheet explaining the significance of each image. Little Sky's traditional calendar and LeBeau's report illuminate what this important site meant to the Lakotas, who made special uses of the fossil resources long before these fossils came to the attention of scientists.[33]

Another outstanding example of the integration of Native culture and paleontology is the state-of-the-art Journey Museum in Rapid City, in the Black Hills of South Dakota, dedicated to the region's geological, paleontological, and Lakota history. The founders of the museum assembled a Lakota Advisory Board to ensure that a Native perspective helped to shape all aspects of the museum. The text for "The Bone Bed" exhibit presents two side-by-side explanations, the "Euro-American Interpretation" and the "Lakota Interpretation." The Lakota text, written by Birgil Kills Straight (Kyle, Pine Ridge Reservation) and Ronnie Theisz (Black Hills State University, Spearfish), was based on oral traditions taped earlier by Kills Straight.

The narrative reads: "At one time in history, the Great Water Spirits, the Unktehi, were trying to defeat the Lightning and Thunder Spirits. The Thunder Beings decided to combine their powers to defeat the Unktehi, their enemies. The fiery bolts consumed the forest and the plains. The waters where the Unktehi lived boiled and then dried up. The Unktehi, big and small, burned and died, leaving only their dried bones in the Badlands, where the bones turned to rocks."[34]

CONSILIENCE

As this book shows, many of the traditional interpretations of fossils were expressed in mythological language, in which perceptive explanations of Earth's history were given in metaphorical terms. Some ideas about fossils, such as the attribution of healing or magical powers to them, seem far removed from science. But even some of the most mystical ideas about geology and the fossil record are not as incompatible with science as they might appear at first glance. So another approach to finding common ground is to seek points of congruence and rapport between established science and Indian natural knowledge. The context of fossils, the lessons they hold, the record of life maintained in rock, and the value of visionary thinking are four such sources of agreement.

Context

Both scientists and traditional Indians agree that *context* is crucial in reading the messages of past life-forms, that something important is lost when creatures of the deep past are torn from their matrix. Johnson Holy Rock, Lakota elder, explained it to me this way: "To take fossils out of the ground *snaps the line of knowledge*." Later at the Sternberg Museum in Hays, Kansas, I mentioned this to paleontologist Greg Liggett. He nodded, "Excavation is information destruction."

This fact is expressed in the 2000 government report *Fossils on Federal and Indian Lands*. "Like a complex tapestry of fragile threads, the fabric . . . of fossils and data together . . . cannot be rewoven once it has been separated. The sediments at a fossil locality cannot be put back in context once they have been dug into and moved." That's why so many tons of fossils gathered by the pioneer paleontologists are useless to science now—the bone hunters failed to record information about the context. Nowadays, complex maps and photos of the position of each bone are made before excavation, and facts about the surrounding sediment are painstakingly detailed, in an effort to save data that will be destroyed.

Why not study more skeletons in the ground, rather than wrenching them from their context? John Allen, Jr., an Assiniboine spiritual leader, points out that whites picked the prairies clean of every bison bone for use as fertilizer, and "now that the buffalo are gone, they take every dinosaur bone they see." He worries that his grandchildren will never see a giant bone in the ground. These great "creatures lived and died before we arrived, so for educational purposes it's okay to take a few dinosaur fossils for museums, but even then, why not use casts and leave the bones in the earth? Think of the future generations." A year later, Morris Chee, Navajo guide at the Moenave dinosaur tracksite near the location of Jesse Williams's discovery, made the same point, "Why don't the scientists make a cast of the fossils and leave the real bones in the ground? Then we could make a museum over them, and people would come here to see the bones and footprints, right where they are."

The trend of building a structure over an important fossil site strongly appeals to Native Americans. Jack Horner's recent remark, during a conversation in March 2003, that erecting skeletons of dead dinosaurs in lifelike poses does not please him—that it feels somehow "too strange"—seemed to echo Clifford Canku's similar feelings. It would be more respectful of both science and cultural sensitivities to show the bones as they appear in the ground, said Horner, who hopes to implement this approach in the planned expansion of the Museum of the Rockies.

But other paleontologists believe excavation and removal is the best course. In 2000, for instance, conflict arose over the discovery of what may be the largest dinosaur ever found in North America, the hundred-foot-long, thirty-five-foot-tall *Alamosaurus* in Big Bend National Park, Texas. Some accused the NPS paleontologists of stealing fossils from public land when they allowed the dinosaur to be hauled to the University of Texas lab in Dallas. Why not leave it in its natural environment? they asked. Why not build a display over it, like Dinosaur National Monument in Utah, "and let people come from around the world to see this magnificent creature"? But NPS scientists brushed aside the idea of a protective structure and protested that allowing the gigantic dinosaur "to slowly erode away in the desert" would leave too many unanswered questions about the specimen.[35]

Dinosaur National Monument in Utah and Hot Springs Mammoth Site in South Dakota offer two fine examples of a structure built over a large deposit of embedded fossils, where paleontologists can be observed at work. Archaeologists, also concerned with avoiding the inevitable damage of excavation, have begun to study ancient artifacts in situ, as well. One impressive example is the Archedome, built over a prehistoric Indian village occupied about seven hundred years ago near Mitchell, South Dakota, where one can watch and talk with working archaeologists.

This approach is in harmony with the traditional Native notion that to understand ancient creatures, we must see *where* and *how* they died. Johnson Holy Rock was fascinated by the panorama of life and death in the masses of jumbled skeletons at Hot Springs, where Columbian mammoths, giant short-faced bears, and other animals died over several centuries in a waterhole about twenty-six thousand years ago. Holy Rock felt that the display was respectful and educational—he singled out the Mammoth Site as a positive model of how traditional Native Americans would like to see fossils treated and interpreted.

Fossil Lessons

The *educational* value of fossils is another concept that paleontologists and Native Americans hold in common. When ethnologist Richard Erdoes was given his Sioux name by Lame Deer and other medicine men, they presented him with a Badlands rock concretion containing opalescent seashells from 200 million years ago, wrapped in red flannel. The medicine men assured Erdoes that "some rocks had a message written on them by nature," but left it to him to decipher the message of the gift. The incident reflects the pervasive idea that fossils contain lessons about the past and future and the brevity of life; they can even warn of environmental dangers.

Why are we so obsessed with what destroyed all the dinosaurs 65 million years ago? As Jack Horner often suggests in his public lectures, it is because we want to know what kinds of disasters might extinguish *us*. The answers might help us to understand and come to terms with our own destiny. Paleontologist Gerta Keller of Princeton observes that those who study fossils realize that "of course, we too will be wiped out eventually." Many of Stephen Jay Gould's essays allude to the lessons humans can glean to avoid the fate of "magnificent beasts in contorted poses among the strata of the earth."

The Native idea that fossils reveal nature's struggle for harmony and balance appeals to many thoughtful biologists and earth scientists. "I think there is much more to paleontology than fangs and bones," Douglas Wolfe observes. "What we call ecology or sustainability is the idea, represented so well in the Zuni creation myth, that nature and cultures are constantly striving toward dynamic equilibrium. We can never achieve this ideal because the foundations are ever-shifting, but we know, or feel, that failing to try will lead to disaster."[36]

"We could learn so much about balance in the environment from extinct animals and the fossils that they left to us," commented Nita Manning, a Northern Cheyenne who put me in touch with the storyteller Albert Grayeagle. In the traditional tale, "Mother Earth's Cries," Grayeagle tells of an old medicine man who, after rains and landslides, often observed the bones of giant creatures that lived no more. Wondering what had befallen them, he asked the Thunder Beings for an explanation. They told him that the extinct creatures had harmed the Earth somehow and that their fate, death by fire and ice, would happen again to the two-leggeds. Humans, they warned, were wounding the Earth, by digging for yellow metal, using giant straws to suck up black water (oil), cutting down forests, and erecting big square lodges that spew dirty smoke. The Earth must survive, and so, although two-leggeds are her favorites, she will cry tears of fire followed by tears of ice to freeze all life.

Grayeagle's story links fossil evidence of mass extinctions to environmental imbalances and cautions that the consequences of mistreatment of the earth could bring about our own destruction. One unexpected, ominous message recently deciphered from the fossil record supports warnings by Indian spiritual leaders about the rapid destruction of the environment and biodiversity. Previously, scientists had assumed that the time it takes for the living world to bounce back after extinction events was in proportion to the damage done. But fossil evidence predicts that the recovery time needed for new creatures to evolve and fill empty niches may actually be about 10 million years, vastly longer than had been proposed earlier. When only a few organisms survive extinction, the scientists learned, then the dynamic "feedback loop" of newly evolving creatures goes off balance. The fossil record is revealing how interdependent diverse life-forms are, and how delicately balanced nature really is, an understanding conveyed in Grayeagle's tale, in the Navajo belief that life cannot exist out of balance, and in all the other Native fossil narratives that relate extinction to disturbances in natural equilibrium.[37]

We need fossils to understand our place on this planet, observes paleontologist Mark Norell (American Museum of Natural History). "Without fossils we would have no indicator of our own species' relative insignificance even during the time that humans have occupied the planet. If this does not strike one as a revelation concerning our place in nature, then it is best to look to mysticism for answers." "All organisms are interrelated through our evolutionary heritage," continued Norell. Everything alive is reciprocally related, and even the "extinct species are not isolated entities from Earth's past. They, like we, are all integrated actors in the drama" of life.

These ideas resonate with Native American insights that everything on Earth is intricately imbricated: nothing is without life and nothing exists in isolation. "Seeing in a sacred manner," explained Lame Deer, means perceiving this dynamic interrelatedness and vitality and not interfering with its flow. Norell's impassioned perspective shows how creative scientists are developing similar holistic conceptions of nature.[38]

Wisdom in Rock

In the traditional Native view, the category of what is alive and has "spirit" includes rock. Scientists normally define rock as inorganic, because it never breathed, metabolized, reproduced, or did any of the other things living, organic material is supposed to do. In American Indian philosophy, by contrast, rock is not lifeless but animate, invisibly pulsating with energy. The Assiniboine spiritual leader John Allen, for example, collects special rocks for sweat lodge ceremonies on his reservation, because he believes that the "kinetic energy stored up for eons" in rocks is released when they are heated to "breathe steam."

In Plains Indian belief, certain stones even have the ability to move. In some sense, one can say that rock does have a kind of life and movement: magnetic rocks jump; crystals grow; stones crack, roll, and topple; radioactive rocks tell time; silicon chips compute; particles whirl and collide; meteors plummet from the sky; boulders and gravels were borne by glaciers hundreds of miles from their sources; gastroliths were transported far from where dinosaurs ingested them; limestone was once teeming with sea life; coal was once flourishing vegetation; amber once oozed as sap from living trees; petrified forests once took root and put out branches; and mineralized bones once supported a flesh-and-blood creature.[39]

But the idea that stone is in some sense *animate* is an enigmatic concept for many non-Indians used to thinking of rocks as dead, inert, the opposite of life. Yet "rocks are made up of vibrating atoms, or they would not exist," Aloma McGaa, archivist at Sisseton-Wahpeton Sioux Reservation, reminded me in 2000. She also pointed out that in classical antiquity, the Greek philosophers Plato and Aristotle considered the question of whether things like rocks contained "spirit." Indeed, Plato saw the universe as a whole, as one living entity, having a body and a soul, and therefore all apparently lifeless matter is part of this living being. Aristotle attributed a "nature" to all animate and inanimate things, such as rocks, whose nature was to be solid and heavy with the ability to move downward. Both philosophers rejected the modern notion of stone as dead, inert matter.[40]

Several Indians remarked in conversations that many great cultures have rock at the core of their beliefs. "All religions have rock as the anchor," said Nita Manning. "To white people, this kind of talk [about the spirit contained in stones] seems strange," acknowledged Lame Deer. But "think of the Rock of Ages, of St. Peter, whose name means rock. Think of Stonehenge. White people have forgotten this and have lost the power which is in rocks." Indeed, the English language used to have an animate word for bedrock: "*living stone*." The novelist Louise Erdrich, an Ojibwe, wrote recently of learning to speak her ancestral tongue. She found that "nouns are designated as alive or dead, animate or inanimate." To her surprise, the word for stone, *asin*, is animate. Once she began thinking of stones as animate, in the Ojibwe way, stones were "not the same as they were to me in English."

In fact, the latest scientific definitions of animate and inanimate objects are evolving rapidly, as modern technology creates virtual realities, exo-sensory devices, animatronic robots, evolving nonorganic superorganisms, bio-mimetics, and artificial intelligence. Humans are developing relationships with "nonbiological objects," in ways that seem to recapitulate some mystical Native American traditions about what is alive. Philosophers of biology who ponder the distinctions between what is alive and what is not are "finding it devilishly difficult." Two examples given by scientists, desert varnish on a rock and proliferating rust on an old car, demonstrate that the differences between living and nonliving are no longer as clear-cut as once assumed. Even rock itself is no longer the icon of lifelessness. New spectroscopy techniques, for example, have revealed carbon signals from microscopic fossil organisms inside rocks 3.5 billion years old.[41]

In Native American mythology, *Inyan*, or Rock, was the most ancient being, "old beyond imagination, ageless, eternal," the origin of life itself. "*Inyan* or Rock is the personified image of primal power," wrote the Sioux ethnologist James Walker; "Rock was there when there was no other." According to the Sioux creation myth, in the beginning, Inyan was surrounded by Darkness. In Clifford Canku's retelling of the myth, Rock was so "lonely" in the primal universe that he sacrificed his "blood," or life force, in order to create something else. From his own blood, Inyan created Earth as a beautiful red disk (a fitting image of the planet as molten rock). Then Inyan made the waters and creatures, using stone and earth to make bones and flesh. As his life force drained into living things, Inyan became stony and seemingly lifeless. To us now, "Inyan now seems hard and helpless, but he is alive in the hills and stones."[42]

"Without rocks, there can be no true grandeur." Few would disagree with Henry Rowe Schoolcraft's sentiment, written as he canoed down the Missouri River in about 1825. But what about the idea of rock as the *originator* of life? Even this mystical notion finds support in recent scientific knowledge. Several new discoveries point to rocks as the cradle of life.

Meteorites, for example, contain many carbon-based compounds, amino acids, the building blocks of primitive life. In 2001, scientists studying two meteorites billions of years old discovered many other organic compounds required for life, simple sugars and amino acids, the key components of RNA, DNA, cell membranes, and energy sources for terrestrial organisms. The discovery bolsters the theory that ingredients delivered by rocks from space contributed to the development of life on Earth. Calcite crystals (a common mineral that often forms on fossilized bones) are now thought to have provided the environment for the biochemistry of primitive life.

In 2003, scientists studying iron sulfide mineral deposits from hydrothermal vents deep in the oceans proposed that "the abundant black mineral might have been the crucial ingredient that first sparked all life" almost 4 billion years ago. They suggest that the origin of life required only rocks, water, and the most basic chemicals. Hot iron sulfide–containing water was "the incubator where life's basic ingredients were concentrated and the first cells were born" and nurtured in cell-like compartments in the rock. At some point, say the scientists, "the rock-cradled life-forms invented the biochemistry" to create their own cell membranes.[43]

Earth scientists and paleobiologists can claim, along with Lame Deer, "I read messages in stones [for] stones bear a hidden message, which they sometimes reveal to us, invisible writing for those who read with their hearts."[44] Fossils may look and feel like lifeless stone, but paleontologists know that they contain the secrets of life, from bacteria to dinosaur bone.

Visionary Paleontology

Like the Natives who intuited some sort of kinship with the extinct beings long buried in the earth, modern paleontologists say that fossils "remind us who we are and how we might have come to be." But "unlike archaeology, which seems near and familiar because we are studying ourselves, paleontology offers a pilgrimage to deep time. It lets us study what natural systems were like before human influence." This insightful phrase from the Department of the Interior's *Fossils on Federal and Indian Lands* would strike a chord with traditional Indians. "A pilgrimage to deep time" is one way to describe a vision quest.[45]

Seeking visions might seem light-years away from scientific inquiry. Yet the most creative paleontologists can be described as visionaries, and many respected scientists have described important theoretical breakthroughs that came to them as revelations while they slept or daydreamed.

Lame Deer described visionary dreams as having a different, eidetic quality, more lucid than ordinary dreams. "You have to work for this, empty your mind for it." The vision is "very real. It hits you sharp and clear like an electric shock." You feel wide awake, and suddenly you see something that your conscious mind tells you can't be there at all. This hyperaware dream state is called "lucid dreaming" or "power dreaming" by neuropsychologists. Paleontologists who trust their dreams about the meaning of fossils are perhaps not so unlike Native American discoverers of fossils during vision quests. Certainly paleontology—solving the mystery of stone creatures that will never be seen walking the earth—inspires dreams and theoretical narratives.

How can people come to know about the distant prehistory of the world? The question was posed in the traditional "History of the Universe" recounted by an Achumawi elder in California. The answer: "It was a dream that told the history." The only way for future people to learn about the monsters and events of the deep past is "by dreams," declares Coyote. "If the people will dream, I will tell them the history."[46]

The interaction of dreaming and telling stories about mysterious, ancient bones was evident in the Iroquois warrior's vision at Big Bone Lick and the Pawnee hunter's dream that led him to a fossil discovery on the Republican River. Native groups that lived near or traveled through conspicuous fossil deposits selected those locales for vision quests where one could decipher nature's messages and receive wisdom and power. Rock art near dinosaur trackways may have been the result of medicine men's visionary attempts to explain the weird prints of unknown creatures. The Crow medicine man Goes Ahead sought understanding of natural mysteries in bone beds in Montana; generations of Piegan vision questers frequented the dinosaur fossils of Alberta; and Lakota men and women seeking the power of ancient bones traveled to Agate Springs on the Niobrara River.

The pioneer paleontologists were susceptible to fossil-inspired dreaming, too. Joseph Leidy, father of American paleontology, became obsessed with the bizarre fossil skulls being discovered by bone hunters in the West. "You can have no idea how much my mind has become inflamed on this subject," he wrote to a friend in 1851. "Night after night I dream of strange forms." A recurrent motif was the image of giant Eocene mammal skulls coming to life. After days spent examining the fossil skulls in his museum, Leidy's unconscious imagined living eyes in the hollow eyesockets.

Edward Drinker Cope was a fossil dreamer too. When he and Charles Sternberg returned to camp each night after exhuming the bones of long-gone beasts, the monsters came to life while Cope slept. "Every animal of which we had found trace during the day played with Cope at night, tossing him in the air, kicking him, trampling upon him," wrote Sternberg. Each time "I waked him, he would thank me cordially and lie down to another attack. But the next morning he would lead the party and be the last to give up at night." The vivid, thrilling visions of extinct creatures apparently spurred Cope on—he wrote of bedding down in camp "to dream of dinosaurs." Interestingly, while most Indian vision quests involved hallucinations and knowledge brought on by fasting, Cope's dreams in the field were perhaps more like peyote-induced visions of southwestern cultures, since his imaginings were enhanced by his favorite remedy, a powerful mixture of opium and belladonna.[47]

There are some striking coincidences in the lucid dreams of fossil hunters across cultures. As the Pawnee doctor Young Bull recounted, sometime before 1830 a Pawnee man fell asleep on a wooded hill on the Republican River of western Kansas and dreamed of a giant being whose race had drowned there. The giant told him to look on the south side of the hill where he would find an immense limb bone. "Take it, wrap it up, and my spirit will be with that bone and will give you great power." Awakening, the man went around to the south slope and found the huge bone from his dream, carried it to his village, and learned its power for the good of his people.

Not so far away, along the Smoky Hill River in western Kansas, in 1867, seventeen-year-old Charles H. Sternberg, the legendary fossil hunter, had a similar experience, just after he had decided to devote his life to collecting "facts from the crust of the earth." His passion for fossils set him dreaming of past life hidden in the earth.

"One night, I dreamed that I was on the river, where the Smoky Hill cuts into its northern bank, three miles southeast of Fort Harker," he wrote. In the dream, he walked up a ravine cutting into the prairie from the base of a clay cliff on the river. "I was at once attracted by a large cone-shaped hill, separated from a knoll to the south by a lateral ravine. On either slope were many chunks of rock, which the frost had loosened from the ledges above." Grass roots had split open the rocks, revealing gigantic prehistoric leaves a foot across, imprisoned "in the heart of the rock for millions of years." On awakening the next morning, Sternberg says, "I went to the place and found everything just as it had been in my dream."[48]

Countering the usual tendency to leave bones buried in the ground, the Pawnee man obeyed a dream that gave him permission to take the bone for its beneficial power, once he understood its history. Seeking to advance science, Sternberg, Leidy, and Cope embarked on comparable missions. The Pawnee and the scientists who followed him were led by dreams about ancient life-forms. Who can say that their dreams did not arise from the same spirit?

Fossil Frauds and

Specious Legends

THE sections below explore the scientific and historical issues surrounding some fraudulent paleontological claims and questionable fossil legends. In some cases, evidence purporting to be related to extinct creatures and Native American legends was deliberately faked, while in other cases misunderstandings of the fossilization process and geological time produced mistaken interpretations of natural evidence.

THE LENAPE STONE

In the late nineteenth and early twentieth centuries, a scientific dispute centered on the question of whether Native Americans could have overlapped with prehistoric elephants and other large mammals of the Pleistocene. The debate arose after Albert Koch of St. Louis claimed to have discovered arrowheads among some mammoth skeletons that he unearthed in 1839 at Kimmswick, Missouri (chapter 4). Today, the best evidence indicates that the last of the large mammals of the Pleistocene probably disappeared on the mainland between eight and ten thousand years ago (and only four thousand years ago on Wrangel Island in the Arctic).

The date of the earliest humans in the Western Hemisphere is still debated, but the latest archaeological and DNA evidence suggests that the first Americans may have arrived as early as thirty to forty thousand years ago. Thus for most of New World human prehistory people coexisted with megafaunas that went extinct after the last Ice Age.

But before this chronology was established, scholars disagreed on whether humans had seen living mammoths and mastodons in the New World. The controversy was at its height in the late nineteenth century, when the so-called Lenape Stone was discovered (in two parts) in 1872 and 1881 on a farm in Bucks County, Pennsylvania. The incised slate stone showed Indians with feathers on their heads fighting a hairy elephant that has trampled one Indian. The artifact was taken as an illustration of the Delaware (Lenape) tradition about the mastodon remains at Big Bone Lick, recorded by Thomas Jefferson (chapter 1). Earlier, in 1836, another controversial discovery was announced: the Wallum Olum, a manuscript purporting to transcribe the history of the Lenape nation's migrations before their arrival in the Northeast. The Wallum Olum was later revealed to be a hoax, perhaps incorporating some scraps of genuine Indian lore.

Henry Mercer, who published a book on his investigations into the authenticity of the Lenape Stone in 1885, believed that the artifact was genuine, but even he noted that when the Lenape Stone was shown to a group of Delaware Indians, they expressed puzzlement about the animal. Meanwhile, many scientists at the time considered the Lenape Stone bogus because the scene showing humans and mastodons together was believed to be impossible. Other scientists, like the paleontologist William Berryman Scott, thought the artifact itself was a fake, but that it depicted a probable scene (Scott believed that mammoths might have survived in the American West until the 1500s).

Finally, in 1926, the discovery of skeletons of mammoths that had been killed and butchered by paleo-Indians in about 9,000–8,000 B.C. at Folsom, New Mexico, clearly demonstrated that North Americans did indeed hunt Pleistocene mammals. Another site, near Clovis, New Mexico, showed that people had hunted mammoths with stone weapons 11,500 years ago. Many other mammoth kill sites by Folsom and Clovis people subsequently found in Mexico, the Southwest, and the Great Plains offered proof that ancient artistic depictions of humans interacting with extinct Pleistocene animals could be authentic. Even Albert Koch's disputed Kimmswick site is now designated a mammoth kill site. But although the elephant-hunting scene on the Lenape Stone turned out to be a real possibility, the artifact is now considered a fake, on artistic and provenience grounds.[1]

ACAMBARO FIGURES AND ICA STONES

The Old Testament creation myth in the book of Genesis has parallels with many other ancient cultures' creation stories: the earth was formed from a dark void; first water creatures and then land animals appeared, followed by humans; and all this took place over six cosmic time periods. And, like the other prescientific creation stories, the Genesis version conveys a sense of the awesome antiquity of Earth and the mystery of life's origins.

Two centuries before Darwin, the Irish archbishop James Ussher "scientifically" calculated the chronology of the biblical creation tradition, by measuring generations from Adam. In 1650, Ussher declared that the earth was created in October 4004 B.C. Fossil remains of the "giants in the earth in those days" were relics left after Noah's Flood of December 2349 B.C., according to his reckoning. Yet Ussher's short duration of time since creation, only about six thousand years, came under increasing pressure as geological and paleontological discoveries advanced and scientists began to grasp deep time.

As this book shows, Europeans of the colonial era strove to reconcile the evidence of gigantic, unfamiliar bones in the New World with the Bible, whose authors were obviously unaware of the Western Hemisphere. Indeed, the growing dissonance between literal faith in Ussher's chronology and the accumulating empirical evidence from around the world was one of the driving forces of the paradigm shift that led to the science of paleontology. By the eighteenth century, thinkers like Cuvier began to approach the problem of "America, with its strange animals, its mysterious bones, and a human race unaccounted for in biblical terms." Cuvier's theory of catastrophism made sense of the "mounting paleontological and geomorphic evidence" without challenging the biblical narrative of a "historical" Flood. After Darwin, many devout Christians found ways to reconcile the symbolic biblical story with developing scientific theories of vast geological ages marked by evolution and extinctions of successive species and the evidence of the fossil record. Their efforts parallel the way many Native Americans revised their myths about monsters by assimilating new information about dinosaurs and mastodons and their extinctions.

But Ussher's calculation that God created Earth and all living things in six twenty-four-hour days about six thousand years ago ossified into dogma for modern creationists, anti-Darwinians whose politically motivated antipathy to science makes them a powerful force in the United States. Like the early Native Americans, creationists must somehow account for mineralized remains of strange creatures never seen alive. But unlike living folklore with its capacity to change and assimilate, the creationist myth cannot accommodate new evidence. To support their literal reading of Genesis, creationists must argue that humans and dinosaurs coexisted.[2]

For proof, creationists cite "ancient" artistic evidence uncovered in Mexico and Peru in the twentieth century. Known as the Acambaro figures and the Ica stones, these artifacts are claimed to have been made by unknown ancient civilizations with *firsthand* knowledge of living dinosaurs.

In 1945, a trove of thousands of clay figures came to light near Acambaro, Guanajuato, ninety miles northwest of Mexico City. In styles unlike any known ancient art of Mexico, the statuettes depict various human races, Egyptian and Sumerian items, Ice Age mammals, fantasy creatures, giant apes, and reptiles said by creationists to represent more than twenty different dinosaur species. The improbable array of figures was amassed by Waldemar Julsrud, an elderly hardware merchant obsessed with the Atlantis myth. He paid a Mexican farmer, Odilon Tinajero, to bring him as many objects as he could find. After Tinajero's initial discovery of twenty thousand objects, the number swelled to over thirty-three thousand. Miraculously, each random pit dug in the region produced more loads of statues, in perfect condition, with no chips, encrusted dirt, or patina of age. Sometime after 1955, Tinajero disappeared.

In 1955, the Acambaro "discovery" was investigated by Charles Hapgood, an anthropology professor from New Hampshire. Marveling that "never in the history of archaeology have such vast numbers of artifacts been found in a few acres," Hapgood nevertheless came away convinced that they were made thousands of years ago by an unknown culture—a conclusion he acknowledged was rejected by reputable archaeologists and paleontologists.

When some large fossil teeth were found among the Acambaro figures, Julsrud at first thought they might have belonged to a mastodon, a logical assumption. In 1955, Hapgood took the teeth to New York to be examined by George Gaylord Simpson, curator of the American Museum of Natural History. Simpson identified the teeth as those of an extinct horse of Pleistocene Mexico. Hapgood also consulted with Harvard paleontologist A. S. Romer about the clay "dinosaur" figures. Romer's opinion was that they were based on living lizards like the iguana. But Hapgood offered several other theories: perhaps the reptile figurines illustrated ancient Indian legends about monsters, or possibly some relict species of gigantic lizard, like the Komodo dragon, had survived from the Cretaceous into the human era—or maybe the figures were inspired by twisted dead trees or by hallucinogens. Meanwhile, however, Hapgood wrote that Julsrud "jumped to the conclusion that dinosaurs and people had lived at the same time."[3]

Shortly thereafter, Mexican workmen reported that "the bones of a monster" had been found in a nearby canyon. Hapgood and Julsrud rushed to the deep *barranca*, where they "actually witnessed the discovery of the *unfossilized* bones of one of these reptiles in an extreme state of decay." The workmen pointed to "strange forms protruding from the canyon wall, . . . large, porous, very decayed . . . but they were not shaped like any bones we knew and they were not fossilized." To Hapgood, they looked like "the bony flanges on the back of the dinosaur Stegosaurus." He showed the "dinosaur bones" to Simpson's AMNH colleague in New York, the paleontologist Harold Anthony.

If the items were bones, they would most likely have been those of mammoths or other Pleistocene mammals, like the teeth found at Acambaro and the abundant Ice Age fossils in the central valleys of Mexico. The unfossilized "Stegosaurus" plates found by the workmen in the barranca sound suspiciously like semimineralized mastodon or mammoth bones, which can have a woody, rotten texture. The circumstances of the discovery recall the mastodon bones collected as "bones of terror" by villagers in ravines in San Luis Potosi, north of Acambaro (described in chapter 2). Mastodon fossils are also found north of Acambaro at San Miguel de Allende, and south around Mexico City. But Harold Anthony at the AMNH identified the "bones" as inorganic concretions of rock. According to Hapgood, "the thought of unfossilized bones of Stegassaurus [sic] was too much for him, as it would have been for any paleontologist."

Since the 1920s in the Americas, many rock art images have been interpreted as ancient depictions of dinosaurs. Rock art is very difficult to date and interpret, and fakes and misinterpretations abound. Viewed from other angles, what appear to be outlines of dinosaurs come into focus as animals that really *were* contemporary with humans, such as giant camels or mastodons, or they turn out to be common symbols in rock art. Some observers have reasoned that the images could be restorations of dinosaur *fossils*, rather than portraits of dinosaurs drawn from life. For example, R. R. Snowden, a scientist who observed the sensational "dinosaur" figure in a petroglyph discovered in 1925 in Havasupai Canyon, near the Grand Canyon, Arizona, wrote at the time: "The carving of a dinosaur by no means shows that the artist had seen the living animal. It is plainly a skeleton of a dinosaur that the artist saw, as evidenced by the absence of forelegs and the hollow abdomen." Snowden noted that genuine dinosaur fossils often weather out of the red sandstone in the vicinity of the petroglyphs.[4]

Could the reptile figures from Acambaro be amazingly accurate ancient *restorations* based on observations of dinosaur *fossils*? Unlikely: the fossils in the state of Guanajuato belong to Pleistocene mastodons and horses, and not to Mesozoic dinosaurs of 250–65 million years ago. No human beings ever saw a living dinosaur, unless they could magically travel back in time more than 65 million years. However, very early people in Mexico and Peru *did* have firsthand knowledge of huge elephants, hulking sloths, and bizarre glyptodonts, ancestral armadillos the size of a sports car. And as we've seen, in later times the Aztecs, Tlaxcaltecas, Incas, and others did come across the fossils of these more recent extinct creatures and created stories about the impressive bones (chapter 2).

Perhaps the natives of Acambaro and Ica honestly assumed that the bones and teeth of large Pleistocene animals belonged to "dinosaurs"—just as Peruvian villagers today associate mastodon and sloth bones with "dinosaurs." For many people, the word "dinosaur" is a catchall term for any large extinct animal. It is a common misconception that all prehistoric species, including early man, overlapped in time—and many popular culture icons have perpetuated this fallacy, from the cartoon caveman Alley Oop to *Turok, Son of Stone* and the Flintstones.

After the discovery of "dinosaur" teeth and bones at Acambaro, locals may have come up with the idea of manufacturing "antique" artifacts depicting fantastic animals based on dinosaur imagery of the day. Perhaps the original idea was to sell curios to tourists, or maybe the plan was to fool or indulge Julsrud, who believed he had found evidence of Atlantis. Then, after Hapgood declared that the artifacts were ancient (despite the failure of dating technology) and suggested that some figures might represent rare "living fossils," the discovery was taken up by creationists in their anti-evolutionist cause.[5]

The story of the Ica stones follows a similar path. Notably, it was Charles Hapgood who announced the 1966 discovery of the "artifacts" by a farmer in a cave in Ica, Peru. The farmer was arrested after selling them to tourists as antiquities, and he admitted that he had carved the relics himself. Despite this inauspicious beginning, the collection of several thousand Ica stones is now housed in the Museo de Piedras Grabadas in Ica (south of Lima, not far from the mysterious earthworks known as Nazca lines, which attract UFO fans from around the world). The smooth andesite (volcanic) Ica stones are engraved with "ancient" scenes. Incised igneous stones are not amenable to dating technologies, so the antiquity claimed for the figures cannot be tested. Not only do the stones depict dinosaurs such as *Stegosaurus* and *Triceratops* (an interesting inclusion, since horned dinosaurs are unknown in South America); they also show ancient brain transplants and heart surgery, sky telescopes, and space travel.

Could the "dinosaurs" be based on fossils found around Ica? No: the fossil remains of that area are of Oligocene to Pleistocene mammals, with no Cretaceous dinosaur remains. Despite the lack of any scientific studies or publications on the artifacts, the Ica stones are hailed by creationists as "scientific" evidence that Native Americans and dinosaurs shared the same time and space. The phenomenal proliferation of Ica stones since 1966, from 10,000 to 50,000, to reports of 100,000 by 2002, outpaces even the rapid reproduction rate of the Acambaro figures, suggesting a profitable chain of forgeries of forgeries to meet the market for pseudo-Indian artifacts that seem to challenge scientific theories. Creating phony fossil legends for political reasons is nothing new. Paul Semonin, in his study of the political uses of paleontology in colonial and early America, shows how an "Indian legend" about mastodons was fabricated for political propaganda in 1795.[6]

In the case of the Lenape Stone, science eventually proved that the faked artifact illustrated a probable scenario. Perhaps creationists hope for a similar turn of events with the suspect Acambaro and Ica figures? The odds are nil. The abyss of time between the extinction of dinosaurs and the appearance of the first humans is stupendous. Whereas in the mammoth-human debate, the scientific evidence had to bridge a gap of only a few thousand years within the Pleistocene epoch, the creationist fantasy must leap across tens of thousands of millennia.

HUMAN AND DINOSAUR FOOTPRINTS

The dinosaurs' extinction more than 60 million years before the appearance of *Homo sapiens* presents a tremendous chronological gulf, forcing literal-minded creationists to squeeze an ever-growing body of geological and biological observations into a severely constricted mythic time frame. Evidence for the coexistence of humans and dinosaurs has also been sought in trackway sites where Cretaceous and Jurassic creatures left footprints in mud that hardened into stone.

The paleontologist William F. Tanner wrote a useful paper for the Paleontological Society's special issue titled "The Evolution-Creation Controversy" in 1984, in which he describes the three types of footprints that can be observed in rock, and explains in detail how even laypeople can learn to distinguish among them. The three types are genuine footprints left by humans or animals; footprints carved by humans; and natural geological features that resemble footprints. The first category is found almost exclusively in sedimentary rocks with a "depositional history prior to lithification"; in only a few exceptional cases have footprints been retained in igneous rock, namely, in hardened lava flows. Real footprints have specific anatomical details and weathering features, as outlined by Tanner.[7]

In 1939 Barnum Brown's fossil hunter Roland Bird, in an article in *Natural History*, mentioned some carved giant-human footprints from Glen Rose, Texas. The Paluxy River bed, now Dinosaur Valley State Park, cuts through layers of limestones, sandstones, and mudstones deposited about 113 million years ago, revealing many dinosaur trackways. Since 1945, the artificial tracks mentioned by Bird and proliferating other tracks have been cited by creationists as evidence that giant humans walked alongside the dinosaurs. One of the "human" tracks is about nineteen inches long. Upon closer examination, the supposed human tracks are attributable to a variety of phenomena, including incomplete or filled-in digits of real dinosaur tracks, weathering, natural depressions, and even some modified and carved specimens on unattached stone blocks.[8]

As discussed in previous chapters, the motivations of Native Americans who carved artificial human, bird, and animal tracks in stone are unknown, but it is certain that the prints were not created as evidence to disprove a prevailing scientific theory. The one point in common between Native American carved prints and creationist "evidence" may be that both groups created tracks in stone in order to illustrate a myth. Many pre-Darwinian cultures, from the ancient Greeks and Judeo-Christians to Native Americans, told stories in which gods or heroes interact with primeval monsters. But those stories were understood as metaphors for the unimaginably long-ago creation of Earth and vanished life-forms, whereas a metaphorical reading of the Judeo-Christian creation story is rejected by strict creationists who insist on a "young earth" and the fixity of all species on Earth created in one fell swoop.

Genuine pre-Darwinian fossil interpretations had no pretensions to formal science, even though the stories can sometimes reveal proto-scientific insights and inquiry based on long-term observations of evidence and the best logic of the time. Indeed, two consistent features of many Native American (and ancient Greek and Roman) fossil legends are *directly* opposed to creationist belief.

First is the awareness that all the creatures known only from their petrified remains had died out in a remote time long *before* the age of present-day humans. Second is the recognition that most of Earth's geological landforms had developed over a vast passage of time. Scientific discoveries now support those ancient insights. Unlike the prescientific Native Americans, classical Greeks, and early Christians, however, today's creationists have access to modern scientific methods for creating and revising hypotheses, as well as the technology for testing and dating. These opportunities were not open to pre-Darwinian cultures, which makes their intuitions about deep time and changing species, and their abilities to assimilate new knowledge into their ancient fossil traditions, all the more impressive.[9]

RED-HAIRED CANNIBAL GIANTS OF
LOVELOCK CAVE, NEVADA

In 1911, miners excavating vast deposits of bat guano in Lovelock Cave, northwestern Nevada, discovered a trove of ancient artifacts—baskets; moccasins; fishing nets; shell, horn, and bead jewelry; and remarkably lifelike duck decoys. The items belonged to a fishing culture that lived about two thousand years ago, when the receding Pleistocene Lake Lahontan created a lush wetlands environment. Naturally mummified human remains, with reddish hair, were also found. In 1911, some enterprising whites claimed that mummified "giants" with reddish hair from Lovelock Cave confirmed an old Paiute myth about a race of red-haired cannibals called *Si-Te-Cahs*.[10]

According to the Paiute elder Sarah Winnemucca's recounting of the Paiute tradition in 1929, a "tribe of barbarians," red-haired cannibals, used to prey on her people when they first arrived in the area, until the Paiute ancestors trapped them in Lovelock Cave and set a big fire to annihilate them with smoke. After some time, the Paiutes returned to the cave, which reeked of burnt bodies.

Sarah Winnemucca possessed some red hair from the bodies of the cannibals in the cave, which had been passed down for numerous generations in her family. Her version of the legend does not mention that the cannibals were giants, but other Paiute versions may have. At any rate, soon after the archaeological discoveries in Lovelock and other dry caves in Nevada, entrepreneurs created bogus tourist displays of the "giant skeletons of Paiute myth." The skeletons were laid out in a pit at Lovelock and were still extant through the 1950s and 1960s.

Certain natural facts help account for the genuine Paiute legend as told by Winnemucca. Archaeologists point out that there are strata of grass and tule in Lovelock Cave that were carbonized from ancient fires. The cave also contained very deep deposits of bat guano, which emits a strong odor often compared to the stench of burnt bodies. The cave, like others in the area, did yield some mummified human remains with red hair, but the skeletons were of normal dimensions. Notably, however, in the Black Rock Desert about a hundred miles north of Lovelock Cave, which was also once covered by Lake Lahontan, there are plentiful fossils of Pleistocene mammoths and cave bears (map 3). The large limb bones of these mammals resemble giant counterparts of human bones and might lead an untrained observer to imagine that giant people once existed in the region.

The Paiutes, who arrived in Nevada after the early lake cultures had disappeared, investigated the dry caves and discovered caches of ancient, unfamiliar artifacts made by unknown people, whose mummified bodies had red hair. The Paiutes created a myth that would account for the archaeological evidence and the natural evidence of ancient fires and the burnt-flesh odor of bat guano. Some versions that described the extinct Si-Te-Cahs race as giants may have assimilated the evidence of giant mammoth bones in the nearby desert.

What about the red hair? Red hair is often prominent in descriptions of long-ago people, monsters, and giants in Amerindian myths. For example, Sioux water monsters were said to be red-haired. Taphonomy (what happens to creatures' bodies after death) helps account for the recurrent detail. As anthropologist Stephanie Livingston points out, melanin and carotene give human and animal hair its color in life, "but these pigments are not stable after death, even though hair is one of the more durable soft tissues of the body."

Depending on variable factors (temperature, light, humidity, acidity, chemical reactions, and minerals in the matrix), dark hair of extreme age often turns rusty red or orange. That is why many Egyptian mummies have red-blond hair, and the hair of well-preserved bodies of extinct mammoths and sloths is reddish, even though they may have been black or brown in life. Paiutes who saw or heard about naturally mummified humans or extinct mammals with bits of reddish hair would attribute this feature to people and creatures of the deep past. Strands of very ancient hair, taken from either human mummies or well-preserved Ice Age fauna, could have been collected and passed down over generations and would show that ancient cannibals or giants were red-haired.[11]

THE BABOQUIVARI MONSTER OF TOHONO O'ODHAM LORE

The Tohono O'odham (Papago) people of northern Mexico and southern Arizona have lived in the Sonoran Desert for millennia. The Tohono O'odhams have several ceremonies that involve Baboquivari Peak, southwest of Tucson, which they claim go back to the days when monsters roamed the earth (see map 3). According to legend, one of the personifications of *Etoi* (*I'itoi*), the spirit that dominates the Baboquivari mountains and valleys, is related to a certain monster.

There are a Mexican band and an Arizona band of the Tohono O'odham nation. The Mexican band practices a secret ritual surrounding an object of particular sacredness. Recently, the object was claimed to be a bone from one of Etoi's manifestations as a *dinosaur*. What is unique about this sacred relic, however, is that it is claimed to be an *unfossilized* dinosaur bone. The story was reported in 1997 by the Sioux scholar Vine Deloria in his book *Red Earth, White Lies*, a critical look at how Indian natural knowledge has been systematically ignored or discredited by establishment science. Deloria cited the Baboquivari bone as a challenge to accepted scientific theories of the chronology of dinosaur extinction (a stance that invites creationist support).

The story summons a swarm of questions. The Baboquivari range consists of Jurassic, Cretaceous, and Tertiary granite with patches of sedimentary rocks that contain dinosaur fossils from the shores of the ancient inland sea. Dinosaur fossils of Mexico are relatively unstudied. Recently, however, Mexican paleontologists have found Cretaceous dinosaur fossils, including ceratopsians, tyrannosaurids, and hadrosaurs, on the Sonora-Arizona border southeast of Tucson, near the border area where in 1942 American paleontologists also found large bones and teeth dating to the Cretaceous. In Sonora southwest of the border, some Late Triassic ichthyosaur fossils were discovered in 1989.

Despite these geological facts, we have to ask, Is the sacred bone really a dinosaur fossil of the Mesozoic era, or could this be another example of the word "dinosaur" applied to a bone of some extinct creature of more recent origin? In that case, the relic could be a semimineralized bone from a Pleistocene beast, perhaps a mastodon. A woody texture could give the impression of a "fresh" bone. And consider the "bones of a monster" discovered in the canyon at Acambaro, Mexico, which were identified by Charles Hapgood in 1955 as unfossilized *Stegosaurus* dinosaur bones: those items were examined by a paleontologist who found them to be nonorganic (above).

But another, much earlier discovery, recounted by Georges Cuvier in 1821, also comes to mind. In Paris, Cuvier examined a startling relic, an elephant's foot said to have been discovered in a cavern in the American West. It was purchased from a *comanchero*, a Mexican trader, who had obtained it from "les sauvages" living somewhere "west of the Missouri River." According to Cuvier, the foot with five toenails looked as though it had been removed from an elephant carcass with a knife. An elephant tooth accompanied the foot. But, wrote Cuvier, "this foot was fresh!" "The find—if authentic—was almost enough to make one doubt that mastodons were extinct," he remarked, "but I could not refrain from suspecting a fraud."

Unfortunately, no dating techniques existed in Cuvier's time, and the geographic location of the cave and the Indian tribe visited by the Mexican trader are unknown. The specimens, which were displayed in Paris in the early nineteenth century, no longer exist. Cuvier's suspicion of fraud was justified, but it is worth noting that Columbian mammoth hair and eight thousand cubic feet of dung, dating to about thirteen thousand years ago, were recently discovered in Bechan Cave in Utah. (See map 3; the quantity of dung is extraordinary: *bechan* is Navajo for "big feces.") It's not impossible that a Mexican trader obtained the foot and tooth of a well-preserved mastodon or mammoth that had been found by southwestern Indians in a very dry cave. Caves in southwestern deserts have also yielded mummified Pleistocene sloths and condors.

Other possibilities could explain the Tohono O'odham belief that they possess a "fresh dinosaur" bone. Perhaps a dinosaur fossil is ritually "transformed" into a "fresh" bone during a religious ceremony. When I contacted Deloria in 2002 about the relic, he pointed out that when he heard the story in Sells, Arizona, the Mexican and American Tohono O'odham groups were estranged. He believes that with the present reunification of the nation, the tradition-keepers will not want to reveal any more secrets of the Mexican band.[12]

There is one more possibility to consider. Could the Baboquivari "fresh" bone have come from a partially petrified or "mummified" dinosaur skeleton? Dinosaur mummies are rare but very exciting finds: skin impressions, cartilage, tendons, and internal organs of an animal that died more than 65 million years ago can be preserved by extremely dry air or sand, or other special conditions. In 1908, for example, two mummified *Edmontosaurus* dinosaurs were found by Charles Sternberg and his sons in the Lance Creek area near Lusk, Wyoming. In Alberta Barnum Brown discovered mummified Cretaceous specimens identified as the crested duckbill *Corythosaurus* and the ceratopsian *Centrosaurus*. In 2000, a desiccated *Brachylophosaurus* (duck-billed dinosaur) was discovered by Nate Murphy near Malta, Montana. The two-ton, twenty-three-foot-long dinosaur is nearly complete, with skin intact and leaves in its stomach.[13]

A relatively unmineralized dinosaur bone from northern Mexico/southern Arizona is "not outside the realm of possibility," comments Arizona paleontologist Douglas Wolfe. He has found some poorly mineralized dinosaur fossils in the Zuni Basin, on the border of Arizona and New Mexico. "Knowledge of such a specimen would be very valuable," says Wolfe. It is an *extremely remote* possibility, but if the Tohono O'odhams of Mexico have made a discovery similar to the very rare finds mentioned above, information about the sacred fossil could contribute to paleontological knowledge.[14]

NOTES

1. I use the terms *Native Americans, Native people, Indians, First Americans, American Indians* and *Amerindians,* and *First Nations* interchangeably, giving the names of specific cultural groups (often called nations in the East and tribes in the West), whenever possible. I use the term *paleo-Indians* for prehistoric, early cultures for which there is archaeological evidence, specifying Clovis, Folsom, Fremont, and so on, whenever known.

2. David Hurst Thomas 2000, chapter 3, argues that the definition of Indians as natural history specimens like mastodon and dinosaur fossils began in eighteenth-century America.

3. The obsidian blade was probably ceremonial. It is in the Sullivan Collection of the Phillips County Museum. Jack Sullivan was a Malta pharmacist who traded medicine for artifacts in the early 1900s.

4. Weishampel and Young 1996, 51.

5. Sternberg 1990, 30–31. Each of Marsh's Yale students hunting fossils in the Bridger Basin in 1870 received "full credit for all his discoveries, and the thought of having one's name attached to some rare specimen in the Yale Museum led to sharp competition." Lanham 1991, 108.

6. Unfortunately Scott did not document his sources in his compilation of legends, including Indian tales, related to extinct elephants and their remains, published in *Scribner's* magazine in 1887.

7. Kindle 1935 credited Indians with several important fossil discoveries but was roundly criticized by Simpson, 1942 and 1943. Simpson referred to Native American involvement in some historic paleontological discoveries but denied that their finds constituted "true" scientific discoveries. Simpson 1942, 132; 1943, 26–27. Occasional, brief references to Native American fossil traditions may be found in paleontological literature since Simpson. For example, Paul Semonin, in *American Monster* (2000), recounted some Indian interpretations of mastodon remains in the colonial era, in order to show how such myths were appropriated by early Americans to create a national identity based on the mastodon as a patriotic totem. Claudine Cohen's *The Fate of the Mammoth* (translated into English

in 2002) focuses on European myths and theories about prehistoric elephants, with passing reference to American Indian legends. Native American scholar Vine Deloria, Jr., pits Native American worldviews against Euro-American science, with some paleontological examples, in *Red Earth, White Lies* (1997). Deloria also presents examples of Native knowledge excluded from orthodox science and history as superstition and fantasy. A few archaeologists have collected evidence for Native American interest in fossils. For example, rock art scholar Peter Faris presented a survey titled "Native American Paleontology: Fossils, Myths, and Imagery" to the Utah Rock Art Research Association in 2001, and his investigations are ongoing. See also Jerry McDonald's 1989 paper "A Collection of Fossils from an Adena Mound in Athens County, Ohio, and Notes on the Collecting and Uses of Fossils by Native Americans." An important 1996 article by Allison Dussias, "Science, Sovereignty, and the Sacred Text: Paleontological Resources and Native American Rights," surveys the history of legal issues surrounding fossils in the western United States, since the era of Cope and Marsh, from the Native American point of view (thanks to Daniel Usner for this reference).

8. Simpson 1942, 132, 134–35; 1943, 26–27. Léo Laporte, per. cor., February 3, 2000. Simpson's personality and career: see Laporte 2000; thanks also to Nate Murphy, interview, July–September 2000; Michael Bell, per. cor., February 3, 2000; Bob Evander, per. cor., February 2000; and Peter Dodson, per. cor., July 20, 2003.

Throughout my endnotes, conversations about specific questions in person or by telephone are cited as per. com.; by letter or email as per. cor. Longer, free-ranging exchanges in person, by phone, or email are cited as interviews. A list of interviewees is included at the end of the bibliography.

9. Simpson 1942, 132–35; 1943, 26–27. The appendix, "Fossil Frauds and Specious Legends," analyzes some notorious false and pseudo-fossil legends, of the sort that apparently led Simpson to deplore all fossil-related traditions as spurious. Simpson 1934, 110, 161.

10. Simpson 1942, 132, 134.

11. Simpson 1943, 26, 37. Anthropologist Loren Eiseley 1945, 84, for example, cited Simpson's critical assessment with approval and suggested that Native American myths about fossils were inspired by European requests for information. Ethnologist Robert Lowie rejected oral traditions as a source of history in 1917: see Echo-Hawk 2000, 274. Deloria 1997, 7, 9, cited Simpson's official history of early paleontology as a prime example of how "scientists have maintained a stranglehold on the definitions of . . . reliable human experiences."

12. Peter Dodson read a draft of this chapter and made these comments in January 2002. Thanks also to Léo Laporte, Simpson's biographer, for helpful comments.

13. The terms *myth*, *legend*, *folklore*, and *tradition* are often used interchangeably, as in this book. Their features overlap, but *mythology* or *myth* typically describes actions of gods or supernatural beings to explain the origins of the world (as in creation myths). *Legends* are less exalted folklore narratives that feature animals and/or human beings pursuing unusual exploits, often set in historical times and/or real places. A legend purports to be true, but it often contains mythological language and allusions. Legendary *traditions* often coalesce around actual events and/or natural facts and were transmitted orally over generations, in some cases never captured in print. This book focuses on legends and traditions that relate to observations of unusual natural phenomena, namely, geological formations and paleontological remains. I discuss creation myths and the like when they provide a relevant background for understanding fossil legends and beliefs. Appropriating modern material into traditional culture: see, for example, Wildschut 1960, 168–69, on the Crow Indians' integration of new, manufactured materials into their traditional medicine bundles.

14. Tylor 1964, 167. Vitaliano 1973. For an Indian perspective on Vitaliano and geomyths, see Deloria 1997, 168–86. For a comprehensive definition and worldwide examples of geomythology, see Mayor 2004.

15. For example, folklore about frozen mammoths is already well covered in the literature: see, e.g., Cohen 2002. South American fossil lore is a rich but little-studied topic; for some examples, see Dozo 1997. Many more Native American fossil accounts await study. For example, when I asked the Blackfeet historian Curly Bear Wagner about the cultural significance of dinosaur bones in Blackfeet traditions, he replied that he himself had not researched that aspect of his people's history, but commented that elders' stories about dinosaur fossils exist in recordings in Blackfeet Reservation archives in Browning, Montana. Wagner, per. com., August 16, 2003.

16. Washburn 1975, 33–35; Emerson 1884, 549.

17. Wayne Archambault, interview, September 7–8, 2000. Emerson 1884, 549: "Les Sauvages," wrote a seventeenth-century French missionary, "have the best memories in the world." See Simpson's memoir of his Patagonian expedition, Simpson 1934, 59, 161.

18. Barbara Mann, interview, June 2002. Lowie cited by Thomas 2000, 99–101. Folklore scholars now generally accept that oral traditions about historical events endure for about a thousand years, although some oral myths about geological and astronomical events can be reliably dated to about seven thousand years. On studies testing the antiquity and accuracy of oral history and traditions, see Echo-Hawk 2000, quotation 267. The processes of creating reliable oral myths about datable geological, historical, or astronomical events thousands of years ago are now analyzed in terms of linguistics and cognition by Barber and Barber 2005.

These issues were broached by Deloria in 1997, 126–36, 39 (observation and accuracy), and 186 (Deloria believed the extent of human memory to be about three thousand years). See also Thomas 2000, chapter 10, on the history of the ethnological debate over whether oral traditions preserve "real history."

19. The *Turok* tales, written and illustrated by writers and artists who were knowledgeable about the latest archaeological and paleontological discoveries of the 1950s and 1960s, told the adventures of two Plains Indians of the 1860s, Turok and his son Andar, who fell into a "medicine hole of time" where they encountered real, live dinosaurs. In 2003, I conducted an informal survey on the Society of Vertebrate Paleontology and Dinosaur Internet discussion lists to elicit memories and comments about the *Turok* comic books. I received more than thirty responses from academic and independent paleontologists and other earth and biological scientists. See also Farlow and Brett-Surman 1997, 691. Native Americans who appreciate *Turok* include John Allen, Jr. (Assiniboine, Montana), Nita Manning (Cheyenne, Black Hills), Todd Tamanend Clark (Seneca/Lenape, Pennsylvania), and Paul Apodaca (Mixtec/Navajo historian, California). Apodaca's comment was typical: "I can tell you I was a reader of *Turok, Son of Stone* while growing up. It was a favorite due to its Native American imagery combined with dinosaurs, favorites for all children and especially for an Indian child." Interview, January 2002. Todd Tamanend Clark began collecting *Turok* comics at age six and now has thousands of Indian-oriented comic books from the 1950s and 1960s. "For its time," says Clark, "the Turok series was a noble, if flawed effort." Despite the stereotypes, Clark believes the comics still have great educational value. Per. cor., August 18, 2000. Nita Manning suggests that the *Turok* illustrations would be a wonderful way to teach paleontology. John Allen, Jr., involved in his reservation's Head Start Program, praised the old comics' spiritual values, as long as one realizes that dinosaurs and humans never really coexisted. This unexpected common bond between Native Americans and paleontologists, a mutual fascination with good storytelling in the style of the old *Turok* adventures, could be a valuable educational tool.

20. In his book on Yuchi traditions, Jason Jackson 2003, chapter 8, addresses conflicting interpretations and contradictions in oral stories, differing effects on hearers and performers, and problems of outsiders' retelling oral myths.

21. Deloria 1997, xiv–xv. Juanita Pahdopony, interview, April–May 2002. Virginia Driving Hawk Sneve, per. cor., May 6, 2002. John Allen, Jr., interview, September 6, 2000. Neeake, elected principal storyteller of the Shawnee Nation United Remnant Band, interview, March–April 2002. I am grateful to Deloria, Pahdopony, Neeake, and Roger Echo-Hawk for valuable discussions of these issues.

22. Fossilization, geological ages, and dinosaur species: Norell, Dingus, and Gaffney 2000, 74–82 (fossilization process); Weishampel and Young 1996, 29–32. For a good survey and illustrations of Ice Age mammals, see Kurten and Anderson 1980. Mammoth and mastodon sites: Lister and Bahn 1994. Tertiary mammals: O'Harra 1920. Paleontological museums: Costa 1994; Halls 1996 and 2005; Palmer 1999; Farlow and Brett-Surman 1997; Norell, Dingus, and Gaffney 2000, 76–80. Skwara 1992 is an invaluable guide to interpreted vertebrate fossil localities in western Canada and the United States.

23. See White 1991 for an account of the accommodating interactions and exchanges of knowledge among Native people and Europeans in the colonial period, in striking contrast to the way Indians were recast as alien others in the nineteenth century. Thomas 2000, chapter 2, also discusses this nineteenth-century transformation in white-Indian relations.

INTRODUCTION
MARSH MONSTERS OF BIG BONE LICK

1. Daubenton's paper was published in 1764. The first illustration of the mastodon teeth found in 1739 was published by Guettard in 1756. French and English discoveries of Big Bone Lick fossils: Kindle 1931 and 1935; Simpson, 1942, 135–39; Simpson 1943, 27–34; Semonin 2000, 87, 111–35; Jillson 1936; Stevens and Kent 1941. Mastodons and mammoths are often confused, especially since the American mastodon was named *Mammut americanum*, while *Mammuthus* refers to the mammoth genus. Both are ancestors of elephants, and both survived till the end of the Pleistocene, but they are not closely related. Mastodons have sharp, pointed molars, while mammoths have flat, ripple-surface molars. See Lister and Bahn 1994. Thanks to Peter Dodson and Barbara Mann, who read and commented on early drafts of this chapter.

2. Cuvier 1821, 208. Simpson 1942, 132–37, and 1943, 28–34: Simpson says Daubenton's testimony about the Indians' discovery "can be granted no weight" because Daubenton was "guilty of special pleading" on their part in order to support his conclusions. Of course, Longueuil does deserve credit for recognizing the fossils' value and escorting them to France. Martin Rudwick's 1976 history of paleontological milestones discusses the 1739 discovery without ever mentioning Native Americans: Rudwick 1985, 105. Cohen 2002, 90, follows Simpson's account (including his erroneous claim that the French defeated the Chickasaws) but leaves out the discovery by "les Sauvages." The combined French forces were defeated by the Chickasaws in 1736, 1739, and again in 1752—and the Chicka-

saws were still victorious at the time of the French surrender to the British in 1763. Waldman 2000, 128.

3. Semonin 2000, 87.

4. Big Bone Lick State Park, Union, Kentucky, museum booklets and brochures published by the Kentucky Department of Parks, 1996, and in March 2000.

5. Since 1936, most historians, apparently unaware of the composition of Longueuil's army—319 Canadian Indians and only 123 Frenchmen—have assumed, along with the historian of Big Bone Lick, W. R. Jillson, that the fossil finders were local Ohio Valley Indians recruited by the French. For example, Jillson (1936, 3) stated: "We may assume without fear of error that [Longueuil] was taken to the remarkable locality by Indian guides," for "this lick . . . was widely known among the aboriginal tribes [of] the Ohio Valley." Only Bell 1949, 169, credited the "Indians in a party of French travelling from Canada" with the discovery. In 2002, 263, Pascal Tassy wrote that the mastodon specimens that initiated the revolution in understanding of fossil species were discovered in 1739 " by the Indians who guided Longueuil's troops on the way to New Orleans."

6. On the French-Abenaki alliance, see Waldman 2000, 121. By 1700, many Algonquians, including Abenakis, were Christianized in Canada and New England, and many were literate in French and Latin. White 1991, 167. By winter of 1739, the combined French armies heading for New Orleans numbered twelve thousand Frenchmen and two thousand Indians and African blacks: Schlarman 1929, 278.

7. French Jesuits helped recruit the Indians for Longueuil's army: Stevens and Kent 1941, 2. The French and their Abenaki allies held important forts in the 1740s–50s. Some Iroquois people lived in Shawnee villages at this time, as reported by French explorers, and few Catholic Iroquois joined French expeditions. Pierre Joseph Celeron was accompanied by Abenakis and a couple of Iroquois on his trip down the Ohio in 1749, and he encountered many hostile villages of Shawnees and Iroquois living together. It is possible that a few Iroquois warriors accompanied Longueuil's army, but the majority were almost surely Abenakis. Celeron 1749, 666, 672, 694, 701, 704, 710.

8. Tsonakwa notes that "ancient animosities between the Abenakis and Iroquois were being fanned into flames by the Europeans." By 1687, the Abenakis and Iroquois were "locked in a death grip," and Abenaki warriors joined the French army in large numbers during the French and Indian Wars. See Tsonakwa and Yolaikia 2001, 104–7.

9. Waldman 2000; Gerard Tsonakwa, interview, February–March 2001; Kindle 1935; Semonin 2000; Jillson 1936. Saline and sulfur springs and bogs occur widely along the Ohio.

10. Gerard Tsonakwa interview. On European explorers instructed to ask about "fossil bones of large animals," see, e.g., Kindle 1935, 451 (David Thompson of the North West Company in 1797); Strong 1934, 86. Fossil ivory trade: Cohen 2002, 65–66, 79–80.

11. Emerson 1884, 338–39. See Spence 1914, 248, for the tale recorded by French Jesuits in the seventeenth century. Creek Indian ivory horn amulets: Gatschet 1899, 259. Fossil ivory in Ohio mounds: thanks to Patricia Mason. Hiscock Site: Chandler 2001. For horned serpents, dragons, and monsters in Native American folklore, see Gatschet 1899; Faris 2001; and Meurger and Gagnon 1988. For the history of Native American and Euro-American relations of this period, see White 1991.

12. Gist, *Journal Through Ohio and Kentucky in 1750–51*, 57–58, cited by Jillson 1936, 5–6. The trader hid the huge tusk in about 1744, five years after Longueuil's men collected the fossils later sent to Paris in 1740.

13. Fossils in London: Simpson 1943, 37. Croghan knew of the salt lick bones in the 1740s and actively collected fossils in the 1760s; he sent some samples collected in 1766 to Benjamin Franklin. See Collinson 1767. Fossils collected by Croghan also ended up in Germany and Holland: Bell 1949, 172–77. Names of the Shawnee chiefs: Croghan 1759. See Croghan 1767; Kindle 1935, 450 and n. 15; Jillson 1936, 15–16; Simpson 1942, 141–42; Semonin 2000, 104–10. Croghan's continuing expeditions are discussed below.

14. On folk memories of living mastodons and Great Elk tales, see Strong 1934; Eiseley 1945; Lankford 1980; Charlevoix 1744, 187; Scott 1887. See also Deloria 1997, 127–32; and Faris 2002. Notably, the Iroquois also had a monster known as Big Elk, described by David Cusick, 1825, 10. Oral history "arguably preserves glimpses and echoes of the long-vanished Pleistocene world of our ancestors," maintains Echo-Hawk 2000, 273. For an excellent analysis of the cognitive, linguistic, and scientific evidence for oral folk memories extending back centuries and even millennia, see Barber and Barber 2005.

15. *Wapapi Adihondagt Aodowoganal* (Record of the Adirondack Wars), cited by Tsonakwa and Yolaikia 2001, 74. When New France fell to the British, "the Jesuits sent many Wapapi (beaded mnemonic records) to the Vatican and France for safekeeping," and many of these wapapi are still stored in Rheims Cathedral (107). For an Abenaki water monster story, see 75–79. Tsonakwa describes the water monster as a prehistoric carnivorous reptile "dreaming" of Permian and Triassic swamps. Horned water monsters are a widespread Amerindian motif: for the history of water monster beliefs, see Meurger and Gagnon 1988; for an example of lake monster tales in Quebec associated with "bones and enormous dinosaur teeth," 101. For illustrations of horned water monsters in Indian rock

paintings of the Great Lakes, see Dewdney and Kidd 1967, 2–3, 81–85, 149; and Ewers 1981.

16. Daubenton may also have received information from the mapmakers de Lery, Bellin, and Mandeville. Simpson believed that "it is probable that some written notation was preserved with the specimens in the Cabinet du Roi." Simpson 1943, 29–31; 1942, 135–39. Pascal Tassy interview, December 7, 2000: Tassy remarked that two "mysterious" Frenchmen associated with Longueuil, Fabri and du Hamel, told Buffon, Daubenton, and Georges Cuvier the circumstances of the Indian hunters' 1739 discovery. Both Fabri and du Hamel stated that the Indians alone found and gathered the fossils. Fabri described the remains as a tusk and a femur, while du Hamel also included the teeth. It was long thought that only two of the molars survived. Fabri served as an officer with Longueuil and wrote to Buffon from New Orleans in 1748, recounting the Louisiana monster tradition, and noting that similar fossils were seen by Natives of Canada. It was Fabri who told Buffon that the Indians referred to mastodon bones as "the grandfather of the buffalo." Cuvier 1821, 209. See also Mercer 1885, 16.

17. Thanks to Josiah Ober for suggesting an investigation of the hippopotamus–water monster analogy. Since many African blacks from the South served with the French forces that merged with Longueuil's Canadian army to fight the Chickasaw War of 1739, it is even possible that African ideas about the fossils contributed to Daubenton's conclusions. Africans would have recognized the ivory tusk as an elephant's but would have noticed that the teeth most resembled those of a hippopotamus.

18. Jennison 1971, 131–40. Wendt 1959, 72–73. Semonin 2000, 72–73, 85, and see fig. 6, a 1682 engraving of a ferocious hippopotamus-behemoth.

19. Pascal Tassy interview. Tassy told me that sometime after World War II, Simpson wrote to the museum requesting a plaster cast of one of Longueuil's specimen molars for his personal collection. The whereabouts of Simpson's cast is unknown. Daubenton 1764. On Cuvier and the Jardin des Plantes museums in Paris, see Rudwick 1976, chapter 3. The inventory number of the femur in Paris is A.C. 2020; the last time it was correctly identified was in 1823. Rice 1951. Interestingly, Rice undertook his study in order to refute George Gaylord Simpson's denigration of Thomas Jefferson's contributions to paleontology (1942, 155). It's revealing that Simpson's scientific gatekeeping placed both Jefferson *and* Native Americans outside "true scientific history." The labels on the femurs in Paris were corrected in 2001. The one on the right now reads: "Proboscidiens— Mastodonte americain (*Mammut americanum*)—Fémur gauche—Gisement de Big Bone Lick (Kentucky, USA). Pleistocène récent—Ce fémur, découvert au bord de la rivière Ohio par le baron de Longueuil en 1739, a été décrit en 1764 par L.J.M. Daubenton qui en démontra les affinités éléphantines." The femur on the

left is now labeled as a *Stegomastodon* from Argentina, a gift of M. Bonnement. Tassy, per. cor., May 15, 2003.

20. In 2002, Pascal Tassy and the museum preparators generously created a set of painted casts of all three molars for me to study. Tassy published his discovery of the mislabeled third tooth (m3 MNHN 1643) in Tassy 2002 and proposed that it become the lectotype of *Mammut americanum*. Tassy interview; Tassy, per. cor., April 6, 2001; July 9, 2002; May 15, 2003.

21. On Morgan, see White 1991, 380–87. Winterbotham 1795, 3:1. The fossils collected by Morgan were drawn by Charles Willson Peale, and what remains of the Morgan collection is kept by the University of Groningen, Germany. Bell 1949. Morgan's transcription was published by William Winterbotham in London in 1795 (and in America in 1796) and was quoted in part by Mercer in 1885, 14–15. Mercer mistakenly attributed the collection of the story to Croghan, however, giving the year as 1748 rather than 1766, and Mercer assumed that the old chief was a Wyandot. Mercer's 1885 book on the notorious Lenape Stone (a faked carving alleged to illustrate the Delaware fossil legend recorded by Jefferson; see appendix) was derided by George Gaylord Simpson, yet in his reading of Mercer, Simpson seems to have missed this genuine historical incident first reported by Winterbotham and discussed by Mercer. Indeed, Simpson dismissed *all* other accounts of the salt lick fossil beds between Longueuil's 1739 expedition and Daubenton's 1762 paper as having "no bearing on paleontological history except to suggest increasing familiarity with the locality among the usually inarticulate frequenters of the disputed wilderness." Morgan's transcription of the Iroquois legend was not mentioned in descriptions of Big Bone Lick by Kindle 1935; Jillson 1936; Simpson 1942, 132 (discussion of Mercer's Lenape Stone), 139 ("inarticulate"); 140–42 (Croghan), and 1943, 37; or by Semonin 2000, 107–8, 163–64, 191–93 (although he mentions that Morgan's bone collection of 1766 went unopened until 1783, when the specimens were drawn by Charles Willson Peale).

22. Wyandots: White 1991, 147, 195–96, 231. Wyandots and Iroquois: Barbeau 1994, 329–31, 345, 353–54; Wyandots vs. Cherokees, 295, 338–39.

23. Andrew Montour, Croghan's Iroquois-French translator, was not present at the meeting described by Morgan, having died in 1752. Croghan's papers, deed books, treaty councils, the papers of Fort Pitt's commander Bouquet, etc., are cited in various sources, see http://www.swcp.com/~dhickman/notes/mingo.html. George Washington was interested in fossils, too: see Semonin 2000, 6–7, 95, 164–66, 176–78. Collinson 1767. Washington 1754.

24. In this book, I use "buffalo" and "bison" interchangeably (technically "bison" refers to the American species). In Iroquois tradition, says Barbara Mann, the "great buffalo"—which she identifies as mastodons—were also known as "Big Shaggies," earth creatures hostile to humans. Mann, interviews, May 27, 2002;

June 12, 2002. The eternal tension between sky and earth-water forces is most clearly seen in Sioux mythology; see chapter 5. Thanks to Patricia Mason for putting me in touch with Barbara Mann, scholar of Native American studies, University of Toledo.

25. Allusions to race were common in Indian oratory at this time, according to White 1991, 282–83. Paul Apodaca, interview, January 2002.

26. Thanks to Eric Buffetaut and Madame Ozanne. Nadaillac 1885; Smith 1883; Spence 1914, 246–48. Echoing Cotton Mather and anticipating George Gaylord Simpson, William Beauchamp (1976, 47–48) noted in 1892 that Mrs. Smith had collected "an allusion" to mastodons in 1890, but stated that Indian "traditions of this creature are of little authority, yet of some interest." Nevertheless, Beauchamp did not relate the story to Ohio fossils.

27. Waldman 2000, 114. Before the eighteenth century, the Tuscaroras lived in Carolina. David Cusick claimed that they warred with the *Oyatoh*, the Iroquois name for the Cherokees, before Columbus. The Iroquois portrayed the early Cherokees as primitive people dwelling in caves and swamps. Beauchamp 1976, 23–25 (Cusick on Ohio explorations), 37, 102. Cusick 1825, 23–25. Schoolcraft 1846, 148–49, 169, 172. Barbara Mann, interview, June 12, 2002. For a Wyandot tale (told by Chief Mandarong, or Joseph White) that begins with the same setting, a war party against the Cherokees in ancient times, and a warrior abandoned on the way home, see Barbeau 1994, 295.

28. Quotation, Schoolcraft 1846, 149. The Iroquois were not the only far-ranging nation: Plains Indians routinely traveled thousands of miles, from Canada to Mexico, for trade, war, and hunting: Wildschut 1960, 169. According to Wyandot tradition recorded in 1870, a Wyandot party crossed the Mississippi heading for the "Backbone" (the Rockies) in 1710–21. Barbeau 1994, 351–52. Shawnee fossil lore is discussed in the next chapter. On Iroquois captives, many from distant nations such as the Cherokees and Shawnees, see Cusick cited in Beauchamp in 1892 (1976, 72; Onondaga chief of Cherokee descent, 102, 109). On Iroquois intermarrying with Cherokees, Parker 1989, 358. Cherokee Ukténa lore: Gatschet 1899, 259. See also "Legend of the Tlanuhwa [Thunder Birds] and Uhktena," an old tradition retold by David Mitchell Wolfe, a Virginia Cherokee, 2000, www.manataka.org/page221.html. I know of no Cherokee legends that directly associate large fossil bones or other remains with these monsters, although Thunder Bird eggs are said to be found in caves along the Tennessee River, and the water monster is said to possess a magical stone or crystal with magical powers. See Hudson 1976, 137–69, figs. 39, 44, 45, for artistic depictions of Cherokee monsters and Thunder Birds. *Ukténa* appears to be linguistically close to the name of the Dakota water monster *Unktehi* (see chapter 5).

29. Scouts and explorers as trustworthy reporters and repositories of oral traditions: Deloria 1997, 39. Cusick 1825, 23–25, cited by Beauchamp in 1892, on the Iroquois expeditions to the West and the Ohio River, 1976, 23–25. On Indian trails and trade routes, see Waldman 2000, 64–65, map. Thanks to Frank Winchell, Varna Boyd, Everett Bassett, and Carole Nash, for information on Indian trails.

30. Wyandot legend of Big Bone Lick: Barbeau 1994, 276–78. Barbara Mann, per. cor., May 27, 2002. Wyandot hunting amulets from petrified monster bones: Barbeau 1994, 116–17, 376.

31. Simpson 1942, 132, 135.

32. Barbara Mann believes that the tradition transcribed by Morgan in 1766 is "so christianized as to lose the actual idea that the speakers were trying to convey, a typical problem in the old records." Mann, interviews, May 27, 2002; June 12, 2002.

33. Simpson 1943, 27.

CHAPTER 1
THE NORTHEAST: GIANTS, GREAT BEARS, AND
GRANDFATHER OF THE BUFFALO

1. Mammoths in Siberia and Asia deposited by the violent action of the winds and waves at the time of the Deluge: Collinson 1767. For biblical doctrines and pre-Darwinian European and American paleontological theories and advances, see Rudwick 1985; Simpson 1942, 1943; Semonin 2000. See Weishampel and Young 1996 for the history of paleontology in the Northeast. Barbara Mann made valuable suggestions on the Iroquois material in this chapter.

2. Stanford 1959. Semonin 2000, 9, 15–40. Tribes: Waldman 2000. Abenaki saying: Tsonakwa and Yolaikia 2001, 41. Weetucks and Maushops giant legends: Simmons 1986, chapter 9. Mohican and Delaware hairless bear: Adams 1997, 27; Bierhorst 1995, 12. W. B. Scott 1887, 477, suggested that these odd "bear" images were based on giant sloths, which would have been observed alive by Ice Age humans. For discoveries of mastodon remains between 1705 and 1923 in New York State, see Osborn 1923, 7, map.

3. Levin 1988, 756–57, 768. Mather's *Life of Eliot*, cited in Neill 1859. Mather did not name the Indians he referred to; they may have been Mohawks, Mohicans, Pequots, Narragansetts, Massachusetts, and/or Wampanoags. *Selected Works* 1974. Semonin 2000, 21–24. The Abenaki historian Gerard Tsonakwa feels that Mather had some "compassion for Native Peoples," since he "took great pains to learn local dialects and foster literacy" and trained interpreters and published reli-

gious texts in Algonquian. Tsonakwa and Yolaikia 2001, 107. *Maughkompos* (*Magoshketomp*) appears to have been a word for "giant man," a variant of the coastal Massachusetts name *Moshops* or *Maushops*, all based on the words *mogke* (great) and *wosketomp* (man). See John Hammond Trumbull's entry in *Natick Dictionary*, compiled in 1903 (Washington, DC), based on seventeenth-century sources, especially the Puritan missionary John Eliot's "Indian Bible." I thank Sam Seibert for this information.

4. Clara Sue Kidwell, Native American Studies Program, University of Oklahoma, per. com., March 2001. Ontario: Coleman and Clark 1999, 110; Cusick 1825, 11.

5. Cusick 1825, 3–4 (apes), and see Beauchamp 1976, 4–15, 47, 50, 61. Cusick's chronologies, derived from ancient oral histories, are probably exaggerated, but they demonstrate the Iroquois sense of deep time and suggest the extent of chronological oral histories, especially in the case of datable phenomena.

6. Cusick 1825, 5–10, 14. Johnson 1881, 41–42, 56–57. There was a major earthquake east of the Great Lakes in 1663: Beauchamp 1976, 103. Cornplanter 1938, 64–65. Seneca Castle fossils: thanks to John Chiment, per. cor., 1999 and 2000. Archaeologists excavating Iroquoian village sites of A.D. 800 to 1650 have found fossils collected as curios and made into pendants; one village of A.D. 1500 yielded 140 such fossils. Robert Pearce, London Museum of Archaeology, Ontario, per. cor., March 25, 1998, November 7, 2001.

7. Parker 1989, 222 (scales from horned serpents worn as medicine amulets). Thanks to Peter Faris for helpful discussions of horned water monsters. Mica: Barbara Mann, interview, June 5, 2002. Later, I learned that the Sioux also visualized Water Monsters covered in scales of glittering mica, but in the Southwest fossil dinosaur scutes were sometimes identified as the armor of a mythic monster called *Yeitso* (chapter 3). Compare a story told by the Sioux medicine man George Eagle Elk, Parmalee, South Dakota, in 1968: Erdoes and Ortiz 1984, 238. Scutes of prehistoric reptiles on the East Coast: Weishampel and Young 1996, 172.

8. Stone Giants: Cusick 1825, 14–16; Parker 1989, 340–41; Emerson 1884, 419. Cardiff Giant: Jaffe 2000, 1–2, 5; Wallace 1999, 54–55; Johnson 1881. See the appendix for other fossil legend hoaxes.

9. On Iroquois tales of horned water monsters, mammoth bears, Stone Giants, and pygmies, see Parker 1989; Cornplanter 1938 (on scales of the horned water monster), 77, 79. Cusick 1825, 10–11, 14, 16, 18. On Algonquian Thunder Bird beliefs collected by Jesuits in 1637 and others, including a reference to finding scattered "bones of serpents" at the nest of a Thunder Bird, see Chamberlain 1890. Delaware horned water monsters: Bierhorst 1995, 11.

10. Cusick 1825, 18, called the Giant Bear *Oyalquoher* and said that it fought a monster lion. Parker 1989, 349–57, 17, 361–62, 222. Tahadondeh's tale was

recorded in 1903 by Arthur Parker, a Seneca born in 1881, who became the director of the Rochester Museum of Science. He commissioned Native artists to illustrate Iroquois traditions in the 1930s.

11. Cornplanter 1938, 105-37. See Osborn 1923, 7, map, for Pleistocene mammoth sites in New York State known to whites since 1705. See Simpson 1942, 157-61, and Semonin 2000, 315-40, for the excitement surrounding mastodon finds in New York. *Arctodus simus* fossils have been found in northwestern Ohio and central Pennsylvania (Seneca lands), and there is evidence of giant bear fossils in New York State, where numerous huge mastodon bones were crushed and gnawed by the jaws of a gigantic predator (thanks to Richard Laub and Bill Parsons of the Buffalo Museum of Science for this information).

12. Uki prints: Barbara Mann, per. cor., June 12, 2002. Great Mosquito Monster: Cusick 1825, 18. Cornplanter's story in Canfield 1902, 59-61. Beauchamp 1922, 225 (tracks of Great Spirit near Jamesville); and 1976, 18, 71 ("until recently" the Great Mosquito tracks could be seen near Brighton, "being often renewed by the Indians," a phrase written in 1892 that suggests the tracks were indeed petroglyphs). Condors in New York: Chandler 2001. Johnson 1881, 58. Canfield 1902. Douglas Schwartz, of the New England Archaeological Research Association, provided photographs of his discoveries of footprints carved in granite, per. cor., May 15, 2000. Connecticut Valley dinosaur footprints were discovered by white settlers in 1802 and recognized as dinosaur prints in 1845: Weishampel and Young 1996, chapter 4 and 106-5; Mayor and Sarjeant 2001, 151. Semonin 2000, 380-81, 397. Sam Siebert, per. cor., March 8, 2001, notes that footprints associated with tribal lore were known in Long Island, New York, and Montville, Connecticut. I thank Rob Schrenck for information about the tracks in Rockland County, and Emma Rainforth for information on Lyell's investigation. On Mesozoic fossil species of the Northeast, see Weishampel and Young. See Tanner 1984 on distinguishing genuine fossil tracks from man-made replicas and natural foot-shaped depressions (thanks to Tony Arnold for this reference).

13. Adams 1997, 40. Quotation from T-rex Natural History Museum pamphlet, Ranchester, Wyoming, July 2003. Wyandot footprint legends: Barbeau 1994, 278, and see 438, photo XA, for the prints at Wendake, Quebec.

14. The Shawnees and Delawares had migrated to the Ohio Valley from the East. The large vertebrate species at Big Bone Lick and related exposures include the giant sloth *Megalonyx jeffersonii*; mastodon *Mammut americanum*; woolly and Columbian mammoths *Mammuthus primigenius* and *M. columbi*; giant bison *Bison antiquus* and *B. latifrons*; and elk, moose, caribou, deer, and musk ox species. See Jillson 1936 for the full history of the discoveries at Big Bone Lick. He estimated that the bones of about 250 individual mammoths alone had been removed from

the site since the eighteenth century (119). The Big Bone Lick surface area was picked clean of bones by 1783, according to Semonin 2000, 196.

15. Buffon 1740–88. See Cuvier 1821, 209. On the concept of "grandfather" as ancestor or master of a species, see Lankford 1980, 299. Blackfeet: see chapter 5. De Jeune cited in Tylor 1964, 180–81 and n. 29. Giant beaver lore: see Harington 1996 (Yukon); Faris 2002; Sandoz 1964, 23; Deloria 1997, 133–4. A giant beaver tooth made into a tool was found in the Hiscock Site, New York (occupied about two thousand years ago): see Chandler 2001. In paleo-Indian mounds in Ohio, archaeologists have found iron meteors imported from Kansas (meteors were a trade item of the Pawnees) that had been hammered into chisels modeled on the shape and size of giant beaver teeth: thanks to Dale Gnidovec, per. cor., June 22, 2003, citing *Michigan History Magazine*, November–December 1994. On giant bison as ancestors of today's bison, see Deloria 1997, 150–51. Winterbotham 1795, 3:139; Mercer 1885, 14–15. Spalding 1999, 22–23. Scott 1887, 477.

16. *Journal of Nicholas Cresswell*, 1774–77, 76, 88–89, cited in Jillson 1936, 22. Beauchamp 1922, 48.

17. *Escape from Indian Captivity* 1982, 12. Big Bone Lick State Park museum texts (seen in April 2001) along the interpretive trail refer to Indians gathering and boiling "magic white sand" (salt) in the 1600s.

18. Wright cited in Simpson 1942, 140, and 1943, 36 and n. 11; Semonin 2000, 100–101; 102: the London naturalist Peter Collinson wrote to John Bartram in 1762 remarking that the Shawnees had referred to the Ohio creatures as "Monstrous Buffaloes ... all struck dead with Lightning." On giant men hunting giant animals, Deloria 1997, 139–41, 147–49. The Shawnee discovery of buttocks-prints in stone is not unique. The Delaware legend below also refers to seat-prints; so does an Assiniboine legend in Montana; and see Lowie 1909, 105, on the buttocks-print left by Iktomi, the mythic trickster of Sioux lore. The Aztecs of Mexico (chapter 2) and Aborigines of Australia have similar accounts. On worldwide folklore about fossil traces, see Mayor and Sarjeant 2001, on buttocks-prints, 156–57. Impressions of dinosaur buttocks in rock have been scientifically recorded (157), but another possibility was suggested to me by Bill Matteson, paleontology student at Sheridan College, Wyoming, in October 2000. He pointed out that large fossil turtle carapaces can leave impressions that resemble human "sitz-marks."

19. Barbara Mann, interview, June 12, 2002. Cf. Dr. William Hunter's view, in a scientific paper of 1769, that the extinction of the American mastodon was a blessing from Heaven, and Dr. James Parkinson's writings in 1804, presenting the successive creation and destruction of species as "phases in the progress of God's nature toward a more perfect form—that of the human species." For these and

other examples of Christian views of evolution and extinction as evidence of God's wisdom, see Semonin 2000, 3, 8, 152, 364–65.

20. Catesby 1743, 2, appendix 7. Cuvier 1806, 55–56; Cuvier 1821, 154–55. Simpson 1942, 132–34 (quotation 134).

21. As Semonin remarked, "even the opinions of African slaves were reported" in the quest to learn the identity of prehistoric fossils. Semonin 2000, 85–86, 193–94. The Africans in America must have been excited to find evidence of familiar-seeming elephants in the New World. As Indians of the South mingled with run-away slaves, they began to absorb African folklore, which resulted in African-like creatures in stories of southeastern tribes. For example, the Choctaws of Mississippi told of giant cannibals who had long ago used mammoths "as their burden bearers," and the Chitimachas of Louisiana described people of the remote past who built houses on scaffolds to escape a "long-nosed monster" that uprooted trees. Alabama Indian legends featured elephantlike creatures and even a gorillalike ogre called "Kolowa." Such stories cannot be considered *fossil legends* since there was no mention of finding bones, but they show how Native American traditions incorporated new zoological information from many sources, a theme evident in chapters ahead. Eiseley 1945, 86–87. For African influences on southern Indian legends, see Lankford 1980, 295, 298–99, citing an article by Alan Dundes on African tales told by Native Americans, in *Southern Folklore Quarterly* (1965). Strong 1934, 86.

22. Jefferson, writing in 1781, 1954, 54. Jefferson learned some Native American vocabularies from Indian trader Col. Gibson: Schoolcraft 1846, 171. Ned Gilmore, Academy of Natural Sciences, Philadelphia, kindly showed me Jefferson's fossil collection in October 2001. Jefferson as paleontologist: Mitchell 1998, chapters 16–17; Lucas 1926; Semonin 2000. Barbara Mann, interview, June 12, 2002. Jefferson on upper Missouri bones: Lucas 1926, 328. Upper Missouri dinosaurs: Wallace 1999, 48–49, 122–23. For early French traders on the upper Missouri in the 1700s, see Grinnell 1923, 1:34–38. Hayden sent the first American dinosaur fossils of the West to Leidy in 1856: they came from the Judith River Formation in Montana.

23. Jefferson 1954, 43–45. Schoolcraft 1884, 1:221. Nez Perce Otis Halfmoon, cited by Ella Clark 1966, 39; for a Shoshone tradition recounted in 1953 by Ralph Dixie, 171. Cuvier 1821, 218. Lewis and Clark were prepared to look for fossil evidence of mastodons in the Northwest: Lewis visited the anatomist Caspar Wistar in Philadelphia, who showed him how to recognize fossils and tracks of large animals, and Clark (with his brother George Rogers Clark) was dispatched to Big Bone Lick to collect mastodon fossils. The Clarks shipped three large crates of fossils to Jefferson by way of New Orleans in 1807. Franklin cited in Simpson 1942, 142; on Stanley, see 169. Stiles: Lucas 1926 and Semonin 2000, 206–11. Leidy 1852, 4.

24. Jefferson 1954, 43; Semonin 2000, 182–85, 196, 292. Eiseley 1945, 86–87, suggests that the Indians told Jefferson and other whites what they wanted to hear. Indian mythology scholar Paul Apodaca agrees with this view; for an opposing Indian view, see Deloria 1997, 128–29. Barbara Mann points out that the motif of the surviving animal was a way of showing that no natural force could completely destroy another. The Choctaws of Mississippi in 1880 told a version of the Delaware-Shawnee tale; see Lankford 1980, 295. On the occurrence of fossil footprints in the region, see Mayor and Sarjeant 2000, 156–57. On the discovery of the dubious Delaware carving known as the Lenape Stone, allegedly illustrating the legend recorded by Jefferson, see Mercer 1885, and the appendix.

25. Cuvier's library was described by the geologist Charles Lyell (1797–1875): Craig and Jones 1985, 144–45. Peter Collinson had sent one of Croghan's fossil specimens and his journal extract to Buffon in 1767: Bell 1949, 170, and see 177 for Cuvier's publication of Peale's drawings. Cuvier 1821, 153–59, 208–24, 266–67. Cuvier 1840, 59; also cited in Rudwick 1985, 216. Ruling out migration and evolution, Cuvier focused on catastrophic extinction—as did the Native Americans—to explain the mass destruction evidenced by the fossils of elephant species. McMillan 1976, 82. Rudwick 1976, 107, 115. Barton's find apparently occurred on the Chemung Creek of the Tioga, near the head of the North Branch of the Susquehannah, where Thomas Jefferson reported the discovery of a very large, spiral tusk in 1808. Rice 1951, 611. *Chemung* and the Lenape (Delaware) word *Shemung* both mean "place of the horns": James Rementer interview, February 9–12, 2001. Hilbert 1975. Chiment quoted in Segelken 2001.

26. Cuvier 1821, 153–59, 208–24, 266–67, 223 (elephant foot). Cuvier 1840, 59; also cited in Rudwick's 1997 translation, 216. Clark's letter: Semonin 2000, 280 n. 37: for an opposing view, see 309. Cuvier 1806, 56 and n.

27. Cuvier on Peale: 1806, 56, and 1821, 155–56, 213–14, 219. Peale 1803 cited "Cary's Museum for 1789 and Winterbotham's History of America" as the sources of the Indian narrative, whose style Peale compared to the style of Ossian's medieval epics. Peale's lurid narrative is a good example of the ways that Indian traditions were reshaped by white translators: like Jefferson, Peale believed that the mastodon was a ferocious carnivore. See also Semonin 2000, 5, 285–86; for a fake Indian legend about mastodons that was created for political propaganda in 1795, see 294–95. Simpson 1942, 179.

28. Adams 1997, 26, 57–58. Bierhorst 1995, 12, 41, 47. The name *Yah Qua Whee* was used for an unknown monster in older traditions, according to Delaware linguist James Rementer. An early expression of the modern controversial idea that the Indians had hunted the mastodons to extinction first appeared in John Filson's book of 1784: see Semonin 2000, 200. Rementer interview.

29. Rementer interview; Bierhorst 1995; Simpson 1943, 27; 1942, 135; Jason Jackson interview, April 2001, and see Jackson 2003, chapter 8, for his discussion of innovation within tradition among contemporary Yuchi Indians, and the way each generation gives new readings of inherited cultural stories. He noted the elders' "strong willingness to make new inquiries" and to "extrapolate deeper interpretations based on further consideration and new evidence" to constantly supplement old oral tales.

30. Thanks to James Rementer, Lenape Language Project, for Homovich 1992, transcribed on tape at the Western Delaware Tribal Complex, Bartlesville, Oklahoma. Bierhorst 1995. Delaware removals from New Jersey: see preface to Adams 1997, xvii–xxxvi.

31. Wyandot tale of making wishes on amulets of burnt and petrified monster bones: Barbeau 1994, 376, and see 288 on relationship with Delawares. European uses of fossils for medicinal purposes included burning jet (petrified coal) to release its curative powers. Petrified wood: Mounier 1974 (thanks to David Parris and Rich White for this reference). According to Ned Gilmore, Academy of Natural Sciences, Philadelphia, many cache-burials of Indian artifacts in New Jersey include marine fossils, such as large brachiopods and shark teeth.

32. Weishampel and Young 1996, 56–57, 68–73, 140–51. William Moraley, an Englishman in New Jersey in the 1700s, wrote in his diary that he "inquired of the Indians" about the huge "Skellitons" in caves along the Delaware River, after he found a gigantic thighbone and tooth (thanks to Billy G. Smith). Pleistocene mammal deposits are also found in New Jersey and Philadelphia. Cretaceous bones are usually very mineralized and quite stony, whereas more recent Pleistocene bones can have a softer, woody texture.

33. "Historic Clay Tobacco Pipes" 1974; Stephen Bray, Olde World Fine Clays, Nova Scotia, per. cor., November 16, 2001. The first clay pipes had a spoon or "ladell" shape: Hitchcock 1999, 12–13, citing William Harrison's "Great Chronologie" (1573).

CHAPTER 2
NEW SPAIN: BONES OF FEAR AND BIRDS OF TERROR

1. La Malinche and the Conquest: Waldman 2000, 90–91, 105–106. Bernal Diaz del Castillo published his eyewitness history of the Spanish Conquest in 1568: Diaz del Castillo 1928, 116–17, 219, 229–30. On the Conquest, see Waldman 2000, 105–6; Grafton 1995, esp. 86–93. Simpson 1942, 133–34. See also Tylor 1964, 183.

2. Thanks to Professor Fernando Quesada Sanz for help in arranging contacts with the museum curators. Museo de America: Concepcion Garcia Sáiz, per. cor., November 20, 2001; Araceli Sánchez Garrido, per. cor., November 14, 2001. Museo Nacional de Ciencias Naturales: Begoña Sánchez Chillon, per. cor., November 26, 2001. It is possible that the records of treasures sent from Mexico exist elsewhere, perhaps in Castile.

3. Acosta (b. 1540) traveled in Mexico in the 1580s: Acosta 1970, 2:452–55. On Aztecs (Mexica), Tlaxcalteca, and Chichimecs, see Smith 1996, 40–41. Antonio Herrera y Tordsillas (b. 1559) gives another version of the Tlaxcalteca legend. This and numerous other early Spanish testimonies to legends of giants and discoveries of their bones in Mexico and Peru are cited in Antelo 2000 (thanks to Barbara Mayor for translating this paper). On the Spanish in the New World: Grafton 1995 (on Acosta, see 1, 207–8).

4. *R. tlascalae* was described by Hugh Falconer in Mexico in 1856. Fossil species in Mexico: Simpson 1942, 133–34. Other Pliocene-Pleistocene mastodon species include *Cuvieronius* and *Cordillerion* (thanks to paleontologist Wade Miller for information on Pleistocene fossils in Mexico). Terra 1957, 30–31 (on Tlaxcalteca tale), 36 (ancient figurines carved from fossil bone), 45 (map), 47 (Valley of Bones, north of Teotihuacan). Barnum Brown's 1910 Mexico expedition reported abundant remains of mastodons, mammoths, horses, and glyptodonts in the central valleys, and referred to reptile bones in the north. Brown, AMNH field report of 1911; AMNH Archives, New York. Brown noted that workers in badlands-type areas found skeletons when collecting salt from ancient lake beds, an activity that would have led people to observe fossils in ancient times, too. Dinosaur fossils are known in a few localities in Mexico. Fossils of large marine reptiles, Cretaceous theropods and tyrannosaurids, sauropods, and duck-billed dinosaurs have been found in Sonora, Baja, Chihuahua, Coahuila, and Neuvo Leon, and Jurassic pterosaurs in Puebla and Tamaulipas. See Rivera 2000, and thanks to James Clark for localities and species, per. cor., November 2001.

5. Simpson thanked paleontologist Edwin Colbert for bringing the Tlaxcalteca discovery to his attention, 1942, 130; 1943, 27. But see Scott 1887, 475. Cotton Mather on Mexican legends: Levin 1988, 767.

6. Popular beliefs about living giants in the New World: Grafton 1995; McEwan et al. 1997, 127–39; Semonin 2000, 30, on giants in Patagonia reported by the explorer Pigafetta in 1520. See Antelo 2000 for a complete summary of early Spanish and European accounts of living giants in Mexico and South America.

7. Cieza de Leon 1964, xii, 189–91. In censoring the Native traditions, Cieza de Leon could be compared to Cotton Mather (see chapter 1). The practice continued among modern ethnologists. In the 1930s, Robert Lowie, for example, translated "obscene" portions of Native narratives into Latin.

8. The Native excavation of 1543 was reported by Agustin de Zárate, *Historia del Peru* (1555), 1.4, cited in Cieza de Leon 1964, 190–91 n. 1. Olmos measured the teeth (four fingers long and three fingers wide) and sent specimens to various cities in Peru. Antelo 2000. Cotton Mather's giant bone reports: Levin 1988, 764–67, quotation 767. Mather's sources for the South American reports: Semonin 2000, 31.

9. Cieza de Leon 1964, 191. Acosta 1970, 1:56. Other Spanish chroniclers recorded the Santa Elena giant legends: see Antelo 2000. In Manta, as at Santa Elena, the giants were men with no women; they practiced homosexuality among themselves and raped the Natives: the women died because they were too small for the giants. See Bierhorst 1988, 190–91, and sources cited in n. 252.

10. On Christian giantology, see Stephens 1989, chapter 2, esp. 75. Cieza de Leon's translator and commentator, Sir Clements Markham, suggested that the Spanish Jesuits elicited "foolish stories" by asking "leading questions," and that they "mixed everything up with Noah's flood" (xlviii). It is important to keep in mind that the local stories were filtered through the Spanish investigators. Yet many other widespread American tales indicate that the giant beings died out or were destroyed because they were dangerous to humans and smaller animals, which seems to confirm that the notion was indigenous.

11. Giantism: Deloria 1997, 151–55. I thank Mary Ann Turner, of the Peabody Museum, for showing me the specimens of Pleistocene fossils and teeth collected by Yale paleontologists in Peru and Ecuador, 1869–1943.

12. There is one dinosaur exposure known in Peru, near the Ecuadoran border, excavated by Philippe Taquet of Paris. Marine reptile fossils at Lima and modern fears of dinosaurs: François Pujos, per. cor., November 24, 2001; April 1, 2002.

13. Sahagun 1970–82, bk. 3, pt. 4, p. 35, and Torquemada, *Segunda parte*, 50, cited by Sahagun's commentators. On foot- and handprints in fossil folklore and rock art, see Mayor and Sarjeant 2001. Dinosaur tracks are known in Michoacan, Coahuila, Puebla, and Oaxaca, Mexico: Rivera 2000.

14. The Pyramid of the Sun was built over a cave, which may have held fossil deposits. Aztec myths refer to the emergence of the first humans from caves, a belief that may have been inspired by "the first archaeologists, native peoples' interpretations of ancient cave deposits" containing extinct mammal bones, human remains, and artifacts, an idea suggested by John W. Hoopes, University of Kansas, per. cor., November 9, 2001. The famous Grottoes of Cacahuamilpa, in Guerrero, southern Mexico, were associated with lore about giant bones: Maximo Salas, interview, February 6, 2002. Recently, in 2001, villagers digging in the "Enchanted Cave" in Morelos, south of Mexico City, found femurs, skulls, and other bones of Columbian mammoths. Southwestern creation myths also refer to humans emerging from underworlds, and many Native American myths say that buffalo and

other animals originated underground: these ideas could be related to discoveries of fossils in caves. See Smith 1996 on Aztec migration from the North, 41. Sahagun 1970–82.

15. Grafton 1995, 140–45. Torquemada 1968, 1:37–38. Carrasco, Jones, and Sessions 2000, 351–52, 359, 375.

16. Leonardo López Luján, interview, September 29, 1999 (thanks to David Carrasco). The Museum of Man, Tepexpan, displays mammoth bones along with obsidian and silex blades and tools. Tepexpan has the southernmost remains of *M. columbi*. Mammoths and humans coexisted in central Mexico until about nine thousand years ago. Tepexpan is also the site of prehistoric human remains dating to between ten and twelve thousand years ago. Terra 1957, 160–71. Brown, AMNH field report of 1911.

17. Smith 1996, 206–7, on Aztec creation myths and the story of grinding up the bones of ancestors.

18. Jones 1942, 162–64 (the "bones of fear" were also dissolved in water and administered during childbirth). Lumholtz 1902, 118–19 (giant bones in Chihuahua). Terra 1957, 96–102. According to an archaeologist's report in 1933, paleo-Indians of Texas may have fortified their pottery by adding pulverized fossil bones to the clay. Fossil deposits around the pottery site near Abilene include Pleistocene mastodon bones and Permian deposits of immense reptiles and amphibians, cotylosaurs and pelycosaurs. Jones 1942, 163–64; Matson 1935. Thanks to Pamela Owen, University of Texas at Austin, for information on the fossil deposits in the area. The 1933 report is controversial: some archaeologists suggest that the bone material added to the clay about seven hundred years ago may have been fresh, not fossilized bone, according to Darrell Creel and Michael Collins, University of Texas at Austin. Tools and arrows made from fossil mastodon and mammoth bones and petrified wood have been found in other archaic Texas sites: see Long 1977, 9 and 16, and figs. 3d; 16a, c, d; 9e.

19. Fossil "dragon bones" (*os draconis fossilia*) have been powdered as medicine in China since antiquity. A dose of dragon bone (*longgu*) is still prescribed for nervous disorders, and dragon's teeth (*longya*) are considered even more effective against anxiety. Invertebrate fossils have also been used for medicine, from Roman to modern times. For Chinese and eighteenth- and nineteenth-century European examples, see Kennedy 1976. Oil of amber, fossilized tree resin, was prescribed by European doctors for gout and bronchitis as recently as 1948, and amber is still used in folk medicine to prevent coughs. Fossil cephalopods and belemnites were fed to English cattle and horses to cure worms and cramp: Craig and Jones 1985, 101. Fossil coral and shells have a high calcium content. According to Maximo Salas, the people, including those of San Luis Potosi, who used fossil bones as strengthening medicines, were "not really giving them any kind of mythi-

cal power, but used them for their calcium content, as a remedy for pregnant and older women. Fossil bone meal was also given to cattle for the mineral content. Old Rx shops used to grind the fossil bones." Salas, interviews, February 6 and September 2002.

20. Collinson 1767 compared mastodon teeth from North America and Peru. Cuvier 1806, 57–58, citing Torrubia, *Apparato para la Historia natural espaniola*, 1:54–79. Cuvier 1821, 157–58, 266–67. For the legendary and scientific saga of the Mexican axolotls—strange larval salamanders that emerge from water onto land, first described by the Spanish in 1570, and studied by Cuvier and later by paleontologist Edward Drinker Cope—see Wendt 1959, 135–40. Humboldt "Vue des Cordilleres," cited in Tylor 1964, 174.

21. Javier Clavijero's account of Rotea's find is given in Antelo 2000. Dinosaur fossils in Baja: Rivera 2000. Thanks also to Tommy Tyrberg and Steve Brusatte. The cave paintings of the Sierra de San Francisco are a UNESCO historical site. Clovis culture: Thomas 2000, 153–63. The Roman emperor Augustus assumed a similar association of mastodon bones and Ice Age tools in the first century B.C., at a site on Capri, where he established a museum for the bones of monsters and the weapons of heroes: see Mayor 2000, 143, 172–75.

22. Humboldt cited in Tylor 1964, 173–74, fig. 19. Mercer 1885. Scott 1887, 469, 476; and see Ashley-Montagu 1944, 568, for Scott's opinion that mammoths lived in the West until the 1500s. See also Winchell 1911, 11–13. Verrill and Verrill 1953, 132–33, plate VII.4.

23. Verrill 1948, 57–60, fig. 27. Verrill and Verrill 1953, plate XIII, center (thanks to Richard Greenwell). For information on pterosaur remains in Mexico, I thank James M. Clark, George Washington University, per. cor., November 2001. Peter Faris helped to evaluate Verrill's "pterodactyl" theory.

24. Turquoise from the Rio Grande Valley, New Mexico, has been found in Teotihuacan, the ancient sacred city of the Aztec Empire: Chronic 1987, 94. On trade between Mexico and North American Indians, Marriott and Rachlin 1975, 97–101; Schultz 1962, 179–93. The *Queztalcoatlus* fossil was found in 1971 by Doug Lawson, a graduate student working with Dr. Wann Langston, Jr., at the Texas Memorial Museum of Science and History.

25. Tapia was recorded at age fifty-five in Pascua, Arizona, in 1942. Giddings 1959, 3, 23, 81–86. Savala 1945. Yaqui is in the Aztec language family. Waldman 2000, 38, and see 57–58 for Yaqui dwellings.

26. Richard White, Tucson, Arizona, per. cor., February 6–7, 2002. Condor remains in the Southwest: Martin 1999, 271–72, and see chapter 3 of this book.

27. Teratorns: Campbell 1980. Giant bird legends: see also Coleman and Clark 1999, 336–38; Musinsky 1997. Other southwestern tales of man-eating raptors occur in Papago (Tohono O'odham), Pima, Shoshone, Ute, Paiute, Navajo, and

Apache traditions. Thompson 1966, 318 n. 151. In central Argentina, the fossils of the largest flying bird known to science were found in 1979. *Argentavis magnificans* lived in the Late Miocene, 5 million years ago; it was over five feet tall, weighed about 170 pounds, and had a wingspan of twenty-five feet. These birds died out millions of years before humans appeared, and so far the remains have been found only in South America. Discoveries of such fossils in later times—if they were recognized as birds—might enter legendary stories told by travelers in Latin America. See Campbell 1980.

CHAPTER 3
THE SOUTHWEST: FOSSIL FETISHES AND MONSTER SLAYERS

1. Thanks to Jim Kirkland, Utah state paleontologist, per. cor., September 8, 1999, for this story, originally told to him by Will Downs, Northern Arizona University, Bilby Research Center; confirmed by Will Downs, per. cor., September 9, 1999. The *Pentaceratops* was excavated south of Farmington in 1974; see the conclusion. On *Pentaceratops*, see Dodson 1996, 115–19. I thank the Navajo healing practitioners Isabelle Walker, Thomas Walker, Jr., and Thomas Walker, Sr., of the Big Water Clan, for reviewing the Navajo material in this chapter for traditional accuracy. Thanks also to Kyril Calsoyas, Flagstaff, Arizona.

2. On the history and culture of Southwest and Great Basin peoples, see Waldman 2000, 37–39, 157–68; on Coronado, 92. Casas Grandes: DiPeso, Rinaldo, and Fenner 1974. Jesuits were expelled from the New World in 1767. On the Franciscans' refusal to learn Native languages and hostility toward Pueblo ceremonies and objects, see Washburn 1975, 118–19.

3. Lanham 1991, 9. See also Simpson 1942, Jaffe 2000, Semonin 2000, Howard 1975, and Wallace 1999 for the early history of scientific American paleontology in the West.

4. For the story of the large-scale acquisition of Native American skulls by the government and museums, see Thomas 2000. For a historical survey of appropriations of fossil resources from Indian lands in the West, see Dussias 1996. See conclusion for further discussion of these conflicts.

5. Cushing 1883, 12–15. See Cushing 1901, 399–411, on "unfinished" proto-humans. On Cushing's life among the Zunis, see Thomas 2000, chapter 8. On the symbolic meaning of Zuni myth, see Young 1992, 80 ("unfinished" humans like salamanders), 81 and n. 18 on Cushing's accuracy. In Navajo myth, humans progress in knowledge in successive worlds, but there is no "evolutionary" relationship between humans and primordial creatures as in the Zuni myth: Reichard 1950, 13–14. "Hearts kept alive": McManis 1998, 6.

6. Cushing 1883, 12, 15. McManis 1998, 5. One wonders what a traditional Zuni would have thought about the fetish power of the dark-red stone "heart" inside the rib cage of a theropod dinosaur skeleton in South Dakota in 2000 (see also chapter 5 on Sioux beliefs about the stone hearts of Water Monsters). The stone dinosaur "heart" is controversial among paleontologists. It was found inside "Willo," a *Thescelosaurus* dinosaur (of 66 million years ago) discovered in 1993 at Buffalo, South Dakota, and acquired by the North Carolina Museum of Natural Science in 1996. One group of paleontologists has identified the object as a heart-shaped iron or sandstone concretion, but another group of paleontologists argues that the concretion may have formed around the actual heart. See Rowe et al. 2001. The find was also reported in *Science* (April 21, 2000).

7. Cushing 1883, 44–45. In California, for example, archaeologists have found belemnites modified for use as gaming pieces at a paleo-Indian site (thanks to John Dougherty for this discovery in cemeteries at site Teh-10, California). Belemnites are associated with ammunition in modern Pakistan, where children gather belemnite fossils that they assign to various bullet "calibers."

8. Cushing 1883, 12–15, 44–45. Concretions form inside sedimentary rocks when minerals collect around a small foreign body. Thanks to Kent McManis, Grey Dog Trading Company, Tucson, for discussing fetishes with me. In similar fashion, among the Blackfeet, small, portable fossils were known as Iniskim, "buffalo-calling" charms, but other rocks and fossils too large to be moved were also called Iniskim. Peck 2002, 148.

9. Douglas Wolfe interviews, October and November 2001. Shells, ripples, and volcanoes: Chronic 2000 and 1987. Permian extinction theory proposed by Gregory Ryskin, Northwestern University, Chicago, 2003. On prescientific concepts of humans evolving from lower life-forms in ancient Greece, Mayor 2000, 214, and on Xenophanes and other natural philosophers on marine fossils, 210–11, 281. Notably, the Wyandot creation myth visualized the primal humans who lived on the island of earth before it was "ripened by the Sun" as sprawling about only half-conscious, in a "torpid state, like turtles and toads and snakes in winter." Barbeau 1994, 273. As noted in chapter 1, Iroquois myth interpreted by David Cusick in 1825 proposed that apes and humans were related: cited by Beauchamp in 1892 (1976, 4).

10. Douglas Wolfe interviews. The "disinterest" of the Native Americans in fossils, and difficulties in obtaining permission to survey or collect on reservation land, are noted by many paleontologists. See conclusion.

11. Harry Manygoats, interview, October 2, 2002. Armer 1937, 60–61. Baylor Brooks (1905–2000), professor of geology, San Diego State University, did field-work in Arizona. Unfortunately, Brooks did not publish any of the narratives he heard, but he did pass them along to his colleague Chester Kennedy, professor

of American literature and folklore at San Diego, who published fossil lore tidbits in twenty issues of *The Fossileer*, the newsletter of the Southwest Fossileers of La Mesa, California; see also Kennedy 1973. Wann Langston, Jr., interview, September 23, 2003.

12. Mearl Kendrew, per. cor., November 2–3, 1999.

13. Reichard 1950; see 158 on withholding lore from outsiders. Anonymous sources, Navajo Reservation, 2001–2. Deloria, per. cor., March 22, 2002.

14. Quotation, Harris n.d. History and geography: Reichard 1950, xvii–xxii, 19, 152. The following summary is based on Reichard 1950; Locke 1989; O'Bryan 1956.

15. Reichard 1950, 21–22, 26, 448–51, 568–73. The twins' names were Monster Slayer and Child Born for Water. I refer to the pair as the Monster Slayers.

16. Chronic 1987, 46–52. There are two Dineh clans with the names *Yei-bi-chei* (Monster people clan) and *Yeii Dine'é* (Giant people clan).

17. Reichard 1950, 104, 206, 392–93. Dinosaur bones sold as petrified wood: Jaffe 2000, 193. Thanks to Vincent Morgan, Granger Papers Project, for information on the big fossil bones near Farmington. Armer 1937, 60–75: work continued on the dam only after a paleontological crew removed the fossils. Phytosaur localities in New Mexico: Chronic 1987, 176, 179, 183.

18. Thanks to Spencer Nesbitt for discussion of fossil scutes. Nodosaur armor discovery reported in the *Arizona Daily Wildcat*, May 2, 2001.

19. Reichard 1950, 404–5, 419, 457. Locke 1989, 116–17. Tylor 1964, 177–80. Thanks to Lorri Hagman for citing Ann Fienup-Riordan, *The Living Tradition of Yupik Masks* (Seattle: University of Washington Press, 1996), 221; Lister and Bahn 1994, 138. Miocene-Pliocene-Pleistocene fossils in Arizona include several mastodon, gomphothere, and mammoth species, saber-tooth cats, glyptodonts, sloths, moose-elk, horned rodents, teratorn birds, and giant camels.

20. Reichard 1950, 383 (the feathers "eventually turned into all kinds of birds"), 420–21, 430. Rustywire 1999. Locke 1989, 117 (black rock like a bird). On Pleistocene raptors and legends of giant birds, see chapter 2 and discussion below.

21. Father Berard Haile cited in Reichard 1950, 107–8, 594, 391, 202, 58, 70, 72.

22. Reichard 1950, 390. Thanks to paleontologist William Parker, Florida State University, for information on colored sediments. A geological *formation* is a basic unit of rock distinctive enough to be mapped in layers. For example, the Kayenta Formation is red sandstone deposited on ancient floodplains during the Late Triassic and Early Jurassic, while Navajo Sandstone is the whitish-pink cliff-forming sandstone made of Jurassic dunes (both contain dinosaur fossils). Zuni centipede: Cushing 1901, 176–85.

23. Yaqui story: Giddings 1959, 171.

24. The story attributed to Bessie Yellowhair was told to me by Gerard Tso-nakwa in Tucson, Arizona, February 11, 2000. See Reichard 1950, 14 (tokens or souvenirs from old world), 198, 490–91, 572 (water monsters). The aversion to disturbing negative legacies from past worlds extends to ancient pottery and beads, too. Traditional children are taught not to touch or pick up any ancient artifacts. Anonymous, Navajo Reservation, March 2002.

25. The Haskie family discovered the *Dilophosaurus* nest, eggs, and tracks: "Tuba City" 2004. The fossil reptile nests in Petrified Forest were discovered by Stephen Hasiotis (University of Colorado at Boulder) and Anthony Martin (Emory University, Atlanta), paper presented at the Geological Society of America annual meeting, Toronto, October 25–29, 1998. Water monsters were "known to the Zuni as Kolowisi, to the Hopi as Palulukon, and to the Tewa as Awanyu." Faris 2001, citing Tyler 1964, 245.

26. Reichard 1950, 21–22, 259. Paleontologists began to study the Chinle For-mation fossil deposits of New Mexico, Arizona, and Texas in 1920–40. "Tuba City" 2004.

27. Reichard 1950, 13, 24, 41–42, 107. When a living thing dies, it should be properly buried or left on the ground so that "it disintegrates and harmonizes with the elements of the earth," 44, 431. The dead monsters "should be disposed of in an orderly manner." Because "the bodies of the enemies [the Monsters] had been left unburied on the surface of the earth," the earth's vitality was impaired, and the people became weak and ill, 22. On "phobia of the dead" and fear of ghosts, 40–43. Timothy Rowe, interview, September 26, 2002.

28. Harry Manygoats, interview, October 2, 2002, with corrections and addi-tions by Manygoats in per. cor., October 28–November 19, 2002. Timothy Rowe interview. Ants: Reichard 1950, 326, 594; and see chapters 4 and 5 of this book. Sternberg and other imaginary trips back into geological time: Spalding 1999, 210–223. Simpson's fantasy: Laporte 2000, 257–66. In "The Last Thunder Horse West of the Mississippi," science fiction writer Sharon Farber (1988) imagines that Cope and Marsh encounter a relict *Brontosaurus* during the Bone Wars, with a wonderful illustration by Robert Walters of cowboys lassoing the rearing sauro-pod. Mitchell 1998, 27–31. Thin membrane of time: the Lakota and Cheyenne concept of Medicine Holes was brought up by Nita Manning when we discussed the plot device of the *Turok, Son of Stone* comic books, interview, March 26, 2000.

29. Harry Manygoats interview. Lame Deer and Erdoes 1994, 56–57; on disas-ters caused by large-scale disruption of earth and water in Sioux lands since the 1930s, see xxvi–xxvii.

30. Reichard 1950, 44–45, 49–51, 70–71, 81–82.

31. Lanham 1991, 125–40, 240. Wallace 1999, 120–21.

32. Psihoyos and Knoebber 1994, 88–89. Welles narrated his story on the University of California Museum of Paleontology, Berkeley, audio Web site, 2002: www.ucmp.berkeley.edu/dilophosaur/discovery.html. Neither Psihoyos nor recent UCMP material credits Jesse Williams with the important find, although Sam Welles's 1984 publication credits Williams with finding the fossil locality. Thanks to Mark Goodwin, Museum of Paleontology, Berkeley, per. cor., September 23, 2003, for information about Welles and Williams. See conclusion for further discussion of the cast given to the Navajos. During the 1998 hearings in the Arizona senate for naming the *Dilophosaurus* the state dinosaur, Williams was credited with the discovery in the senate fact sheet and research memo for H.B. 2133. Fischer 1998 and Gerard Tsonakwa, interview, February 11, 2000. Wann Langston interview.

33. Anthony R. Garcez, interview, February 22, 2002. Garcez publishes contemporary Native American ghost and witchcraft lore about the Southwest, with Red Rabbit Press, Truth or Consequences, New Mexico. Manygoats interview, October 2, 2002. Isabelle Walker brought the European shark tooth to her father, Thomas Walker. Walker interview, October 2, 2002.

34. Reichard 1950, 8. Frisbie 1987, 30, 59, 61–62, 66–68. Under the Native American Graves Protection and Repatriation Act (NAGPRA), the jish containing a fossil shell was repatriated to Roman Hubbell's grandson, Sherwin Curley, in 1996, as sacred objects necessary for the continued practice of traditional Navajo religion (thanks to Patricia Mason for this information). On NAGPRA and fossils, see the conclusion.

35. Psihoyos and Knoebber 1994, 159–61.

36. Lockley 1991, 184–85. For color photos of dinosaur tracks, see Psihoyos and Knoebber 1994, 136–41, 158, 160.

37. *Gee-tow-ta-own-lay-new* is the name of the ancient ruin near Jemez, according to William Whatley, Jemez tribal archaeologist (thanks to Keith Foster). On fossils near Jemez Pueblo, see Chronic 1987, 156.

38. Lockley 1991, 185 and 186. Mayor and Sarjeant 2001, 151, figs. 5 and 6.

39. Peter Faris, per. com., October 11–14, 2003; per. cor., November 17–23; Faris 2004. In the Cub Creek petroglyphs, the giant lizards are six and three feet long, approaching a human figure about one foot tall. On the dinosaur tracks in northeastern Utah, see Hamblin, Bilbey, and Hall 2000, citing Lockley; see also Costa 1994, 57–61.

40. "Tuba City" 2004 (thanks to Peter Faris). Harry Manygoats interview. Morris Chee, Jr. (b. 1976), interview, October 2, 2002.

41. Look 1981, 30, pointed out that the three-toed tracks on many of the costumes are rounded at the bottom like dinosaur tracks found near Hopi villages. See also Lockley 1991, 185–86, fig. 14.1 (Hopi dancers' kilts). Thanks to Ray

Stanford for his recollection of the Hopi dinosaur track story. Palulukon: Tyler 1964, 245. Three Hopi and Zuni figures with dinosaur track designs may be seen in the collections of the Museum of Northern Arizona: Hopi Wuyaqtaywa (broad-faced katsina), ca. 1930; Civolo/Zuni Buffalo Dancer Katsina, ca. 1930 E3781 Zuni; and Unidentified Zuni Kachina, Snake Dancer, pre-1940 (probably 1880–1900) E3753.

42. Reichard 1950, 558, citing ten references, 133. Rustywire 1999: when he was a boy, Rustywire's father demonstrated how Changing Woman made children's footprints with the side of her fist and fingertips to fool a monster.

43. Tuba City tracks: Chronic 2000, 238–39. Charles A. Repenning, a geologist who was mapping the Navajo Reservation in 1948–55, told me about this trick in 1999: see Mayor and Sarjeant 2001, 157. Prayer Rock brochure, Britton, South Dakota, has a photo of an Indian praying with his hands placed in the carved prints. Reichard 1950, 558. On ceremonial set of human footprints carved in about 1600 on a cliff above the Mississippi River, see Schoolcraft 1975, 173–79; Tanner 1984, 122–23.

44. "Person" or "people" in many Native American tales is often translated as "man" or "humans," but also refers to primal animals in the old days when the earth was young. Woiche 1992, xxi–iv, 1–3, 85–86, 115–16, 127–41, 150, 155–60. Note that the body of the Giant Water Dragon was cast into the ocean, so its remains were never seen, a detail that parallels the explanation in the old English epic *Beowulf* for why the monster Grendel's bones were never found—they too had been hurled into the sea.

45. Frank Day's painting (1964) shows a giant serpent (*Hicky*) entwined around *Hum*, a "large lizard type of animal." Dobkins 1997, 72, plate 39 (thanks to Zeese Papanikolas). I thank Tracy Ford for information on California fossils; see Hilton 2003 for mosasaur, ichthyosaur, plesiosaur, crocodile, and lizard fossils in California.

46. Wilson 1998, 14, 79–80, 96–99, 114–15, 121–22, 128 (thanks to Zeese Papanikolas). Dene storyteller's reference to dinosaurs: Spalding 1999, 248. Geochronology: Lanham 1991, 15–16. "Time is long": Jaffe 2000, 17. California has plenty of Pleistocene mammal fossils, but because the region was underwater during the Cretaceous, dinosaur exposures are few (mostly hadrosaurs).

47. Laporte 2000, 260 and nn. 15–16. Simpson 1934, 109–10.

48. "Stone Mother": information from Pyramid Lake Paiute Tribe, August 1, 2001. Loud and Harrington 1929.

49. Footprints: Lockley 1991, 185 and n. 3; see Lockley and Hunt 1995, 117, fig. 4.5.

50. Drilled trilobites worn as amulets (as in the ancient burials) were called *shugi-pits napa t'schoy*, "lizard foot bead things." The Paiutes have the same names for the trilobites. Taylor and Robison 1976.

51. Wallace 1999, 61–62, 81; Jaffe 2000, 35–36, 75, 368; Lanham 1991, chapter 11. Grinnell 1932 recounts his memories of the 1870 expedition and mentions the Shoshone guide. Schuchert and LeVene 1940, 100–124, map 110. Cope's comment: Wallace 1999, 176.

52. For a map of railroads and trails west, see Waldman 2000, 203–5; and for a map of fossil locations along railroads, see Brown 1919, 425.

53. Information about the fossils at Homol'ovi: thanks to Douglas Gann, University of Arizona, per. cor., December 12, 1999.

54. Fewkes 1898, 730. Spence 1914, 92.

55. Moqui marbles: thanks to information from the Rock Shed, 515 First Street, Keystone, South Dakota.

56. Ray Stanford told me about gastrolith burnishers, a practice he heard about from Pueblo and Hopi potters in Arizona in 1960–67, per. cor., February 2002. Gregory Wood, a Colorado archaeoceramist who reproduces Anasazi pottery in the traditional ways, collects gastrolith burnishers from dinosaur sites in Utah. Tony Semallie, Cameron Trading Post, Arizona, per. com., October 2, 2002. The Big Horn Basin site was excavated by the University of Wyoming.

57. Conover 1997. Ball 1941, 33–34. In preparation for its being knapped like flint, petrified wood may have been charred first, which offers an alternative explanation for the charred petrified wood found in paleo-Indian sites (chapter 1). Agate House, on the Long Logs Trail in the southern part of Petrified Forest National Park, was reconstructed in 1934. Petrified wood is also abundant north of Chaco Canyon, east and north of Gallup, in the Zuni Mountains, and along the Rio Puerco near Jemez; fossil palm wood is found west of Truth or Consequences, New Mexico. A site near Cerrillos has very large logs, up to 6 feet in diameter and 135 feet long. Sinkankas 1959, 367. On the history of removals of petrified wood from the forest by commercial interests and tourists in modern times and the forest's designation as a national park, see Conover 1997 and the conclusion.

58. Conover 1997. Paul Apodaca, interview, January 6, 2002.

59. Opler 1994, 269–72. Goddard 1911, 209.

60. Thanks to Patrica Mason for the Apache story in Russell 1898, 255, reprinted in Thompson 1966, 101–3. In the Apache origin myth, Taos was the Apache birthplace, and "Taos" in the Apache tale might refer to Taos Pueblo, the second-oldest continuously populated village in America. When I contacted Taos Pueblo, the Pueblo historian Joe S. Sando indicated that he knows of no other written records of the great wing preserved at Taos, "but oral tradition may have similar stories being handed down by individual elders." Sando, of Jemez Pueblo, relayed his comments via the Pueblo Cultural Center, January 6, 2002.

61. Some paleontologists speculate that rare, complete specimens of pterosaurs might exist in shale formations near Abiquiu, southwest of Taos, New Mexico, and east of the Sangre de Cristo Mountains. Thanks to Paul Bauer for information on pterosaur remains. Tommy Tyrberg, per. cor., January 14, 2002. Teratorns: Campbell 1980. According to Alison Stenger, archaeologist, Woodburn Paleoarchaeological Project, Portland, Oregon, per. cor., June–July 2000, her team came across a humerus so large that that they first thought it was the leg bone of an elk in an excavation near Portland, Oregon. After more of the skeleton emerged, it was identified as a teratorn with a wingspan of over twelve feet.

62. Martin 1999, 267–72, and fig. 8.4, preserved condor, Stevens Cave, Grand Canyon National Park, 12,500 years old. Paul Martin, interview, February 9, 2000.

63. Puerco Pueblo petroglyph: thanks to Steve Pavlik and Hallie Larsen, National Park Service ranger, Petrified Forest, per. cor., February 17, 2003. In the 1930s, Father Berard Haile recorded an interesting Navajo account of Monster Slayer overcoming an enormous carrion bird that was "in charge of evil" in the time "when the earth was still dominated by monsters." The giant vultures declared, "Wherever Monsters are killed and decay, we . . . will be present as scavengers." Cited in Reichard 1950, 104–5; see also 489. Daniel Boone claimed to have seen a gigantic raptor on the Tennessee River, which the Cherokees said was the home of the Thunder Bird, and modern cryptozoologists maintain records of giant bird sightings from the time of Boone up to the present: the reports cluster along the Rio Grande and in Alaska. See, e.g., Coleman and Clark 1999, 236–38.

64. Simpson 1942, 132–33. Simpson published photos of the Gobernador fossils in the AMNH collections (photo 32661, fossil fragment of lower jaw of unidentified carnivore, and photo 32660, upper jaw of *Phenacodus primaevus*).

65. Spencer Lucas, curator of paleontology, New Mexico Museum of Natural History, Albuquerque, per. cor., September 21, 1999. Blackfeet forays into the Southwest and Mexico: Schultz 1962, 180, 351–54. Jack T. Hughes, per. cor., January 13, 2000.

CHAPTER 4
THE PRAIRIES: FOSSIL MEDICINE AND SPIRIT ANIMALS

1. Some historians locate Quivera on the Platte River in Nebraska; others put it near Lyons or Wichita, Kansas. Pawnee elders of the 1880s recalled old traditions about the arrival of the Spanish in Kansas, according to Grinnell 1928, 39. Marsh, public lecture, 1877. Several helpful people in the Kansas State Historical Society suggested references for this chapter. I'm grateful for the corrections

and constructive suggestions of Roger Echo-Hawk, who reviewed the Pawnee material in this chapter.

2. Young Bull had been a Pawnee Scout in the 1870s, known as Koo-Tah-Wee-Kootz-Tah-Kah. He was photographed in 1913 at Otoe Reservation, Oklahoma, with his medicine man regalia: his hat is in the anthropological collections, Mathers Museum, Indiana University, Bloomington. Dorsey collected more than Native American folklore; he also collected numerous Indian skulls from fresh graves across the Northwest; see Thomas 2000, 62. Murie (b. 1862) never knew his father, a Scot who commanded a battalion of Pawnee Scouts under Major Frank North; his mother was a Pawnee of the Skidi band. Murie's Pawnee name was Ri-tahkacihari, Young Eagle. See Douglas Parks's biography of Murie in Murie 1981, 21–25.

3. Dorsey 1906, 7, 10, 241; story no. 81, 294–95. Young Bull led the Buffalo Doctors ceremony in 1902. Pawnee priests were concerned with astronomy, while Pawnee doctors dealt with earth phenomena, such as fossils. Dorsey 1906, 265. Murie 1981, 394–98. Parks and Wedel 1985 omitted Young Bull's tale from their survey of Pawnee sacred geography, even though they mention the place of the bone's discovery, Swimming Mound, in connection with healing rites, 158–59, table 1; on animal lodge medicine, see 151–53; historical locations of Pawnee bands, 146–51.

4. Pawnee earth lodges: Waldman 2000, 59. Custer wrote in *My Life on the Plains* (1874): "Our march was completed to Medicine Lodge Creek, where . . . scouting parties were sent up and down the stream as far as there was the least probability of finding Indians. The party . . . scoured down the valley of Medicine Lodge Creek [to] the famous 'medicine lodge,' an immense structure erected by the Indians . . . as a council house, where each year the various tribes of the southern plains were wont to assemble in mysterious conclave to consult the Great Spirit as to the future and to offer up rude sacrifices and engage in imposing ceremonies, such as were believed to be appeasing and satisfactory to the Indian Deity. . . . The Medicine Lodge was found in a deserted but well-preserved condition. . . . Hanging overhead, were collected various kinds of herbs and plants, vegetable offerings no doubt to the Great Spirit; while, in strange contrast to these peaceful specimens of the fruits of the earth, were trophies of warpath and the chase, the latter being represented by horns and dressed skins of animals killed in the hunt, some of the skins being beautifully ornamented in the most fantastic of styles peculiar to the Indian idea of art."

5. In 1889, Grinnell (1961, 350–53) described Pawnee medicine bundles, blackened with smoke and age, some of which were said to date back to the distant time when the Pawnees lived in the Southwest. Sadie's medicine bundle was donated to the museum in the 1970s. Thanks to Richard Gould, curator, Pawnee

Indian Village Museum, Republic, Kansas, interviews, February 3, 2000, and October 17, 2002. Kansas State Historical Society, information on the "Sacred Pawnee Bundle," 1999. The 1873 battle is commemorated at Massacre Canyon Monument, Trenton, Nebraska.

6. Dorsey 1906, story no. 81, 294–95; story no. 35, 134–35; and story no. 82, 296–97. Buffalo was of the Skidi band of Pawnees. Making a fossil-powder tea parallels the practices of the Delawares (chapter 1), those of the people of Mexico (chapter 2), and the Navajo jish (chapter 3).

7. Besides an interest in fossils, the Pawnees were also keenly aware of meteorites, which they located and collected after observing their trajectories. Indeed, the Kansas prairie is one of the best places on Earth to find meteorites. I thank Roger Echo-Hawk for information on Wonderful Bone Creek, at the Pawnee city known as the Stabaco Site (25HW16). Thanks to Mike Everhart for a photo and information on the point with fossil inclusions, found in south-central Kansas in 1972.

8. Young Bull and Fighting Chief were of the Pitahawirata band of Pawnees. Hyde 1951, 65–67; see his "Map of Pawnee Land, 1300–1725," showing Pawnee villages along the Republican River. Bruce 1932, 16, and see British map of 1755 showing Pani (Pawnee) villages in Kansas. Smallpox: Hyde 1951, 84, 127; Catlin 1973, 24.

9. Dorsey 1906, story no. 79, 265–71. Young Bull and his grandmother placed Swimming Mound in western Kansas or Nebraska. The new state borders between Nebraska and Kansas meant little to the Pawnees. The Republican River valley flows east across southern Nebraska and into central Kansas; its South Fork is in northwestern Kansas. The North Fork crosses the corner of Colorado, Kansas, and Nebraska: it is another possible site for Swimming Mound, since maps of 1725 indicate "Big Timbers" on the banks; see Hyde 1951.

10. Mike Everhart, interview, December 30, 1999; also see Everhart's informative Web site, www.oceansofkansas.com. Greg Liggett, interview, October 16, 2002.

11. On fossils of Kansas, see Buchanan and McCauley 1987, 6–15, 145, 177–78, 181–87. Republican River fossils: Osborn 1921, 348–49, 483. Charles H. Sternberg collected vertebrate fossils on the Solomon, Smoky Hill, and Republican rivers in the 1870s for Cope, who visited the Smoky Hill beds in 1871. Sternberg 1990. Webb 1872, 325–29, 339–65. Hatcher sent many crates of Smoky Hill fossils to Marsh. Lanham 1991, 198–200. For a history of fossil collecting in the Niobrara Formation of Kansas, see Williston 1898; Lanham 1991, chapter 8; Jaffe 2000, 52–66. The *Stegomastodon* found near Trenton, Nebraska, a few miles from the massacre site, was excavated in 1997 by the University of Nebraska State Museum, Lincoln. *Williams Stegomastodon Site*, brochure, Trenton, Nebraska, n.d. If

it lay further west, Swimming Mound may have been submerged in 1953, under the waters of Swanson Reservoir. Thanks to Brenda Daniel, historian for Hitchcock County, Nebraska, for archaeological and topographical information, and Robert Hunt, per. cor., October 30, 2002. *Mammuthus imperator* in Hitchcock County: Colton 1935, 1. For information on and drawings of fossils of the badlands region, Boyce and Haag 1991.

12. Webb 1872, 384–85 (thanks to Patricia Mason). On Webb, see Wallace 1999, 93–94; Jaffe 2000, 62–66 and n. 11. About 60 million buffalo were slaughtered in the government's systematic destruction of the herds in the late 1800s. Later, trainloads of bison bones were collected for fertilizer. Dwindling bison herds: Waldman 2000, 209–10; Sternberg 1990, 9; Webb 1872, 311–14, 492; Leidy 1852, 4. William Webb also reported that huge birdlike footprints were impressed on a rock ledge in western Kansas; possibly these belonged to Cretaceous creatures, or maybe they were petroglyphs. Cope examined a set of "human" footprints near Bavaria, central Kansas, and concluded that they were either carved by an Indian or else left by an early mammal, such as a bear or sloth. Bird tracks and human prints that resemble fossil tracks in stone were frequently carved by Native Americans for various reasons: to call out genuine fossil trackways, to illustrate mythic tales, or to signal a sacred place. The northern plains have many examples of this kind of fossil-related rock art. Webb 1872, 37, 104–10.

13. On North's recruitment of one hundred Pawnee Scouts, see Bruce 1932. Schuchert and LeVene 1940, 100–105, 102 (for different spellings of the scouts' names), 105 (Marsh's paleontology lesson). Betts 1871, 664. Lanham 1991, 81–83, 86. Jaffe 2000, 30–31. See Grinnell 1972, 32–36, on the Pawnee scouts. Roger Echo-Hawk, interview, March 6, 2003.

14. The 1868 treaty at Fort Laramie, designating all of South Dakota west of the Missouri River as a "permanent reservation" for the Sioux, was violated as soon as it was signed. Jaffe 2000, 115, 117. Fossil hunting in Dakota Territory: Grinnell 1972, 85–88, 103–4; in Montana, 120; in Wyoming, 130, 133–34, 144; working in the paleontology lab at Yale, 122, 125, 166 n. 27. Wortman's find: Gries 1998, 133–34, and 130, map. See chapter 5 for more on Cope's dinosaur finds.

15. On Sternberg's encounters with Indians in the 1870s, see Sternberg 1990, 10–12, 36–37, 47–48, 63–68, 78, 82, 151–53, 191–200, 222–25. Grinnell 1961, 358–59.

16. Grinnell 1928, 246–47. The unnamed medicine man had been a Pawnee Scout in 1869. Hyde 1951, 66–67. Waconda (Pahowa): Webb 1872, 397–99, 403. White Bone Mound: Parks and Wedel 1985, 162 and n. 45.

17. Simpson discussed the puzzling Lewis and Clark find of 1804, in the cave on Soldier's Creek flowing into the Missouri just north of Council Bluffs, Iowa: Simpson 1942, 169–70. David Parris interview, August 4, 2000, and per. cor., December 29, 2000, and May 30, 2003.

18. Virginia Wulfkuhle, Kansas State Historical Society, and Donald Blakeslee, Wichita State University, helped with spirit mounds. Parks and Wedel 1985, 153–63, and figs. 3–8, attempted to locate all of the sacred mounds mentioned by Pawnees; they failed to identify Swimming Mound or White Bone Mound. *Silvisaurus*: Ottawa County Historical Museum, Minneapolis, Kansas. Everhart's *Pteranodon* dig, www.oceansofkansas.com.

19. Giant bird: Curtis 1966, 258. Water monster medicine lodges: Murie 1981, 39, 168, 174–75. Water serpent eggs: Grinnell 1923, 2:97–98. Mosasaurs as sea serpents: Betts 1871, 671; Marsh 1877, 14. Ellis 2003b, 37, and Ellis 2003a. Greg Liggett interview. Today's snakes may be the surviving branch of extinct mosasaurs: Ellis 2003b, 38–41.

20. Silverhorn's 1891–94 sketch is one of many ledgerbook drawings, manuscript 4252, National Anthropological Archives, inv. no. 09059900, Smithsonian Institution, Washington, DC. Another of Silverhorn's water monster drawings (1887) appears in Boyd 1983, 92–93. Water monster paintings on Kiowa tipis were collected in 1904 by James Mooney in Oklahoma; see Faris 2001. The *Piasa*, a giant devouring monster or bird described by Father Marquette in 1673, was depicted in a large colored painting on a rock bluff on the Mississippi near Alton, Illinois. According to Marquette, the monster had antlers and red eyes, a semihuman face, a body covered in scales, and a long tail. Musinsky 1997; Coleman and Clark 1999, 201. Meurger and Gagnon 1988, 189–93. North American water monster legends: Mackal 1980; Meurger and Gagnon; Faris 2001.

21. Grinnell writing in 1889, 1961, 354–56. Once again, Grinnell refrained from mentioning that the evidence the Pawnee elders spoke of corresponded to the abundant deposits of very large bones found in hills and canyons of Kansas and Nebraska. Dorsey 1906, 296. Other Pawnee stories associate giant bison with catastrophic floods, which may point to memories of great lakes that formed at the edges of the retreating glaciers in the Late Pleistocene, according to Pawnee historian Roger Echo-Hawk. Echo-Hawk 2000, 276–77, has found that Grinnell's manuscripts differ from the published versions in this respect, for example in identifying "mythic" mountains with actual mountain ranges.

22. Roger Echo-Hawk interview. See Thomas 2000, chapter 10, for anthropologists' rejection of oral tradition as "real" history.

23. Jones 1942, 162, citing Carlson and Jones 1939, 534n. On Comanches, see Waldman 2000, 173–76. The ingredients of plaster of paris are gypsum and water.

24. Oklahoma fossil information provided by Keith Manasco, J. P. Cavigelli, Bill May. Sauropod information comes from Mathew Wedel; the Oklahoma Museum of Natural History, Norman; Reeds 1926; and Halls 1996, 100–101. Wallace and Hoebel 1952, 171.

380   NOTES TO PAGES 198-208

25. Thanks to Daniel Gelo for information about Piamupits, per. cor., January 2000. Jones 1972, 51–52. Juanita Pahdopony and Harry Mithlo, interviews, April–May 2002. *Pia Mupitz, Mu pitz, Mu peetz* are various pronunciations for the bogeyman who sniffed out children who soiled their beds or were noisy in the tipi at night. Thanks to Mike Everhart, Ken Carpenter, David Marjanovic, Doug Wolfe, and many others who offered useful information about the hydroscopic effect of mineralized bone.

26. McDonald 1989, 297; Leidy 1852, 12–13 (thanks to Paul Martin). Leidy's collection: Leidy 1869. On Leidy, see Lanham 1991, 18–22. Cuvier 1821, 222.

27. Koch 1840–41.

28. Cuvier's molar from the Osage River: Cuvier 1821, 222. Pascal Tassy, per. cor., May 15, 2003. See Cuvier 1834 cited in Simpson 1942, 172–73; on Koch see 165 and 173.

29. Ashley-Montagu 1944, 568–71. Koch excavated in Benton County, along the Bourbeuse River southwest of St. Louis, and at Kimmswick, just south of St. Louis, now the Kimmswick Mastodon Kill Site. See Leidy 1852, 16, on mastodon and ox fossils from Big Bone River. Henry Schoolcraft examined "human footprints" in limestone at St. Louis in 1821: Schoolcraft 1975 [1825], 172–79. See also the appendix.

30. Ashes and bones: Jones 1874, 73, 74 (weapons). Historians of paleontology follow Simpson in dismissing Koch: see, for example, Simpson 1942, 165, 168, 173 (Koch's "extravagant nonsense" has "little scientific value"); and Semonin 2000, 382–86. Koch was a complex character, a bit of a charlatan, but the scientific importance of Koch's finds was reconsidered by McMillan 1976, 81–93, and see Wood and McMillan 1976, 5, 71–73, map, 48, fig. 3.1; 90 (Koch's mastodon skeleton is now correctly assembled in the British Museum; many individual fossils and related Clovis artifacts from Missouri are in Berlin). Mastodon bones have been found in prehistoric dwellings south of St. Louis: Jones 1942, 163.

31. For Vine Deloria's discussion of this story, see 1997, 131–33, and see 127 for the constellation. Shirley, a traditional Osage in Oklahoma, interview, August 4–5 and September 30, 2002.

32. By 1673, the Osages had migrated to Missouri from the Ohio Valley. Waldman 2000, 197–209, 220.

33. The dam was begun in 1964, and the valley was flooded in 1979. Wood and McMillan 1976, 5, 10. Koch's Kimmswick dig is now the Mastodon State Historic Site, south of St. Louis, near Imperial.

34. Jason Jackson interview, March 2, 2001. Another Yuchi version mentioning dinosaurs was given by Chief Simon Harry in 1996. Jackson 2003, chapter 8. The motif of a giant lizard that nests in a hollow tree is widespread in northeastern Indian lore; cf. the Iroquois tale in chapter 1, recounted by David Cusick in 1825.

35. Littlechief's "Ancient Evil Beast" (1975): Boyd 1983, 92–93, 44. Thanks to James Farlow for pointing out (per. cor., March 22, 2000) that Littlechief's monster is "nearly a dead ringer for Charles Knight's famous Field Museum restoration of *Triceratops*."

36. On Cheyennes, see Waldman 2000, 169–73. Grinnell 1923, 2:95–99. Hoebel 1960, 86. Fear of springs: John Allen, Jr., interview, September 6, 2000.

37. Grinnell 1923, 2:95–99. Kroeber 1983, 438, 442.

38. Grinnell 1923, 2:95–99. White River fossils: O'Harra 1920, 26, 78–87, 128–31, 110–17. Thanks to George Engelmann, paleontologist at the University of Nebraska, Omaha, for sharing ideas about the identity of the double-toothed bull. *Agate Fossil Beds* 1980. Greg Liggett interview. "Terminator Pig" and paleontology of Pawnee Buttes: information from Steven Wade Veatch.

39. Marsh often used the phrase "flying dragons" for pterosaurs: see Jaffe 2000, 52; Schuchert and LeVene 1940, 123–24 ("I uncovered . . . the giant wing of the ancient dragon"). "Sea serpents": Marsh 1877, 14. Cope: Wallace 1999, 74; Lanham 1991, 99. Webb 1872, 326.

40. Stands In Timber and Liberty 1967, 117, 122, 13–14, 53. Grinnell 1923, 2:44–45 (Yellow Haired Woman), 119–20 (stone bone powder), 122–23 (baculites). See "Cheyenne Stone Buffalo-Horn" 1927. On ocher and pigments in western fossil beds, I consulted Charles Repenning, Desmond Maxwell, Patrick Norton, and Chandler Good Strike. The Crow elder Old Coyote also bade an emotional farewell to an old medicine bundle; see Wildschut 1960, 112.

41. Nita Manning, interviews, 2000–2002. The number of fossils in the rattle matched the number of medicinal plants (405) known to the Sioux and Cheyennes. Lame Deer and Erdoes 1994, 5, 113, 135–36; yuwipi ceremony, 191–207, esp. 205, and glossary, 305–6. Assiniboine and ants: John Allen, Jr., interview, September 6, 2000. Badlands, 1965, ant discoveries: Clark 1974, 73–74. Crow Indians and ants: Snell 2000, 36–37. Abenakis and ants: Tsonakwa and Yolaikia 2001, 96–97.

42. Hatcher: Lanham 1991, 198–213 (anthills, 208–9). Webb 1872, 381–82. Michael Flynn, interview, October 4, 2000.

CHAPTER 5
THE HIGH PLAINS: THUNDER BIRDS, WATER MONSTERS,
AND BUFFALO-CALLING STONES

1. One of the earliest written descriptions of a tornado was by a traveler from the East in 1814, who compared its shape to "a cone with its apex downward, rather like a speaking-trumpet. [The cloud was] black as pitch and appeared to boil." Schoolcraft 1975 [1825], 183. "Thunder cracked in deafening peals with

tongues of electricity," wrote Charles Sternberg (1917, 70), about being overtaken by a storm on the prairie. Forked lightning ignited grass fires all around him and killed a calf nearby. See also Sternberg 1990, 121. An Assiniboine holy man, Bull's Dry Bones, described an ancient tradition about his people's first encounter with a tornado (the Assiniboines arrived in the West in the 1500s): a whirlwind like a black column that carried people over the sea; Denig 1930, 614. The Crow chief Plenty Coups described a tornado during his vision quest: a black cloud formed with "streaks of mad color" as all Four Winds and Thunders rushed together "to make war" on a beautiful forest, leaving nothing but tangled trees, twisted like blades of grass. Linderman 1962, 65–66.

2. Reptiles and insects as the first creatures: Walker 1983, 236, 240 (cold-blooded), 243 (fossils of Water Monsters). The Blackfeet also say reptiles were the first creatures (Spalding 1999, 248), as do the Zunis; see chapter 3. For another Lakota version of how the bones of giants and water monsters came to be buried in the Badlands, how the Badlands were formed, and the creation of Thunder Birds, see Virginia Driving Hawk Sneve's story "Badlands Bones," Sneve 2000, 101–5. Thanks to Erin Howley, Badlands National Park ranger, per. com., September 21, 1999, for suggesting references and contacts. The nostalgic illustration, by R. F. Peterson, of Sioux discovering a *Pteranodon* skeleton appeared in Geis 1959, 10–11.

3. The general term *badlands* means any dry, elevated, sparsely vegetated region characterized by bare rocks, pinnacles, hoodoos, hills, knife-sharp ridges, and ravines intricately sculpted by the forces of erosion. The "Big Badlands" or "White River Badlands" of South Dakota refers to the valley of the White River, which contains Miocene and Oligocene mammals. The Hell Creek Formation badlands of the western Dakotas and eastern Montana contain Cretaceous dinosaurs. The badlands along the Missouri River contain Cretaceous marine reptiles. Lanham 1991, 24–25; history of Badlands fossil discoveries, 26–46. See Boyce and Haag 1991 for descriptions and sketches of Dakota fossils. Erdoes and Ortiz 1984, 222; and Lame Deer and Erdoes 1994, 136, 239. Unktehi bones in the Badlands: Erdoes and Ortiz 1984, 220–22, 94, 240; and Lame Deer and Erdoes 1994, 136, 251–52. Walker 1991, 108. LaPointe 1976, 19.

4. Lakes 1997, 10–15; Jaffe 2000, 185–89. Lanham 1991, 97–98; and see 29, for exposed fossils weathering away. Anyone searching the tops of badlands ravines will often find the spine of "some monster of the ancient sea," wrote Edward Cope in 1875, with "the vertebral column running far into the limestone that locks him in his last prison." In October 2003, I visited the Hogback, where Lakes discovered his specimens: special thanks to Peter and Charlotte Faris, and the curators at Dinosaur Ridge Museum and the Morrison Natural History Museum.

5. For the early history of paleontological discoveries in the Badlands and west-ern states, see Osborn 1921 and 1929; Froiland and Weedon 1990, 46–54; Lan-ham 1991; Jaffe 2000. South Dakota geology: Gries 1998. For excellent old geo-logical and paleontological survey maps of the West, see *US Geological Survey Bulletin*, nos. 257 (Judith River Beds, 1905); 612 (Overland Route, 1916), 613 (Santa Fe Route, 1916).

6. Parts of the reported plesiosaur vertebrae found by Lewis and Clark were supposedly sent to the Smithsonian but have not yet been located. David Parris, interview, August 5, 2000, and per. cor., May 30, 2003. Pompey's Pillar is a monu-mental outcrop of Cretaceous sandstone: Alt and Hyndman 2000, 377. In 1825, Henry Rowe Schoolcraft spoke with Clark about his find on the Yellowstone: Schoolcraft 1975, 294. See also Weishampel and Young 1996, 57–58; Gries 1998, 89. The earliest verified dinosaur remains found by whites in America were taken from a quarry in 1818 in Connecticut. Thought to be human remains, they were not identified as dinosaur fossils until 1915.

7. Lee Azure: David Parris, Crow Creek Reservation field notebook, entries and photos, August 27, 1993; and Parris and Shelton 2000.

8. Fosha 1993 on Iniskim in ancient South Dakota sites. For a survey of Iniskim traditions in several ancient Plains cultures: Peck 2002, and see 155–62 for archae-ological evidence of baculite collection in the Dakotas, Montana, and Canada. Chandler Good Strike, interview, March and August 2000. Schultz 1962, 306–11, for Many Tail Feathers's version of the first buffalo-calling stone; see 370 for the buffalo-calling ritual. See Grinnell 1962, 125–26, for a brief version of the ritual. Not surprisingly, when Grinnell lived among the Blackfeet, he did not ask them about the abundance of dinosaur fossils in their lands. See Russell 1998 (Charlie Crow Eagle's Iniskim); see also Kroeber 1983, 443; Barrett 1921; Reeves 1993; Kehoe 1965; and Wissler 1912. Thanks to Greg McDonald, Darren Tanke, and David Reese for references for Iniskim. Baculites are now mined in Canada by Korite Minerals, Ltd., as a gemstone called "ammolite." For a horn coral fossil Iniskim, see "Cheyenne Stone Buffalo-Horn" 1927.

9. Bull's Dry Bones: Denig 1930, 613. Lanham 1991, 97; Catlin 1973, 85. DeSmet: Wayne Archambault, interview, September 7, 2000.

10. Lame Deer and Erdoes 1994, 252, 254. Belemnites and Zunis, chapter 3; and Cheyennes, chapter 4. See Geis 1959, 11.

11. See chapter 4 for "blue vision." Catlin 1973, 204–5.

12. Louis Agassiz first proposed the theory of glacial transport in the early 1800s, but it was not accepted until the 1870s. Sioux ideas about moving stones exist in many old traditions, but the earliest account I know of was reported in 1834 by Pond 1986, 87, 89. Lame Deer and Erdoes 1994, 194; Walker 1983, 144–45 (moving stone); 228 (the action of water created gravel and sand). Moving

stones in Montana: Alt and Hyndman 2000, 35 (quotation and map); see 288 for a forty-mile path of distinctive rocks that were carried by a glacier from Snake Butte, Montana. See also Parks and Wedel 1985, 170, on traveling rocks. Moving stones: Clifford Canku, interview, July 28, 2000; Callahan 2000–. See Heinlein 2000, citing Assiniboine (Nakota) leader John Allen, Jr.; on the Assiniboines and traveling rocks: Lowie 1909, 120; Blackfeet stories of traveling rocks: Grinnell 1962, 165–66. Geological forces much earlier than glaciers also moved stones: zircons and other minerals in Utah's Navajo Sandstone were carried from the Appalachians by ancient river systems 275–150 million years ago, as reported in *Science News* 164 (August 30, 2003): 131–32. See conclusion for further discussion of rocks as animate objects.

13. Durand 1994, 101 and map. Thanks to Keith Lekness, curator at the Nicollet Tower, Coteau des Prairies, South Dakota, for information on Nicollet's maps, July 2000. Lame Deer and Erdoes 1994, 252; Catlin 1973, 164–65, 168, 206. In 1859, Edward Neill of the Minnesota Historical Society visited another site that the Sioux called "Thunder Tracks." Neill 1859, 58. I visited three Thunder nest and track sites mapped by Nicollet: in the sand hills near Hankinson, North Dakota; in Brown's Valley, Minnesota (thanks to Shirley Ecker at Sam Brown Park); and near Peever, South Dakota. I also observed human hand- and footprints and Thunder Bird tracks carved on boulders, "Prayer Rocks," at Britton, Ipswich, and Pierre, South Dakota; and Medicine Rock, now in Gettysburg, South Dakota, visited by white explorers in 1825 at its original site at the mouth of the Little Cheyenne River on the Missouri; the boulder was later moved to avoid inundation by the Oahe Dam. Brad Tennant, per. cor., August 2, 2000. Ipswich Prayer Rock and photo: Gries 1998, 46–47, 77–78 (pipestone). Many other carved tracks on rocks exist in the prairies, described by Lewis and Clark and other early travelers. Thanks to Rick Gebhart and Kevin Callahan and the Upper Midwest Rock Art Research Association for information on petroglyph boulders. Lame Deer on George Catlin and pipestone: Lame Deer and Erdoes 1994, 273–74. Other legends accounted for blood-red pipestone, see, e.g., Erdoes and Ortiz 1984, 94. I visited Pipestone National Monument on July 5, 2003.

14. Clifford Canku interview, and his teaching handouts "Dakota Spirits" and "Circle of Evil Spirits." Thanks also to Aloma McGaa, Sisseton-Wahpeton tribal archivist. Carved tracks in rock are easily distinguished from genuine footprints: see Tanner 1984. Black Hills *Pteranodons*: Boyce and Haag 1991, 12. Paleontologist Jim Martin has found remains of *Pteranodons* with six- to ten-foot wingspans around Edgemont, South Dakota, south of the Black Hills, interview, August 4, 2000. The day I arrived in Sisseton to interview Canku, the tribe was preparing to evacuate the next day, because of Environmental Protection Agency fears that tons of TNT buried by the U.S. government on the reservation in 1938 had de-

graded into unstable nitrogycerin and might explode. The EPA ordered that the dynamite be located and detonated (see conclusion for much more extensive unexploded munitions dangers on Pine Ridge Reservation, South Dakota).

15. Lightning power: Lame Deer and Erdoes 1994, 253–54.

16. The Great Lakes region was under water during dinosaur days, so Cretaceous exposures are practically unknown, although some Cretaceous fish and turtle fossils have turned up in Minnesota. St. Anthony Falls: Parkman 1905–11, 11; Parks and Wedel 1985, 170–71.

17. Pond 1860–67, 220; Pond 1986, 98, 87. See also Neill 1859, on "Oanktayhee, bones of the mastodon." See Callahan 2000– on water monsters in Minnesota lore.

18. Indiana legend: Mackal 1980, 210–11; Lister and Bahn 1994, 158 (mammoth site at Jonesboro, Indiana). C. Richard Harington's Yukon find: Bélanger 1988. For Native legends about Alaskan and Canadian mammoths, frozen and skeletal, see Cohen 2002; Lister and Bahn 1994.

19. Pond 1860–67, 220; Pond 1986, 98, 87. Neill 1859, 63. The concept of wakan is defined by various medicine men in Walker 1991, e.g., 68–74. See also Medicine Crow 2000, 112–14, on concept of manitou, wakan, baxbe. "Irresistible influence" exerted by fossils: interestingly, some fossils are actually magnetic, owing to iron pyrite crystals that form during mineralization (thanks to Patricia Mason and Paul Hlava). Magnets are used in alternative medicine today. Winchell 1911, 259, on elephant fossils in Minnesota; on pottery and mastodon remains in burial mound at Stillwater, southern Minnesota, 274. There were several small lakes around Shakopee.

20. Schoolcraft 1884, original vol. 4:643–45. Chingwauk: Meurger and Gagnon 1988, 170–71; Dewdney and Kidd 1967, 81–83. Chingwauk made the sketches from his memory of rock art on Lake Superior recounting a war expedition of five canoes, led by a shaman-warrior named Myeengun, and their encounters with Water Monsters in Lake Superior.

21. Riggs 1992, 485. See also Durand 1994, 96, 100. Pond 1860–67, 217, wakan; 217–23, Onkteri.

22. Sioux migrations: Waldman 2000, 177–82; Froiland and Weedon 1990, 61–68. The mosasaur from Frederick and the mammoth from Wetonka are both exhibited in the South Dakota School of Mines Museum, Rapid City: see Gries 1998, 76–77, 45–46 (photos of both).

23. Unktehi's back like a "crosscut saw": see also Clark 1966, 301. LaPointe 1976, 19, 38.

24. Lakota myth of the crystal heart of Unktehi; Null 1998, 96–98. The discovery of the dinosaur heart (displayed in the North Carolina Museum of Natural Science) is controversial, but what is interesting for a folklorist is the paleontolo-

gists' eagerness to find the *heart* of a dinosaur and the meaning they ascribe to it. On the stone heart debate, see Rowe et al. 2001. Badlands fossils: O'Harra 1920. For interpreted fossil sites in western North America: Skwara 1992; see also Costa 1994; Halls 1996 and 2005.

25. Walker 1983, 28, 158, 218, 337 (Unktehi), 82, 212 (teeth in beak of Thunder Bird); 115 (nest of bones), 123–24 (tracks). Pond 1860–67, 228–30 ("shiver the oak"). Samuel Pond tried to grasp the mystic concept of the Thunder Bird, whose voice was thunder and whose weapon was lightning. He witnessed dances around effigies of Thunder Birds: Pond 1986, 87, 102. On pictographs and petroglyphs of Thunder Birds in Minnesota, see Winchell 1911, pt. 5 and plates. The four types of Thunder Birds were also described by Lame Deer: Erdoes and Ortiz 1984, 218–20; Lame Deer and Erdoes 1994, 252–53; by the Oglala elder George Sword, in Walker 1983, 82; and by Seven Rabbits, in Walker 1991, 118. The first, black Thunder Bird calls to mind *Hesperornis*, which stood nearly five feet tall and had a very long beak with teeth and very small wings. Pterosaur fossils have six joints in the wing (plus the shoulder joint); the "hand" is elongated into three claws and one long "finger" with four joints. Modern birds have four joints in the wing plus the shoulder joint, although the interphalangeal joint is not very conspicuous. Ptersosaur and bird anatomy clarified by Tommy Tyrberg, per. cor., January 14, 2002; and Greg Liggett, interview, October 16, 2002.

26. Landslips along the Missouri: Mails 1996, 93. Clifford Canku interview. Pond 1860–67, 230. Neill 1859, 58. See also Chamberlain 1890: the ancient foes of Thunder Birds were the "Un-kche-ghi-la or water monsters, whose bones are now found in the bluffs of Nebraska and Dakota." On Thunder Birds, see Faris 2001 and Musinsky 1997.

27. Darren Naish, per. cor., January 28 and March 6, 2000. The *Diatryma* model in the California Academy of Sciences, San Francisco, may have been observed by the Yakimas. The incident recalls the Yuchi identification of the allosaurid dinosaur in the Oklahoma museum as the giant lizard of their mythology; see chapter 4. Northwest Coast Indians also have Thunder Bird tales in which the gigantic birds carried whales from the Pacific Ocean to mountaintops. Peter Faris suggests that people who saw Ice Age megafauna fossils identified them with the largest creatures they knew—whales—and imagined that birds huge enough to carry off whales had dropped the skeletons far from the sea. Faris 2001. John Alexander, AMNH, has pointed out that it does not take more than a few centuries for mythology to coalesce around an animal: for example, he notes that the Plains legend of the "thunder or big dog" (horse) developed after horses were brought to America by the Spanish in the sixteenth century. Per. cor., February 2001. See Denig 1930, 412, for a version of this myth.

28. Lame Deer and Erdoes 1994, 252. Neihardt 1961, 22–25, 188–90. Spence 1914, 110. Clark 1974, 73. Cook 1957, 115, 196–97; and for Cook's full story see Osborn 1929, xxi–xxii (thanks to Andrew Hemmings for this reference). The name "Young Man Afraid of His Horses" meant that he was so fearsome in battle that the enemy fled when they saw his horse: Lame Deer and Erdoes 1994, 116. Cope and Marsh: Lanham 1991, 86, 149–53; Jaffe 2000, 113–23, 131–43.

29. After the Custer Military Expedition in the Black Hills to find gold, the Sioux believed that "fossil hunting" was often a cover story for gold prospecting: Scott 1939, 155; Wallace 1999, 96–97, 100; Dussias 1996, 115, 118. The Sioux hunter's explanation of the Thunder Horse tooth given to Marsh in 1877 was apparently garbled: it was said to be that of a "big horse struck by lightning." See Matthew 1926, 460–61, and Lull 1926, 460–61. LaPointe 1976, 62–63; Jaffe 2000, 65. Beach 1877, 259 (thanks to Patricia Mason). Marsh and Red Cloud: Schuchert and LeVene 1940, 164–68, plate XII. Lanham 1991, 86, 149–53; Jaffe 2000, 113–23, 131–43. Titanotheres and brontotheres: Lanham 1991, 147–48; Mader 1994; Osborn 1929. *Brontosaurus* (now *Apatosaurus*) sonic boom: Myhrvold and Currie 1997.

30. Cook 1957, 196, 234–38. *Agate Fossil Beds* 1980; history of excavations, 38–39; museums with Agate Springs fossils, 86–87.

31. LeBeau 2001. Ruthann Knudson, interview, October 28 and November 1, 2002. I am grateful to Ruthann Knudson for sending me LeBeau's official report and a photocopy of his original field notebook of the cultural survey, completed December 14, 2001. A Blackfeet cultural evaluation was also produced by Curly Bear Wagner of Montana in 2000. A vision seeker made a circle of rocks or a narrow pit: see, e.g., Lame Deer and Erdoes 1994, 1–7; Snell 2000, 46; Medicine Crow 2000, 80–83. James Walker's references to Gnaski's demonic powers and "*Hmuǧma* wizards" are less informative and say nothing of fossils or bones. Walker 1983, 106, 243 (Gnaski); Walker 1991, 51, 80, 94.

32. See Neill 1859, 62–63, for a Sioux magical "shooting" ceremony and medicine bags containing animal claws with the power to inflict pain and death on others. See also Pond's description of a Sioux "shooting" ceremony using shells in 1834: Pond 1986, 94–95, 106. Lame Deer referred to spells cast and sickness inflicted by magical "shooting" of tiny blades, quills, jagged rocks, and other sharp objects: Lame Deer and Erdoes 1994, 159, 175. Deloria, per. cor., June 2–4, 2003. Warnings: Null 1998, 98. The only other recorded collection of fossils for evil intent that I found was the reputed use of fossils for witchcraft among Navajos (chapter 3).

33. Hayden's "intensity no threat," Howard 1975, 154–55; Indians "thought Hayden insane, and thus a holy man, not to be harmed," Lanham 1991, 35, 38–39. Hayden was "some sort of crazy, white mystic," Jaffe 2000, 25. According to

Kindle 1935, fossil hunters were thought "queer," 451–52. Dussias 1996, 112–13, citing Osborn's biography of Cope (1931), 21. Clark 1974, 78: "hewing to their tradition of not harming the mentally ill, they left him alone." Wallace 1999, 52: Hayden's "harmless lunacy."

34. Deloria 1997, 207–8. Wallace 1999, 50–51. *Agate Fossil Beds* 1980, 35–37. See Mitchell 1998, 30: "the landscape of the American West was a veritable boneyard," the late nineteenth century could be called "the age of bones," and the landscape of the era evokes the biblical "valley of dry bones."

35. Froiland and Weedon 1990, 194; LaPointe 1976, 16–19, 51. See also Deloria 1997, 207, on Sioux tales of volcanoes in the Black Hills. Boyce and Haag 1991, 8–9, 32–33. Gries 1998, 218–21; see 220 for Red Valley "Racetrack."

36. It was the beaver skeletons inside the corkscrews that finally led the paleontologists to identify them as burrows. *Agate Fossil Beds* 1980; see 33, 70 on beaver burrows, photo 69. O'Harra 1920, 59–61, discusses the enigma of *Daemonelix*. Skwara 1992, 161–62. LeBeau 2001; see 7–8, 11, 13, 14 for Beaver's lodges. The giant beaver tooth would have come from a Pleistocene *Castoroides ohioensis* or *Paleocastor*, which reached the size of a bear, not from the smaller Miocene beavers at Agate Springs. Giant beaver fossils exist in loess deposits in South Dakota and Nebraska. Sandoz 1964, xiii–xiv (thanks to Peter Faris). Richard Harington, per. cor., August 21, 2000; June 16, 2003. In Dene legends of the Northwest Territories, Canada, gigantic beavers were destroyed by the culture hero Yamoria. Walt Humphries, per. cor., December 6, 1999; May 12, 2000; Dene legend information from Prince of Wales Northern Heritage Centre, Yellowknife, Northwest Territories, Canada.

37. Eldon Little Moon interview, October 14, 2002. Dorsey 1894, 393, 438–41; Lame Deer and Erdoes 1994, 251–52. Battle of the Little Bighorn and Wounded Knee: Waldman 2000, 179–82; Lame Deer and Erdoes 1994, 11–13.

38. Johnson Holy Rock, interview, October 14, 2002. Dave Bald Eagle, interview, June 25, 2000. Information on Pawnee Buttes fossils from Steven Wade Veatch and Scott E. Foss. David Parris, per. cor., June 2, 2003. The Plains tribes routinely traveled very long distances. For example, the Blackfeet knew "practically all of the great West from Mexico north to Saskatchewan" and regularly traded in the Southwest: Schultz 1962, 351.

39. Devil's Tower legends: Clark 1966, 305–6; Deloria 1997, 204–5; LaPointe 1976, 65–67; Boyd 1983, 88–93; and see Levendorsky 1996. Devil's Tower fossil information: thanks to Bill Matteson, interview, October 10–11, 2000; William Monteleone, per. cor., April 26, 2002; and John Foster, Museum of Western Colorado, per. cor., April 22–23, 2002. For the geology, see Lageson and Spearing 1988, 96–101. Kiowa interest in fossils is also demonstrated in the name of a Kiowa

medicine man painted by George Catlin, Quay-ham-kay, or Stone Shell. Catlin 1973, 75.

40. Johnson Holy Rock interview. David Parris, interview, August 4 and 6, 2000. Photos of Silas Fills the Pipe are in the Sinclair Papers, New Jersey State Museum, Trenton.

41. Culbertson and Evans: Clark 1974, 74–75; Lanham 1991, 32–33; on Leidy, see 18–22; see also Schultz 1962, 349. Leidy 1869, 23–24; see 361–446 for Leidy's valuable bibliography of all publications on extinct mammals of North America, 1717 to 1869. Hayden's guides: Howard 1975, 155; Lanham 1991, 38–46, and see 85 (Marsh).

42. Dussias 1996, 113–23, on the paleontologists' reliance on Indian accounts of fossils and Indian guides; on Cope, see 120–23, Cope quoted on 122. Lanham 1991, 159, 161–62; 268 (Cope). Peter Dodson pointed out that as a pacifist Cope usually declined to ride with armed escorts. See Lanham 1991, 156–59. In 1871, Cope was furnished with a five-man military escort from Fort Wallace, Kansas, but he refused to carry the gun they offered him. Jaffe 2000, 59.

43. Lanham 1991, 159, 161–62; 268 (Cope). Wallace 1999, 124, 263–64 (Cope). Cope and Marsh: Jaffe 2000, 65, 112, 114, 121–22, 177, 352. Standing Rock Sioux often find dinosaur fossils along the Grand and Moreau riverbanks after spring floods, according to Deloria 1997, 222.

44. Cope's *T. rex* find rediscovered: Barrett 2000. Neal Larson, per. cor., August 5, 2003. Rule of priority in naming fossils: Lanham 1991, 113–16. On Grinnell and Wortman, see chapter 4.

45. Scott 1939, 155–57, 161–64. Scott 1887. Agnew 1890, 15–17, 26, 28, 54–59. Wounded Knee: Waldman 2000, 181–82. Joel Minor, the archivist at Oglala Lakota College, Pine Ridge Reservation (October 15, 2002), helped me try to learn what happened to Alick Mousseau.

46. Scott 1939, 155–57, 161–64. White Bear became important in tribal politics and was a friend of Charles M. Russell, according to the Crow medicine woman Alma Hogan Snell, interview, August 14, 2003. Little People made stone arrows: Linderman 1962, 40–41; stone arrows originally the shattered stone bones of Red Woman, 53. Geology of Wyoming: Lageson and Spearing 1988. Tim McCleary, Little Big Horn College, and Marvin Stewart, Crow Agency, Crow Reservation, Montana, read and made helpful comments on the Crow section of this chapter.

47. Thompson had obtained his fossil bundle—the largest rock medicine bundle he'd ever seen—in Los Angeles, in the 1980s, from a collector who said it was originally from Hardin, a town ten miles north of the trading post. Putt Thompson, interview, October 12, 2001. I attempted to photograph Thompson's medicine rock, but the three photos did not turn out; some would say that the bundle

"did not want to be photographed." Cf. Lame Deer and Erdoes 1994, 275, on a sacred pipe that was "impossible to photograph." Thanks to artifacts trader Jeb Taylor of Buffalo, Wyoming, for comments on fossils in amulets and bundles, per. com., October 8, 2000. Lisa Brahm-Lindberg and Sheryl Ley, Washakie Museum, Worland, Wyoming (July 24, 2003), showed me the Crow amulet, which was obtained from Putt Thompson in 1999. The documentary film *Contrary Warriors* (Rattlesnake Productions, 1990) records the ceremonial unwrapping of the sacred medicine bundle of Marvin Stewart's ancestor, Living Bull, which contains fossil ammonites and baculites.

48. I met with Roger Colten, collections manager, Anthropology Department, Peabody Museum, Yale University, on November 29, 2001. Gall's bundle, YPM 049254, collection notes, Peabody Museum, New Haven, Connecticut. Landman 1982–83, published photographs and descriptions of the Crow and Sioux fossil medicine bags at the Peabody, as well as the ammonite acquired by Marsh. Since the passage of NAGPRA legislation (see conclusion), it is no longer acceptable to publish photographs of sacred medicine bundles without permission of the relevant tribes. Fossil dentalia: Alex and Martin 1993. Crow rock medicine bundles: Marvin Stewart, interview, March 22, 2004; Wildschut 1960, esp. 90–114; testing, 12–13; skull medicine bundles, 16; exotic trade items in medicine bundles, 169; Pretty Coyote's fossil bundle, 113–14 and figs. 44 and 45.

49. Lowie 1983, 250–56, quotation 261–62. Baaxpee: Snell 2000, 46 n. 4; Medicine Crow 2000, 80–82. Peck 2002, 153; Wildschut 1960, 92, 93; on maxpe, 2, 12. Baco'ritsi'tse or bacoritse in Crow legend: Peck 2002, 152–53; Wildschut 1960, 90–97.

50. Linderman 1962, 43, 61, 74. Heavy Blackfeet bundle: Schultz 1962, 14, 306.

51. Maxwell 1999–2000; Desmond Maxwell, per. cor., December 18 and 28, 1999. Maxwell and Taylor 1994; there is also evidence that highly polished quartz, chert, and chalcedony gastroliths of the dinosaurs were selected for tools by prehistoric Plains cultures. Michael Flynn, per. com., March 24, 2004. Michael Fosha, assistant state archaeologist, South Dakota School of Mines and Technology, per. cor., September 14, 1999. Lakota and Assiniboine spiritual leaders tell me that volcanic rocks that can withstand high heat are selected by traditional Indians for sweat lodge ceremonies, while river rocks are avoided because they tend to explode when heated (thanks to Eli Tail, Sr., and John Allen, Jr.). Interest in collecting fossils began several millennia ago in America. In a paleo-Indian dwelling site near Fossil, Oregon, a research team from the Oregon Museum of Science and Industry's Hancock Field Station discovered a trove of fossils collected about eleven thousand years ago. Many of the (unidentified) fossils were pierced for stringing as ornaments and amulets, and in one corner of the site, there was a neat stack of

five rock slabs containing fossil leaf impressions. "Were Early American Indians the First Fossil Enthusiasts?" 1988 (thanks to Bill Matteson).

52. As reported in *Acta Palaeontologica Polonica* 49, 2 (2004): 197–210, Jerry Harris and Peter Dodson named the sauropod *Suuwassea emilieae*, combining *suu* (thunder) and *wassa* (ancient) to mean "ancient thunder." Harris later learned from a Crow speaker that the single word *suuwassa* means " 'the first thunder heard in Spring,' . . . a beautiful sentiment lacking any comparably romantic term in English." Harris, per. cor., 2003. Michael Flynn and Bill Matteson, interviews, October 4 and 11, 2000.

53. Medicine Crow 2000, 2. Lowie 1983, 3, 112; Linderman 1962, 188, 194. "Alligator" water monster: Linderman 1972, 126–28. Water monsters: Clark 1966, 301. Chief Medicine Crow's drawings: see 1930.23 of the ledger drawings in the Barstow Collection, Crow Indian Illustrations, Montana State University–Billings, Special Collections, Online Image Database http://libmuse.msu.edu/epubs/nadb/. Large fossil bones were noted by the former Little Bighorn Battlefield historian Neil Mangum and the archaeologist Dr. Richard Fox. William Boyes, interview, August 19, 2003. Marvin Stewart, interview, March 22, 2004.

54. Alma Hogan Snell, interview, August 14, 2003. Plenty Coups's experience: Linderman 1962, 192–95. Head Start word for giant dinosaur: Tim McCleary, interview, March 2004.

55. Medicine Crow 1998. Medicine Crow spoke of dinosaur eggs at Little Big Horn College, Crow Agency, in the late 1990s. Two claws: Medicine Crow's text accompanying the display of Crow shields at the Museum of the American Indian, New York City, June 2000; and see Medicine Crow 1998, 28.

56. Alma Snell interview; and Snell 2000, 46–47 and n. 7 (Snell did not publish Boyes's photo or sketch); 199 n. 5. On vision quest beds visible in the Wolf Mountains, Medicine Crow 2000, 80–83. In the 1990s, Snell and others tried to locate the tree with the carving, using William Boyes's map, but many trees on Squaw Butte had burnt in forest fires since 1973. Dragonflies were admired by Native Americans for their swift precision flight—the Blackfeet, for example, thought the dragonfly was never hit by hailstones or lightning, and therefore its spirit could protect one from being struck by lightning or missiles. Curly Bear Wagner, per. com., August 16, 2003. Before the publication of Goes Ahead's vision by Snell in 2000, Wayne George, an Ashishinabe artist (northern Minnesota), described a "vision" to me that curiously parallels Goes Ahead's vision. George was sitting on a rock in a kind of trance "watching large dinosaurs moving in the distance"; then his "eye caught a movement far on the horizon." It came near him—it was a very large dragonfly. Per. cor., December 18, 1999.

57. William Boyes interview, and per. cor., September 15, 2003.

58. See Chief Medicine Crow's sketch, 1930.23, Barstow Collection. The wings on his snake are more like the crest on a spinosaurid dinosaur. Alma Snell interview. As an example of translation problems, Wildschut 1960, 11, mentions the Crow "water monster" known as the "Long Bug." According to Alma Snell, however, "Long Bug" is the word for otter, whose underwater touch is feared by swimmers as a bad omen. Snell 2000, 69–70. The word for the supernatural otter is *Baapuxte*, which means a "mesh" pattern like the texture of some insects. Tim McCleary, interview, March 2004. Jeff Hecht, per. cor., June 5, 2003. Triassic red beds near Crow Reservation: Alt and Hyndman 2000, 235–36. Cary Easterday and Conrad Labandeira, per. cor., June 9, 2003. Jerry Harris, per. cor., August 2003. Michael Flynn, per. com., June 23, 2004.

59. Bill Snell, August 14, 2003, told me the fate of Goes Ahead's medicine bundle; see also Snell 2000, 51.

60. Linderman 1972, 48–54. Alma Snell interview. The stone Vs of old buffalo drives can be seen throughout western Montana. See Schultz 1962, on the use of baculite fossils to lure bison into the Vs and over the cliffs, 309–19; and see 317 for emerging awareness among the Blackfeet that the practice was environmentally unsound. Oregon legend: Saylor 1900. Cope and the Modocs: thanks to Alison Stenger and William Orr, per. cor., June 15, 2003. Waldman 2000, 153–54 (Modoc War).

61. Sediments in the vicinity of the Yellowtail Dam reservoir are Triassic, Jurassic, Cretaceous, and Pleistocene: Alt and Hyndman 2000, 373–77, map on 374 and photo of a typical Cretaceous sandstone cliff in the area on 375. I first visited the Fort Smith Dam on July 23, 2003, and spoke with Theo Huggs, a Crow woman who works for the National Park Service. I am grateful to Ellyn Nadeau, Fort Smith Fly Shop, for arranging for me to talk with Huggs and with Alma Hogan Snell. If the dark stain in the cliff indicated the presence of alluvial organic matter of the Quaternary age, however, then it's possible that the girls found part of the skull of a Pleistocene musk ox, whose remains occur in Montana. Male specimens have a deep, straight groove running down the center of the skull (see fig. 58). But would a musk ox skull stand out in a pile of bison skulls? Pretty Shield did not mention any horns on the giant skull. Musk ox: Dale Gnidovec, per. cor., June 10, 2003. Alma Snell interview. Marvin Stewart interview. Skulls piled at Dryhead Cliff buffalo jump: Medicine Crow 2000, 82, 87. On the geology of the Dryhead Cliff area, see Alt and Hyndman 2000, 234–35, and see 234 for map of Dryhead area.

62. Linderman 1972, 48–54. Iktomi credited with making stone arrows and piling them in heaps: Pond 1986, 88; and Lowie 1909, 105.

63. Wayne Archambault, interview, September 7–8, 2000. Coming Day (b. ca. 1860–70?) died in about 1940; he was also known as Old Warrior, according to

Minerva Allen, Assiniboine storyteller at Fort Belknap. As a boy, Wayne Archambault recalled that many people were afraid of the holy man, who always painted his face red. Bill Snell remembered that Coming Day's face and body were daubed with red ocher, and that he told good stories; interview, August 14, 2003. On man-eating bison of ages past, Grinnell 1962, 140; and for a man-eating mammoth tale of Alaska, Teit 1917. Denig 1930, 615–17. John Allen, Jr., interview, September 6, 2000.

64. Lowie 1909, 169–70. Wayne Archambault interview. Gerta Keller, paleontologist at Princeton University, is the chief proponent of the new theory. Hedges 2003; Achenbach 2003.

65. Jim Kennedy, interview, May 11, 2004. Bullchild 1985. Kindle 1935, 449–50, citing Richardson 1854, 101–2; Hind 1860, 2:60 (Ta-wa-pit); Tyrrell 1892. L'Heureux 1871; thanks to Clive Coy for the typescript translation of L'Heureux's original handwritten manuscript. Hind 1860 1:312–13. Tokaryk 1997. Spalding 1999, 16–17, 22–23, 248, citing Bullchild 1985. Red Deer dinosaurs: Norell, Dingus, and Gaffney 2000, 203–6. See also Spalding 1993. The Selwyn Geological Survey of Canada, 1877, hired as assistants and guides "Indians" named Baptiste Lafleur, Ahquon, and Mastie, and "half-breed" voyageurs Thomas Hillier, Robert Todd, Morice Deschamps, Luzion, Joe Grey, and Jim. On Bylot Island in the Arctic, an Inuit youth named Joshua Enookolook (of Pond Inlet, Northwest Territories) found a dinosaur bone on an expedition with Phil Currie and Dale Russell in the 1980s. Thanks to Darren Tanke for information on several First Nations fossil guides and finders, per. cor., November–December 1999; April 5, 22, 23, 2000. Dinosaur Provincial Park: Donald Brinkman, curator of vertebrates, Royal Tyrrell Museum, per. cor., January 28, 2000.

66. Blackfeet baby dinosaur: McGill 2003. Bill Snell interview, August 14, 2003. Hell Creek Formation: Norell, Dingus, and Gaffney 2000, 201–2. Nate Murphy, interview, September 6, 2000. On the stony dinosaur mummy, see Perkins 2002, and chapter 3. Cope and Sternberg in the Judith Badlands: Lanham 1991, 154–64; Jaffe 2000, 171–84; and Sternberg 1990. Blackfeet and Assiniboines (once known as Cutthroat Sioux) were much feared in the area during Cope's day.

67. John Allen, Jr., interview, September 6, 2000. I am grateful to Minerva Allen for sharing the story told by Coming Day. Bill Snell interview. Among Crows, Sioux, Assiniboines, and other northern groups, stories were always reserved for winter entertainment, not to be told in summer. Barnum Brown 1919 referred to fossil collecting as "hunting big game of the past." Mitchell 1998, 30, 143, points out that modern-day dinosaur fossil *hunters* are still seen as courageous "big-game" hunters. Cope: Jaffe 2000, 61. Sternberg 1990, 203–4. Simpson 1934, 83.

CONCLUSION
COMMON GROUND

1. Paleontological historian Martin Rudwick, in his preface to the 1985 edition of *The Meaning of Fossils*, characterized all paleontological knowledge before the "Renaissance of Western civilisation" as nothing but a "diffuse awareness of fossils." "Irascible": Peter Dodson, per. cor., July 13, 2003. Michael Novacek, per. cor., April 3, 1998.

2. Native American worldview and attitudes toward stones and fossils in the living culture today: Dussias 1996, 97–107, 154–55. On hostilities in western South Dakota during the Bone Wars, see, for example, Jaffe 2000, 112–20.

3. Lame Deer and Erdoes 1994, 194–95. Wovoka and Curly cited on Indigenous Peoples Literature Web site, www.indigenouspeople.net. Holy Rock interview, October 14, 2002. Clifford Canku interview, July 28, 2000. Harry Manygoats interview; see chapter 3. Dussias 1996, 97; see 100–107 on the inviolability of the earth. See Wildschut 1960, 90, on Crows leaving rocks and fossils in the ground, or collecting them for personal medicine.

4. See Deloria 1997, 206–7, and Sneve 2000. Lakota interpretation of geology, museum text written by Birgil Kills Straight (Kyle, Pine Ridge Reservation) and Ronnie Theisz (Black Hills State University, Spearfish, South Dakota), Journey Museum, Rapid City, South Dakota. In the late 1800s, about a hundred petrified logs were taken from the site by the AMNH and the South Dakota School of Mines in Rapid City. In 1935, Weiland returned to excavate numerous logs from underground, too. Cycad National Monument: quotations from Santucci and Hughes 1998; see also Boyce and Haag 1991, 31; Gries 1998, 286–87. Weiland was "criticized by some colleagues for taking more specimens than he needed to conduct his research." Santucci, NPS paleontologist, interview on earthsky.com, 1999. I was unable to learn where the Peabody stores the hundreds of logs collected by Weiland. In the same era, trainloads of immense logs from Arizona's Petrified Forest went to the Smithsonian; see chapter 3 and Conover 1997.

5. Marsh: see chapter 4. The NPS "tries to ensure that all visitors to parks . . . are able to see the fossils for which park units were created by allowing the collection of fossils for scientific or research purposes." But in actuality, this restriction excludes everyone except academic paleontologists from seeing the fossils "protected" by the NPS sites. *Fossils on Federal and Indian Lands* 2000.

6. Michael Flynn, interview, October 4, 2000. See *Skull Wars* by Thomas 2000. Army collections of skulls: Dussias 1996, 157 n. 476. Skulls collected by Marsh (and his student Grinnell) in 1870: Jaffe 2000, 31; Betts 1871.

7. Marsh's student Betts 1871, 665, included a sketch of the Yale team removing an Indian skull from a burial scaffold. Cope's collection of Native American skulls: Lanham 1991, 164; Dussias 1996, 121, citing Cope's letters home. Charles Sternberg 1990, 94–95, recounted a "funny experience" described by Cope: On the way down the Missouri to Omaha, Cope went ashore and found the grave of a Crow man wrapped in a blanket surrounded by a log framework to keep scavengers away. "It was an easy matter to pick up the skull," wrote Sternberg, but when Cope returned with the skull and began to lecture the passengers about the cranial characteristics of the tribe, the deckhands protested that bad luck would dog the boat unless Cope returned the skull to the grave. Travels of Cope's skull: Psihoyos and Knoebber 1994.

8. One small example of a report filed under NAGPRA in the Federal Register of 1999 gives a sense of the incredible scale of the grave robberies: the Peabody Museum at Harvard and the Peabody Museum at Phillips Academy, Andover, Massachusets, reported that they still have in their possession the skeletal remains of 1,921 Native American individuals that had been dug up from Pecos Pueblo and mission church cemeteries in New Mexico in 1915–29, along with hundreds of grave goods that had been buried with the bodies. Thomas 2000, 107–10. NAGPRA: Thomas 2000, 209–38; and Dussias 1996, 123, 150–54, see 154 n. 454, and 157 on the overlap between paleontology and archaeology. An acrimonious dispute over possession of a profoundly significant human fossil arose in the case of Kennewick Man, a skeleton estimated to be about ninety-two hundred years old, found eroding out of the Columbia River bank in Washington State in 1999. See Thomas 2000. A coalition of five Native American tribes requested custody of the "Ancient One" under NAGPRA, in order to rebury the skeleton. They were opposed by a coalition of eight scientific researchers who wanted to study Kennewick Man. The Interior Department's decision in favor of reburial was overturned in 2002 by a federal judge who decided that Kennewick Man was so ancient that "cultural affiliation" with any modern tribes was too tenuous to justify his return for reburial. On Indian antagonism toward "bonediggers," see Watkins 2000. Marla Big Boy, attorney for one of the tribes, sees the case as another fight between "scientific arrogance and validating traditional knowledge." Marla Big Boy, per. cor., December 9, 1999; and see Gease 2002a.

9. Shoshone and Bannock notions: anonymous tribal council member, Fort Hall Indian Reservation, Idaho, April 29, 2000. Thanks also to John Blahna, Shawnee, interview, April 29, 2000. Lame Deer and Erdoes 1994, 30.

10. Dussias 1996, pt. 3, 110–23, 156–57; quotations 117, 125; on the relationship of scientists and the U.S. military in removing fossils in the West, see 112–20, 157. Greg MacDonald, Paleontology Program coordinator, NPS, remarks,

"There is no question that the relationship between tribes and the government has never been the best, so tribes tend to question the government's motives in most situations." Per. cor., September 12, 2003.

11. Aureliano Flores quoted in a Reuters news story, July 16, 2001. Jensen 2003; further information on the Santee dispute from Lawrence Bradley, University of Nebraska graduate student, November 11, 2003.

12. Reeds 1926, 467–78. Reeds's article was subtitled "The Fossil Collector's Happy Hunting Ground." His map shows his collection site in the Hunton Formation on Coal Creek within the Chickasaw nation border. On November 18, 1918, the AMNH purchased Reeds's collection from the Hunton Formation for three hundred dollars; the archives contain no record of John Seeley, rightful owner of the specimens. Thanks to Bushra Hussaini, collections manager, Fossil Invertebrates, AMNH, per. cor., February 4–5, 2004. Indian displacements and land cessions: Waldman 2000, 200–208. For a modern analogue to Reeds's attitude, see Whybrow 2000, 200–202, on British paleontologists' collection of rare frog fossils from Yemeni-owned land. On the Greek and Roman plunder of local fossil bones in classical antiquity, and in modern Greece by paleontologist Barnum Brown in the 1920s, see Mayor 2000, 95–96 and n. 34.

13. Mike O'Neill, National Paleontology Program director, BLM, Washington DC, per. cor., April 23, 2003. So far, O'Neill continued, "no tribal entity has officially identified fossils as sources of cultural or religious values." Actually, in 1992 the Cheyenne River Sioux tribe claimed an interest in the disputed *T. rex* named Sue as part of the tribe's cultural heritage, but this consideration was ignored by the courts; see below. I know of one repatriation under NAGPRA of a Navajo medicine bundle, or jish, that happened to include a small marine fossil, but the fossil was only incidental to the case (see chapter 3, n. 34).

14. Dussias 1996, on *T. rex* Sue, 90–91; on the lack of legislation regulating fossil collecting, see 123–25 and notes; on NAGPRA as model for fossil resources on reservations, 147–54, quotations 153–54; on ARPA's specific exclusion of fossils from archaeological resources, 147–48.

15. Red Cloud: Lanham 1991, 152. LaPointe 1976, 71, discusses the "rules of life" explained by Standing Bear, Lakota leader: "Children [are] taught to sit still and enjoy the silence [and] the constant talker [is] considered rude and unthinking." Silence "was meaningful to the Lakota [and] in the presence of the great [or wakan], silence was the mark of respect. More powerful than words was silence with the Lakota." Interest in fossils is recent: O'Neill, per. cor., April 23, 2003. William Boyes, interview, August 19, 2003. The lack of clear laws for cultural resource management on federal and public lands: Knudson 2000.

16. Lanham 1991, 29. Boyce and Haag 1991, i–ii. Bakker quoted in Verrengia 2000. On the laws governing fossil collecting and the burgeoning market for fossils, see McFarling 2001.

17. For example, invertebrate and plant fossils may be gathered in "reasonable amounts" without permits on BLM land, but permits are required on NPS land. Vertebrate fossils may be gathered only for educational use by qualified scientists on BLM and NPS lands. Reservations contain three kinds of land: tribal land, land privately owned by Indians or whites, and state land. Because of the delicate relationship between some tribes and the BIA, it would be prudent for a researcher to check with the tribal council and the BIA to legitimize the permission, according to Mike O'Neill, National Paleontology Program director, BLM, interview, September 15, 2003.

18. See the principles, recommendations, and definitions outlined in the report of the secretary of the Interior Department, *Fossils on Federal and Indian Lands* 2000. Several government agencies consulted with members of the Society of Vertebrate Paleontology on how to structure a national policy for vertebrate fosssils on public lands. See also the valuable "Fossil Legislation" Web site, www.colossal-fossil-site.com. Article 9 of the SVP bylaws sets forth professional guidelines for the proper treatment of fossils: "By-laws on Ethics," SVP *News Bulletin* 180 (Spring 2001): 145; summary of the Interior Department's 2000 report, 35–37. I thank David Parris, Greg McDonald, and Mike O'Neill for information about reservation permits for paleontologists.

19. "Like cocaine": Verrengia 2000. Douglas Wolfe, per. cor., September 10, 2003. Williams received $7.6 million from the auction. Monastersky 1997. Dussias 1996, 88. The Sue case is especially complex because the ranch land was outside the reservation and allotted to Williams in trust by the government. Thanks to Mike O'Neill for clarifying some legal aspects of the Sue case, interview, September 15, 2003.

20. Dussias 1996, 86, 93–95, 97–102. For other points of consilience between traditional Indian perspectives and science, see the final section of this chapter.

21. Benton 2003, 10; Rachel Benton, per. cor., September 15, 2003. NPS cultural resource specialist Marianne Mills and park superintendent William Supernaugh also claimed that the source of the controversy was a simple misunderstanding over the nickname "Titanothere Graveyard." Henderson 2002. Notably, the NPS consistently refers to the Stronghold Unit as the "South Unit" and to the fossils as titanotheres, avoiding the more common name, brontotheres, given by Marsh to commemorate the Sioux Thunder Beasts. Johnson Holy Rock is involved in trying resolve the issue. Kent 2000–2001. As Holy Rock remarked to me, the government announcement was imperious and secretive—"Why didn't

they work in peace, try to get some agreement first? That land is not government land, that is Indian land." Interview, October 14, 2002. On the Stronghold controversy, see Henderson 2002; Gease 2002a, b, c; and Steen 2003.

22. *Prairie Preamble* (official Badlands National Park newspaper), Summer 2003, 4 and 8. Beads found near ancient human remains: Gease 2002a. Rachel Benton, per. cor., September 15, 2003. Geo-archaeological surveys cited by NPS cultural resource specialist Marianne Mills: Former Badlands Bombing Range Restoration Advisory Board 1999. On August 9, 2002, the Oglalas filed under NAGPRA for possession of "all human remains and burial objects" in the Stronghold Unit. For Executive Order 13007, May 24, 1996, see www.colossal-fossil-site.com. David Rains Wallace poked around the Stronghold Unit in 1997 and was questioned about fossil hunting by Lakotas: 1999, 51

23. Ghost Dance: Waldman 2000, 181–82. See Gease 2002a, citing Margaret Lemley Warren, *The Badlands Fox* (1991) for oral history of white militia killing Ghost Dancers at the Stronghold and selling artifacts.

24. "Badlands Gunnery Range" [Stronghold Unit] n.d., information sheet; and *Prairie Preamble* 2003, 4 and 8. See also Former Badlands Bombing Range Restoration Advisory Board 1999. The unexploded ordnance blanketing the Stronghold recalls the tons of TNT that were buried on the Dakota Sisseton-Wahpeton Reservation in eastern South Dakota in 1938 by the Bureau of Indian Affairs. Fears that the dynamite had degraded into explosive nitroglycerin caused the evacuation of the reservation in 2000 (see chapter 5, n. 14). Lame Deer and fellow Sioux leaders expressed deep anger at the appropriation of the Stronghold Unit: Lame Deer and Erdoes 1994, 97, 119–20. The Lakotas have never accepted the 1868 treaty giving away the Black Hills, and the appropriation of the Stronghold into the national park also remains a flashpoint. Henderson 2002; Gease 2002b and c. Rachel Benton remarked to me that "many of the demonstrators openly admit that they actively poach fossils in the South Unit." Per. cor., September 15, 2003.

25. "Because we have to": F. A. Calabrese, archaeologist and regional NPS director, Gease 2002b. Removing fossils is "exactly as if they were still in the ground": Brian Kenner, Badlands chief of resource management, Gease 2002a. Benton 2003, 10. William Supernaugh interview, June 30, 2004. The "fossils had been deteriorating for thousands of years" before scientists became interested in them, admitted Barbara Beasley, U.S. Forest Service paleontologist, in "Poachers Illegally Taking Fossils" 2003.

26. Parris and Shelton 2000.

27. Michael Flynn teaches geology, paleontology, and psychology, and is the curator of the Geology Museum in the Science Building of Sheridan College. Interview, October 4, 2000. Thanks also to Bill Matteson, paleontology student, for a tour of the museum and useful information. Interview, October 11, 2000.

28. Timothy Rowe, interview, September 26, 2002, and see www.DigiMorph .org. The Eco-Scouts, based at Seba Dalkai School on the reservation, were established as a way to offer Navajo youth incentives to take an interest in the ecology and history of Navajo land. Kyril Calsoyas, former principal of Seba Dalkai School, interview, October 2, 2002. So far no Navajos have taken up the offer of scholarships to study paleontology with Rowe, although many Navajos study for geology degrees. Rowe points out that economics is a factor, since geology careers are more lucrative than those in paleontology. Educational outreach sensitive to Native American traditions would help. The dearth of Indians entering the fields of paleontology and archaeology may stem from obvious historical reasons. There were fewer than ten Native Americans with Ph.D.'s in archaeology in 2000, for example, and even fewer academically trained paleontologists who are Native American. Paleontologists could help change those statistics, by making their science more attractive to Indian youth. See Watkins 2000: the author is a Choctaw archaeologist who explains the double bind of Indians who enter such fields as paleontology and archaeology. Thomas 2000, chapters 22–24 and his epilogue, discusses how archaeology could be enriched by Native American perspectives.

29. Bessie Yellowhair was an assistant to tribal president Thomas Atcitty: Fischer 1998. The senate countered that the legislation might assist the tribe in retrieving the fossils from Berkeley some day (so far the tribe has not formally requested the specimens, but they own a cast; see below). As a compromise, the senate proposed two state dinosaurs, the *Dilophosaurus* and the *Sonorasaurus*, discovered by amateur fossil hunters on state lands in 1994, now in the Sonora Desert Museum, Tucson. The only known specimens of the famous *Dilophosaurus* remain in Berkeley, although part of another dilophosaur was recently discovered in China. Arizona State Senate research memo, April 17, 1998, and the revised fact sheet for H.B. 2133. The *Sonorasaurus* was suggested as an alternative by the Abenaki storyteller and amateur paleontologist Gerard Tsonakwa, interview, February and March 2001.

30. Timothy Rowe, per. cor., September 8, 2003. Sam Welles excavated the *Dilophosaurus* specimens in 1942 under a permit issued by the Department of the Interior and "thereby saved [them] from destruction by the weather." There was no provision for the skeleton's return to the Navajos; instead it was to be kept "for perpetuity" at Berkeley. Joseph T. Gregory, curator of the University Museum, Berkeley, to Navajo tribal chairman Raymond Nakai, April 17, 1970. Thanks to Mark Goodwin for copies of the correspondence concerning the *Dilophosaurus* excavation and the gift of the cast, in the Sam Welles Archives, Museum of Paleontology, Berkeley, California. Since 1996, paleontologist Mark Goodwin has corresponded with Gary Kmett, a non-Indian who teaches a year-long course in paleontology at Tuba City High School on the reservation. Goodwin has contributed

400   NOTES TO PAGES 317-324

scientific journals, articles, and casts of dilophosaur limb bones for study by Najavo youth. Goodwin, per. cor., September 15 and 23, 2003. The Navajo Nation Minerals Department is now responsible for negotiating with paleontologists. Recently, they revised the standard open-ended time for the return of fossil specimens in a contract with the University of New Mexico, Albuquerque. In this case, the Cretaceous fossil was to be returned in five years, and in the meantime a cast was to be created for the Navajo nation. Geoffrey Brown, director, Navajo Nation Museum, interview, March 24, 2004.

31. Timothy Rowe, interview, September 26, 2002. Wann Langston, Jr., interview, September 23, 2003. Clarenda Begay, curator, Navajo Nation Museum, Window Rock, Arizona, interview, September 10, 2003. Geoffrey Brown interview.

32. Jim Kennedy, interview, May 11, 2004. The baby tyrannosaurid may be an *Albertasaurus* or a *T. rex* (meat-eating dinosaurs look similar when young). It is nearly complete, missing only the tip of the tail and feet. The Museum of the Rockies holds other fossil specimens in trust for the Blackfeet tribe. Jack Horner, interview, March 24, 2003. McGill 2003.

33. See chapter 5. LeBeau's evaluation was undertaken in compliance with the National Historic Preservation Act, which requires federal agencies to document and evaluate the cultural legacies of historic landscapes. Ruthann Knudson, per. cor., October 28 and November 1, 2002. Dawn Little Sky's winter count information sheet was compiled by NPS ranger Anne Wilson, 2000. According to Dan Johnson, assistant to Marianne Mills, NPS cultural resource specialist, no cultural evaluation report has been undertaken at Badlands National Park, although a draft of an "ethnographic survey" by David White (2001) mentions Sioux traditions about Thunder Birds and Water Monsters in relation to fossils. William Supernaugh, interview, June 30, 2004. See also Former Badlands Bombing Range Restoration Advisory Board 1999.

34. I visited the Journey Museum on August 9, 2000. As far as I know, it is the only museum to offer Native American fossil traditions on an equal basis with established science. Ronnie Theisz provided information about the creation of the Lakota text, per. cor., September 8, 2003. The Lakota Advisory Board included Virginia Driving Hawk Sneve, Nellie Two Bulls, and Birgil Kills Straight, among others. In 1999, Birgil Kills Straight managed the fossil resources on Pine Ridge Reservation.

35. Johnson Holy Rock, interview, October 14, 2002. Morris Chee, interview, October 2002. John Allen, Jr., interview, September 6, 2000. Greg Liggett, interview, October 16, 2002. Jack Horner, interview, March 24, 2003. The *Alamosaurus* dispute was reported on CNN.com, June 2000.

36. Epilogue in Lame Deer and Erdoes 1994, 299, and see 112-14. Keller cited in Hedges 2003. Gould 1985, chapter 28, quotation 426. Douglas Wolfe, per.

cor., September 8, 2003. See also Semonin 2000, 409–11, on myth and metaphor as essential elements in understanding nature's past and extinctions.

37. Nita Manning, per. cor., March 26, 2000. Albert Grayeagle, "Earth Mother's Cries," posted on his Story Page Web site, aol.com, March 2000. Yoon 2000.

38. Norell, Dingus, and Gaffney. 2000, 96. Lame Deer and Erdoes 1994, xiv–xv.

39. John Allen, Jr., interview, September 6, 2000. "Spirit" speaks in the steam when water is poured on red-hot rocks: Lame Deer and Erdoes 1994, 2, 113, 4. In the 1830s, the Ponds collected the earliest references to Sioux worship of the spirit of stone, called "Taku-Shkan-shkan, that which moves." Rocks were thought to have attributes of life. Samuel Pond 1986, 87–89. Interestingly, Pond also recorded instances of skepticism about the sacredness of rocks among some Sioux; see 89, 106. On Sioux and Blackfeet ideas about animate rocks, see Parks and Wedel 1985, 171. Silicon is man-made quartz, used in watches and computers. The traditions about the wisdom stored in rock are modernized in "The Sacred Stone," by Hawk, posted by Sid Byrd, an Indian activist at Lovelady Prison, Texas, on the Indigenous Peoples Literature Web site, September 17, 2000 (thanks to Glenn Welker). He tells of an old medicine man who explains the knowledge contained in stone to a young boy by pointing out that his watch and computer are animated by silicon quartz. Thus "The smartest men in the world today still use the sacred aspects of stone," without realizing that they "gain, keep, and gather their knowledge and share it with the world" by means of a sacred "stone," the silicon chip.

40. Aloma McGaa, per. cor., September 27, 2000. "The earth, the rocks, the minerals, all of which you call 'dead,' are very much alive," maintained Lame Deer. He felt that considering these geological entities "dead and inert and inanimate" made them vulnerable to "exploitation as a resource." Lame Deer and Erdoes 1994, 120, xv. On scientific definitions and studies of rock, see Palmer 1999, 170–73. Thanks to Christian Wildberg, classical philosopher, Princeton University, for clarifications of the ideas of Plato, *Timaeus* 30B-D, and Aristotle, *Physics* and bks. 3 and 4 of the *On the Heavens*.

41. Nita Mannng, per. cor., March 26, 2000. Lame Deer and Erdoes 1994, 195. Erdrich 2000. Evolving definitions of what is animate and/or "almost alive": Hafner 2000; Angier 2001. Desert varnish is a little-understood process involving iron and manganese oxide in a possible biological interaction with clay and rocks in arid landscapes. Paleobiologist J. William Schopf used new Raman spectroscopy to confirm the biological origin of the earliest known fossils, as reported in *Nature*, March 7, 2002.

42. Walker 1983, 159, 206–7. Clifford Canku, interview, July 28, 2000. Inyan story in museum text, Cultural Heritage Center, Pierre, South Dakota; the text

consultants included Ben Black Bear, Jr., Martin Broken Leg, Marvin Holy, and others.

43. Schoolcraft 1975 [1825], 296. On rocks and the origin of life, see Palmer 1999, 50–53. The discovery by NASA scientists of crucial amino acids and sugars in meteors was reported by the BBC, *Nature*, and *Science News*, December 2001. Amino acid building blocks of life in earthbound calcite minerals, reported in *Science News*, May 5, 2001. Iron sulfide rocks as the "spawning ground of life": Morgan 2003.

44. Lame Deer and Erdoes 1994, 112, 193.

45. *Fossils on Federal and Indian Lands* 2000.

46. Woiche 1992, 114, 159.

47. Wallace 1999, 48, 126. Jaffe 2000, 122, 179, 352. Opium and belladonna: Lanham 1991, 123. Lame Deer and Erdoes 1994, 56–60. The term "lucid dreaming" to describe the technique of controlling dreams and following them to a desired conclusion was coined by the nineteenth-century Dutch psychiatrist Frederik van Eeden. Another technique for reaching into the subconscious to solve complex problems while in an altered state of mind has been called "integration": scientists such as Albert Einstein, John Nash, and Richard Feynman are said to have used the method.

48. See chapter 4 for Young Bull's narrative. Lanham 1991, 76–77. Sternberg 1990, 18–19. Few paleontologists will ever be able to embrace the concept, expressed by Assiniboine John Allen, Jr. (chapter 5), that there is no need to possess fossils other than in telling the story of their discovery. But in recent years, scientists are coming to recognize the value of storytelling, as a way of "identifying some of the questions scientists must ask," and as "a legitimate tool of interpretation." Speculation, scenario building, storytelling, creative logic—these "are the easiest, most colorful, most untrustworthy, most maligned, but sometimes most fruitful approach" for understanding the fossil record. Spalding 1999, 211; see also 261. Fossils bestow "intangible gifts to the imagination and curiosity in the same ways that art and music enrich our lives": *Fossils on Federal and Indian Lands* 2000.

APPENDIX
FOSSIL FRAUDS AND SPECIOUS LEGENDS

1. On the debate over the question of the first North Americans hunting mammoths, see Thomas 2000, 145–66; McMillan 1976, 90–93; Winchell 1911, 11–13; Deloria 1997, 127–34; Jones 1874, 73–74; and see Ashley-Montagu 1944, 568, for Scott's opinion that mammoths lived in the West until the 1500s; see

569–71 on Albert Koch's discovery in 1838 of elephant skeletons and stone tools in Missouri (discussed in chapter 4). See also Scott 1887, 474–76. On the Wallum Olum, see Oestreicher 1994. For other contemporary expert opinions on the inauthenticity of the Lenape Stone carving, and the reaction of contemporary Indians, see Mercer 1885, 14, 17–18. On a "woolly mammoth" carved on a thousand-year-old shell found in Delaware, see Griffith et al. 1988. Mammoth kill sites: Waldman 2000, 1–4. Chronic 1987, 97–98 (Folsom); *Agate Fossil Beds* 1980, 16–17. Terra 1957, 19–28 (Mexico). Extinction of mammoths: Lister and Bahn 1994; see also Martin 1999. Clovis sites have been found in every mainland state. Clovis, Folsom, and other paleo-cultures of the end of the Ice Age: Waldman 2000, 2–4.

2. Quotations from McMillan 1976, 82. Ussher: Semonin 2000, 16; Rudwick 1985, 70, 135; Glass, Temkin, and Straus 1968, 4, 364–65; Weishampel and Young 1996, 52–53. See also Gould 1985, 115, 124–25, The most recent version of creationist dogma, "intelligent design," expands the age of Earth beyond six thousand years and acknowledges minor changes in life-forms over time, but still adheres to creationist religious belief and is antagonistic to scientific methods of experiment and proof. See *Natural History*, special issue 2002.

3. See Hapgood 1972, with photos of the collection. A few stone artifacts and pottery shards found at Acambaro may be genuinely ancient. Thanks to Léo Laporte and Robin Cox, curator at the American Philosophical Society, Philadelphia, for help in determining Simpson's role. Although Hapgood was not a creationist, his notion that the Acambaro figures might represent living dinosaurs, whose "unmineralized" bones were buried in the area, continues to attract creationists to the collection.

4. Snowden 1925 (thanks to Juliet Burba). George Gaylord Simpson also rejected the authenticity of alleged Indian reconstructions in southwestern petroglyphs of dinosaur images from observations of fossils, 1942, 132. Havasupai Canyon petroglyphs: Deloria 1997, 224–25. Lister and Bahn 1994, 103, 126, suggest that a rock painting near Moab, Utah, shows a mammoth, but others, such as rock art specialist Peter Faris, believe it may depict a bear. On extinct animals in rock art, see Faris 2002. See Feliks 1998 for a fascinating argument that observations of plant and invertebrate fossils inspired the invention of rock art, as an effort to imitate nature's replication of familiar life-forms in rock. Feliks's paper is illustrated with rock art symbols from Europe that appear to replicate marine and plant fossils.

5. Thanks to paleontologist Dan Chure for discussions of the artifacts from Acambaro, and "dinosaurs" in rock art, per. cor., November 2001, March 2002. The fossils of Guanajuato are mostly Pleistocene horses and rhynchothere and gomphothere mastodons, according to Wade Miller, a paleontologist who works in the region, per. cor., April 2, 2002.

6. Hapgood was shown the Ica stones in 1972: Hapgood 1972, 11. On the lack of horned dinosaurs in South America (except for one very questionable jaw fragment found in Patagonia in 1918), see Dodson 1996, 284. Thanks to François Pujos and Rodolfo Salas for discussion of the Ica Stones and the Pleistocene fossils of Peru. Pujos, per. cor., April 1, 2002. See Semonin 2000, 294–95.

7. Tanner 1984, 117–18. Mayor and Sarjeant 2001. Fossil footprints of humans and extinct mammals have been found in volcanic stone in Nicaragua and Guatemala, for instance. See Terra 1957, 141–42; Mayor and Sarjeant 2001, 157–58, and on footprints of humans and hogs in lava in Hawaii, 158–59.

8. Roland T. Bird in *Natural History* 43, 5: 254–61. Norell, Dingus, and Gaffney 2000, 181–83. Information on Paluxy River tracks from Dr. Stephen Myers, and see Glen Kuban, papers delivered at the First International Symposium on Dinosaur Tracks and Traces in Albuquerque, New Mexico, published in Gillette and Lockley 1989.

9. Ancient Greek creation myths were taken symbolically: see Mayor 2000, 194, and see 202–7 for the sense of deep time expressed in Greek myth.

10. Compare the Cardiff Giant hoax of 1869, based on Iroquois myth, see chapter 1.

11. About ten thousand artifacts, along with human mummies, were excavated from Lovelock Cave by the Hearst Museum beginning in 1912. *Lovelock Cave. Formerly Known as Sunset Guano Cave*, BLM report NV-CH-18, Hearst Museum, Berkeley, California, n.d. (thanks to Laurie Bryant, BLM, Salt Lake City, Utah). Loud and Harrington 1929, and appendix 3, "Sarah Winnemucca's Account of Lovelock Cave." I thank Stephanie Livingston, University of Nevada, Reno, for helpful information. Mark Twain viewed one of the "giants" of Paiute myth displayed in Virginia City, Montana. On red, orange, and dun hair of preserved mammoths, see Lister and Bahn 1994, 70; Semonin 2000, 316. Recently, the remains of a larger-than-average Columbian mammoth and a young mammoth that perished between thirteen and twenty thousand years ago were found in the Black Rock Desert near Winnemucca, once covered by Lake Lahontan. The skeleton is on display at the Nevada State Museum in Carson City.

12. The dinosaurs of Mexico are relatively unstudied. I learned of Mesozoic remains known so far from Rivera 2000. Thanks also to Tracy Ford, per. cor., April 2002. Deloria 1997, 220. Deloria has had no luck in tracking down the Tohono O'odham person who worked at the tribal office and told him the story, per. cor., January 9 and March 22, 2002. Cuvier 1821, 223. On Mexican traders and western tribes, Marriott and Rachlin 1975, 97–98. Bechan and Cowboy Caves are near Moab, Utah: Lister and Bahn 1994, 71, 75–76, 157; Martin 1999, 267–76, esp. 268–70 on sloths and condors.

13. Sternbergs' find: Norell, Dingus, and Gaffney 2000, 154–55. Leonardo, the 77-million-year-old dinosaur mummy found near Malta (described in chapter 5) was first reported at the Society of Vertebrate Paleontology annual meeting in Norman, Oklahoma, October 10, 2002, by Nate Murphy, curator of the Phillips County Museum; Mark Thompson, geologist; and Dave Trexler, Timescale Adventures. Mummified dinosaur skin found in the Grand Staircase–Escalante National Monument in southern Utah was on display in 2001 in the Museum of Northern Arizona in Flagstaff. Another discovery of well-preserved dinosaur skin occurred in the Big Horn Basin in 2004.

14. According to Douglas Wolfe, "Cretaceous shoreline sediments contain arkosic (derived from granite) sediments in large abundance indicating that Cretaceous shorelines in Arizona were close to granitic source rocks. It is possible that 'remnant' Cretaceous terrace deposits still exist on granitic terrains around the Baboquivari area, as is the case at several localities in Arizona-Mexico. If the bone deposits were never deeply buried then the extent of mineralization we see in the Morrison Formation, for instance, would not occur. Some dinosaur bones I've seen in the Zuni Basin are only poorly permineralized." Wolfe also cautions that "many people use 'dinosaur' as a phrase to capture any fossilized or inexplicable bone." Wolfe, interview, February 6–10, 2002.

BIBLIOGRAPHY

Achenbach, Joel. 2003. "Fire and Ice: Big Rocks, Raging Volcanoes, and a Big Chill." *Washington Post*, reprinted in *National Geographic*, April 2003.

Acosta, Father Joseph [José] de. 1970 [1604]. *The Natural and Moral History of the Indies*. 2 vols. Trans. Edward Grimston. Ed. Clements R. Markham for the Hakluyt Society. New York: Burt Franklin.

Adams, Richard Calmet. 1997 [1905]. *Legends of the Delaware Indians and Picture Writing*. Ed. Deborah Nichols. Syracuse: Syracuse Univ. Press.

Agate Fossil Beds. 1980. National Park Handbook no. 107. U.S. Dept of the Interior. Washington, DC: GPO.

Agnew, Cornelius Rea. 1890. Logbook of the Princeton Scientific Expeditions, 8th Geological Expedition, Box 2, Folder 3, Mudd Manuscript Library, Princeton University.

Alex, Lynn Marie, and James Martin. 1993. "Occurrence of Fossil and Recent Dentalium [in] Western South Dakota." *Plains Anthropologist* 38, 145, Memoir 27: 131–43.

Alt, David, and Donald W. Hyndman. 2000. *Roadside Geology of Montana*. 9th ed. Missoula, MT: Mountain Press.

Angier, Natalie. 2001. "Defining the Undefinable: Being Alive." *New York Times*, December 18, Science Times 1, 6.

Antelo, Jesús H. 2000. "Gigantes en la mitologia, el arte, la ciencia y la historia." Anillo Espanol de Historia, Coruña, Spain.

Armer, Laura Adams. 1937. *The Trader's Children*. New York: Longman's, Green.

Ashley-Montagu, M. F. 1944. "An Indian Tradition relating to the Mastodon." *American Anthropologist* 49:568–71.

"Badlands Gunnery Range." N.d. Information sheet. Badlands National Park, National Park Service, Dept. of the Interior. Washington, DC.

Ball, Sydney. 1941. "The Mining of Gems and Ornamental Stones by American Indians." *Bulletin of the Bureau of American Ethnology* 120:1–77.

Barbeau, Charles Marius. 1994. *Mythologie huronne et wyandotte*. Montreal: Univ. of Montreal Press.

Barber, Elizabeth Wayland, and Paul T. Barber. 2005. *When They Severed Earth from Sky: How the Human Mind Shapes Myth*. Princeton: Princeton Univ. Press.

Barrett, S. A. 1921. "The Blackfoot Iniskim or Buffalo Bundle, Its Origin and Use." *Public Museum of Milwaukee Yearbook* 1:80–84.

Barrett, Steven. 2000. "Scientists Don't Dig New Name: Name of Older Fossil May Predate 'Tyrant Lizard King.' " Associated Press story on ABCnews.com.

Beach, William Wallace, ed. 1877. *The Indian Miscellany, containing papers on the history, antiquities . . . etc.* Albany: Munsell.

Beauchamp, William M. 1922. *Iroquois Folk Lore.* Reprint, Port Washington, NY: Ira J. Friedman, 1965.

———. 1976 [1892]. *The Iroquois Trail, or Foot-Prints of the Six Nations, in Customs, Traditions, and History [including] David Cusick's Sketches of Ancient History of the Six Nations.* Reprint, New York: AMS Press.

Bélanger, Nick. 1988. "The Whitestone Mammoth." *Biome* 8, 3:4.

Bell, Whitfield J. 1949. "A Box of Old Bones: A Note on the Identification of the Mastodon, 1766–1806." *Proceedings of the American Philosophical Society* 93, 2 (May): 169–77.

Benton, Rachel. 2003. "Fossil Resources: Hidden Treasures." *Prairie Preamble* (official newspaper of Badlands National Park, Department of the Interior) (Summer): 10.

Betts, Charles. 1871. "The Yale College Expedition of 1870." *Harper's New Monthly Magazine* 43, 257 (October): 663–71.

Bierhorst, John. 1988. *The Mythology of South America.* New York: William Morrow.

———. 1995. *Mythology of the Lenape: Guide and Texts.* Tucson: Univ. of Arizona Press.

Boyce, Japheth B., and Terri Haag. 1991. *Japh's Pretty Good Fossil Book of the Dakota Territory.* Rapid City, SD: RJB Rock Shop.

Boyd, Maurice. 1983. *Kiowa Voices.* Vol. 2, *Myths, Legends, and Folktales.* Fort Worth: Texas Christian Univ. Press.

Brown, Barnum. 1919. "Hunting Big Game of Other Days." *National Geographic Magazine* 35, 5 (May): 407–29.

Bruce, Robert. 1932. *The Fighting Norths and Pawnee Scouts.* Lincoln: Nebraska State Historical Society.

Buchanan, Rex, and James McCauley. 1987. *Roadside Kansas: Traveler's Guide to Its Geology and Landmarks.* Lawrence: Univ. Press of Kansas.

Buffon, Georges Louis Leclerc de. 1740–88. *Histoire naturelle, générale et particulière.* Paris: Imprimeries royale.

Bullchild, Percy. 1985. *The Sun Came Down: The History of the Earth as My Blackfeet Elders Told It.* New York: Harper & Row.

Callahan, Kevin L. 2000–. Web site on Midwestern Rock Art and Archaeology. Anthropology Department, University of Minnesota. www.geocities.com/ Athens/Acropolis/5579/.

Campbell, Kenneth E. 1980. "The World's Largest Flying Bird." *Terra* 19, 2 (Fall): 20–23.

Canfield, William W. 1902. *The Legends of the Iroquois Told by "The Cornplanter."* New York: Wessels.

Carrasco, David, Lindsay Jones, and Scott Sessions, eds. 2000. *Mesoamerica's Classic Heritage: From Teotihuacan to the Aztecs.* Boulder: Univ. Press of Colorado.

Catesby, Mark. 1743. *The Natural History of Carolina, Florida and the Bahama Islands.* Vol. 2. London, n.p.

Catlin, George. 1973 [1844]. *Letters and Notes on the Manners, Customs, and Conditions of North American Indians.* Vol. 2. New York: Dover.

Celeron, Pierre Joseph. 1749. "Journal of Expedition." *Ministère des Colonies.* Collection Moreau St. Mery, Canada, vol. 40 (1741–1749), fol. 318, and in *English Translation of Margry,* 6:666–721.

Chamberlain, A. F. 1890. "The Thunder-Bird amongst the Algonkins." *American Anthropologist* (January): 51–54.

Chandler, James M. 2001. "The Hiscock Site: A Lovely Jumble of Discoveries." *Mammoth Trumpet* (Center for the Discovery of the First Americans) 16, 4: n.p.

Charlevoix, Father de. 1744. *History of New France.* Vol. 5. Paris: n.p.

"Cheyenne Stone Buffalo-Horn." 1927. *Indian Notes* 4, 2:150–53.

Chronic, Halka. 1987. *Roadside Geology of New Mexico.* Missoula, MT: Mountain Press.

———. 2000. *Roadside Geology of Arizona.* Missoula, MT: Mountain Press.

Cieza de Leon, Pedro de. 1964 [1553]. *The Travels of Pedro de Cieza de Leon, A.D. 1532–50, Contained in the First Part of His Chronicle of Peru.* Trans. and ed. Clements R. Markham for the Hakluyt Society. New York: Burt Franklin.

Clark, Champ. 1974. *The Badlands.* N.p.: Time-Life.

Clark, Ella E. 1966. *Indian Legends of the Northern Rockies.* Norman: Univ. of Oklahoma Press.

Cohen, Claudine. 2002. *The Fate of the Mammoth.* Trans. W. Rodarmor. Chicago: Univ. of Chicago Press.

Coleman, Loren, and Jerome Clark. 1999. *Cryptozoology A to Z.* New York: Simon and Schuster.

Collinson, Peter. 1767. "An Account of Some Very Large Fossil Teeth Found in North America." *Philosophical Transactions of the Royal Society of London* 57: 464 and 468.

Colton, Ray E. 1935. "Recent Flood Waters Revealed Much to Science: Mastodon and Reptilian Bones of Great Antiquity Are Found in Republican River." *Republican Leader* (Trenton, Nebraska), October 11, 1.

Conover, Adele. 1997. "Petrified Forest National Park: The Object at Hand." *Smithsonian* (June).

Conway, Thor. 1993. *Painted Dreams: Native American Rock Art*. Minocquia, WI: Northword Press.

Cook, James H. 1957 [1923]. *Fifty Years on the Old Frontier*. Norman: Univ. of Oklahoma Press.

Cornplanter, Jesse J. 1938. *Legends of the Longhouse*. Philadelphia: Lippincott.

Costa, Vincenzo. 1994. *Dinosaur Safari Guide: Tracking North America's Prehistoric Past*. Stillwater, MN: Voyageur Press.

Craig, G.Y., and E. J. Jones. 1985. *A Geological Miscellany*. Princeton: Princeton Univ. Press.

Croghan, George. 1759. "Minutes of Conferences Held by Capt. George Croghan." B.M., Add. MSS. 21655, f73–75. Glenn A. Black Laboratory of Archaeology, Ohio Valley–Great Lakes Ethnohistory Archives, Miami Collection, Indiana University.

———. 1767. Ohio Valley, Letter to Lord Shelbourne, Secretary of State for the Southern Department, American Colonies, London. Cited in Kindle 1935.

Curtis, Natalie. 1966. *The Indians Book: Song and Legends of the American Indian*. New York: Dover.

Cushing, Frank H. 1883. "Zuni Fetiches." *Second Annual Report of the Bureau of American Ethnology, 1880–1881*, 3–45. Washington, DC: GPO.

———. 1901. *Zuni Folk Tales*. Reprint, Univ. of Arizona Press, 1999.

Cusick, David. 1825. *Sketches of Ancient History of the Six Nations, Comprising . . . the Foundation of [North America]. . . the Creation of the Universe . . . the Wars, Fierce Animals, Etc.* Fayetteville, NY: Recorder Print.

Custer, George Armstrong. 1977 [1874]. *My Life on the Plains*. Norman: Univ. of Oklahoma Press.

Cuvier, Georges. 1806. "Sur les éléphans vivans et fossiles." *Annales du Museum d'Histoire Naturelle* (Paris) 8:3–58.

———. 1821. *Recherches sur les ossemens fossiles*. 2nd rev. ed. Vol. 1. Paris: Belin.

———. 1840 [1812]. *Discours sur les révolutions de la surface du globe*. 8th ed. Paris: Cousin.

Daubenton, Louis Jean Marie. 1764 [1762]. "Mémoire sur des os et des dents remarquables par leur grandeur." *Académie Royale Scientifique Mém. Année*, 206–29.

Deloria, Vine, Jr. 1997 [1995]. *Red Earth, White Lies: Native Americans and the Myth of Scientific Fact*. Golden, CO: Fulcrum.

Denig, Edwin Thompson. 1930. "Indian Tribes of the Upper Missouri: The Assiniboin." *Forty-sixth Annual Report of the Bureau of American Ethnology, 1928–29*, 375–628. Washington, DC: GPO.

Dewdney, Selwyn, and Kenneth E. Kidd. 1967. *Indian Rock Paintings of the Great Lakes*. 2nd ed. Toronto: Univ. of Toronto Press.

Diaz del Castillo, Bernal. 1928 [1568]. *The Discovery and Conquest of Mexico, 1517–21*. Trans. A. P. Maudslay. London: Routledge & Sons.

DiPeso, C. C., J. B. Rinaldo, and G. J. Fenner. 1974. *Casas Grandes: A Fallen Trade Center of Gran Chichimeca*. Vol. 7. Flagstaff, AZ: Northland Press.

Dobkins, Rebecca. 1997. *Memory and Imagination: The Legacy of Maidu Indian Artist Frank Day*. Oakland: Oakland Museum of California.

Dodson, Peter. 1996. *The Horned Dinosaurs*. Princeton: Princeton Univ. Press.

Dorsey, George A. 1894. "A Study of Siouan Cults." *Eleventh Annual Report of the Bureau of American Ethnology*. Washington, DC: Smithsonian.

———. 1906. *The Pawnee: Mythology (Part I)*. Carnegie Institution Publication no. 59. Washington, DC: Carnegie Institution of Washington

Dozo, Maria Teresa. 1997. "El Significado de los Fosiles para los Antiguos Habitantes de la Patagonia." *Revista Museo* (Fundacion Museo de La Plata, Argentina) 2, 10:41–43.

Durand, Paul. 1994. *Where the Waters Gather and the Rivers Meet: Atlas of the Eastern Sioux*. Faribault, MN: Paul Durand.

Dussias, Allison. 1996. "Science, Sovereignty, and the Sacred Text: Paleontological Resources and Native American Rights." *Maryland Law Review* 55:84–159.

Echo-Hawk, Roger C. 2000. "Ancient History in the New World: Integrating Oral Traditions and the Archaeological Record in Deep Time." *American Antiquity* 65, 2:267–90.

Eiseley, Loren. 1945. "Myth and Mammoth in Archaeology." *American Antiquity* 11:84–87.

Ellis, Richard. 2003a. *Sea Dragons: Predators of the Prehistoric Oceans*. Lawrence: Univ. Press of Kansas.

———. 2003b. "Terrible Lizards of the Sea." *Natural History* (September): 36–41.

Emerson, Ellen Russell. 1884. *Indian Myths or Legends, Traditions, and Symbols of the Aborigines of America*. Boston: Houghton Mifflin.

Erdoes, Richard, and Alfonso Ortiz, eds. 1984. *American Indian Myths and Legends*. New York: Pantheon Books.

Erdrich, Louise. 2000. "Two Languages in Mind, but Just One in the Heart." *New York Times*, Writers on Writing, May 22, E1–2.

Escape from Indian Captivity: The Story of Mary Draper Ingles and Son Thomas Ingles. 1982. As told by John Ingles. Ed. R. I. Steele and A. L. Ingles. 2nd ed. Radford, VA: n.p.

Ewers. John C. 1981. "Water Monsters in Plains Indian Art." *American Indian Art Magazine* (Autumn): 38–45.

Farber, Sharon. 1988. "The Last Thunder Horse West of the Mississippi." *Isaac Asimov's Science Fiction Magazine* 12 (November): 20–44.

Faris, Peter. 2001. "Native American Paleontology: Fossils, Myths, and Imagery." Paper presented at the Utah Rock Art Research Association annual meeting, Moab, October 5–7.

———. 2002. "Native American Paleontology: Extinct Animals in Rock Art." Paper presented at the Utah Rock Art Research Association Symposium, November 3.

———. 2004. "The Influence of Fossil Footprints on Rock Art." Paper presented at the Colorado Rock Art Association annual meeting, Denver, May 22.

Farlow, James O., and M. K. Brett-Surman, eds. 1997. *The Complete Dinosaur.* Bloomington: Indiana Univ. Press.

Feliks, John. 1998. "The Impact of Fossils on the Development of Visual Representation." *Rock Art Research* 15, 2:109–34.

Fewkes, Jesse W. 1898. "Archaeological Expedition to Arizona in 1895." *Seventeenth Annual Report of the Bureau of American Ethnology,* 730–42. Washington, DC: GPO.

Fischer, Howard. 1998. "Attempted Diplomacy in Designating State Dinosaur Doesn't Suit Navajos." Capitol Media Services, Phoenix, April 24.

Former Badlands Bombing Range Restoration Advisory Board. 1999. Meeting Minutes, September 16, Kyle, South Dakota.

Fosha, Michael. 1993. "Two Iniskims from the Anton Rygh Village Site in Campbell County, South Dakota." *South Dakota Archaeological Society Newsletter* 23, 4:3–5.

Fossils on Federal and Indian Lands. 2000. Report of the Secretary of the Department of the Interior. Washington, DC, May.

Frisbie, Charlotte. 1987. *Navajo Medicine Bundles or Jish.* Albuquerque: Univ. of New Mexico Press.

Froiland, Sven G., and Ronald R. Weedon. 1990. *Natural History of the Black Hills and Badlands.* Sioux Falls, SD: Center for Western Studies, Augustana College.

Gatschet, Albert. 1899. "Water-Monsters of American Aborigines." *Journal of American Folklore* 13:255–60.

Gease, Heidi Bell. 2002a. "Badlands Fossil Dig Mired in History, Opposing Views." *Rapid City* [SD] *Journal,* August 5.

——— 2002b. "Badlands Fossil Dig Delayed." *Rapid City* [SD] *Journal,* August 8.

———. 2002c. "National Park Service Officials Postpone Dig." *Rapid City* [SD] *Journal,* August 30.

Geis, Darlene. 1959. *Dinosaurs and Other Prehistoric Animals.* New York: Grosset & Dunlap.

Giddings, Ruth Warner. 1959. *Yaqui Myths and Legends.* Tucson: Univ. of Arizona Press.

Gillette, D., and M. Lockley, eds. 1989. *Dinosaur Tracks and Traces*. Cambridge: Cambridge University Press.

Glass, Bentley, Owsei Temkin, and William Straus, eds. 1968. *Forerunners of Darwin, 1745–1859*. Baltimore: Johns Hopkins Press.

Goddard, Pliny Earle. 1911. "Jicarilla Apache Texts." *Anthropological Papers of the American Museum of Natural History* 8: 208–9.

Gould, Stephen Jay. 1985. *The Flamingo's Smile: Reflections on Natural History*. New York: Norton.

Grafton, Anthony. 1995. *New Worlds, Ancient Texts: The Power of Tradition and the Shock of Discovery*. Cambridge: Harvard Univ. Press.

Gries, John Paul. 1998. *Roadside Geology of South Dakota*. 2nd ed. Missoula, MT: Mountain Press.

Griffin, J. B., D. Meltzer, B. Smith, and W. Sturtevant. 1988. "A Mammoth Fraud in Science." *American Antiquity* 53, 3:578–82.

Grinnell, George Bird. 1923. *The Cheyenne Indians: Their History and Ways of Life*. 2 vols. New Haven: Yale Univ. Press.

———. 1928. *Two Great Scouts and Their Pawnee Battalion*. Cleveland: Clark.

———. 1932. "From Yale to the Wild West." *Journal of Natural History* 23:329–36.

———. 1961 [1889]. *Pawnee Hero Stories and Folk-tales*. Lincoln: Univ. of Nebraska Press.

———. 1962 [1892]. *Blackfoot Lodge Tales: The Story of a Prairie People*. Lincoln: Univ. of Nebraska Press.

———. 1972. *The Passing of the Great West: Selected Papers of George Bird Grinnell*. Ed. John F. Reiger. New York: Winchester Press.

Hafner, Katie. 2000. "What Do You Mean, 'It's Just Like a Real Dog'?" [things that are "almost alive"]. *New York Times*, May 25, G1 and 7.

Halls, Kelly Milner. 1996. *Dino-Trekking: The Ultimate Dinosaur Lover's Travel Guide*. New York: Wiley.

———. 2005. *Jurassic Park Institute Dinosaur Activity Guide*. New York: Random House.

Hamblin, Alden, Sue Ann Bilbey, and James Evan Hall. 2000. "Prehistoric Animal Tracks at Red Fleet State Park, Northeastern Utah." *Utah Geological Association Publication* 28:1–10.

Hapgood, Charles. 1972. *Mystery in Acambaro*. Kempton: Adventures Unlimited Press.

Harington, C. R. 1996. "Giant Beaver." *Beringian Research Notes* (Yukon Beringia Interpretive Centre) 6 (March): 1–4.

Harris, Richard. N.d. "Sacred Mountains of the Dineh, parts 1 and 2." *Four Corners Magazine*. www.fourcornersmagazine.com.

Hedges, Chris. 2003. "Where Dinosaurs Roamed, She Throws Stones." *New York Times*, December 17, B3.

Heinlein, Parker. 2000. "Along the Hi-Line." *Daily Chronicle* (Bozeman, MT), August 6.

Henderson, Dierdtra. 2002. "Fossil Clash Digs Up Deep Indian Anger." *Denver Post*, December 30.

Hilbert, Alfred. 1975. "That Word 'Chemung'—What It Means." *Chemung Historical Journal* (March): 2473.

Hilton, Richard P. 2003. *Dinosaurs and Other Mesozoic Reptiles of California*. Berkeley and Los Angeles: Univ. of California Press.

Hind, Henry Y. 1860. *Narrative of the Canadian Red River Exploring Expedition of 1857 and of the Assiniboine and Saskatchewan Expedition of 1860*. 2 vols. London: n.p.

"Historic Clay Tobacco Pipes." 1974. *Bulletin of the Archaeological Society of New Jersey* (Spring–Summer): 171–19.

Hitchcock, J. A. 1999. "Clay Pipes Then and Now." *Tobacco Times* 4 (November): 12–13.

Hoebel. E. A. 1960. *The Cheyennes*. New York: Holt, Rinehart & Winston.

Homovich, Esther. 1992. "The Story of Mahtahis." Transcribed at the Western Delaware Tribal Complex, Bartlesville, OK, by James Rementer, Lenape Language Project, January 23.

Howard, Robert West. 1975. *The Dawnseekers: The First History of American Paleontology*. New York: Harcourt Brace Jovanovich.

Hudson, Charles. 1976. *The Southeastern Indians*. Knoxville: Univ. of Tennessee Press.

Hyde, George E. 1951. *Pawnee Indians*. Denver: Univ. of Denver Press.

Jackson, Jason. 2003. *Yuchi Ceremonial Life: Performance, Meaning, and Tradition in a Contemporary American Indian Community*. Lincoln: Univ. of Nebraska Press.

Jaffe, Mark. 2000. *The Gilded Dinosaur: The Fossil War between E. D. Cope and O. C. Marsh and the Rise of American Science*. New York: Crown Publishers.

Jefferson, Thomas. 1954 [1781]. *Notes on the State of Virginia*. Ed. and notes William Peden. Chapel Hill: Univ. of North Carolina Press.

Jennison, George. 1971. *Noah's Cargo: Some Curious Chapters of Natural History*. New York: Benjamin Blom.

Jensen, Andy. 2003. "Dinosaur Fossil Becomes Issue of Ownership." *Daily Nebraskan*, November 11.

Jillson, Willard Rouse. 1936. *Big Bone Lick: An Outline of Its History, Geology and Paleontology to Which Is Added an Annotated Bibliography of 207 Titles*. Big Bone Lick Association publication no. 1. Louisville, KY: Big Bone Lick Association.

Johnson, Elias. 1881. *Legends, Traditions and Laws, of the Iroquois, or Six Nations, and History of the Tuscarora Indians.* Lockport, NY.: Union Printing Co.

Jones, Charles C. 1874. "Antiquity of the North American Indians." *North American Review* 118, 242 (January).

Jones, David E. 1972. *Sanapia: Comanche Medicine Woman.* N.p.: International Thomson Pub.

Jones, Volney H. 1942. "Fossil Bones as Medicine." *American Anthropologist*, n.s., 44:162–64.

Kehoe, Thomas. 1965. " 'Buffalo Stones': An Addendum to 'The Folklore of Fossils.' " *Antiquity* 39, 155 (September): 212–13.

Kennedy, Chet [Chester B.]. 1973. "The Folklore of Fossils." *The Fossileer* 14 and 20 (April and October): 6–7.

———. 1976. "A Fossil for What Ails You." *Fossils Magazine* 1 (May): 42–57.

Kent, Jim. 2000–2001. "Lakota Protest National Park Service Badlands Dig." *Native American Times* [Oklahoma Indian Times], nativetimes.com.

Kindle, E. M. 1931. "The Story of the Discovery of Big Bone Lick." *Kentucky Geological Survey*, 6th ser., 41:195–212.

———. 1935. "American Indian Discoveries of Vertebrate Fossils." *Journal of Paleontology* 9, 5 (July): 449–52.

Knudson, Ruthann. 2000. "Cultural Resource Management in Context." In *Science and Technology in Historic Preservation*, ed. Ray Williamson and Paul Nickens, 267–90. New York: Kluwer Academic/Plenum.

Koch, Albert. 1840–41. *Description of the Missourium, or Missouri leviathan; together with its supposed habits. Indian traditions concerning the location from whence it was exhumed; . . .* Pamphlet. St. Louis, MO. Cited in Simpson 1942.

Kroeber, Alfred L. 1983. *The Arapahoe.* Lincoln: Univ. of Nebraska Press.

Kurten, Bjorn, and Elaine Anderson. 1980. *Pleistocene Animals of North America.* New York: Columbia Univ. Press.

Lageson, David, and Darwin Spearing. 1988. *Roadside Geology of Wyoming.* Missoula, MT: Mountain Press.

Lakes, Arthur. 1997. *Discovering Dinosaurs in the Old West: The Field Journals of Arthur Lakes.* Ed. M. Kohl and J. McIntosh. Washington, DC: Smithsonian.

Lame Deer, John (Fire), and Richard Erdoes. 1994 [1972]. *Lame Deer, Seeker of Visions.* New York: Washington Square Press.

Landman, Neil H. 1982–83. "Powerful Plains Indian Medicine: Invertebrate Fossils, a Selection from Two Yale Peabody Collections." *Discovery* 16, 2:21–23.

Lanham, Url. 1991 [1973]. *The Bone Hunters: The Heroic Age of Paleontology in the American West.* New York: Dover.

Lankford, George E. 1980. "Pleistocene Animals in Folk Memory." *Journal of American Folklore* 93, 369:293–304.

LaPointe, James. 1976. *Legends of the Lakota*. San Francisco: Indian Historian Press.

Laporte, Léo. 2000. *George Gaylord Simpson*. New York: Columbia Univ. Press.

LeBeau, Sebastian C. [Bronco]. 2001. "Wico'cajeyate: Traditional Cultural Property Evaluation." Prepared for Agate Fossil Beds National Monument, 301 River Road, Harrison, Nebraska, Dept. of Interior, National Park Service, December.

Leidy, Joseph. 1852. "Memoir of the Extinct Species of American Ox." *Smithsonian Contributions to Knowledge* 5:3–20.

———. 1869. "The Extinct Mammalian Fauna of Dakota and Nebraska." *Academy of Natural Sciences* [Philadelphia] *Journal*, vol. 7. Philadelphia: J. B. Lippincott.

Levendosky, Charles. 1996. "How Can a Place Named 'Devils' Be Holy?" *Casper* [WY] *Star-Tribune*, August 18.

Levin, David. 1988. "Giants in the Earth: Science and the Occult in Cotton Mather's Letters to the Royal Society." *William and Mary Quarterly*, 3rd ser., 45:751–70.

L'Heureux, Jean. 1871. "Description of a Portion of the Nor'West and the Indians" [Geographical survey of Alberta and the Indians]. Translations by the Glenbow Foundation, Glenbow-Alberta Archives, Jean L'Heureux Papers, Calgary. Original French manuscripts in the Public Archives of Canada, Ottawa.

Linderman, Frank B. 1962 [1930]. *Plenty-coups, Chief of the Crows*. Lincoln: Univ. of Nebraska Press.

———. 1972 [1932]. *Pretty-shield: Medicine Woman of the Crows*. Lincoln: Univ. of Nebraska Press.

Lister, Adrian, and Paul Bahn. 1994. *Mammoths*. New York: Macmillan.

Locke, Raymond Friday. 1989. *The Book of the Navajo*. Los Angeles: Mankind.

Lockley, Martin. 1991. *Tracking Dinosaurs: A New Look at an Ancient World*. Cambridge: Cambridge Univ. Press.

Lockley, Martin, and Adrian Hunt. 1995. *Dinosaur Tracks and Other Fossil Footprints of the Western United States*. New York: Columbia Univ. Press.

Long, Russell J. 1977. "McFaddin Beach." *Patillo Higgins Series of Natural History and Anthropology* (Spindletop Museum, Lamar University [TX]), no. 1: 1–35.

Look, Al. 1981. *The Hopi Snake Dance*. Grand Junction, CO: Crown Point.

Loud, Llewellyn L., and M. R. Harrington. 1929. "Lovelock Cave." In *University of California Publications in American Archaeology and Ethnology*, vol. 25, ed. A. Kroeber and R. Lowie, 1–83. Berkeley and Los Angeles: Univ. of California Press, 1931.

Lowie, Robert H. 1909. "The Assiniboine." *Anthropological Papers of the American Museum of Natural History* 4, pt. 1. New York.

———. 1983 [1935]. *The Crow Indians.* Lincoln: Univ. of Nebraska Press.

Lucas, Frederick. 1926. "Thomas Jefferson—Paleontologist." *Natural History* 26, 3:328–30.

Lull, Richard S. 1926. "Early Fossil Hunting in the Rocky Mountains." *Natural History* 26, 5:455–61.

Lumholtz, K. 1902. *Unknown Mexico.* Vol. 1. New York: n.p.

McDonald, Jerry N. 1989. "A Collection of Fossils from an Adena Mound in Athens County, Ohio, and Notes on the Collecting and Uses of Fossils by Native Americans." In *In the Light of Past Experience: Papers in Honor of Jack T. Hughes*, ed. B. C. Roper. [Texas] Panhandle Archaeological Society publication no. 5: 295–306.

McEwan, Colin, Luis A. Borrero, and Alfredo Prieto, eds. 1997. *Patagonia: Natural History, Prehistory and Ethnography at the Uttermost End of the Earth.* Princeton: Princeton Univ. Press.

McFarling, Usha Lee. 2001. "Ancient Bone Sales Thrive in Capitalist Era: Trading of Relics Riles Scientists." *Los Angeles Times*, January 22, A1, A15.

McGill, John. 2003. "Baby Dinosaur Back in Browning." *Great Falls* [MT] *Tribune*, October 27.

Mackal, Roy P. 1980. *Searching for Hidden Animals.* New York: Doubleday.

McManis, Kent. 1998. *A Guide to Zuni Fetishes and Carvings.* Vol. 1, *The Animals and the Carvers.* Rev. ed. Tucson: Treasure Chest Books.

McMillan, R. Bruce. 1976. "Man and Mastodon: A Review of Koch's 1840 Pomme de Terre Expeditions." In Wood and McMillan 1976, 81–96.

Mader, Bryn. 1994. "Distant Thunder." *Natural History* 103, 4 (April): 61–62.

Mails, Thomas E. 1996. *The Mystic Warriors of the Plains.* New York: Marlowe and Co.

Marriott, Alice, and Carol Rachlin. 1975. *Plains Indian Mythology.* New York: New American Library.

Marsh, Othniel C. 1877. "Introduction and Succession of Vertebrate Life in America." An address before the American Association for the Advancement of Science, Nashville, TN, August 30.

Martin, Paul. 1999. "Deep History and a Wilder West." In *Ecology of Sonoran Desert Plants and Plant Communities*, ed. R. Robichaux, 255–90. Tucson: Univ. of Arizona Press.

Matson, F. R. 1935. "Identification of the Aplastic Present in Pottery Sherds from Texas." *Texas Archeology and Paleontology Society Bulletin* 7:68–69.

Matthew, W. D. 1926. "Early Days of Fossil Hunting in the High Plains." *Natural History* 26:449–61.

Maxwell, Desmond. 1999–2000. "Days of the Deinos." *Natural History* (December–January): 60–65.

Maxwell, W. Desmond, and John Taylor. 1994. "Dinosaurian Bone Used as Fire Rock in Indian Hearths, South-Central Montana." *Archaeology in Montana* 35, 2:1–4.

Mayor, Adrienne. 2000. *The First Fossil Hunters: Paleontology in Greek and Roman Times.* Princeton: Princeton Univ. Press.

———. 2004. "Geomythology." In *Encyclopedia of Geology,* ed. R. Selley, R. Cocks, and I. Palmer. Oxford: Elsevier.

Mayor, Adrienne, and William A. S. Sarjeant. 2001. "The Folklore of Footprints in Stone: From Classical Antiquity to the Present." *Ichnos* 8, 2:143–63.

Medicine Crow, Joe. 1998. *Brave Wolf and the Thunderbird: Tales of the People.* National Museum of the American Indian, Smithsonian Institution, Washington DC. New York: Abbeville Press.

———. 2000 [1992]. *From the Heart of the Crow Country: The Crow Indians' Own Stories.* Lincoln: Univ. of Nebraska Press.

Mercer, Henry C. 1885. *The Lenape Stone, or the Indian and the Mammoth.* New York: Putnam's Sons.

Meurger, Michel, and Claude Gagnon. 1988. *Lake Monster Traditions: A Cross-Cultural Analysis.* London: Fortean Tomes.

Mitchell, W.J.T. 1998. *The Last Dinosaur Book.* Chicago: Univ. of Chicago Press.

Monastersky, Richard. 1997. "Psst . . . Wanna Buy a *T. rex*? Paleontologists Fret about Dinosaur Sales." *Science News* 152 (December 13): 382–83.

Morgan, Kendall. 2003. "A Rocky Start: Fresh Take on Life's Oldest Story." *Science News* 163 (April 26): 264–66.

Mounier, R. Alan. 1974. "Aboriginal Use of Petrified Wood in New Jersey." *Bulletin of the Archaeological Society of New Jersey* 30 (Spring–Summer): 25–26.

Murie, James R. 1981. *Ceremonies of the Pawnee.* Washington, DC: Smithsonian.

Musinsky, Gerald. 1997. "The Thunderbird: Living Fossil or Living Folklore." Unpublished paper. P.O. Box 514, North Bend, PA 17760.

Myhrvold, Nathan P., and Philip J. Currie. 1997. "Supersonic Sauropods? Tail Dynamics in the Diplodocids." *Paleobiology* 23, 4:393–409.

Nadaillac, Marquis de. 1885. "Les Légendes des Iroquois." *La Nature: Revue des Sciences* (Paris), 149–51.

Neihardt, John G. 1961 [1932]. *Black Elk Speaks: Being the Life Story of a Holy Man of the Oglala Sioux.* Lincoln: Univ. of Nebraska Press.

Neill, Edward D. 1859. *Dahkotah Land and Dahkota Life.* Philadelphia: Lippincott.

Norell, Mark, Lowell Dingus, and Eugene Gaffney. 2000. *Discovering Dinosaurs: Evolution, Extinction, and the Lessons of Prehistory.* Rev. ed. Berkeley and Los Angeles: Univ. of California Press.

Null, Gary. 1998. *Secrets of the Sacred White Buffalo.* Paramus, NJ: Prentice Hall.

O'Bryan, Aileen. 1956. "The Diné: Origin Myths of the Navaho Indians." *Bulletin of the Bureau of American Ethnology* 163.

Oestreicher, David. 1994."Unmasking the Walam Olum: A Nineteenth Century Hoax," *Bulletin of the Archaeological Society of New Jersey* 49:1–44.

O'Harra, Cleophas C. 1920. *The White River Badlands.* South Dakota School of Mines, Bulletin 13. Rapid City: South Dakota School of Mines.

Opler, Morris Edward. 1994. *Myths and Tales of the Jicarilla Apache Indians.* Lincoln: Univ. of Nebraska Press.

Osborn, Henry Fairfield. 1921. *Age of Mammals.* New York: Macmillan.

———. 1923. "Mastodons of the Hudson Highlands." *Natural History* 23 (January–February): 3–24.

———. 1929. *The Titanotheres of Ancient Wyoming, Dakota, and Nebraska.* Vol. 1, Monograph 55. Washington, DC: GPO. Reprint, New York: Arno Press, 1980.

Palmer, Douglas. 1999. *Atlas of the Prehistoric World.* New York: Discovery Books.

Parker, Arthur C. 1989 [1923]. *Seneca Myths and Folk Tales.* Lincoln: Univ. of Nebraska Press.

Parkman, Francis. 1905–11. *Francis Parkman Works.* Vol. 2, *Jesuits.* New York: Little, Brown.

Parks, Douglas R., and Waldo R. Wedel. 1985. "Pawnee Geography: Historical and Sacred." *Great Plains Quarterly* 5 (Summer): 143–76.

Parris, David, and Sally Shelton. 2000. "Fossil Vertebrate Resources: An Outreach to Native Americans." Proposal of the Outreach Committee of the Society of Vertebrate Paleontology, Third Conference on Partnership Opportunities for Federally Associated Collections, November 13–15, Austin, TX.

Peale, Rembrandt. 1803. *A Historical Disquisition on the Mammoth, or Great American Incognitum, an Extinct, Immense, Carnivorous Animal Whose Fossil Remains Have Been Found in North America.* London: E. Lawrence. Reprinted in *Selected Works* 1974.

Peck, Trevor R. 2002. "Archaeologically Recovered Ammonites: Evidence for Long-Term Continuity in Nitsitapii Ritual." *Plains Anthropologist* 47, 181:147–64.

Perkins, S. 2002. "Rare Fossil Reveals Common Dinosaur's Soft Tissue." *Science News* (October 19): 243–44.

"Poachers Illegally Taking Fossils in South Dakota." 2003. Associated Press news story, September 22.

Pond, Gideon. 1860–67. "Dakota Superstitions" and "Dakota Gods." In *Collections of the Minnesota Historical Society* (St. Paul), 2:215–55.

Pond, Samuel W. 1986 [1870–71]. *The Dakota or Sioux in Minnesota as They Were in 1834.* Intro. Gary Clayton Anderson. St. Paul: Minnesota Historical Society Press.

Psihoyos, Louie, and John Knoebber. 1994. *Hunting Dinosaurs*. New York: Random House.

Reeds, Chester A. 1926. "The Arbuckle Mountains, Oklahoma: The Fossil Collector's Happy Hunting Ground." *Natural History* 26, 5:463–74.

Reeves, Brian. 1993. "Iniskim: A Sacred Nitsitapii Religious Tradition." In *Kunaitupii: Coming Together on Native Sacred Sites*, ed. Brian O. K. Reeves and Margaret Kennedy, 194–259. Calgary: Archaeological Society of Alberta, Canada.

Reichard, Gladys A. 1950. *Navaho Religion: A Study of Symbolism*. Princeton: Princeton Univ. Press.

Rice, Howard C. 1951. "Jefferson's Gift of Fossils to the Museum of Natural History in Paris." *Proceedings of the American Philosophical Society* 95, 6:597–627.

Richardson, Sir John. 1854. *The Zoology (of the) voyage of H.M.S. Herald: Vertebrates, including fossil mammals*. London, n.p. Also in *Boston Society of Natural History, Proceedings*.

Riggs, Stephen R. 1992 [1852]. *Dakota-English Dictionary*. Ed. James Owen Dorsey. St. Paul: Minnesota Historical Society Press.

Rivera, René Hernandez. 2000. "Los Dinosaurios en Mexico." *Revista Digital Universitaria* (online journal) 1, 1 (July 1). www.revista.unam.mx/vol.1/dino/creta.html.

Rowe, Timothy, Earle F. McBride, Paul C. Sereno, Dale A. Russell, Paul E. Fisher, Reese E. Barrick, and Michael K. Stoskopf. 2001. "Dinosaur with a Heart of Stone." *Science* 291 (February 2): 783.

Rudwick, Martin. 1985 [1976]. *The Meaning of Fossils: Episodes in the History of Paleontology*. Chicago: Univ. of Chicago Press.

———. 1997. *Georges Cuvier, Fossil Bones, and Geological Catastrophes*. Chicago: Univ. of Chicago Press.

Russell, Frank. 1898. "Myths of the Jicarilla Apache." *Journal of American Folklore* 11, 43 (October–November). Reprinted in Thompson 1966.

Russell, Loris S. 1998. "The First Fossil Hunters." *Alberta* 1, 1:11–16.

Rustywire, John. 1999. "Shiprock and Tse Nalyehe and the Twin Heroes." *Star Mountain-Navajo Life* (online journal).

Sahagun, Bernardino de. 1970–82 [1566–69]. *Florentine Codex. General History of the Things of New Spain*. Trans. Arthur J. O. Anderson and Charles E. Dibble. 2nd rev. ed. 12 vols. Santa Fe, NM: School of American Research.

Sandoz, Mari. 1964. *The Beaver Men, Spearheads of Empire*. Lincoln: Univ. of Nebraska Press.

Santucci, Vincent, and Marikka Hughes. 1998. *Fossil Cycad National Monument: A Case of Paleontological Resource Mismanagement*. In *National Park Service Paleontological Research*, ed. V. L. Santucci and L. McClelland, 3:84–89. Technical Report NPS/NRGRD/GRDTR-9801.

Savala, Refugio. 1945. "The Legend of Skeleton Mountain." *Arizona Quarterly* 1 (Spring). Reprinted in *The South Corner of Time*, ed. Larry Evers, 227–29. Tucson: Univ. of Arizona Press, 1980.

Saylor, F. H. 1900. "Coyote Kills a Dragon." *Oregon Native Son* 2, 6 (November). Portland: Native Son Pub. Co.

Schlarman, Joseph H. 1929. *From Quebec to New Orleans: The Story of the French in America*. Belleville, IL: Buechler.

Schoolcraft, Henry R. 1846. *Notes on the Iroquois*. New York: Bartlett & Welford.

———. 1884 [1851–57]. *Indian Tribes of the United States: Their History, Antiquities, Customs . . . Oral Legends and Myths*, 2 vols. [orig. 6 vols.] Ed. Francis Drake. Philadelphia: Lippincott.

———. 1975 [1825]. *Travels in . . . the Mississippi Valley*. New York: Collins and Hannay. Reprint, Millwood, NY: Kraus.

Schuchert, Charles, and Clara Mae LeVene. 1940. *O. C. Marsh: Pioneer in Paleontology*. New Haven: Yale Univ. Press.

Schultz, James Willard. 1962. *Blackfeet and Buffalo: Memories of Life among the Indians*. Norman: Univ. of Oklahoma Press.

Scott, W[illiam] B[erryman]. 1887. "American Elephant Myths." *Scribner's Magazine* 1 (January–June): 469–78.

———. 1939. *Some Memories of a Paleontologist*. Princeton: Princeton Univ. Press.

Segelken, Roger. 2001. "Mastodon Mania." *Cornell Chronicle* (February 1).

Selected Works in Nineteenth-Century North American Paleontology. 1974. Intro. Keir B. Sterling. New York: Arno Press.

Semonin, Paul. 2000. *American Monster: How the Nation's First Prehistoric Creature Became a Symbol of National Identity*. New York: New York Univ. Press.

Simmons, William. 1986. *Spirit of the New England Tribes*. Hanover, NH: Univ. Press of New England.

Simpson, George Gaylord. 1934. *Attending Marvels: A Patagonian Journal*. New York: Macmillan.

———. 1942. "The Beginnings of Vertebrate Paleontology in North America." *Proceedings of the American Philosophical Society* 86:130–88.

———. 1943. "The Discovery of Fossil Vertebrates in North America." *Journal of Paleontology* 17, 1 (January): 26–38.

Sinkankas, John. 1959. *Gemstones of North America*. Princeton: Van Nostrand.

Skwara, T. 1992. *Old Bones and Serpent Stones: A Guide to Interpreted Fossil Localities in Canada and the United States*. Vol. 2, *Western Sites*. Blacksburg, VA: McDonald & Woodward.

Smith, Erminnie A. 1883. "Myths of the Iroquois." *Second Annual Report of the Bureau of American Ethnology, 1880–81*, 51–116. Washington, DC: GPO.

Smith, Michael E. 1996. *The Aztecs*. Oxford: Blackwell.

Smith, Teresa. 1995. *The Island of the Anishnaabeg: Thunderers and Water Monsters in the Traditional Ojibwe Life-World*. Moscow: Univ. of Idaho Press.

Snell, Alma Hogan. 2000. *Grandmother's Grandchild: My Crow Indian Life*. Ed. Becky Matthew. Lincoln: Univ. of Nebraska Press.

Sneve, Virginia Driving Hawk. 2000. *Grandpa Was a Cowboy and an Indian*. Lincoln: Univ. of Nebraska Press.

Snowden, R. R. 1925. [Havasupai pictograph]. Letters in Record Unit 7084, William Henry Holmes Papers, 1870–1931, Smithsonian Institution Archives, Washington, DC.

Spalding, David A. E. 1993. *Dinosaur Hunters: 150 Extraordinary Discoveries*. Toronto: Key Porter Books.

———. 1999. *Into the Dinosaurs' Graveyard: Canadian Digs and Discoveries*. Toronto: Doubleday Canada.

Spence, Lewis. 1914. *The Myths of the North American Indians*. New York: Dover.

Stands In Timber, John, and Margot Liberty. 1967. *Cheyenne Memories*. Lincoln: Univ. of Nebraska Press.

Stanford, Donald E. 1959. "The Giant Bones of Claverack, New York, 1705." *New York History* 40:47–61.

Steen, Jomay. 2003. "Resolution on Badlands Plan Eludes Park Service." *Rapid City Journal*, October 3.

Stephens, Walter. 1989. *Giants in Those Days: Folklore, Ancient History, and Nationalism*. Lincoln: Univ. of Nebraska Press.

Sternberg, Charles H. 1917. *Hunting Dinosaurs*. Lawrence, KS: World Company Press.

———. 1990 [1909]. *The Life of a Fossil Hunter*. Bloomington: Indiana Univ. Press.

Stevens, Sylvester K., and Donald H. Kent, eds. 1941. *The Expedition of Baron de Longueuil*. 2nd rev. ed. Harrisburg, PA: Erie County Historical Society, Pennsylvania Historical Commission.

Strong, W. D. 1934. "North American Traditions Suggesting a Knowledge of the Mammoth." *American Anthropologist* 36:81–88.

Tanner, William F. 1984. "Human and Not-So-Human Footprint Images on the Rocks." In "The Evolution-Creation Controversy," ed. R. Gestaldo and W. F. Tanner. *Paleontological Society*, special issue, 1:117–33.

Tassy, Pascal. 2002. "L'émergence du concept d'espèce fossile: le mastdonte américain (Proboscidea, Mammalia) entre clarté et confusion." *Geodiversitas* 24, 2:263–94.

Taylor, M. E., and R. A. Robison. 1976. "Trilobites in Utah Folklore." *Brigham Young University Geology Studies* 23, 2 (July): 1–5.

Teit, James A. 1917. "Kaska Tales." *Journal of American Folk-Lore* 30.

Terra, Helmut de. 1957. *Man and Mammoth in Mexico*. London: Hutchinson.

Thomas, David Hurst. 2000. *Skull Wars: Kennewick Man, Archaeology and the Battle for Native American Identity*. New York: Basic Books.

Thompson, Stith. 1966. *Tales of the North American Indian*. Bloomington: Indiana Univ. Press.

Tokaryk, Timothy T. 1997. "Facing the Past: A Cursory Review of Paleontology in Southern Saskatchewan." In *Canadian Paleontology Conference Field Trip Guidebook no. 6: Upper Cretaceous and Tertiary Stratigraphy and Paleontology of Southern Saskatchewan*, ed. L. McKenzie-McAnally, 9–27. N.p: Geological Association of Canada.

Torquemada, Fray Juan de. 1968 [ca. 1557–1664]. *Monarquia indiana*. 4th ed. 3 vols. Mexico City: Editorial Porrua.

Torrubia. N.d. *L'Apparato para la Historia natural espaniola: Gigantologie espagnole*. Cited in Cuvier 1806.

Tsonakwa, Gerard, and Yolaikia Wapitaska. 2001. *Seven Eyes, Seven Legs: Supernatural Stories of the Abenaki*. Walnut, CA: Kiva Pub.

"Tuba City: Where Dinosaurs Roamed." 2004. *Arizona Republic*, www.azcentral.com/travel/arizona/features/articles/archive/tubadino.html.

Tyler, Hamilton A. 1964. *Pueblo Gods and Myths*. Norman: Univ. of Oklahoma Press.

Tylor, Edward Burnet. 1964 [1865]. *Researches into the Early History of Mankind*. London. Reprint, Chicago: Univ. of Chicago Press.

Tyrrell, J. B. 1892. "Report on Northwestern Manitoba, with Portions of the Adjacent Districts of Assiniboia and Saskatchewan." *Geological Survey Canada, Annual Report* 5:129E.

Verrengia, Joseph. 2000. "As T. rex Is Unveiled, Discoverer Lies Low." *Minneapolis Star Tribune*, May 14, A19, 24.

Verrill, A. Hyatt. 1948. *Strange Prehistoric Animals and Their Stories*. New York: L. C. Page.

Verrill, A. Hyatt, and Ruth Verrill. 1953. *America's Ancient Civilizations*. New York: G. P. Putnam's Sons.

Vitaliano, Dorothy. 1973. *Legends of the Earth*. Bloomington: Indiana Univ. Press.

Waldman, Carl. 2000. *Atlas of the North American Indian*. Rev. ed. New York: Checkmark Books.

Walker, James R. 1983. *Lakota Myth*. Ed. Elaine Jahner. Lincoln: Univ. of Nebraska Press.

———. 1991. *Lakota Belief and Ritual*. Ed. Raymond DeMalle and Elaine Jahner. Lincoln: Univ. of Nebraska Press.

Wallace, David Rains. 1999. *The Bonehunters' Revenge*. Boston: Houghton Mifflin.

Wallace, E., and E. A. Hoebel. 1952. *The Comanches*. Norman: Univ. of Oklahoma Press.

Washburn, Wilcomb. 1975. *The Indian in America*. New York: Harper & Row.

Washington, George. 1754. "Major George Washington's Journal to the River Ohio." *Maryland Gazette* (March 21, 28).

Watkins, Joe. 2000. "Writing Unwritten History: An Archaeologist and American Indian Walks the Tightrope of a Double Life." *Archaeology* (November–December): 36–44.

Webb, W. E. 1872. *Buffalo Land: An Authentic Narrative of . . . a Scientific and Sporting Party upon the Great Plains of the West*. Chicago: Hannaford.

Weishampel, David, and Luther Young. 1996. *Dinosaurs of the East Coast*. Baltimore: Johns Hopkins Univ. Press.

Wendt, Herbert. 1959. *Out of Noah's Ark: The Story of Man's Discovery of the Animal Kingdom*. New York: Houghton Mifflin.

"Were Early American Indians the First Fossil Enthusiasts?" 1988. *Earth Science* (Spring): 11.

White, Richard. 1991. *The Middle Ground: Indians, Empires, and Republics in the Great Lakes Region, 1650–1815*. Cambridge: Cambridge Univ. Press.

Whybrow, Peter, ed. 2000. *Travels with the Fossil Hunters*. Cambridge: Cambridge Univ. Press.

Wildschut, William. 1960. *Crow Indian Medicine Bundles*. New York: Museum of the American Indian Heye Foundation.

Williston, Samuel W. 1898. "A Brief History of Collecting in the Niobrara Formation. Addenda to Part I." *University of Kansas Geological Survey* 4:28–32.

Wilson, Darryl Babe. 1998. *The Morning the Sun Went Down*. Berkeley, CA: Heyday.

Winchell, Newton H., ed. 1911. *The Aborigines of Minnesota, a Report Based on the Collections of Jacob V. Brower and the Field Surveys and Notes of Alfred J. Hill and Theodore Lewis. Collected, augmented, and described by N. H. Winchell*. St. Paul: Minnesota Historical Society.

Winterbotham, William. 1795. *An Historical, Geographical, Commercial, and Philosophical View of the United States of America*. 4 vols. London: Ridgeway.

Wissler, Clark. 1912. "Ceremonial Bundles of the Blackfoot Indians." *Anthropological Papers of the American Museum of Natural History* 7, 1–2:65–289.

Woiche, Istet. 1992 [1928]. *Annikadel: The History of the Universe as Told by the Achumawi Indians of California*. Ed. C. Hart Merriam. Tucson: Univ. of Arizona Press.

Wood, W. Raymond, and R. Bruce McMillan, eds. 1976. *Prehistoric Man and His Environments: A Case Study in the Ozark Highland*. New York: Academic Press.

Yoon, Carol Kaesuk. 2000. "Study Jolts Views on Recovery from Extinctions." *New York Times*, March 9.

Young, M. Jane. 1992. "Morning Star, Evening Star: Zuni Traditional Stories." In *Earth and Sky: Visions of the Cosmos in Native American Folklore*, ed. Ray A. Williamson and Claire R. Farrar, 75–99. Albuquerque: Univ. of New Mexico Press.

INTERVIEWS

John Allen, Jr., Assiniboine, spiritual leader, Fort Belknap Reservation, Montana

Paul Apodaca, Navajo/Mixtec, scholar of Native American myth, Chapman University, Orange, California

Wayne Archambault, Assiniboine, fossil hunter and photographer, Zurich, Montana

Dave Bald Eagle, Miniconjou Lakota chief, Cheyenne River Sioux Reservation, South Dakota

Clarenda Begay, Navajo, curator, Navajo Nation Museum, Window Rock, Arizona

John Blahna, Shawnee/Omaha, Landfall, Minnesota

William Boyes, Custer Battlefield historian, Rockville, Maryland

Geoffrey Brown, director, Navajo Nation Museum, Window Rock, Arizona

Kyril Calsoyas, former principal, Seba Dalkai and Tuba City schools, Flagstaff, Arizona

Clifford Canku, Dakota Sioux, teacher Sisseton-Wahpeton College, Sisseton, South Dakota

Morris Chee, Jr., Navajo, dinosaur track guide, Navajo Reservation, Moenave, Arizona

Vine Deloria, Jr., Standing Rock Sioux, Indian activist and historian, Boulder, Colorado

Roger Echo-Hawk, Pawnee, historian, Longmont, Colorado

Michael Everhart, paleontologist, Sternberg Museum, Hays, Kansas

Michael Flynn, paleontologist, Sheridan College, Sheridan, Wyoming

Antonio R. Garcez, Apache, writer, New Mexico

Mark Goodwin, paleontologist, University of California Museum of Paleontology, Berkeley, California

Chandler Good Strike, Gros Ventre, artist, Fort Belknap Reservation, Hays, Montana

Richard Gould, curator, Pawnee Village Museum, Republic, Kansas

Johnson Holy Rock, Oglala Lakota Sioux, elder, Pine Ridge Reservation, South Dakota

Jack Horner, paleontologist, Museum of the Rockies, Bozeman, Montana

Jason Jackson, folklorist, University of Oklahoma, Norman

Mearl Kendrew, Navajo, San Bernardino, California

Jim Kennedy, Blackfeet, tribal council, Blackfeet Reservation, Browning, Montana

Ruthann Knudson, NPS superintendent, Agate Fossil Beds, Harrison, Nebraska

Wann Langston, Jr., paleontologist emeritus, University of Texas, Austin

Greg Liggett, paleontologist, Sternberg Museum, Hays, Kansas

Eldon Little Moon, Lakota Sioux, Pine Ridge Reservation, Wounded Knee, South Dakota

Leonardo López Luján, archaeologist, Mexico City

Ambrose McBride, Sioux, Crow Creek Reservation, Fort Thompson, South Dakota

Tim McCleary, librarian, Little Big Horn College, Crow Reservation, Crow Agency, Montana

Greg McDonald, Paleontology Program coordinator, National Park Service, Washington, DC

Barbara Mann, scholar of Iroquois culture, University of Toledo, Ohio

Nita Manning, Northern Cheyenne, Rapid City, South Dakota

Harry Manygoats, Navajo, spiritual leader, Navajo Cultural Center, Navajo Reservation, Tuba City, Arizona

Jim Martin, paleontologist, Museum of Geology, South Dakota School of Mines and Technology, Rapid City

Paul Martin, ecologist, Tucson, Arizona

Bill Matteson, paleontology student, Sheridan College, Sheridan, Wyoming

Harry Mithlo, Comanche, storyteller, Lawton, Oklahoma

Nate Murphy, paleontologist, Phillips County Museum, Malta, Montana

Mike O'Neill, National Paleontology Program director, Bureau of Land Management, Washington, DC

Neeake (Fred Shaw), Shawnee, elected storyteller, Shawnee United Remnant Band, Ohio

Juanita Pahdopony, Comanche, storyteller and artist, Lawton, Oklahoma

David Parris, paleontologist, curator, Natural History Museum, Trenton, New Jersey

James Rementer, Delaware Language Project, Delaware Tribal Headquarters, Bartlesville, Oklahoma

Timothy Rowe, paleontologist, University of Texas, Austin

Maximo Salas, paleontological artist and architect, Mexico City, Mexico

Vincent Santucci, National Park Service paleontologist, Washington, DC

Shirley, Osage, Oklahoma

Alma Hogan Snell, Crow, medicine woman, Crow Reservation, Fort Smith, Montana

Bill Snell, Assiniboine, Crow Reservation, Fort Smith, Montana

Marvin Stewart, Crow, elder and keeper of the Living Bull medicine bundle, Crow Reservation, Montana

William Supernaugh, superintendent, Badlands National Park, South Dakota

Eli Tail, Jr., Oglala Lakota, spiritual leader, Pine Ridge Reservation, Porcupine, South Dakota

Pascal Tassy, curator of vertebrate fossils, Museum of Natural History, Paris, France

Putt Thompson, Custer Trading Post, Crow Reservation, Crow Agency, Montana

Gerard Tsonakwa, Abenaki, storyteller and artist, Tucson, Arizona

Isabelle Walker, Navajo, medicine woman, Flagstaff, Arizona

Glenn Welker, manager, Indigenous Peoples Literature Web site

Douglas Wolfe, paleontologist, Zuni Basin Dinosaur Project, Mesa, Arizona

INDEX